Real Estate Investment Trusts

FINANCIAL MANAGEMENT ASSOCIATION
Survey and Synthesis Series

The Search for Value: Measuring the Company's Cost of Capital
Michael C. Ehrhardt

Managing Pension Plans: A Comprehensive Guide to Improving Plan Performance
Dennis E. Logue and Jack S. Rader

Efficient Asset Management: A Practical Guide to Stock Portfolio Optimization and Asset Allocation
Richard O. Michaud

Real Options: Managing Strategic Investment in an Uncertain World
Martha Amram and Nalin Kulatilaka

Beyond Greed and Fear: Understanding Behavioral Finance and the Psychology of Investing
Hersh Shefrin

Dividend Policy: Its Impact on Form Value
Ronald C. Lease, Kose John, Avner Kalay, Uri Loewenstein, and Oded H. Sarig

Value Based Management: The Corporate Response to Shareholder Revolution
John D. Martin and J. William Petty

Debt Management: A Practitioner's Guide
John D. Finnerty and Douglas R. Emery

Real Estate Investment Trusts: Structure, Performance, and Investment Opportunities
Su Han Chan, John Erickson, and Ko Wang

Trading and Exhanges: Market Microstructure for Practitioners
Larry Harris

Real Estate Investment Trusts

Structure, Performance, and Investment Opportunities

SU HAN CHAN
JOHN ERICKSON
KO WANG

2003

OXFORD
UNIVERSITY PRESS

Oxford New York
Auckland Bangkok Buenos Aires Cape Town Chennai
Dar es Salaam Delhi Hong Kong Istanbul Karachi Kolkata
Kuala Lumpur Madrid Melbourne Mexico City Mumbai Nairobi
São Paulo Shanghai Singapore Taipei Tokyo Toronto

Published by Oxford University Press, Inc.
198 Madison Avenue, New York, New York 10016

www.oup.com

Library of Congress Cataloging-in-Publication Data

Chan, Su Han, 1956–
Real estate investment trusts : structure, performance, and investment opportunities / Su Han Chan, John Erickson, Ko Wang.
p. cm.—(Financial Management Association survey and synthesis series)
Includes bibliographical references and index.
ISBN 0-19-515534-3
1. Real estate investment trusts. I. Erickson, John, 1944– II. Wang, Ko, 1955– III. Title. IV. Series.

HG5095 .C48 2002
332.63'247—dc21 2001059810

9 8 7 6 5 4 3 2 1

Printed in the United States of America
on acid-free paper

To our parents, with love and gratitude.

S.H.C.
J.E.
K.W.

Preface

A recent survey conducted by the National Association of Realtors indicates that more than half of the household wealth in the United States is in real estate. This has been the case even in the late 1990s and early 2000s, when Internet business has attracted the attention (and financial resources) of most investors. Surveys ranking the richest people in the world always report that a majority of them have wealth tied to real estate or are in real estate-related businesses. In sum, regardless of the wealth level of an individual, real estate is one of the most important assets—if not *the* most important asset—for any investor.

Ironically, despite its dominant position in most investors' portfolios, real estate is probably the subject that receives the least attention among finance scholars and in the investment community. For example, although there are several academic journals devoted to the study of real estate, top-tier mainstream finance journals rarely publish real estate–related research. Moreover, when compared to industrial firms, the real estate sector has not received as much attention from the financial analysts of major investment firms. This lack of attention may be due to the difficulty of gathering information on real estate markets.

Possibly because of this lack of attention from the investment community, both the public and private real estate markets traditionally have been viewed as being less efficient than the general stock market. However, given the important role real estate plays in our economy, we believe in making an effort to enhance the understanding of the general investing public about real estate markets. Acting on this belief, we decided to write a book that draws on our own research in real estate markets over the years and on the works of other respected professionals and scholars in the real estate field. Specifically, we concentrate our effort on the *real estate investment trust (REIT)* market, which is considered to be the most transparent among all real estate markets.

Most existing REIT books are written in a way that provides narrowly focused technical knowledge on how to conduct business in REITs. Some books survey the REIT literature, but in a fragmented manner. Our book has a different objective. We convey important lessons that real estate and finance academics have learned about REITs to both the general public and real estate practitioners, including REIT managers and advisors. We survey the academic literature on REITs and synthesize the findings in a way that is both understandable and useful to academicians and general investors alike. We provide not only explanations of various problems REITs have had over the years, but also the solutions that managers and lawmakers have developed to make the REIT a more effective vehicle for managing real estate assets. We provide our own insights into the structure and performance of REITs to inform the reader about their future development. Finally, we illustrate many of the issues we discuss with data from our own unique, comprehensive database, which tracks the changes in organizational form and REIT stock performance since information on the earliest REITs first became available in 1962.

We hope that, by providing this comprehensive examination of the industry, our book will energize the investment community's interest in REITs and provide useful information to the policy- and lawmakers who enact regulations governing REITs. We also hope that, by highlighting the problems and improvements associated with past REITs, REIT executives will be able to manage their trusts more efficiently and transparently so that this market will become an important vehicle for investing in real estate. Finally, it is our hope that this book will stimulate students' interest in the subject matter and provide a solid foundation for our colleagues to conduct additional quality research on real estate markets.

Acknowledgments

We wish to express our sincere appreciation to those who have given constructive comments and suggestions for the book. Specifically, we are indebted to the 12 individuals who have devoted a significant amount of their time to review the draft of each chapter of the book. Those individuals are Brent Ambrose (University of Kentucky), Dennis Capozza (University of Michigan), David Downs (University of Georgia), Robert Edelstein (University of California–Berkeley), George Gau (University of Texas–Austin), John Glascock (George Washington University), Joseph Gyourko (University of Pennsylvania), Youguo Liang (Prudential Real Estate Investors), David Ling (University of Florida), Jianping Mei (New York University), Glenn Mueller (Johns Hopkins University and Legg Mason), and Kerry Vandell (University of Wisconsin–Madison). Their comments greatly improved the quality of the book.

We also would like to thank Paul Donnelly, Kenneth Eades, Arthur Keown, and John Martin for their encouragement and assistance. Their guidance made it possible for us to write this book for the Financial Management Association and Oxford University Press Survey and Synthesis Series. This book could not have been completed without the support of our universities. In this regard, we express our special thanks to Kam-hon Lee (former dean of the Faculty of Business Administration at the Chinese University of Hong Kong), Anil Puri (dean of the College of Business and Economics at the California State University–Fullerton), and Richard Wong (director of the School of Business at the University of Hong Kong).

Finally, we would like to acknowledge research assistance from Jacob Ming Yan Chan, Eveline Irwandi, Shiu-Ming Kan, Joe Haoming Liu, and

Daniel Yau. Their hard work and tireless effort have allowed us to provide many up-to-date statistics, which are essential for supporting the main arguments of this book. W. K. Leung, a dear friend of Ko Wang and Su Han Chan, has provided a helping hand in generating some of the data. We also thank Virginia Unkefer and Diana Plattner for providing capable editorial support for this book.

Contents

Real Estate Investment Trusts

1

Introduction

Is a REIT a Stock or Real Estate?

A traditional *real estate investment trust (REIT)* is essentially a closed-end fund created exclusively for holding real properties, mortgage-related assets, or both. This investment vehicle was created by the U.S. Congress in 1960 for the express purpose of providing investors with an opportunity to invest in real properties and, at the same time, to enjoy the same benefits provided to shareholders in investment trusts. In order to make REITs a more attractive investment, Congress waived the corporate-level income tax on REITs if they met the conditions set by tax laws governing them. Among the conditions are that REITs must be widely held and that they must distribute most of their taxable income as dividends to shareholders.

Before the creation of REITs, investors could purchase real properties only from the property market (and not from the stock market). However, with the creation of REITs, it is possible to trade properties in the stock market since they are now in a form of a corporation or trust. In other words, investors can buy REIT stocks from the stock market with the intention of buying a pool of real properties and/or mortgages. Thus, the REIT concept made it possible and convenient for small investors to invest in real estate.

In recent years, the changes in tax laws have allowed REITs to manage their own properties and provide related services to their tenants. In this regard, some of the modern REITs can also be viewed as operating companies (rather than as pure closed-end funds, like traditional REITs). However, even for the modern REITs, real estate holdings are still the most significant part of their assets. Given this, it is fair to say that most REITs (traditional or modern) can be viewed as pools of properties (and/or mortgages) traded in the stock market. REIT investors need to understand both the property market and the stock markets in order to make sound investment decisions. Although some investors have substantial experience investing in the real property market and others might understand the stock market quite well, only a few are proficient at investing in both markets.

There are, in fact, quite a few differences between the property market and the stock market. On the surface, we see that the pattern of price movements in the stock market is significantly different from that in the real estate market. For example, we know that the price of a stock can change every minute, while the price of real property does not change quite so fast. We frequently observe that the prices of REIT stocks move significantly within a day while the prices of the underlying properties stay the same.

We can use an extreme case to illustrate this situation. We know that the stock prices of REITs dropped more than 20% on what is now called Black Monday in October 1987. However, the price of the underlying properties did not drop on that day. Although the price of a REIT is supposed to reflect its underlying property value, the prices of REITs either before or after Black Monday did not reflect their underlying property values. (It is also possible that neither prices reflected the underlying property values of REITs.) In any case, from this particular example, we know that a REIT's stock price might differ significantly from its underlying property value, at least in the short run.

While we cannot—and will never—know which REIT price (before or after Black Monday) tells us more about the underlying value of the property, we might wonder why few investors arbitraged the profits. For example, if the investors believe that the price of the REIT stock has dropped far below its underlying property value, they should, in theory, buy up all the REIT's stocks (or enough shares to control the REIT), disband the REIT, and sell off its properties in the property market. Indeed, if managers of REITs believe that REIT stock prices are valued far below the value of their underlying properties, they should sell all the properties and give the money to their stockholders. It seems that, depending on the market conditions, smart investors should move between the property market and the REIT stock market to arbitrage the profits.[1]

Obviously, besides transaction costs, there must be some structural issues associated with the organization of REITs that prohibit investors from arbitraging profits between the two markets. For example, REIT managers and the advisors of a REIT might be able to control the important corporate decisions regarding the REIT, making it difficult for outsiders to intervene in management decisions. It is also possible that the price information on the underlying properties or mortgages might not be readily available. This is especially true for some mortgage REITs with special provisions on income or appreciation participation. (That is, the owners of mortgages may receive not only debt service but also income from properties based on certain conditions.)

The problems of valuation uncertainty and the lack of understanding about the actual value of the underlying properties can be amplified by the nature of the REIT. Congress enacted laws governing REITs with the intention of creating an investment vehicle for small investors to invest in real estate. In fact, the tax law governing REITs specifically limited the number of large investors a REIT could have and also encouraged diversified REIT ownership. However, without help from sophisticated institutional investors, it would be difficult for small investors to analyze the REIT market on their own. (Of course, this observation applies to most stocks in the market.)

The complicated valuation issues inherent in REITs together with their unique fund-type organizational structure, the constraints on corporate policies imposed by tax regulations, and their diversified ownership structures make REITs a unique group of stocks in the stock market. In fact, several researchers in the field of finance (especially those studying initial public offerings, or IPOs) specifically exclude REITs from their samples when they seek to analyze special phenomena in the stock market. It is clear that the stock market does not understand REITs to the extent that it should.

Over the past 40 years, the REIT stock market experienced several ups and downs—but it has also experienced unprecedented growth. Prior to 1986, total REIT capitalization stayed well below $10 billion even though REITs had been in existence for 25 years by that time. At one recent point, it was estimated that the equity market capitalization of REITs was close to $160 billion.

This explosive growth suggests that experience has taught investors lessons on how to evaluate REIT stocks. Regulators and REIT managers have also learned from past mistakes and are striving to revise the REIT structure to serve investors better. However, all the evidence on REIT valuation and performance and the lessons that investors and REIT managers have learned are currently documented only in a piecemeal fashion. There is a need to summarize past experience and to synthesize the evidence about REIT investments in a systematic way to provide guidance for the future development of the REIT market. This book aims to fulfill this need.

Why REITs Deserve Our Attention

Although we do not know the exact amount of real estate wealth in the world, we can safely conclude that real estate comprises a significant portion of the world's wealth. The consensus is that real estate comprises 40–50% of the total wealth in the United States.[2] Most U.S. families own their own homes, but the majority of commercial properties are still in the hands of investors. What would happen if most of the commercial properties were traded (via REITs) in the stock market? Is there any reason to believe that this will not happen?

We know that the values of many large commercial properties are higher than the values of many of the companies traded in the stock market. If companies with small capitalizations can be traded in the stock market, then so should properties with large capitalizations. Indeed, we see no reason that properties should not be traded in the stock market just as companies are. As the size of the REIT market increases, it will be important for us to understand this market much better than we do currently.

Increasing REIT IPO Activities

Will some of the commercial properties currently available be securitized and traded in the stock market? The answer is probably yes. How quickly the process of the securitization will move is another question. Given the size of the real property market, it will take a long time for the stock market to securitize even a small portion of the properties in the real estate market. From the existing evidence on real estate securitization, we believe that there is momentum for this activity.

Table 1.1 reports the funds raised through the IPO activities of REITs and by non-REIT firms from 1970 to the end of October 2001. One can see that, as a single industry, REITs contribute a significant portion to the IPO pool. During the 1970–2000 period, the total funds raised from REIT IPOs was about 7.57% of the total funds raised by IPOs in all other industries. This percentage exceeded 20% in 4 of the 30 years under investigation. This is, indeed, a very significant percentage for a single industry.

This percentage is also steadily increasing. Between 1970 and 1979, the percentage was 7.02, but it grows to 9.08% during the 1990–99 period. Although REIT IPO activity is quite cyclical (e.g., there are many IPOs in 1993–94 and 1997 but none in 2000–01 [as of October 31]), there is no reason to believe that in the long run the increasing trend of real estate securitization will slow down. As REITs continue to move into the market, it will become even more important for investors and REIT managers to have a better understanding of them.

REITs Are Different from Other Stocks

One might ask why it is necessary to study the literature on REITs. Couldn't we simply study the finance literature that covers all stocks in the market to gain an understanding of REITs? After all, REITs are part of the general stock market, are they not? Although REITS are traded in the general stock market, they have not been treated as general stocks by researchers. As mentioned earlier, many finance researchers specifically exclude REITs in their samples because they believe that REITs behave differently from other operating companies in the general market.

More important, many studies have found that REITs either behave differently from other types of stock in the market or have certain unique

Table 1.1 Comparison of Equity Funds Raised through Initial Public Offerings by REITs and by Non-REIT Firms

Year End	Funds (in $ millions) Raised from IPOs		Funds Raised by REIT IPOs Relative to Funds Raised by Non-REIT IPOs (%)
	By REITs	By Non-REIT Firms	
1970	61	780	7.82
1971	182	1,655	10.98
1972	170	2,724	6.24
1973	59	330	18.02
1974	0	51	0.00
1975	0	264	0.00
1976	0	237	0.00
1977	0	151	0.00
1978	0	247	0.00
1979	10	429	2.40
1980	30	1,404	2.14
1981	50	3,200	1.56
1982	215	1,334	16.12
1983	68	13,168	0.51
1984	237	3,932	6.04
1985	2,706	10,450	25.89
1986	905	17,571	5.15
1987	539	13,841	3.89
1988	964	4,514	21.35
1989	500	5,721	8.74
1990	350	4,749	7.37
1991	208	16,202	1.28
1992	878	22,989	3.82
1993	8,469	30,587	27.69
1994	6,614	19,039	34.74
1995	923	29,422	3.14
1996	1,133	43,150	2.63
1997	6,216	34,010	18.28
1998	2,236	35,052	6.38
1999	292	65,653	0.44
2000	0	66,480	0.00
2001[a]	0	n.a.	n.a.
1970–79	482	6,868	7.02
1980–89	6,213	75,135	8.27
1990–99	27,319	300,853	9.08
1970–2000	34,015	449,336	7.57

Source: For REITs, the data are based on the authors' REIT sample and various publications by NAREIT. For non-REIT firms, the data are based on an updated version (as of April 16, 2001) of Ibbotson, Sindelar, and Ritter's (1994) table and are available on Jay Ritter's Web site, http://bear.cba.ufl.edu/ritter.

[a]Data are as of October 31, 2001.

characteristics (or factors) that other stocks do not share. These studies examine topics such as return prediction, price-generating processes, dividend policies, capital structure, initial and seasoned public offerings, and merger activities. Indeed, given REITs' unique trust structure and tax regulations, it would be surprising if they behaved exactly the same as other stocks. The uniqueness of REITs underscores the need for a synthesis of existing REIT studies to better understand them. In other words, if a student of the market simply applied his or her knowledge gained from the general stock market to that for REIT stocks, this student might be in for a surprise.

Bringing the Evidence Together

Virtually all currently available books on REITs either address the REIT industry solely from the perspective of the investor in REIT stocks or present advice on how to organize a REIT from the perspective of a future REIT operator. Some books on the subject are compiled from individual articles on REITS without providing an integrative discussion of the issues surrounding them. Not many texts in the market present what is currently known about REITs in a comprehensive, organized, and documented fashion.[3] Furthermore, no books before now have used detailed, up-to-date data to describe the REIT industry.

In addition, individual knowledge of the REIT industry that is based on limited observations and ad hoc information is useful, but will not by itself provide a comprehensive understanding of the many complicated issues surrounding REITs. The industry can best be understood through an analysis of the empirical evidence provided by existing academic research on REITs. Our purpose in this book is to analyze the REIT market in a systematic manner by synthesizing the extensive evidence derived from academic research with relevant views expressed by finance and real estate practitioners in the popular press.

Survey and Synthesis of Evidence

This book is designed to serve as a bridge connecting practitioners in the REIT field with researchers in real estate and finance. There is currently a large body of finance and real estate literature (more than 400 academic and practitioner articles) examining the characteristics of REITs in a rigorous and scientific manner. This literature addresses issues that are of particular interest to the real estate and general investor communities. For the most part, the literature on REITs is not well known outside academic real estate and finance circles. But it does provide important information for investors and managers by documenting the characteristics of REITs that are responsible for the phenomenal growth of the industry. This book synthesizes this large body of literature in a systematic and comprehensive way to provide useful information to investors, REIT managers, academics, and students who are interested in learning more about REITs.

A Comprehensive Database

The most serious problem researchers face when summarizing results from academic studies is the lack of synchronization of sample periods used in those studies, which makes the comparison of their results difficult. In addition, few published empirical studies in the academic literature use the most recent data available (which, in those studies' defense, could partially be due the fact that it takes a long time to publish an academic study). To minimize these two problems, we have established a large and up-to-date database on REITs created over the last 10 years. Where necessary, we use the most recent data from this database to replicate and update some of the results reported in other studies. By so doing, we have the most up-to-date information available for our discussions.

The database we use in this book is very large; it includes information on the publicly traded REITs presently in existence, as well as information on the REITs that have not survived during the past 40 years. This means that, other than the National Association of Real Estate Investment Trusts (NAREIT), we have the largest database on REITs we know of, comprisinga total of 486 REITs that have trading information between 1962 and 2000. In addition, with our database, we eliminate the survivorship bias that can distort discussions of the issues surrounding REITs (especially on REIT stock performance). As a side benefit, we also used this database to generate a comprehensive return index for the REIT industry; it is included in the appendix. This index will give the reader a useful and quick reference on the return performance of REITs over the 1962–2000 period. Our analyses required the use of a massive amount of stock return and firm performance data, which are available only from the Center for Research in Security Prices (CRSP) and COMPUSTAT tapes. Because CRSP updates its data once a year, the data available in the tape as of October 2001 goes only up to 2000. Thus, our analysis covers the period from 1962 to 2000.

Issues of Interest

Our intention is to provide a thorough analysis and synthesis of the existing research on REITs in a way that will enable managers to improve their investment decisions and the REITs' operating performance. Our analysis is designed to give practitioners a more thorough understanding of the changes in the industry that have affected REIT operating performance in the past as well as the factors that can be expected to affect their performance in the future. With this in mind, we will focus only on issues that are relevant to managing and investing in REITs. We first identify the important issues that we believe deserve our attention; we then classify them into three categories: understanding REITs, managing REITs, and investing in REITs.

Understanding REITs

Before we can analyze REITs in detail we have to understand the basic structure of the REIT market—how it evolved and the reasons for its past failures and successes. To accomplish this, we focus on the following seven issues.

- Do REIT stocks resemble non-REIT stocks in the general market?
- Should we view REITs as stocks or property?
- Does the REIT organizational form reduce the cost of capital for real estate companies relative to that of traditional real estate operating companies?
- Is the performance of REIT stocks different from the performance of the stocks of master limited partnerships (MLPs) or commingled real estate funds (CREFs)?
- What is the effect of institutional investor participation on REIT performance?
- How does the number of financial analysts following REIT stocks affect REIT stock performance?
- How efficient is the market for REIT stocks in providing liquidity, information dissemination, and price determination?

Managing REITs

Both traditional REITs (similar to closed-end mutual funds) and modern REITs (similar to operating companies) are governed by special tax laws. Although these laws provide significant tax benefits on the corporate income tax level, they also require that REITs pay out a significant portion of their earnings. This requirement has put a constraint on REIT financial policies. There are at least eight important issues surrounding the financing of REITs that deserve the attention of REIT managers. These issues are as follows:

- How do REIT financial policies, such as policies on dividend and capital structure, affect their performance?
- How does REIT market capitalization affect performance?
- How do property acquisitions and dispositions affect the market value of REITs?
- What is the impact of REIT merger and acquisition decisions on share values?

- How do agency issues (potential conflicts of interest among shareholders, managers, and creditors) affect shareholder wealth?
- What is the trend in institutional investments in REITs, and what are the implications of such investments on the agency and on corporate control issues prevailing in the REIT stock market?
- When and why do REITs make secondary offerings?
- Should REITs pay more dividends than is required by the tax laws?

Investing in REITs

We will examine the characteristics of the various types of REIT stocks and document the factors that affect their performance. This book will also add to the existing literature on the subject by providing an analysis and synthesis of REIT performance as influenced by organizational structure, asset type, management style, and the financial policies of REITs. Ten issues are important to REIT investors. They are the following:

- Which type of REIT stock has performed the best, and which type can be expected to show superior performance in the future?
- Does investing in a number of different REITs with alternative asset holdings improve diversification and stock performance?
- How can REITs play an essential diversification role under classic portfolio theory?
- What are the top performing sectors of the equity REIT industry?
- To what extent is the market for REITs efficient?
- Is the potential conflict of interest between the managers and the shareholders of REITs really a problem for shareholders?
- Do REIT stocks provide more diversification for investment portfolios than direct investments in real estate or investments in private pooled real estate vehicles, such as CREFs?
- Do the recent changes in REIT organizational structure affect REIT performance?
- Can we predict REIT returns? If we can, how?
- How do REIT IPOs perform in the short run and in the long run?

Where We Are Headed

To begin our analysis, in chapter 2 we first review the evolution of the REIT concept. From our discussion of the ups and downs of REITs, we are able to identify the problems they face and to see whether the solutions to those problems have been effective. This chapter will provide us with basic information for the analysis in later chapters. We then move, in chapter 3, to a discussion of the organizational structure of REITs. We pay special attention to the recent changes in REIT structure and the issues related to their optimal structure. The creation of the operating format for REITs might change the way REITs perform in the stock market.

Chapter 4 is devoted to a unique issue faced by REITs. Similar to a stock mutual fund that needs a fund manager, a REIT also needs an advisor or manager for its day-to-day operations. The use of an advisor has created a great deal of controversy in the REIT industry. We tell you why and offer potential solutions. There has also been much debate recently in the REIT industry on the optimal size of a REIT. Should a REIT be as big as possible? Chapter 5 will give you the answer.

We believe that one of the most important changes in the REIT industry during the past 40 years is the increasing presence of institutional investors in the REIT stock market. REITs were originally designed to be an investment vehicle for small investors. We know, however, that small investors lack bargaining power. In chapter 6, we discuss the problems of having small investors and the changes institutional investors have brought to the REIT industry. Chapter 7 addresses another timely issue: Should a REIT concentrate its investments in one property type and/or in a small geographical area? Although there is no absolute answer to this question, there seem to be some commonly agreed upon principles, which we report in that chapter.

Chapter 8 discusses REIT dividend and financing policies. Because REITs are required to pay out high dividends and do not pay tax at the corporate level, the considerations of their dividend and financial policies must be different from those of industrial firms. In chapter 9 we discuss another unique characteristic of REITs: their IPOs. Empirical evidence tells us that REIT IPOs behave differently from industrial firm IPOs. We show the reader how they are different and review the factors causing the difference.

Chapter 10 offers focused and practical advice for readers who are interested in investing in REIT stocks. In that chapter, we examine the various issues related to the performance of REIT stocks. The issue of whether an investor can earn abnormal returns by predicting the stock movements of REITs is examined in chapter 11. Chapter 12 is our concluding chapter. We talk about the future directions of the REIT industry and the potential boom of REIT markets outside the United States, especially in Asia, and offer our opinions about the future of the REIT industry using our own crystal ball.

A Book for Wiser Decision Making

Although the REIT concept dates back to the 19th century, the history known to investors is still relatively brief. However, the REIT industry has been expanding and has the potential to expand further. This rapid evolution has been driven, to a large extent, by tax changes—but it is also the result of innovations in organizational form that reflect the industry's desire to adapt to the needs of investors. The unprecedented growth in the number of REITs, their market capitalization, and institutional interest in recent years suggest that managers have learned to avoid the types of problems that have plagued REITs in the past. In other words, managers may be wiser and investors may now be significantly more knowledgeable about the characteristics of REITs. This is the knowledge we would like to share with our readers. In addition, we believe that it is important for us to understand the problems facing REITs before we suggest how they can be overcome. Hence, we pay particular attention to the cause of a problem before we talk about the solution.

We have designed this book for the general reader and investor (large or small) interested in investing in REITs and for sophisticated REIT practitioners interested in learning more about their industry and its future directions. Because the book provides insights useful to REIT managers, it should also be of interest to consultants and lawyers who practice in the area of corporate law governing REITs or in real estate law, and to government regulators who work in the area of real estate securitization. Finally, the book will be of interest to finance and real estate students and the academic community alike.

NOTES

1. We observe that several REITs took their companies private when the stock market conditions were poor. We can assume that part of the motivation was to arbitrage the profits between public and private real estate markets.
2. See, for example, Ibbotson and Siegel (1983) and Apgar (1986).
3. However, we like two books on REITs that we have read. One is by Block (1998)and discusses investing in REITs, and another is by Garrigan and Parsons (1998) and contains a collection of good articles on the subject.

REFERENCES

Apgar, Mahlon. 1986. A strategic view of real estate. *Real Estate Issues* 11 (Fall-Winter): 7–8.

Block, Ralph L. 1998. *Investing in REITs: Real estate investment trusts.* Princeton, N.J.: Bloomberg Press.

Garrigan, Richard T., and John F. C. Parsons, ed. 1998. *Real estate investment trusts: Structure, analysis, and strategy.* New York: McGraw-Hill.

Ibbotson, Roger G., and Lawrence B. Siegel. 1983. The world market wealth portfolio. *Journal of Portfolio Management* 19 (Winter): 5–7.

2

The Origins and Evolution of Real Estate Investment Trusts

How Far Have We Come and Where Do We Go from Here?

The REIT as we know it today is in fact the revival of an older idea in real estate investment, the roots of which lie in 19th-century New England. That idea—called the Massachusetts trust—had lain dormant for 25 years before investors revived its spirit in 1960. The REIT industry has gone through several ups and downs since then. Some of the downturns were caused by changes in the operating environment, such as changes in tax laws. Some of the problems, however, arose from the inexperience and greed of some past REIT managers and owners. Because of the lessons learned from these mistakes and the changes made as a result, the REIT environment is much more efficient today than when it was established in 1960. It remains far from perfect, however, and as we shall see, the REIT industry will have to keep evolving in order to survive in a changing environment.

The History of the REIT Concept

The basic concept of the REIT originated with the business trusts that were formed in Boston, Massachusetts, in the mid-19th century, when the wealth created by the industrial revolution led to a demand for real estate investment opportunities. State laws at the time prevented a corporation from owning real estate unless the property was an integral part of the business. This made it impossible to use a corporation as a vehicle for investing and dealing exclusively in real estate. The *Massachusetts trust,* designed in response to these laws, was the first type of legal entity allowed to invest in real estate. This entity provided benefits similar to those of a corporation: transferability of ownership shares, limited liability, and centralized management expertise.

The Massachusetts trust also offered another benefit that was crucial to its attractiveness as an investment vehicle: favorable tax treatment that eliminated federal taxation at the trust level and that allowed investors to receive distributions of rental income free of taxes at the individual level. Although originally formed to provide wealthy investors with a conduit for income from equity investments, the Massachusetts trust soon became available to general investors as well.[1]

After their success in Boston, the trusts began to provide capital to develop real estate in other cities such as Chicago, Omaha, and Denver. The Massachusetts real estate trust remained a conduit for real estate investment until 1935, when the U.S. Supreme Court's removal of its favorable tax status resulted in its demise along with that of many similar trusts.

By the 1940s, the remaining trusts were competing directly for capital with tax-favored regulated investment companies (closed-end mutual funds, created by the Investment Company Act of 1940) and with real estate syndicates. The concept of the Massachusetts trust form of real estate investment was revived in the 1950s when its advocates, including one of the remaining trusts—the Real Estate Trust of America—lobbied the federal government for tax treatment equal to that of investment companies created by the 1940 act.

These efforts were rewarded in 1960 when the tax law was amended to give real estate trusts tax treatment similar to that for closed-end mutual funds. This gave small investors an opportunity to invest in real estate through a vehicle that provided investment expertise at a reduced cost, reduced risk, and a significantly lower minimum initial investment. By the time the first REIT came on the market in 1961, the underlying concept had actually been around for more than 100 years.

REITs in the 1960s–80s

The 1960 law originally defined a REIT as *an unincorporated association with multiple trustees as managers and having transferable shares of beneficial interest.* This definition intentionally patterned REITS after closed-end investment companies. Like these companies, REITs could issue shares to the public, and the value of those shares would vary above or below the net asset value of the REITs themselves.

The legislation creating REITs also placed significant restrictions on their operations and investments. In order to maintain their tax-favored status, a REIT was required to meet the following restrictions:

1. Pay out a minimum of 90% of its taxable income to its shareholders every year;
2. Have at least 100 shareholders with no more than 5 of these owning more than a combined 50% of the trust's outstanding shares (the "5/50 rule");
3. Be an *investor* in real estate, as opposed to a broker;
4. Derive at least 90% of its gross income from rent and interest income, gains on the sale of property or shares of other trusts, and other real estate sources;
5. Derive a minimum of 75% of its gross income from real property interests, gains on the sale of real property, and shares of other trusts and other real estate sources; and
6. Have at least 75% of total assets in real estate properties or mortgages, cash, and government securities.

Failure to meet any of these restrictions would either subject a REIT to disqualification for special tax-exempt treatment purposes or disqualify a portion of its earnings from tax-exempt treatment at the corporate level.

The asset and trading restrictions on REITs were designed to make them long-term investments, in contrast to real estate syndicates and real estate corporations. The profitability of the latter companies depends on their ability to manage their assets actively through continuous purchase and sale. However, because REITs were designed as passive investment vehicles, they were prohibited from actively turning over their properties or directly managing them. Instead, they were required to either employ property management firms or lease their properties.

Until recently, most REITs employed advisory firms to determine their management and investment policies. These advisors received a fee, typically a percentage of total assets, in return for their services. In most cases, the advisory firms were the original sponsors of the REITs. McMahan (1994) observes, moreover, that managers who worked for REIT advisory firms were unlikely to have any significant investment in the stocks of the REITs they managed. This created a potential conflict of interest within the early REIT structure because managerial decisions were not necessarily aligned with those of the shareholders.

Like their predecessors that were built on the Boston model, the early REITs initially invested in real property. Despite their predecessors' popularity, however, REITs did not catch on at first, in large part because of the stock market decline in May of 1962. In addition, investors and analysts were unfamiliar with REITs, and neither federal nor state laws had been developed to deal with them. Elliot (1965) reports that by 1965 there were approximately 65 REITs in existence, most of which had been created prior to the market downturn of 1962. Schulkin (1971) indicates that between 1963 and 1968, total capitalization grew slowly, with only a handful of new REITs raising more than $10 million in their initial offerings.

REITs initially focused on traditional property investments financed primarily with equity, but toward the end of the 1960s the growth of earnings (cash flows) was becoming an increasingly important objective of their managers and shareholders. As a result, REITs began to rely more heavily on short-term borrowing as well as on their traditional sources of financing: long-term debt, convertible debt, and warrants. In addition, a significantly larger number of new REITs focused on mortgage lending rather than simply on direct property investments. Almost all REITs created between 1968 and 1970, in fact, were mortgage REITs.

The 1960s: REITs Attract Investor Attention

As investment vehicles, REITs did not become popular until the late 1960s. Between 1968 and 1970, REIT assets more than quadrupled from an estimated $1.0 billion to $4.7 billion. Records of new issues between 1968 and 1970 indicate that the number of new REITs increased dramatically—from approximately 61 to 161.[2]

This growth in the number of REITs and in their assets was due to several factors. First, not only were capital markets becoming more comfortable with REIT securities, but changing credit conditions and the higher interest rates that prevailed in 1968–70 and 1973 created a significant shortage of funds for construction and development companies. During that period, banks, thrifts, and insurance companies could not directly engage in construction and development (C&D) lending activities because of regulations and statutory restrictions. This gave them an incentive to set up publicly funded REITs to engage in these activities.

In addition, banks, thrifts, and other traditional providers of mortgage loans and C&D credit faced restrictions on their ability to raise funds by paying higher rates on deposits. *Mortgage REITs,* which have at least 75% of their holdings in such direct financial assets as mortgages and short-term loans (compared to *equity REITs,* which invest at least 75% of their assets directly in real property) were in a position to take advantage of these changing conditions by financing the purchase or construction of real estate properties. That is, because their rates were not regulated, mortgage REITs were able to pay the higher interest rates necessary to finance riskier mortgage and C&D loans. As a result, many banks and a number of developers set up their own mortgage trusts to satisfy the demand for short-term and higher risk C&D loans. These banks also frequently acted as the advisors to their trusts. These activities in late 1960s and early 1970s marked the beginning of a period of significant growth in the REIT industry.

Analyzing data from 114 REITs obtained from the National Association of Real Estate Trusts (NAREIT) and from standard sources of financial information, Schulkin (1971) found that 45 REITs had invested primarily in C&D loans and that 60 had invested primarily in long-term equity property investments. In addition, 55 of these REITs were advised by commercial banks, insurance companies, and financial conglomerates, whereas 13 were advised by mortgage bankers.

Although most of the REITs created during this period were of the mortgage and equity type, a third type also appeared. This was the *hybrid REIT,* which represented a mixture of the equity and mortgage REITs because it invested in both real estate property and mortgages. (Table 2.1 and figure 2.1 give an idea of the trends in the growth in average and total REIT capitalization.)

The 1970s: Rough Times for REITs

Although REIT returns were respectable in the early years, a number of problems soon surfaced—especially for mortgage REITs specializing in (C&D) loans and the higher risk mortgage segments of the industry during the early 1970s. The boom in building that had accompanied the significant increase in REIT financing for these types of loans ended in the way that many real estate booms frequently end: through poor investment decisions and overbuilding.

By 1973, mortgage REITs that financed C&D and longer term loans for condominiums and apartments faced markets in which properties were in excess supply. At the same time, interest rates were rising along with construction costs (due primarily to rising inflation and a shortage of construction materials). Hines (1975) suggests that these conditions led to a significant number of mortgage defaults and builder bankruptcies.

This situation was due in part to competition among lenders, which had caused many REITs to finance questionable projects. In many cases, REIT managers were inexperienced in real estate investing, and very few of them understood the limitations of the REIT vehicle as a source of funding for real estate development. As a result, most new REITs were financing long-term mortgages using short-terms sources of funding, such as commercial paper with maturities ranging from 30 to 60 days. The short maturity of their sources of financing forced them to borrow at increasing rates, putting a strain on profitability and, in many cases, creating negative spreads between the cost of funds and the return on REIT investments.

Furthermore, the investment advisors for many C&D lenders were banks, which often lacked expertise in real estate markets. Robertson (1975) reports that these problems, coupled with the inherent conflict of interest among banks, REITs, and REIT advisors, created pressure on these REITs to make loans of questionable quality. This conflict of interest was motivated—predictably—by the desire of banks and REIT advisors to earn fee income. Since advisor fees were based on the gross amounts of funds loaned, advisors had a strong incentive to push REITs to borrow so that they could make new loans.

Table 2.1 Annual Equity-Market Capitalization and Return Performance of Publicly Traded REITs

	Capitalization ($ thousands)		Total Return		
Year-End	Mean	Total	Annual Mean (%)	Index	Number of REITs
1962	21,010	42,020	22.64	122.64	2
1963	20,637	41,274	−2.58	119.48	2
1964	21,073	63,219	26.27	150.87	3
1965	33,138	132,554	14.52	172.78	4
1966	26,993	107,974	−12.79	150.67	4
1967	32,926	164,631	25.57	189.20	5
1968	68,379	341,895	65.96	314.01	5
1969	64,702	711,717	9.12	342.66	11
1970	51,216	1,587,699	8.06	370.29	31
1971	62,575	3,253,912	29.45	479.36	52
1972	59,823	6,939,422	14.65	549.60	116
1973	37,290	5,034,176	−29.62	386.79	135
1974	11,912	1,548,590	−66.89	128.05	130
1975	13,239	1,628,377	21.70	155.84	123
1976	18,048	2,219,856	56.12	243.31	123
1977	20,399	2,407,057	36.12	331.19	118
1978	19,939	2,292,997	13.32	375.28	115
1979	25,499	2,804,876	43.69	539.25	110
1980	31,449	3,490,866	33.68	720.86	111
1981	32,113	3,050,707	7.61	775.73	95
1982	46,337	4,170,314	28.35	995.67	90
1983	58,615	4,982,276	32.80	1,322.21	85
1984	70,218	5,757,841	12.68	1,489.92	82
1985	74,824	8,006,183	13.33	1,688.54	107
1986	91,518	10,158,482	12.45	1,898.78	111
1987	79,941	9,832,693	−12.43	1,662.73	123
1988	89,918	11,149,880	10.41	1,835.78	124
1989	94,854	11,287,613	−7.46	1,698.81	119
1990	72,426	8,473,844	−24.40	1,284.26	117
1991	92,910	12,635,755	26.86	1,629.27	136
1992	111,969	15,563,732	12.66	1,835.50	139
1993	177,075	32,758,840	39.19	2,554.81	185
1994	194,138	44,457,700	2.66	2,622.68	229
1995	252,195	56,239,464	21.69	3,191.62	223
1996	409,898	83,209,306	37.30	4,382.24	203
1997	630,108	132,322,628	24.54	5,457.67	210
1998	635,573	138,554,856	−14.24	4,680.47	218
1999	611,895	128,498,029	−2.39	4,568.44	210
2000	725,714	140,062,860	15.96	5,297.44	193

Source: Information prepared by the authors using the REIT sample described in the appendix.

Note: The return index series is based on December 1961 = 100.

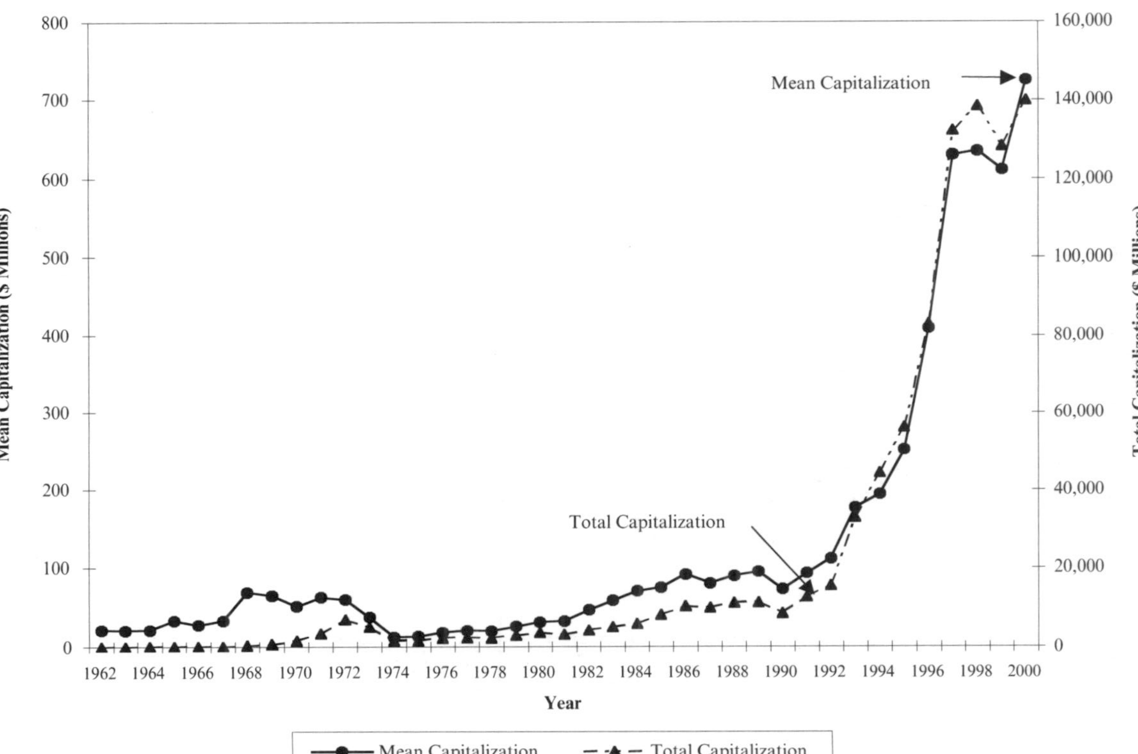

Figure 2.1 Annual Mean and Total REIT Capitalization

Poor investment judgment, high levels of leverage, and the conflicts of interest that existed between banks sponsors and their REIT subsidiaries were not the only problems. The rigid requirements necessary to qualify as a REIT worked to reduce significantly the flexibility of the REIT to adjust to declining markets. For example, although REITs can use the "like-kind" exchange provisions of section 1031 of the Internal Revenue Code to exchange properties in their portfolios, restrictions on the acquisition and sale of REIT assets at least constrain their ability to diversify their asset portfolios adequately or to eliminate poorly performing properties from them altogether.

In 1975, REIT earnings were squeezed further when the accounting profession imposed new, more conservative accounting standards requiring REITs to recognize both the cost of carrying loan losses and their estimated future costs. By the beginning of 1975, REITs owed $11 billion to banks, which represented more than half of all REIT assets. Many REITs had financed their activities based on the expectation that their earnings (cash flows) would grow significantly. Stevenson (1977) observes that some REITs even issued convertible debt in the expectation that the debt would be converted to equity as earnings growth pushed up REIT share prices. As the number of bankruptcies by developers rose, however, mortgage REITs were left with an increasing number of nonperforming loans in their portfolios.

According to the 1986 *REIT Fact Book,* published by NAREIT, total REIT assets declined by 40% between the end of 1973 and the end of 1975. Similarly, the value of total REIT common equity declined by 68% between the end of 1973 and the end of 1975, while the return performance index plunged 60% during the same period (see table 2.1 and figures 2.1 and 2.2). This significant decline could be attributable to the problems mentioned above.

Non-Mortgage REITs During the 1970s

As suggested previously, most of the losses experienced by the REIT industry as a whole during the early 1970s were concentrated in the mortgage sector, which had participated in making C&D and longer term loans to developers in overbuilt condominium and apartment markets. In general, while the returns in all the sectors of the REIT industry declined, equity REIT performance fared the best.

For example, in 1972 the total returns to mortgage and hybrid REIT investors were 10% and 18%, respectively. In 1974 they were –50% and –76%, respectively, as table 2.2 and figure 2.3 illustrate. The returns to equity REITs declined from +11% in 1972 to –57% at the end of 1974. Those REITs that continued to specialize in direct equity investments based on conservative investment valuations and using low levels of leverage were able to maintain their profitability. As a new form of real estate investment vehicle, REITs were going through a period of growing pains, forcing their

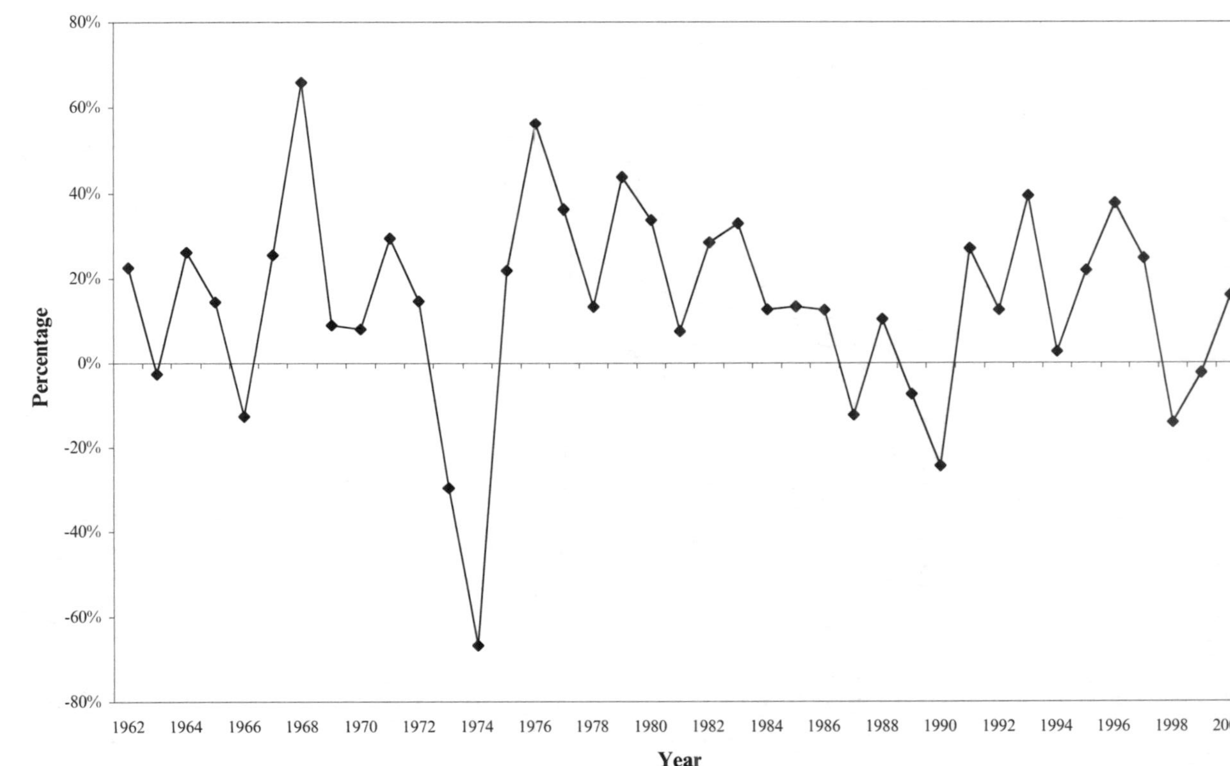

Figure 2.2 Annual Mean Total Returns for All-Publickly-traded REITs

Table 2.2 Annual Mean Total Return by REIT Type

Year End	Equity REIT (%)	Number of Obs.	Hybrid REIT (%)	Number of Obs.	Mortgage REIT (%)	Number of Obs.
1962	22.64	2	—	0	—	0
1963	−2.58	2	—	0	—	0
1964	45.86	2	−9.99	1	—	0
1965	−0.08	2	13.21	1	45.25	1
1966	−13.27	2	−15.60	1	−12.37	1
1967	16.03	3	−0.70	1	49.33	1
1968	42.27	3	88.05	1	135.82	1
1969	−13.38	5	68.20	4	−11.05	2
1970	17.55	10	2.50	18	9.09	3
1971	17.41	15	37.10	30	7.56	7
1972	11.48	44	17.64	58	10.21	14
1973	−21.30	54	−34.43	65	−23.15	16
1974	−56.79	50	−76.14	65	−49.65	15
1975	23.82	52	14.95	57	−7.47	14
1976	51.25	52	53.83	57	72.64	14
1977	45.00	52	31.84	52	16.75	14
1978	16.76	51	12.33	50	2.21	14
1979	52.09	51	41.07	46	2.90	13
1980	45.55	55	25.41	42	14.53	14
1981	10.81	51	0.19	29	4.19	15
1982	25.22	48	28.85	29	37.85	13
1983	35.74	46	36.08	28	−11.02	11
1984	17.52	47	9.19	21	2.18	14
1985	13.27	63	15.66	22	−0.49	22
1986	7.93	65	16.07	20	20.78	26
1987	−10.76	76	−12.44	21	−14.86	26
1988	11.72	69	18.43	21	2.62	34
1989	−3.30	67	−9.62	22	−6.77	30
1990	−25.82	67	−32.33	21	−15.21	29
1991	22.42	87	20.87	21	−0.82	28
1992	14.75	91	8.97	22	8.04	26
1993	46.77	134	42.36	21	9.44	30
1994	4.15	181	−2.50	21	−3.29	27
1995	19.30	179	16.65	18	10.60	26
1996	37.06	167	25.91	15	46.77	21
1997	22.29	171	36.71	13	34.28	26
1998	−11.01	174	−8.67	13	−34.52	31
1999	−2.90	167	0.15	14	−1.53	29
2000	17.31	156	12.86	13	8.79	24

Source: Information prepared by the authors based on the REIT sample described in the appendix.

Note: The series for Equity REITs, Hybrid REITs, and Mortgage REITs begins in July 1962, May 1964, and June 1965, respectively.

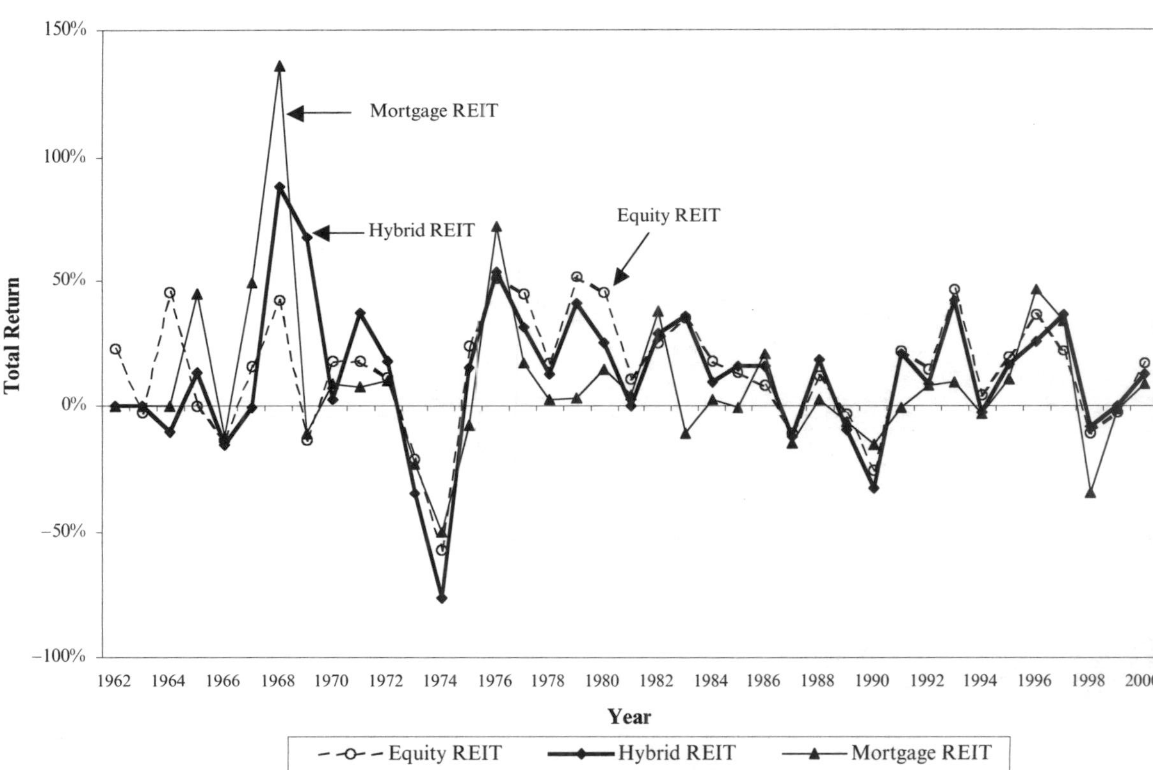

Figure 2.3 Annual Mean Total Return by REIT type

sponsors and their investors to recognize their limitations and adjust their investment strategies accordingly.

The Tax Reform Act of 1976

Most mortgage REITs that had problems during this period sought to recover by renegotiating bank loans, swapping or selling properties to reduce bank debt, and improving the quality of properties in their portfolios. In recognition of the difficulties REITs faced during this period, Congress made a number of substantial changes in the tax provisions that applied to REITs through the Tax Reform Act of 1976 (TRA 76). These changes were not entirely satisfactory in terms of providing REITs with the flexibility needed to deal with the problems of earnings losses (e.g., the new law increased the dividend payout requirement from 90 to 95%). Nonetheless, the changes did provide some flexibility that allowed REITs to adapt to downturns in economic conditions. Among other things, TRA 76 reduced the likelihood that a REIT would inadvertently lose its tax status because of a failure to meet the strict qualification requirements. The new law eliminated disqualification as the penalty for unintentionally failing to meet the 75% and 90% gross-income tests. The accounting treatment of operating losses and capital gains was also modified to allow eight years of losses to be carried forward, which reduced the incentive for a REIT to voluntarily disqualify itself in order to carry forward such losses.

REITs were also given the right to hold property for sale, although they were subject to a special excise tax of 100% on the income produced when these properties were sold unless REITs acted as investors rather than dealers. The law presumptively concluded that a REIT would not incur the excise tax if it satisfied a number of criteria, including a limit on the number of sales and a minimum four-year holding period for the sold property.[3]

Nevertheless, many REITs with significant losses gave up their REIT status and became corporations in order to gain an operating company's greater flexibility in dealing with the losses they were incurring. In a study of the impact of tax reform on the performance of REITs and other real estate assets, Sanger, Sirmans, and Turnbull (1990) provide evidence that TRA 76, along with other changes in the laws affecting REITs in 1975 and 1976, improved their performance while effectively reducing their risk relative to the overall securities market.

The adjustments to the laws governing all REITs—along with the REIT industry's recognition of the excesses associated with many mortgage and hybrid REIT lending practices and the difficulties created by the excessive use of leverage—provided the basis for the industry's recovery. However, because of the magnitude of the problem, the recovery process was slow. Total REIT assets fell from their high of $20.48 billion in 1974 to $7.10 billion in 1981.[4] Nossiter (1982) estimates that the total number of public and private REITs in existence declined from 250 in 1972 to 124 in 1982. Likewise, the total market capitalization of publicly traded REITs in 1972 was $7 billion. The industry did not reach this level again until 1985.

Those REITs that survived the poor real estate markets of the early 1970s took advantage of the significantly lower prices that were due to the large numbers of properties put on the market by C&D REITs and their bank sponsors who sought to recover. This led to a large improvement in REIT returns after 1975. For example, from its lowest point in 1974, the REIT total return index rose by 193% by 1978 and by another 107% between end of 1978 and the end of 1981 (see table 2.1). Much of this recovery was due to surviving equity REITs that had purchased low-priced properties made available by financially distressed mortgage REITs. In addition, many mortgage REITs evolved into equity REITs when they foreclosed on properties and took over ownership.

The 1980s: A Changing Market Environment

Although REIT returns had recovered from their lows of 1974, the recovery in the popularity of REITs as investment vehicles took longer, as evidenced by the relatively slow increase in total REIT capitalization. By 1982, investors viewed REITs as significantly undervalued. These perceptions were fueled by the recognition that REITs had been out of investor favor for almost a decade. Moreover, Edmunds (1982) suggests that REITs in general failed to revalue the carrying costs of their older properties. Instead of realizing loan losses in earnings and reducing their reserves, REIT managers chose a more conservative view and maintained their reserves in anticipation of the possibility of declining market values. Only after properties were sold at prices generating extraordinary gains could REIT managers recognize increased property values.

These factors, along with the sudden jump in the general popularity of REIT stocks that occurred in 1982, helped propel average total capitalization upward by 119% between 1981 and the end of 1984 while the index of total REIT returns increased by 92% (see table 2.1). How had REITs changed? In addition to paring down their debt and ceasing to lend to risky C&D projects, many mortgage REITs had returned to real property investments. Mortgage REITs also made significant inroads into less risky mortgage lending as insurance companies and savings and loan organizations (S&Ls) reduced their loan originations in this area.

In addition, in 1981 the Economic Recovery Act provided significant new tax breaks for property investors in the forms of operating loss pass-throughs and shortened depreciation periods. This gave a significant impetus to the creation of *real estate limited partnerships (RELPs)* and encouraged a major boom in real estate investing. With the advent of the RELP, the competition for real estate investment capital helped reduce the popularity of REITs even though their average annual returns were more than 20% between 1981 and 1984.

Investors were attracted to RELPs because of the high tax-sheltered returns they could offer through the higher levels of leverage they took on, and because of the more generous tax write-offs they provided as a result of their ability to pass their losses through to investors. Moreover, because RELPs sold for less than their net asset values and with the assumption that there would be no subsequent declines in their asset values, their limited lives were intended to ensure that investors would realize a capital gain upon their termination when the underlying real estate assets were sold.[5]

Traditional REITs, on the other hand, resemble closed-end investment vehicles that can sell at either a discount or a premium to their net asset values. The fact that REITs did offer significantly greater liquidity than RELPs was not enough to overcome their limited attractiveness to investors until 1986, when changes in the tax laws limited many of the tax-shelter benefits of RELPs.

The 1980s also saw the creation of another limited-partnership investment vehicle that competed with REITs for investor dollars. This was the *master limited partnership (MLP),* which provided both liquidity and an investment concept similar to that of a REIT. In addition, the MLP provided investors with tax benefits similar to those of the traditional limited partnership. Originally designed to roll a number of smaller oil and gas partnerships into one publicly traded entity, the MLP concept was also used for a number of different types of real estate assets such as mortgages, diversified equity real estate properties, and specialized real estate assets (e.g., restaurant properties, hotels, and motels). Although first launched in 1981, the MLP did not become popular until the mid-1980s.

In response to these competing investment vehicles, the REIT industry successfully began to market an alternative investment vehicle called a *self-liquidating finite-life REIT (FREIT),* the first one of which was sponsored in 1976 by the Landsing Corporation. However, FREITs did not catch on with investors until they began to trade publicly in the 1980s. The FREIT was marketed as a way to eliminate one of the disadvantages of REITs relative to RELPs by promising investors that their assets would be liquidated after a finite period of time, typically averaging around 10 years. Although the liquidity of FREIT shares was similar to that of REITs, an FREIT also had the ability to terminate early in the event that market conditions made early termination desirable. This flexibility was intended to improve the likelihood that investors would receive a capital gain upon liquidation of the FREIT's assets.[6]

In addition to introducing the FREIT, the industry was in the process of adapting to changing market conditions in other ways. For example, many mortgage REITs sought to make participating mortgage loans that provided investors with additional income if property prices increased. Some REITs specialized in project lending to improve their returns, while others invested in properties through joint ventures to spread their risks.

Tax Reform Changes REITs Once More

Despite the espoused advantages of the FREIT vehicle, the changes in REIT debt structures, and more conservative investment policies, the primary impetus for the increased popularity of REITs was the Tax Reform Act of 1986 (TRA 86). This law and subsequent changes in the tax laws affecting REITs in 1987 and 1988 effectively eliminated the tax advantages that had underpinned most RELPs and MLPs prior to that time. Knight and Lee (1992) point out that, among other things, TRA 86 eliminated the ability to use passive income losses from partnerships to offset gains in other active or passive income, which had been one of the major advantages of limited partnerships. They also indicate that for REITs the law suspended both the minimum 100-shareholder requirement and the 5/50 rule for a REIT's first taxable year after the beginning of operations. It also allowed property that did not qualify as real estate for tax purposes to be treated as such for one year after investment by the REIT.

These changes made REITs attractive investments similar to RELPs and MLPs—but they also had other effects. For example, TRA 86 provided REITs with increased managerial flexibility. It amended the independent-contractor rule and allowed REITs to provide certain customary services to tenants without using independent contractors. This allowed REITs to capture the fees they had previously paid to independent contractors for these services. Nevertheless, REITs still had the problem that, if they provided services that were not "customary," all of the income earned from a tenant that might previously have been considered qualified income was considered tainted and thus was disqualified for income tax purposes.[7]

The significance of this change was that REITs were given greater managerial control over their properties and could make substantial investment decisions internally rather than externally. TRA 86 allowed REITs to be actively managed instead of externally advised, which provided a greater alignment of management and shareholder interests. Having an internal management helped reduce some of the conflicts of interest that had existed between REITs and their shareholders and brought the REIT entity closer to the operating level of management decision making. The change also provided REIT managements with the opportunity to improve the efficiency of their operating decisions, and was a major step toward the creation of the fully integrated REIT.

The 1990s: Growth and Change—Again

Real estate markets and prices saw a significant downturn during late 1989 and the early 1990s.[8] The nominal annual mean returns to the REIT industry, which had rebounded initially from their 1987 lows, fell from a positive 10% in 1988 to a negative 24% in 1990. The large number of properties thrown on the market by failed banks and S&Ls was a significant factor in pushing down direct real estate prices and REIT returns. As in the past, those REITs that suffered most through this period were mortgage and hybrid REITs with excessive leverage. This was particularly true for those REITs specializing in lending for offices, condominiums, and hotels because the markets for these properties were significantly overbuilt.

The REIT Boom

With the collapse of property prices in 1990, the REIT industry was set once again for a significant recovery. Between the end of 1990 and the end of 1995, the REIT return index rose by 149%, and total REIT equity-market capitalization rose from $8.5 billion to more than $56 billion (see table 2.1), with most of the gain coming from price appreciation and new-share issuance. During this same period, total REIT assets rose from $44 billion to $97 billion. The total number of publicly traded REITs rose from 117 at the end of 1990 to 223 at the end of 1995.

The majority of this growth came from an increase in the number of equity REITs during the period. The total number of equity REITs increased from 67 in 1990 to 179 in 1995, while the total number of mortgage and hybrid REITs fell from 50 to 44 (see table 2.2). The size of the average REIT as measured by its total capitalization also increased significantly. For example, the average capitalization of all publicly traded REITs rose from $72 million in 1990 to $252 million in 1995 and to $726 million in 2000 (see table 2.1). More important, equity REITs became an even more significant player in the REIT market. In 1990, the capitalization of equity REITs accounted for 64% of the capitalization of all REITs, an amount that increased to 87% by 1995.

The decline in the number and relative capitalization of mortgage and hybrid REITs during this period was part of a longer term secular trend that can be attributed to at least two factors. The first is the significant volatility of mortgage REITs combined with their lower average annual returns relative to those of equity REITs. Although the annual returns of mortgage REITs often surpassed those of equity REITs in good years, the average annual returns to mortgage and hybrid REITs have traditionally been below those of equity REITs measured over longer periods of time.

According to Brown (2000), the particularly weak performance of certain mortgage REITs during the late 1980s and early 1990s was the result of high leverage combined with the ownership characteristics of the properties on which the REITs were lending, resulting in significant financial problems during market downturns. This financial distress led to a large number of foreclosures of nonperforming loans because mortgage REITs had little or no incentive to renegotiate these loans to prevent foreclosure.[9] As a result, a large number of foreclosed properties were put on the market at low prices and purchased by equity REITs, resulting in a significant shift in asset values and market capitalization away from mortgage REITs and toward equity REITs.[10]

In addition, a major factor propelling the growth of equity REITs during the 1990s was the organizational innovation of the umbrella partnership REIT (discussed later). Because the umbrella partnership REIT structure facilitated the acquisition of private real estate property by equity REITs, it became enormously popular and attracted a significant amount of investor capital. The nature of this innovation meant that it was confined to equity REITs and could not be matched by mortgage or hybrid REITs because of differences in their assets.

Factors in the Growth of the REIT Industry

Aside from the low property prices that spurred the REIT recovery, several changes during this period significantly contributed to the increase in REITs' total capitalization. The first change was the Omnibus Budget Reconciliation Act of 1993, which changed REIT shareholder ownership requirements as they applied to pension funds. Because REITs are stocks with high-dividend yields, they are naturally desirable long-term investments for pension funds. However, prior to this law, REITs had had to meet the conditions of the 5/50 rule, which required that no fewer than five individuals could own more than a combined 50% of all shares outstanding. The rule reduced the attractiveness of REITs to pension funds because a pension fund's investment in a REIT counted as that of one individual investor rather than as the investments of the multiple owners of the pension fund. The 1993 act, however, modified the 5/50 rule for pension funds so that they were allowed to count all of their own investors in the fund as individuals for REIT investment purposes and thus avoid violating the 5/50 rule as long as the REIT had at least 100 shareholders. This change in legal requirements helped spur pension investment in REITs, which contributed to the growth of REIT capitalization and led to increased interest by investment banking firms and their securities analysts. This in turn had the effect of increasing the number of traders investing in REITs, which contributed to the increased liquidity of the REIT stock market.

The second change that has contributed to REIT growth was the structural innovation of the *umbrella partnership REIT (UPREIT).* An UPREIT consists of two entities: the REIT and an *operating partnership (OP),* both of which issue ownership units. The REIT issues stock shares to the public and uses the funds it raises to purchase properties and an interest in the OP (usually a controlling interest); thus, in an UPREIT structure, the REIT owns its properties indirectly through the OP. The operating partners (who frequently include the REIT's management and who owned the properties before swapping them into the REIT) are issued OP units for the real estate assets they contribute to the REIT. Existing owners of properties can swap their current real estate investments for OP units using the Internal Revenue Service (IRS) tax-deferred exchange rule 731. Operating partnership unit holders have the right to convert these shares into the REIT's shares, but this conversion is a fully taxable event. The contributing partner must be careful not to lose his or her share of debt in the contributed properties or else risk immediate taxation.

The UPREIT structure facilitates the securitization of real estate by allowing the operating partners to defer capital gains taxes until a time when the tax benefits of such a conversion are the greatest. It is this benefit that provides the motivation for owners of private real estate to move their properties into an UPREIT. In 1993 and 1994, 67% and 89%, respectively, of all new equity REIT capital was raised through IPOs that used the UPREIT vehicle.

A third change of significance during this period was the increase in the number of REITs specializing in distinct types of property such as apartments, office and industrial properties, shopping malls, self-storage properties, hotels and motels, and others. Most of the REITs that came to the market in 1993 were self-advised and their managers took significant equity positions in them. Furthermore, McMahan (1994) notes that many of the individuals on REIT management teams had worked in specific property sectors for years prior to their IPOs. This trend has proven beneficial to the industry and its shareholders because it means that REIT management is more focused and more knowledgeable about the specific property sectors in which they operate, which should lead to improved managerial efficiency and increased profitability.

The REIT Simplification Act and the REIT Modernization Act

Another set of important changes that have recently affected REITs are embodied in the Taxpayer Relief Act of 1997, also called the REIT Simplification Act (REITSA), and the REIT Modernization Act (RMA) of 1999. REITSA contained 12 provisions directly affecting REITs. Among other things, REITSA eliminated certain provisions that would have disqualified REIT rental income for tax purposes if the REIT performed certain nonqualifying services for tenants. REITSA also eliminated the tax on shareholders who receive retained capital gains distributed at a later date, and it repealed the rule requiring that a REIT not earn more than 30% of its gross income from the sale of assets not held as long-term investments.[11]

The RMA of 1999 went into effect in 2001 and carries the changes initiated by REITSA even further. Among other things, it allows REITs to own taxable subsidiaries that can provide their tenants services that REITs cannot currently provide without disqualifying their rents from favorable tax treatment. Edwards (2000) also reports that the law allows REITs that own nursing homes (healthcare REITs) to hire independent contractors to run the homes. Finally, the RMA of 1999 reduces the taxable earnings distribution requirement of REITs from 95 to 90%. Both of these changes to the tax laws are a continuation of the process that began with the TRA of 1976. The REIT industry continues to lobby Congress to improve the competitive position of REITs as owners and operators in real estate markets. On June 4, 2001, the IRS released a revenue ruling (no. 2001–29) reaffirming that a REIT can operate an active trade or business as part of its typical real estate rental activities.

The Modern REIT

It is clear that changes in the tax laws governing REITs over the last 40 years have had mixed effects on the growth of the REIT industry. The good news is that the more recent of these changes have increased the efficiency of REITs' operations by eliminating or modifying many of the burdensome tax-related compliance restrictions that reduced their ability to compete in their markets.

The increased specialization of REITs in particular property sectors, the recent change in structural organization, and the increased attractiveness of REITs to institutional investors have also contributed to the significant increase in the efficiency and profitability of the average REIT. The greater transparency and lower debt levels compared to those for privately held real estate make REITs a better investment vehicle for small investors. Furthermore, the industry has become increasingly aware that its future lies in direct property investments. In 1999 about 80% of all publicly traded REITs were equity REITs, which accounted for 95% of total REIT capitalization.

Many REITs have also recognized the benefits of size, which gave rise in the mid-1990s to an increase in consolidation not only in the form of single-asset and portfolio acquisitions but also in the form of REIT mergers. The following appear to be the advantages of consolidation:

1. increased operating efficiency and higher flow of funds from operations;
2. economies of scale, which can lead to a lower cost of capital;
3. greater access to capital resulting from the increased attention of financial analysts;
4. increased liquidity of the shares, which is an essential condition for a stock to attract institutional investors' attention; and
5. the benefits of both horizontal and vertical integration.[12]

In addition, there is increasing awareness that size is beneficial in allowing REITs to gain a significant share of their markets. In effect, the modern REIT has become more like the modern operating company in pursuing the goals of strategic advantage and long-term profitability.

The Future of the REIT Concept

The REIT concept has evolved significantly since its creation more than 100 years ago. Today's REITs are very different from both the 19th-century Massachusetts real estate trusts and, to a large extent, the first REITs that Congress envisioned when it created the REIT industry in 1960.

Yet although the REIT industry has come a long way and has seen many changes in organizational and operating structures, it is clear that the core REIT concepts and the incentives to establish REITs will remain the same in the foreseeable future. The demand from real estate capital users to access public capital markets and the demand on the part of investors, both large and small, for a liquid and fungible real estate investment vehicle will persist, especially when this vehicle is characterized by the absence of the double-taxation of income. However, because change is necessary for the survival of REITs in changing markets, the organizational characteristics, ownership structures, and investment strategies that REITs adopt are also likely to continue evolving as long as the tax laws governing them allow for such changes.

NOTES

1. See Valachi (1977) for a discussion of the origins of REITs as Massachusetts business trusts.
2. See REIT Fact Book (1976) and Korobow and Gelson (1972). These estimates undoubtedly include both publicly traded and private REITs. This accounts in part for the discrepancy between the number of REITs found on the CRSP and COMPUSTAT tapes and reported in table 2.1 When using COMPUSTAT tapes, researchers should be aware that the tapes routinely identify other entities as REITs.
3. See Wurtzebach (1977) and Phillips and Cowen (1977) for a detailed discussion of these issues.
4. See various issues of the REIT Fact Book.
5. This did not happen, however, and many RELPs were compelled to sell their assets at distressed values.
6. Nevertheless, FREITs turned out to be poor investments relative to traditional REITs. See Goebel and Kim (1989).
7. See Edwards (1997) for a discussion of these changes.
8. For a detailed discussion of why real estate markets are always overbuilt, see Wang and Zhou (2000).
9. For a detailed discussion of why lenders do not have an incentive to negotiate with borrowers, see Wang, Young, and Zhou (2002).
10. It should be noted that equity REITs bought a substantial proportion of their properties from distressed equity owners, banks, foreign investors, and mortgage REITs.

11. For a detailed discussion of REITSA, see NAREIT, *The Real Estate Provisions of the Tax Payer Relief Act of 1997,* (1997).

12. See Mahan and Galloway (1997) and Baird and Donahue (1996) for a discussion of these issues. It should also be noted that some argue that large size will decrease earnings-per-share growth (see Mueller 1998).

REFERENCES

Bailey, Norman F. 1966. Real estate investment trusts: An appraisal. *Financial Analysts Journal* 22 (May/June): 107–14.

Baird, Blake, and Paul J. Donahue Jr. 1996. The future of consolidation. *REIT Report* 16 (Autumn): 28.

Bergson, Steven M. 1983. Send in the clones: REITs come up with new twists to attract investors. *Barron's* (13 February).

Brown, David T. 2000. Liquidity and liquidation: Evidence from real estate investment trusts. *Journal of Finance* 55 (1): 469–85.

Doherty, Edward. 1983. Ex-REIT's back from the brink. *Financial World* 152 (15 August): 28.

Edmunds, John C. 1982. Why REIT stocks are undervalued. *Real Estate Review* 12 (Fall): 96–99.

Edwards, Tony. 2000. At your service: REITs modernized. *Real Estate Portfolio* (March/April): 43–46

Edwards, Tony. 1997. REITs simplified. *REIT Report* XVIII (Autumn): 35–39.

Elliot, Richard J., Jr. 1962. More room at the top? Real estate investment trusts have come to Wall Street and Main Street. *Barrons National and Business Financial Weekly* 30:3+.

Elliot, Richard J., Jr. 1965. Fresh appraisal: The rewards and risks in real estate investment trusts. *Barrons National and Business Financial Weekly* 45:3+.

Goebel, Paul R., and Kee S. Kim. 1989. Performance evaluation of finite-life real estate investment trusts. *Journal of Real Estate Research* 4:57–69.

Hines, Mary Alice. 1975. What has happened to REITs? *Appraisal Journal* 43:252–60.

Knight, Ray A., and Lee G. Knight. 1992. REITs reemerge as attractive investment vehicles. *Real Estate Review* 22:42–48.

Korobow, Leon, and Richard J. Gelson. 1972. REITs: Impact on mortgage credit. *Appraisal Journal* 40:42–54.

McMahan, John. 1994. The long view: A perspective on the REIT market. *Real Estate Issues* 19:1–4.

McMahan, John, and Margaret Galloway. 1997. A strategic alliance: The BRE-RCT merger. *REIT Report* 17:27–33.

Menna, Gilbert G. 1998. *The UPREIT structure after two years: Where do we go from here?* Washington D.C.: NAREIT.

Mueller, Glenn. 1998. REIT size and earnings growth: Is bigger better or a new challenge? *Journal of Real Estate Portfolio Management* 4 (2): 149–57.

National Association of Real Estate Investment Trusts (NAREIT). 1976. *REIT Fact Book / 1976.* Washington, D.C.: NAREIT.

National Association of Real Estate Investment Trusts. 1997. *The real estate provisions of the Taxpayer Relief Act of 1997.* Washington, D.C.: NAREIT.

National Association of Real Estate Investment Trusts. 1999. *White paper on funds from operations.* Washington, D.C.: NAREIT.

National Association of Real Estate Investment Trusts. 2000. *Statistical digest.* Washington, D.C.: NAREIT.

Nossiter, Daniel D. 1982. Building values: REITs adapt to changes in the business climate. *Barrons National and Business Financial Weekly* 62:11+.

Phillips, Lawrence C., and Scott S. Cowen. 1977. Tax reform implications for real estate investment trusts. *Tax Magazine* 55:84–91.

Reier, Sharon. 1985. The return of the REITs. *Institutional Investor* 19:31+.

Robertson, Wyndham. 1996. How the bankers got trapped in the REIT disaster. *Fortune* 91:113–15+.

Rogers, Ronald C., and James E. Owers. 1985. The investment performance of real estate limited partnerships. *AREUEA Journal* 13 (2): 153–66.

Sagalyn, Lynne. 1996. Conflicts of interest in the structure of REITs. *Real Estate Finance* 13:153–56.

Sanger, Gary C., C. F. Sirmans, and Geoffrey K. Turnbull. 1990. The effects of tax reform on real estate: Some empirical results. *Land Economics* 66:409–24.

Schulkin, Peter A. 1971. Real estate investment trusts. *Financial Analysts Journal* 27:33–40+.

Seligman, Daniel. 1964. Personal investing: The rise of the R.E.I.T.'s. *Fortune* 69:177–78.

Smith, Keith, and David Shulman. 1976. The performance of equity real estate investment trusts. *Financial Analysts Journal* 31:61–66.

Smith, Keith V. 1980. Historical returns of real estate equity portfolios. In *The investment manager's handbook,* ed. Sumner Levine, 426–42. Homewood, Ill.: Dow Jones-Irwin.

Stevenson, Howard H. 1977. What went wrong with the REITs? *Appraisal Journal* 45:249–60.

Thomas, Dana L. 1974. Real estate fall-out: REIT collapse puts lots of property up for grabs. *Barrons National and Business Financial Weekly* 54:3+.

Valachi, Donald J. 1977. REITs: A historical perspective. *Appraisal Journal* 45:440–45.

Vinocur, Barry. 1986. Master limited partnerships, REITs both gain from tax reform. *Barrons National and Business Financial Weekly* 66:78.

Wang, Ko, Leslie Young, and Yuqing Zhou. 2002. Non-discriminating foreclosure and voluntary liquidating costs. *Review of Financial Studies* 15:959–85.

Wang, Ko, and Yuqing Zhou. 2000. Overbuilding: A game-theoretic approach. *Real Estate Economics* 28:493–522.

Wurtzebach, Charles. 1977. An institutional explanation of poor REIT performance. *Appraisal Journal* 45:103–09.

3

Organizational Structure

Is There Such a Thing As a Free Lunch?

A company can choose among a wide variety of organizational forms for holding real property and mortgages. For publicly held companies, these forms include the REIT, the master limited partnership (MLP), the business trust, and the corporation. If a firm elects to hold real properties using a REIT as the vehicle, then the tax at the corporation level is exempted. Given this tax benefit, one would argue that if there are no costs associated with this particular organizational form, then all corporations should use it to hold real properties and mortgages.

In reality, of course, this is not the case—many property companies elect to be corporations, partnerships, or business trusts. The question, considering the REIT's tax benefits, is why?[1] Apparently, certain costs are preventing some firms from adopting this particular organizational form.

Briefly, a firm that elects to be a REIT loses management flexibility. How costly that is varies according to the characteristics of the firm. Any firm entertaining the idea of becoming a REIT must consider whether the positive attributes (the tax benefits and the benefits of being a public company) will outweigh any potentially negative consequences, and which REIT type will be in a position to capture the former while avoiding the latter. This chapter answers these important questions.

The Costs of Being a REIT

As mentioned in chapter 2, a firm must meet some requirements to become a REIT. Although these requirements change over time, we can roughly group them into four categories:

1. *Restrictions placed on the ownership structure.* For example, no more than 50% of the shares of a REIT can be held directly or indirectly by any group of five or fewer investors (a restriction that has been relaxed in recent years, as discussed in chapter 2).
2. *Restrictions on the type of income a REIT can generate and the type of assets a REIT it may hold.* For example, certain percentages of income and assets must be property or mortgage related. (These percentages have changed over time.) There is also a limitation on the percentage of income in a given year that can come from the sales of properties held for the short term.
3. *Restrictions on the company's management structure.* In the past, for example, a REIT could not manage its own business and had to hire an outside advisor to do so.
4. *Restrictions on financial policies.* For example, to qualify as a REIT the company must distribute 90% of its taxable income, which includes capital gains.

As discussed in previous chapters, Congress established the REIT as a vehicle through which the small investor could participate in real estate investment. The subsequent limitations placed on REITs, although well intended, have imposed real costs that may be problematic for the very investors Congress originally intended to help. The following sections will point out and elaborate upon some of these costs.

Reduced Benefits of Using Debt

It is well documented in the finance literature that the advantages of using debt are the tax-deductibility of interest and the reduction of free cash flow (and hence the lowering of agency costs). Because REITs do not pay corporate income taxes, however, the tax benefits of using debt do not apply to them; and because REITs must compete with regular firms in the market for debt capital, the after-tax cost of using debt will be higher for REITs than for other firms. Given these considerations, REITs have less incentive to use debt.[2]

Reducing the free cash flow (the other benefit of using debt) means there will be less need for stockholders to incur costs to monitor a manager's decisions. Because the compensation of many managers is based on the size of the company, there is an incentive for managers to invest in projects even if they are not profitable. When a company uses debt, however, a significant amount of income is committed to making debt payments and managers are unable to use the income to pursue unprofitable investments. In addition, the debt holders also have incentives to monitor the manager's decisions, which helps reduce the agency problems faced by the firm.

One might argue that the reduction of the free cash flow is not particularly important for REITs because REITs have to pay out 90% (95% before 1999) of their taxable income. However, Wang, Erickson, and Gau (1993) point out that this might not be the case. After paying out 95% of taxable income, a REIT still may have a significant amount of cash on hand because depreciation is not a cash-outflow item. Hence the reduction of free cash flow (and thus of agency costs) is still an important benefit of using debt, even if the dividend policy of REITs is restricted.

Reduced Growth Potential

The requirement that REITs pay out 90% of their taxable income means there is little internal capital left to facilitate the growth of the company. Given this and the fact that real estate is a capital-intensive business, a REIT will have to rely on external capital if the firm wishes to expand its property portfolio. This can be accomplished in only two ways: by issuing new stocks or issuing new debt. We already know that REITs are in a disadvantaged position to issue debt because deductions on interest payments no longer apply. From the finance literature, we also know that an issuance of equity securities will normally depress a firm's stock price. With these facts in mind, it is clear that one of the most important costs of electing to be a REIT is the limitation on future growth.

This is a particularly serious problem given the empirical evidence that the stocks of finite-life REITs perform much worse than other REITs (Goeber and Kim 1989). Finite REITs are those that will be liquidated after a certain period (say, 10 years after its establishment). Clearly, finite REITs have no growth potential, which is proof that the stock market emphasizes a firm's growth opportunities and values them accordingly. Thus the inability to use internal capital (retained earnings) to facilitate growth translates into a significant cost to REITs.

Conflicts of Interest between Shareholders and Managers

The conflict between advisor/managers and REIT shareholders has also been a detriment to growth in the property sector. Without the ability to manage their own assets actively, traditional developer/operators risk losing control of their properties upon conversion to REIT status. In addition, since the advisor of a REIT gives advice on the REIT's investment and financing decisions while also serving as the party who buys or sells properties and mortgages to that REIT, there is an inherent conflict of interest.

More seriously, since the compensation of REIT managers can be tied to the size of the REIT, the managers have an incentive to maximize their welfare by investing in unprofitable assets (as mentioned previously).

In 1986, private-letter rulings from the IRS allowed REITs to assume responsibility for selecting investment properties and managing assets, allowing them to obtain "self-advised" and "self-managed" status. The importance of eliminating the conflicts of interest was not widely recognized until after the Kimco REIT initial public offering (IPO) in 1991. Some people attribute the surge in IPOs of REITs in the early 1990s to the change in advisor regulations in 1986. However, it is interesting to note that the two competing organizational structures (internally advised vs. externally advised) existed concurrently during the period of rapid growth in the 1990s, and that both are prevalent even now. This dual structure provides an interesting laboratory to study which type of REIT is more suitable for absorbing the agency costs associated with REIT advisors.

The Problem of Market Timing

Most investors prefer to "time the market" if possible, meaning that they prefer to make purchase or disposition decisions based on perceived cycles in the real estate market. Moreover, investors choose at certain times to hold cash and dispose of their properties. Since REITs are required to hold a significant part of their assets as either properties or mortgages, unfortunately, they cannot time the market to the extent that a regular corporation might.

In addition, there is a restriction on the disposition of REIT properties. A REIT's lack of freedom to dispose of properties acquired with a short holding period (say, four years for properties and six months for mortgages) represents a significant risk for its portfolio. Although REITs might be able to use 1031 transactions (tax-free) to exchange properties in their portfolios, the restriction will at least put some constraints on their ability to move quickly from a cold market to a hot market or to get out of a distressed market altogether.

Conversion Costs

IRS section 351(e) stipulates that the conversion from a partnership to a corporate form, such as a REIT, is a taxable event. That is, converting from a partnership to a REIT requires the partnership to pay capital gains on the difference between the fair market value and the tax basis of the properties it holds. When the tax basis of a partnership is low compared with the market value of the properties, using the REIT structure will represent a significant cost to a partnership. In fact, this cost has prevented many partnerships from converting to REITs and is an important reason for the creation of UPREITs (discussed in the previous chapter).

The Net Effect of the REIT Organizational Form

Given the trade-off between the costs and benefits of using the REIT organizational form, it is worth questioning whether the net benefit is positive or negative. Although the benefits and costs vary for individual REITs, two recent studies consider whether the structure is beneficial to the average REIT.

The Tradeoff between Tax Benefits and Flotation Costs

Gyourko and Sinai (1999) present a convincing case that, using reasonable parameter values, the overall benefit of being a REIT outweighs the cost. In their trade-off analysis they consider two positive factors and one negative factor of the REIT structure. First, they consider the tax savings of being a REIT. They estimate that tax savings alone contribute about 4% percent of industry market capitalization. Furthermore, a REIT does not need to engage in potentially costly tax-avoidance strategies to the extent that a regular corporation does; Gyourko and Sinai estimate the cost savings on those strategies to be 1–4%. The total benefit of being a REIT adds up to around 5–8%. (Gentry, Kemsley, and Mayer (2002) provide direct evidence on the positive relationship between tax basis and firm value. Their findings indicate that investors capitalize future dividend taxes into the share prices of REITs.)

On the negative side, because REITs are required to pay out most of their taxable income, they have to raise capital to finance growth. Gyourko and Sinai (1999) estimate that the finance-related cost of raising capital is about 2.5% of industry market capitalization. Given this, the net benefit of being a REIT is about 2.5–5.5% of the industry equity market capitalization—a tremendous amount given the amount of total REIT capitalization. Furthermore, it is apparent that low-payout firms will benefit more from the REIT structure.

One might argue that a REIT could change its organizational structure to that of a corporation, or vice versa, based on its needs. However, Gyourko and Sinai (1999) believe that this strategy might create more harm than good. It is well documented in the finance literature that low–tax bracket investors tend to invest in stocks with high-dividend payout ratios because they do not mind paying ordinary income tax. On the other hand, high–tax bracket investors tend to invest in stocks with low dividend payout ratios because they prefer to avoid the tax on ordinary income.

Since REITs pay out high dividends, one would expect that their shareholders are mostly tax-exempt investors or investors in low tax brackets. Thus, if a REIT switches to a corporation, the tax-exempt or low–tax bracket shareholders will be upset. When the company switches back from corporation to REIT, the investors in the new corporation, who will probably be from higher tax brackets, will be upset.

It should be noted that Maris and Elayan (1991) provide empirical support for the tax-induced clientele hypothesis later proposed by Gyourko and Sinai (1999). Maris and Elayan found a negative relationship between investor tax rates and the dividend yield of a REIT stock. This means that tax-exempt investors or investors in low tax brackets tend to invest in REITs with high dividend-payout ratios. In addition, Damodaran, John, and Liu (1997) study organizational-form changes of REITs. They find few circumstances in which a firm changed organizational form twice during the 1966 to 1989 period. It seems likely that Gyourko and Sinai are correct—that switching back and forth from REIT to corporate status cannot reduce the costs and restrictions imposed on the REIT structure.

However, it should be noted that the comparison made by Gyourko and Sinai (1999) focuses only on the trade-off between tax shelters and the restriction on dividend payouts. Other costs, such as the restriction on assets and ownership, are not addressed. A second study, discussed in the next section, offers additional insights into the costs and benefits of the REIT structure.

Changes in Organizational Structure

Damodaran, John, and Liu (1997) report very interesting findings related to the REIT organizational structure. They document that when REITs are in distress, they tend to switch to the corporate structure. After changing from a REIT to a corporation, the firm will pay substantially smaller dividends than before and will restructure its assets. Specifically, such firms will sell a significant portion of their existing assets and replace them with new assets. This evidence indicates that the REIT structure does impose costs on a firm. Those costs are high for distressed firms, which need more flexibility in financial policies and asset acquisitions in times of distress.

On the other hand, Damodaran, John, and Liu also find that firms switching from a corporate to a REIT structure normally have significant amounts of free cash flow on hand. After a firm elects to be a REIT, it will pay out much larger dividends than before. Firms that change from a corporation to a REIT tend to restructure fewer assets than the REITs that change to corporations.

To summarize, Damodaran, John, and Liu find that firms changing from the REIT to the corporate structure are motivated by the advantage of having dividend-policy and asset-restructuring flexibility. This normally happens when firms are in distress. When a firm changes from a corporation to a REIT, the tax benefits are normally the motivation. From this we can conclude that firms with large cash flows to be paid out as dividends should elect to be REITs to avoid income taxes. Firms in distress should not use the REIT structure as a vehicle to hold real estate in order to avoid restrictions on their financing and operating policies. If our conclusion is accurate, we can further conclude that the net benefit of the REIT organizational structure is positive because, all other things being equal, there will be more healthy firms than distressed firms.

Whether to Take Advantage of the REIT Structure

Damodaran, John, and Liu (1997) report that the stock market responds to firms undergoing structural change—that is, when a firm makes an announcement about such a change, the market reacts positively. The profitability of such firms also increases following those changes. This indicates that the type of organizational structure has an impact on the value of a firm. Consequently, it pays for a corporation to choose the correct structure in the real estate market.

Table 3.1 provides some interesting information. In the table, we report the number of firms listed as REITs and de-listed as REITs in each year during the 1962–2000 period using the sample of 486 firms.Column (1) indicates how many REITs began trading in the stock market during the specified year. Column (2) presents the number of REITs that were dropped from the stock market. Column (3) reports the net number of REITs that traded on the stock market each year during the 1962–2000 period. As column (3) shows, 2 REITs were traded on the stock market in 1962; in 2000, however, there were a total of 211 REITs with stocks traded in the major stock markets. This shows that the REIT organizational structure is gaining support from the stock markets.

Note, however, that the number of publicly traded REITs does not always increase over time. From the table it is clear that many firms elected to be REITs or were de-listed as REITs in each year during the period under examination. We see that a significant number of firms became publicly traded REITs during the 1970–73, 1985–88, and 1993–98 periods; yet we also see that a significant number of REITs were de-listed during the 1979–83 and 1994–2000 periods. Similar patterns can also be observed from table 3.2, in which we partition REITs by the type of assets they hold. Since this pattern holds for both equity and mortgage REITs, the significant change in the number of REITs should not be due to the influence of the mortgage or property markets. This also gives clear evidence that the REIT organizational structure has fallen in and out of fashion several times during the 1962–2000 period.

Although these dramatic movements could be due to the cycles in the market at large, it is also possible that the REIT organizational structure might be more beneficial to certain investors at certain periods. This is especially true if we look at the 1993–2000 period, during which many corporations became publicly traded REITs at the same time that many other

Table 3.1 Number of REITs Listed, Traded, and De-listed in Each Year During the 1962–2000 Period

Year	Number of REITs That Began Trading (1)	Number of REITs That De-listed (2)	Number of REITs Traded (3)
1962	2	0	2
1963	0	0	2
1964	1	0	3
1965	1	0	4
1966	0	0	4
1967	1	0	5
1968	1	1	6
1969	6	0	11
1970	21	0	32
1971	22	0	54
1972	66	0	120
1973	22	4	142
1974	4	2	142
1975	1	3	141
1976	3	3	141
1977	2	9	140
1978	3	5	134
1979	2	10	131
1980	8	13	129
1981	4	20	120
1982	5	14	105
1983	5	12	96
1984	7	9	91
1985	33	8	115
1986	18	11	125
1987	11	3	125
1988	17	18	139
1989	6	8	127
1990	3	4	122
1991	22	2	140
1992	7	5	145
1993	49	4	189
1994	51	10	236
1995	8	17	234
1996	10	28	227
1997	30	19	229
1998	26	18	236
1999	7	15	225
2000	1	18	211
Total	486	293	

Table 3.2 Number of Equity, Mortgage, and Hybrid REITs Listed, Traded, and De-Listed Each Year During the 1962–2000 Period

	Equity REIT			Mortgage REIT			Hybrid REIT		
Year	Number to Begin Trading	Number to De-list	Total Number Traded	Number to Begin Trading	Number to De-list	Total Number Traded	Number to Begin Trading	Number to De-list	Total Number Traded
1962	2	0	2	0	0	0	0	0	0
1963	0	0	2	0	0	0	0	0	0
1964	0	0	2	1	0	1	0	0	0
1965	0	0	2	0	0	1	1	0	1
1966	0	0	2	0	0	1	0	0	1
1967	1	0	3	0	0	1	0	0	1
1968	1	1	4	0	0	1	0	0	1
1969	2	0	5	3	0	4	1	0	2
1970	5	0	10	15	0	19	1	0	3
1971	6	0	16	12	0	31	4	0	7
1972	29	0	45	30	0	61	7	0	14
1973	10	0	55	8	3	69	4	1	18
1974	2	1	57	2	1	68	0	0	17
1975	1	0	57	0	1	67	0	2	17
1976	3	1	60	0	2	66	0	0	15
1977	0	2	59	2	7	66	0	0	15

1978	1	2	58	2	2	61	0	1	15
1979	2	4	58	0	5	59	0	1	14
1980	4	2	58	3	11	57	1	0	14
1981	2	7	58	1	13	47	1	0	15
1982	2	7	53	2	4	36	1	3	16
1983	1	2	47	3	7	35	1	3	14
1984	4	3	49	0	6	28	3	0	14
1985	19	3	65	5	4	27	9	1	23
1986	11	6	73	2	4	25	5	1	27
1987	10	2	77	0	0	21	1	1	27
1988	6	12	81	2	2	23	9	4	35
1989	1	2	70	1	1	22	4	5	35
1990	1	1	69	1	1	22	1	2	31
1991	22	1	90	0	0	21	0	1	29
1992	5	2	94	1	0	22	1	3	29
1993	45	2	137	0	1	22	4	1	30
1994	51	7	186	0	0	21	0	3	29
1995	8	12	187	0	4	21	0	1	26
1996	8	19	183	0	2	17	2	7	27
1997	21	13	185	1	3	16	8	3	28
1998	14	12	186	3	3	16	9	3	34
1999	5	12	179	2	1	15	0	2	31
2000	1	12	168	0	1	14	0	5	29
Total	305	150		102	89		78	54	

Table 3.3 Summary Statistics of the Duration of Publicly Traded REIT Stocks

	Equity REITS	Mortgage REITs	Hybrid REITs	All REITs
Average number of days	2,854	3,696	2,701	3,081
Maximum number of days	10,426	9,773	10,040	10,426
Minimum number of days	343	201	265	201
Number of observations	150	89	54	293

REITs were de-listed from the stock market. Note that 1993–2000 is the period in which the REIT industry underwent a significant change in organizational structure. Firms chose whether to be REITs or not based on whether they could take advantage of those changes.

Furthermore, the average life of a publicly traded REIT is not very long. Table 3.3 indicates that, for the 293 REITs that were listed and de-listed during the 1962–2000 period, their average life is only eight years—that is, 3,081 days (days are more specific than fractions of years for our purposes). For those de-listed REITs, the maximum number of days is 10,426 and the minimum is 201. Equity, mortgage, and hybrid REITs trade on the stock market for 2,854 days, 3,696 days, and 2,701 days, respectively. This evidence (the short duration of REIT stocks) suggests that it might pay for a firm to take advantage of the REIT structure when situations allow—that is, to strike while the iron is hot.

A Comparison with the MLP and Corporation Structures

Besides the REIT organizational structure, the partnership structure also enjoys similar tax benefits. An *MLP* (or *master limited partnership,* mentioned earlier) is a limited partnership that is traded on a stock exchange. Apache Petroleum Company was the first MLP with units traded on a major stock market. Although it might be difficult to identify which companies are limited partnerships, Wang and Erickson (1997) point out that about 178 firms listed on the CRSP and COMPUSTAT tapes are companies whose names end with the word *partnership.*

After a detailed examination of the 178 companies, Wang and Erickson reported that 144 were MLPs during the 1981–91 period. Among the 144 MLPs traded on the stock market, 60 were real-estate related. Of these 60, 19 invested primarily in mortgage debt instruments (similar to mortgage REITs) and 41 invested in real properties (similar to equity REITs). Comparing these figures in to those in table 3.1, we can see that the number of real estate MLPs was significantly lower than the overall number of REITs during the same period.

However, even though the MLP organizational structure offers tax advantages similar to those of a REIT, it also suffers from burdensome administrative costs and agency issues. Partnerships need to keep very good accounting records for tax purposes. In addition, limited partnerships have little operational control over the business decisions of the partnership. This problem is even greater if the partnership is formed by a parent company—when the parent company acts as the general partner of an MLP, there is serious potential for a conflict of interest.

It should be noted that, unlike a traditional REIT, a partnership is an operating company just like any other industrial firm. However, because of agency issues and heavy administrative costs, empirical evidence indicates that a limited partnership might not be a good organizational form for holding real estate. Kapplin and Schwartz (1988) examine 119 real estate partnership transactions occurring on the National Partnership Exchange in 1985, and they find that the average internal rate of return of the transactions is only 3.5%—far below the return for common stocks during the same period. Roger and Owers (1985) conclude that, on a before-tax basis, real estate partnerships have not performed well relative to comparable real estate investments.

Wang and Erickson (1997) examine the stock performance of the 144 MLPs discussed earlier, which include 60 property and mortgage MLPs. They find that the 144 MLP stocks significantly underperformed the market on a risk-adjusted basis during the 1981–91 period. This indicates that the stock market does not seem to like this particular organizational form. However, they also find that, during the same period, the performance of the units of real estate MLPs seems to be comparable with that of REITs. Nevertheless, the empirical evidence on the performance of real estate MLPs seems to indicate that an MLP has not been a good vehicle for this particular purpose.

Empirical evidence also indicates that the limited-partnership organizational structure in real estate might be beneficial only to investors in high tax brackets (Roger and Owers 1985). Martin and Cook (1991) find that publicly traded limited partnerships perform worse than other common stocks. They report that the weak performance was especially evident after the passage of the Tax Revenue Act of 1987, which restricted the tax benefits of limited partnerships. Given the fact that REITs are now dominated by institutional investors who do not need to pay taxes, it is quite clear that the MLP form will fall out of favor when investors are looking for an organizational structure for holding real estate.

Since the empirical evidence clearly indicates that MLPs underperform the stock market and that the organizational structure is designed for investors in very high tax brackets, a natural question is why real estate partnerships do not change their organizational structure from an MLP to a corporation or a REIT. It is difficult to answer this question fully, because it is very difficult to identify firms that use the corporate form to hold real estate. Chan, Gau, and Wang (1995), for example, report that many non–real estate firms also hold a significant amount of assets in real estate such as headquarters, plants, and land. Moreover, it is difficult to compare the stock performance of real estate corporations with that of MLPs. However, Gyourko and Keim (1992) report that the stocks of 64 real estate–related companies (26 general contractors and 38 developers) perform similarly to other stocks in the market on a risk-adjusted basis. If we can use the stock performance of general contractors and developers as a proxy for real estate holding corporations, then it appears that using the corporate form to hold real estate is at least as good a vehicle as using an MLP.

It would be interesting to know whether MLPs should change their organizational structure to that of the REIT, given the fact that there are many institutional investors in the real estate stock market. Given what we already know about MLPs, the answer to the question is probably yes. The next section focuses on this important issue.

New Structures: The UPREIT and DOWNREIT

There are many ways to establish the initial portfolio of a REIT. An existing REIT can raise funds and then buy properties or mortgages to establish its portfolio. Alternatively, a corporation can convert to—or spin off part of its corporate assets to form—a REIT. However, a partnership that would like to convert to a REIT will face certain tax disadvantages. After all, moving properties from a partnership to a REIT involves property transactions; it is, therefore, a taxable event.

A natural way to avoid this tax is not to make transactions at the property level. Instead, the partnership can sell its units (stocks), not the actual properties, to a REIT. Under this circumstance, the REIT still owns the underlying properties of the partnership through its ownership of the partnership itself. Since there is no transaction of properties, this should not be a taxable event. We call this type of REIT an UPREIT—an umbrella partnership REIT—and to avoid taxes is basically the motivation for establishing one.

To put it simply, an *UPREIT* is a REIT that owns an operating partnership and serves as the general partner of an operating partnership. Most, if not all, of the assets of the REIT are held through the ownership of the operating partnership. Under this structure, an UPREIT format basically provides two forms of ownership, in that an equity holder of the firm can be either a *shareholder of the REIT* or a *unit holder of the operating partnership.* Both REIT stockholders and partnership unit holders will own the same underlying portfolio of properties.

Even though the underlying properties of the partnership units and REIT stocks are the same, there are important differences between the two types of ownership. A limited partner of the operating partnership is not entitled to the same rights and protections that a REIT shareholder enjoys. The tax treatment is not the same, and the units of the operating partnership are not the same as the shares of the REIT. Given this, the welfare of partnership unit holders is in the hands of the REIT. How to align the interests of the REIT shareholders and those of the partnership unit holders becomes an important issue. This is especially true when there are many different types of partners under one REIT. Figure 3.1 provides an illustration of the UPREIT concept.

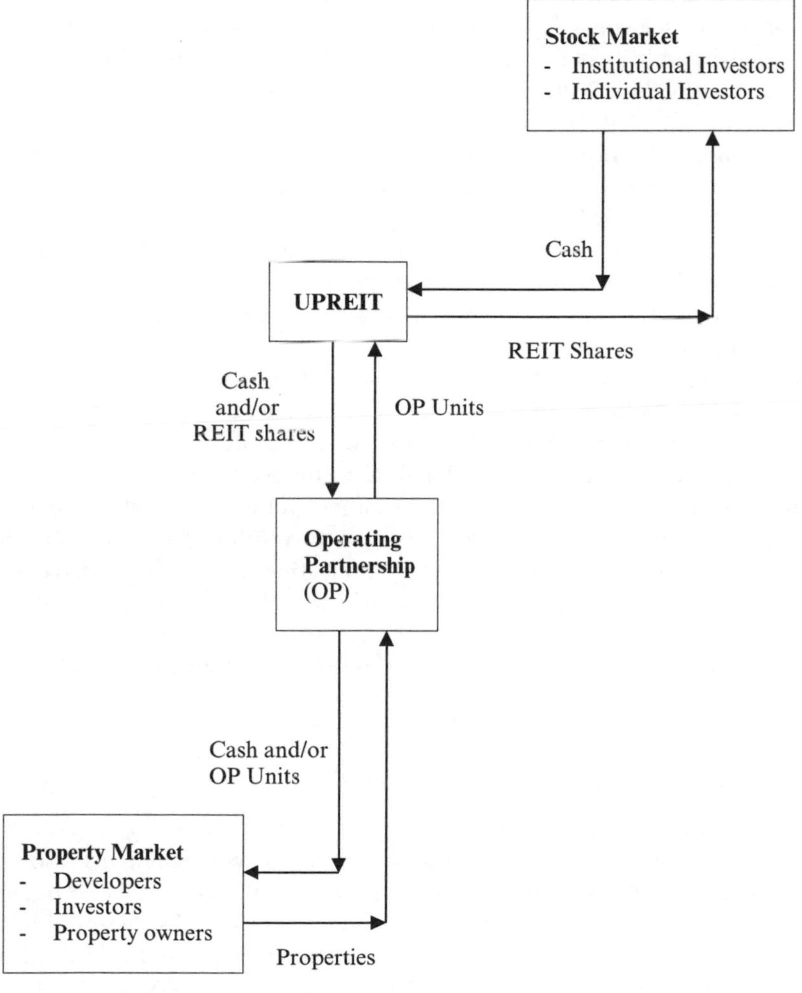

Figure 3.1 An Illustration of the UPREIT Concept

It can be seen that there are many advantages to using the UPREIT structure. First, a REIT can acquire properties in a way that offers special tax advantages to the seller. Second, it can purchase properties using either cash or partnership units (or a combination of the two). This will substantially reduce a REIT's need for capital. As previously noted, a REIT is required to pay out a substantial portion of its taxable income as dividends. An UPREIT has certain advantages over traditional REITs in making property acquisitions because of the ability to offer partnership units to purchase property.

The *DOWNREIT* structure is a variation of the UPREIT structure. Similar to the UPREIT, a DOWNREIT also allows a REIT to acquire property on a tax-deferred basis through the issuance of partnership units. Unlike an UPREIT, a DOWNREIT can own multiple partnerships at the same time and may own assets at both the REIT and the partnership levels. This structure gives additional flexibility over the UPREIT structure because it can form partnerships with each property acquisition.

Since not all REITs are currently using the UPREIT and DOWNREIT structures, one can safely guess that they must have certain disadvantages. Similar to any partnership structure, the cost of maintaining tax records for UPREITs and DOWNREITSs is significant and the task complex. This is particularly true when a REIT owns multiple partnerships or acquires properties by issuing operating partnership units.

Although this increase in administrative cost is significant, it is still measurable. The other major cost of the UPREIT structure, however, is more significant and is difficult to measure. This is the *conflict of interests* among stakeholders. Remember that the tax advantages are what draw the limited partners to the UPREIT structure. To protect the tax advantages of some limited partners, a REIT will have to take the partners' interests into consideration when it makes decisions on the debt level of the firm and on dispositions of properties. Since the disposition of a particular asset or the use of more debt might have tax implications on certain limited partners, it will be difficult for a REIT manager to make a value-maximization decision for the firm as a whole. Just like everything else in the world, there is no free lunch. The use of this newly invented structure also has its costs.

The Net Effect of the UPREIT and DOWNREIT

As discussed, an UPREIT can reduce the tax consequence when a partnership is converted to a REIT, but the conversion process inevitably creates additional conflicts among REIT stakeholders. In 1993 and 1994, 52 out of the 66 new REITs used an UPREIT as their organizational structure. Table 3.4 shows that in 1995, a total of 172 traditional REITs and 65 UPREITs were listed on the stock market. The number of UPREITs grew significantly in more recent years. In 1999, the number of new UPREITs (106)

Table 3.4 Number of Traditional REITs, UPREITs, and DOWNREITs during the 1995–2000 Period

	2000	1999	1998	1997	1996	1995
Traditional REITs	116	97	108	118	157	172
UPREITs	109	106	104	80	69	65
DOWNREITs	18	14	11	9	0	0
Total	233	217	223	207	226	237

Note: In this table the number of REITs in each year could be more or less than the number of REITs listed in table 3.1 because we do not have specific information on several of the REITs and because some of those listed here are not publicly traded. Those REITs are excluded from the sample.

surpassed that of traditional REITs (97). Clearly, there are benefits to using the UPREIT structure—the question is, are its tax benefits outweighed by the additional agency costs that go along with it?

Sinai and Gyourko (2000) use a very interesting method to answer this question. They investigate the impact of the capital gains tax cut under the Taxpayer Relief Act of 1997 on the price movements of REITs and UPREITs. Building owners who sold properties to UPREITs are able to defer paying capital gains taxes without penalty until they choose to sell their stake in the UPREIT. Given this tax advantage, Sinai and Gyourko hypothesize that traditional REITs will have to pay a higher price for properties than will UPREITs. This benefit should be reflected in the share price of the UPREITs.

Given this hypothesis, a reduction in the capital gains rate caused by the Taxpayer Relief Act of 1997 will reduce the benefit of being an UPREIT. This will, in turn, reduce the share price of UPREITs. Sinai and Gyourko find that the capital gains tax-rate changes under the Taxpayer Relief Act of 1997 led to an average 14.6% decline in the share price of UPREITs that are active in property acquisitions, as compared to other REITs. This means UPREITs that are active in property acquisitions are the ones that will enjoy the tax benefits. Table 3.4 provides additional evidence supporting Sinai and Gyourko's argument by showing that the number of UPREITs stays almost the same after 1997.

Clearly, the UPREIT structure adds value to the traditional REIT structure. The amount of value added depends on the tax benefits derived from the property acquisitions. Realizing that the UPREIT structure also carries certain costs, however, REITs that do not acquire properties should have no need to convert to UPREITs. This is probably why approximately half of the REITs in the stock market in 1999 were still traditional REITs. It is likely that the traditional REIT and the UPREIT will continue to coexist in the future, as REIT managers continue to select the most appropriate structures for their firms based on their individual REITs' characteristics.

What Have We Learned?

As with most things in life, being a REIT has both benefits and costs, as discussed earlier in this chapter. All things considered, the net effect of being a REIT tends to be positive, although the benefits and costs do vary depending on REIT characteristics and management strategies. Although in general it is a good idea to use the REIT structure to hold real assets, companies with the following characteristics might not find it suitable to use this particular organizational structure:

- *Firms adopting a high-growth strategy.* The dividend payout constraint under this strategy increases the cost of being a REIT.
- *Firms needing flexibility on property acquisitions.* The limitations on the type of assets in which a REIT can invest will be more serious in this case.
- *Firms investing in speculative assets or operating in dynamic markets.* Regulations prohibit a REIT from buying and selling properties in a short period.
- *Firms using high debt levels.* Since REITs do not pay corporate taxes, the tax benefits of using debt no longer apply under this circumstance.
- *Firms having institutional investors as their basic clientele.* Since institutional investors do not pay corporate taxes, the tax advantage to the investors diminishes under this circumstance.

Will the REIT Structure Survive?

Although the REIT structure was designed to offer small investors a chance to invest in real estate, it has evolved into a vehicle for holding properties and mortgages for both individual and institutional investors. The structure has evolved several times over the years. Thus it might pay to ask whether the REIT organizational structure will survive in the future.

To answer this question we refer to a report by Morrissey (2000) in the *Dow Jones Newswire.* (Morrissey's report came after the Lehman Brother's "Future of REITs" conference held in New York in February 2000.) In the report Morrissey observed that, after two years of stock price turmoil in the REIT market, the heads of five of the country's most successful REITs still say that they have no regrets in adopting the REIT structure. Morrissey also notes that Steven Roth, chairman of Vornado Realty Trust, believes that real estate companies would not perform better as corporations. Roth reported that the stock price of Starwood Hotel and Resorts Worldwide continued to go down after the company converted from a REIT to a C-corporation in January 1999. At the conference, five well-known executives indicated that they are looking forward to the REIT Modernization Act's becoming effective. (The act will allow REITs to set up taxable units to provide non-real-estate-related services to tenants.)

Because of the tax benefits, it is highly likely that investors will take advantage of the REIT organizational structure, in particular because it has evolved to minimize agency costs and reduce the regulations attached to REIT operations. We can safely conclude, then, that the REIT organizational structure will be with us in the foreseeable future. However, the operational aspects of the structure will certainly change in order to maximize the tax benefits and reduce the agency (and other) costs of being a REIT.

NOTES

1. Joseph Gyourko, who reviewed a draft of this chapter, kindly offered his thoughts on this question. He points out that it makes sense for a firm to be a REIT only if it wants to be publicly traded. If a firm chooses to remain private it typically can use much more leverage than a public company can. Thus if a firm remains private without choosing the REIT status, it can reduce its tax liabilities through the interest-payment deductions resulting from its high debt usage. Therefore, it is possible that the reason for choosing the REIT status is not only for tax benefits but also for the purpose of raising funds in the public market.
2. See Chapter 8 for a detailed discussion of this issue.

REFERENCES

Chan, Su Han, George Gau, and Ko Wang. 1995. Stock-market reaction to capital investment decisions: Evidence from business relocation announcements. *Journal of Financial and Quantitative Analysis* 30:81–100.

Damodaran, Aswath, Kose John, and Crocker Liu. 1997. The determinants of organization form changes: Evidence and implication from real estate. *Journal of Financial Economics* 45:169–92.

Gentry, William, Deen Kemsley, and Christopher Mayer. 2002. Dividend taxes and share prices: Evidence from real estate investment trusts. *Journal of Finance*, Forthcoming.

Goebel, Paul, and Kee Kim. 1989. Performance evaluation of finite-life real estate investment trusts. *Journal of Real Estate Research* 4:57–69.

Gyourko, Joseph, and Todd Sinai. 1999. The REIT vehicle: Its value today and in the future. *Journal of Real Estate Research* 18:355–75.

Gyourko, Joseph, and Donald Keim. 1992. What does the stock market tell us about real estate returns? *AREUEA Journal* 20:457–85.

Kapplin, Steve, and Arthur Schwartz. 1988. Public real estate limited partnership returns: A preliminary comparison with other investments. *AREUEA Journal* 16:63–68.

Maris, Brian, and Fayez Elayan. 1991. A test for tax-induced investor clienteles in real estate investment trusts. *Journal of Real Estate Research* 6:169–78.

Martin, John, and Douglas Cook. 1991. A comparison of the recent performance of publicly traded real property portfolios and common stock. *AREUEA Journal* 19:184–211.

Morrissey, Janet. 2000. REIT executives see brighter outlook for sector. *Dow Jones Newswires* (February 17).

Rogers, Ronald, and James Owers. 1985. The investment performance of real estate limited partnerships. *AREUEA Journal* 13:153–66.

Sinai, Todd, and Joseph Gyourko. 2000. The asset price incidence of capital gains taxes: Evidence from the Taxpayer Relief Act of 1997 and publicly-traded real estate firms. University of Pennsylvania. Working paper.

Sagalyn, Lynne. 1996. Conflicts of interest in the structure of REITs. *Real Estate Finance* 13:34–51.

Wang, Ko, and John Erickson. 1997. The stock performance of securitized real estate and master limited partnership. *Real Estate Economics* 25:295–319.

Wang, Ko, John Erickson, and George Gau. 1993. Dividend policies and dividend announcement effects for real estate investment trusts. *AREUEA Journal* 21:185–201.

4

Advisor Puzzle

Is Doing It Yourself Better Than Outsourcing?

Imagine that you hire a broker to purchase a property or to arrange the financing of the property for you, only to find in the end that the seller of the property or the bank who loans you the money is actually the broker you hired. This scenario seems unthinkable in the real world; however, a similar type of conflict of interest has been endemic to the REIT industry for a long time, even today.

This problem arose because when the Congress created REITs, it envisioned them as passive investment vehicles much like mutual funds. That is, REITs were not intended to engage in the operating activities of a traditional company. Consequently, a REIT must hire outside individuals to manage its day-to-day operations. This includes making decisions on the purchase and financing of properties for a REIT. These external-management and external-advisor requirements were mandatory for REITs until 1986, when Congress changed the tax codes to allow REITs to manage their own portfolios.

Common sense teaches us that the external-advisor arrangement cannot work. When the advisor is also the seller of the property, it is easy to guess that the interests of the REIT stockholders may not be the advisor's top priority during a negotiation. However, it is interesting to note that, after Congress relaxed the tax codes to allow REITs to manage their firms internally, not all of them converted to internally advised REITs. Thus, the REIT industry presents an interesting case in which two competing management structures have coexisted for a long period of time—from 1986 to the present.

This issue is important to investors and managers of REITs for at least two reasons. First, given the obvious conflict of interest for the externally advised REITs, why do some REITs still elect to use this type of structure? Second, given the coexistence of the structures, which structure is most likely to perform better than the other? This chapter answers these important questions.

The Evolution

Managing investment and property through an external advisor has created several conflict-of-interest situations between shareholders and advisors. As early as the 1970s, Schulkin (1971) pointed out the conflict of interest in the REIT structure. This problem tarnished the reputation of the REIT industry and may have been part of the reason for the REIT market collapse in the early 1970s.

The conflict of interest resulted from the regulations governing REITs. Prior to 1986, REITs were viewed as passive investment vehicles. Given this status, their day-to-day business operations (property management and investment decisions) had to be conducted by outside entities. Consequently, REITs had to hire property managers to handle matters related to the leasing, management, maintenance, and operational aspects of their properties. Since REITs also needed to acquire and dispose of their properties over time, they had to have advisors (who normally carried out functions similar to mutual fund portfolio managers) to select their properties and to execute their investment strategies. Sometimes, the advisors also served as managers of the properties.

Clearly, advisors were in a key position to influence the timing of property acquisitions, dispositions, tenant leases, property management contracts, and debt-financing choices. In addition, the advisors had the ability to affect the decisions on who would be awarded the contract or the business. Since the advisor was normally not excluded from the deal making, it is not surprising that the advisor's related party or affiliated entity received favorable terms from transactions that the advisor recommended.

This potential for self-dealing made investors wonder whether it paid to invest in REITs. This might explain the relatively slow growth of the REIT industry prior to 1986. The conflict between advisors and REIT shareholders was also detrimental to the growth of the REIT industry. Without the ability to manage their assets actively, developers and major property owners risked losing control of their properties if they elected to use a REIT as the vehicle for holding their properties. For this reason, they often hesitated to convert their firms to REITs.

In 1986, private-letter rulings from the IRS allowed REITs to assume responsibility for selecting investment properties and managing assets. The 1986 Tax Reform Act clarifies that a REIT "may directly select, hire, and compensate those independent contractors who will provide customary services that may be provided by a REIT in connection with the rental of property, rather than hiring an independent contractor to hire other independent contractors." This effectively allowed a REITs to gain self-advised or self-managed status, or both.

New Plan Realty Trust might have been the first REIT to convert from external-advisor to internal-advisor status in 1988 (although several other REITs also claimed that they were working on converting as early as 1986). This conversion process gradually gained momentum as the benefits became evident. For example, in 1991, Meridian Point Real Estate Investment Trust decided to replace their external advisors with internal advisors and began to manage their properties internally. This was a big move in the industry because the trusts consisted of seven publicly traded finite-life REITs with total assets exceeding $450 million. Reeder (1992) reports that, during the 12 months after the change, the seven REITs incurred about $3.5 million less in ongoing operating costs.

However, the importance and the benefit of eliminating these conflicts were not widely recognized until after Kimco Realty's IPO in 1991. Kimco's sponsor was able to mitigate the agency problems through a carefully designed incentive plan for the REIT. As a consequence, after three to four years of a cold REIT IPO market that had no new issues, Kimco Realty was able to attract the attention of a large number of investors with the launch of a new breed of REIT (a REIT with a self-advised structure).[1] The Kimco IPO set the standard for other REIT IPOs to follow. As shown in table 3.1 of the previous chapter, there was tremendous growth in the REIT market in the early 1990s. It is fair to say that the remarkable growth of REITs during the 1990s could have been partially caused by the creation of the internally advised structure.

Ambrose and Linneman (2001) report that, during the 1990–96 period, most internally advised REITs were aggressively pursuing growth strategies via the acquisition and development of properties. In addition, they find that most internally advised REITs in their sample are infinite-life REITs. (As a comparison, only 21% of externally advised REITs are finite-life REITs.) This might underscore the difference in management philosophy between an internally advised REIT (operating company) and an externally advised REIT (investment manager). Consequently, Ambrose and Linneman's report that the average size of internally advised REITs is much larger than that of externally advised REITs during the 1990–96 period is not surprising.

Internally advised REITs have been rapidly dominating the real estate industry since the change in regulations. Tables 4.1 and 4.2 report the speed of conversion from externally managed/advised REITs to internally managed/advised REITs.[2] Table 4.1 indicates that the number of internally managed REITs grew from 41 in the 1993 to 164 in 1997. The number of externally managed REITs declined significantly during the period. The number of REITs operated by management-affiliated companies decreased

Table 4.1 REITs Categorized by Property Management Structure during the 1993–97 Period

Management Structure	1997	1996	1995	1994	1993
Internally managed	164	120	118	73	41
Management affiliate	54	70	71	51	76
Unrelated third party	50	62	77	58	67
More than one type	0	0	6	11	12
Total	268	252	260	171	172

Source: Various issues of NAREIT publications. NAREIT began publishing information on internally and externally managed REITs after 1992. REIT publications in 1998, 1999, and 2000 do not contain explicit information on REITs' management structures. The sample of REITs used in this table includes both private and publicly traded REITs, which is different from the REIT sample reported in tables 3.1–3.3, which includes only publicly traded REITs.

from 76 in 1993 to 54 in 1997; the number of REITs managed by unrelated companies also decreased from 67 to 50 during the same period. From the table, we can see clearly that most of the newly created REITs were internally managed.

There is also a trend in REIT conversions from externally advised to internally advised, although this trend is not as evident as that from externally to internally managed. Table 4.2 reports that the number of internally advised REITs increased from 83 in 1993 to 174 in 2000. While this shows a clear increase in internally advised REITs during the period, it is not clear whether externally advised REITs were completely out of favor at the time. However, the negative story of the relationship between Transcontinental Realty Investors and its advisor (Basic Capital Management) reported by Dean Starkman (2001) will certainly motivate more REIT shareholders to demand a change to internal advisors.

Given the perceived benefits of using internal experts, several leading REIT experts in the industry began to think that the self-advised and self-

Table 4.2 REITs Categorized by Advisor Style during the 1993–2000 Period

Advisor Style	2000	1999	1998	1997	1996	1995	1994	1993
External advisor	25	105	87	93	100	112	n.a.	n.a.
Internal advisor	174	189	194	193	186	178	133	83
Total	269	294	281	286	286	290	133	83

Source: Various issues of NAREIT publications. NAREIT began publishing information on internally/externally advised REITs after 1992. However, in 1993 and 1994, the publications do not report on REITs with an external advisor structure. The sample of REITs used in this table includes both private and publicly traded REITs, which is different from the REIT sample reported in tables 3.1–3.3, which includes only publicly traded REITs.

managed types of REIT would dominate the industry (see, e.g., Linneman 1997). This view was driven by the belief that internally advised REITs, similar to operating companies, would be able to improve profits by expanding revenues or controlling expenses. Linneman (1997) argues that, in a highly competitive industry, a firm that has a distinct long-term competitive advantage (as internally advised REITs have) should eventually dominate the industry. This is a plausible argument; however, we observe few conversions from external to internal advisors after 1996. The reason for this is not clear. We will need to see more empirical evidence supporting Linneman's hypothesis.

The Problems with Using External Advisors

It appears that the conflict of interest caused by the use of external advisors is not simply a topic for academic discussion. Empirical evidence indicates that agency problems do exist in the real world. For example, Cannon and Vogt (1995) report that all of the 23 externally advised REITs they examined during the 1987–92 period had some form of interrelationship among trustees, advisors, and managers. Another piece of evidence is provided by Golec (1994), who, after examining the compensation policies of 66 REITs during the 1962–87 period, reports that

> In most cases, formula [i.e., externally advised] REIT managers and board members, who also serve as advisors, are paid solely through the advisory contract and receive no direct compensation from the REIT. Contracts are renewed annually by boards of directors, usually without changes. Most can be canceled with as little as 60-days notice by either the REIT or the advisor; however, cancellations are rare. Since formula advisors are free to work with other REITs or invest on their own, most REIT advisors' contracts explicitly state that advisors are not obligated to first offer real estate opportunities to the REIT. (182)

The Potential Costs

Solt and Miller (1985), Howe and Shilling (1990), Hsieh and Sirmans (1991), Cannon and Vogt (1995), Wei, Hsieh, and Sirmans (1995), and Sagalyn (1996), provide extensive discussions about the conflicts of interest faced by externally advised REITs. These situations are briefly summarized in the following sections.

Revenue Allocation

In the case in which an advisor/manager serves several REITs—which is legal—it is interesting to see how the advisor allocates revenues. For example, when and if this advisor finds a good investment opportunity, to which REIT will he or she give the investment opportunity? Viewed from another angle, if the advisor owns a property that he or she would like to sell, to which REIT will the advisor give the property?

A similar situation also exists for externally managed REITs. When a property manager who serves several REITs finds a good tenant, which REIT will get this tenant's contract? Apparently, the contract will go to the REIT that maximizes the manager's benefit. Under this scenario, the welfare of the other REITs will be sacrificed.

Self-Dealing

Recall from our earlier discussions that the external advisor can affect the decisions on who will be awarded the contract or the business. Since the advisor could also be a participant in the deal making, the related party or affiliated entity of the advisor could receive favorable terms from the REIT. If this happens, it is the shareholders of the REIT who will suffer the loss.

In addition, since the advisors have the ability to shuffle benefits around, there is a serious conflict of interest when external advisors are used. How can the shareholders of a REIT make sure that the advisor obtains the best available terms when the REIT purchases a property from its own advisor? The conflict of interest might be the most serious problem for the REIT organizational structure. Since investors are not sure that the advisors of a REIT are working for the benefit of the shareholders, their concern will be reflected in their valuation of the REIT's stock price.

Poor Stock Performance

Howe and Shilling (1990) were the first to investigate whether advisors affect the stock performance of REITs. They classify REIT advisors into seven categories and find that REITs advised by different types of advisors perform very differently. They first find that all externally advised REITs perform badly during the sample period—that is, after compensating for risk, externally advised REITs perform worse than the general stock market.

Furthermore, Howe and Shilling (1990) also find that those REITs that are advised by more well-known advisors (such as syndicates, real estate advisors, and insurance companies) perform better than REITs advised by less well-known advisors (such as an unknown person or a mortgage banker). One interpretation is that those better known advisors have a reputation to maintain and thus will not extract personal benefits to the extent that other, lesser known advisors will. Howe and Shilling's finding provides strong evidence that the use of external advisors affects REIT stock performance. The negative impact is greater for REITs hiring less well-known advisors who have less need to worry about maintaining a reputation in the field.

The Worst-Case Scenario: Captive REITs

When a sponsor creates a REIT and forms a wholly owned subsidiary to serve as its advisor, the result is a *captive-financing affiliate* of the sponsor (or a *captive REIT*). Since a third company is used as the advisor of the REIT, a captive REIT must be an externally advised REIT. However, the agency issues of captive REITs are more profound than those of non-captive REITs, although both (captive and non-captive) REITs can also be externally advised. Figure 4.1 illustrates the concept of a captive REIT.

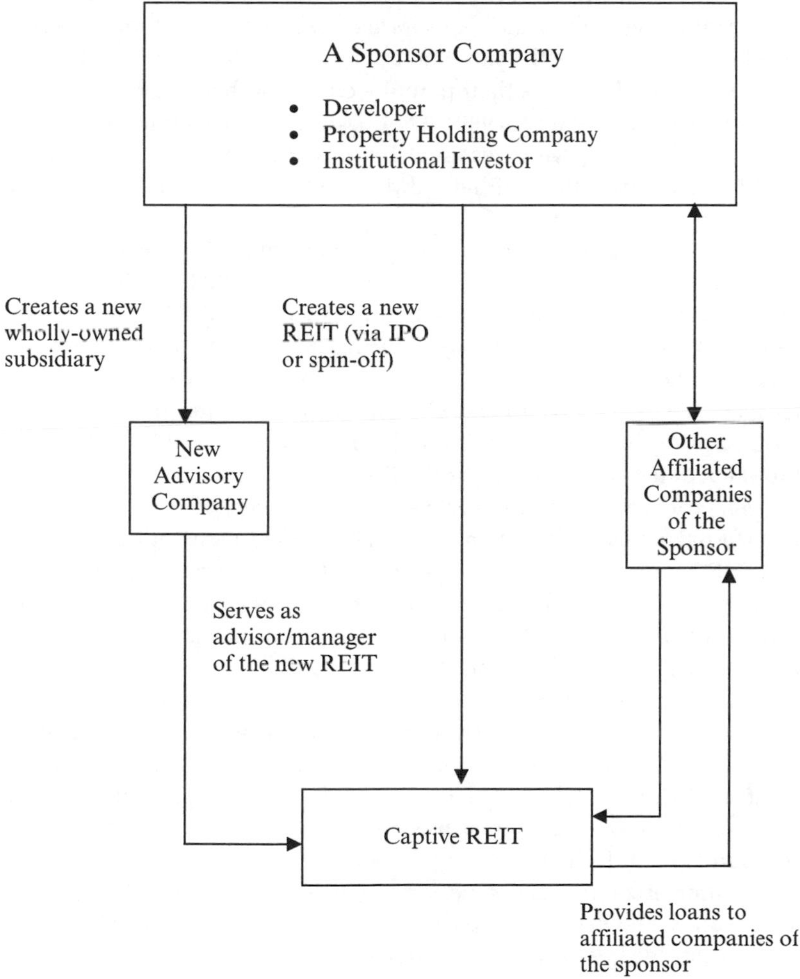

Figure 4.1 An Illustration of the Concept of a Captive REIT

Hsieh and Sirmans (1991) believe that captive REITs are created to serve the financial needs of the sponsors, and thus that the unique type of agency cost due to the sponsor-shareholder conflict, alone, will lower the value of the REIT. Moreover, on top of the regular agency issues that apply to all externally advised REITs, two more additional concerns apply to captive REITs. Both are related to transactions with a REIT's parent company (or the sponsor).

First, there is a suspicion that captive REITs pay too much to buy properties from the sponsor. To illustrate this situation, Hsieh and Sirmans (1991, p. 181) cite a *Wall Street Journal* article (August 28, 1989) that claims "some REITs are advised by developers who might use them to unload properties at high prices." Second, a captive REIT might provide financing to other affiliates of the same sponsors at a cost lower than the market rate. Hsieh and Sirmans use the suit filed by the shareholder of VMS Mortgage Investment Fund to prove their point by citing another article in the *Wall Street Journal* (January 12, 1990). They argue that the conflicts of interest between VMS Mortgage Investment Fund and its affiliates existed such that the trust's loans to its affiliate "did not approximate arm's length business transactions" (p. 181).

Given this additional agency cost, the financial performance of captive REITs should be far inferior to that of non-captive REITs. Hsieh and Sirmans (1991) examine the financial performance of 55 REITs traded on the New York Stock Exchange (NYSE) during the 1968–86 period. Not surprisingly, they find that the stocks of non-captive REITs perform much better than those of captive REITs. Their evidence indicates that the agency costs imposed by external advisors of the REIT are eventually reflected in the value of the stocks of captive REITs.

Wei, Hsieh, and Sirmans (1995) examine another type of cost imposed by external advisors of captive REITs. They examine the bid-ask spreads of 42 REITs during the 1985–86 period and find that captive REITs have larger bid-ask spreads than non-captive REITs. Their finding suggests that captive REITs are subject to a greater degree of information asymmetry than non-captives. (The financial literature indicates that the greater the information asymmetry associated with a stock, the larger the bid-ask spread.) The result probably makes sense, because the sponsors control captive REITs and should have more information than all other outsiders associated with the REITs. The larger bid-ask spread represents a significant cost to captive REIT investors since the transaction fee for buying those stocks will be higher.

To summarize, the use of external advisors has a negative impact on stock value. The negative impact is more evident when a REIT sponsor forms a subsidiary to serve as the advisor of the REIT.

The Problem of Using Internal Advisors

The UPREIT creates a conflict of interest due to the issue of the deferment of tax liability, which may cause UPREIT partnership-unit holders and REIT stockholders to reach different conclusions regarding which properties should be sold and when. In addition, some UPREITs were structured such that unit holders of the partnership have greater proportional voting power than ordinary REIT investors. With this structure, the disposition decision is more likely to maximize the value of the unit holder's property rather than the stockholders'.

Conflicts of interest can also occur among unit holders when a REIT holds multiple partnerships (as with the case of DOWNREITs). Again, because sellers of the original property to the REIT can defer their tax liability on the property's sale, the disposition decision could be a function of which partners have more say in the structure. Therefore, an advisor now might need to serve stockholders with different interests. The larger shareholders that can influence the hiring decisions of internal advisors are more likely to receive more attention from the advisor than the small, individual investors. Therefore, it is fair to say that, similar to externally advised REITs, internally advised REITs also have their own agency problems.

However, it should be noted that, although internally advised REITs also suffer from some agency costs, those costs cannot be avoided even if the REIT uses an external advisor. In other words, any type of advisor (internal or external) will have to deal with this particular agency problem. Since externally advised REITs have additional agency problems, it is fair to say that internally advised REITs are better equipped to handle agency costs than externally advised REITs.

Which One to Use: External or Internal?

If the use of externally advised REITs results in undesired agency costs, it is reasonable to expect that these agency costs will affect the REIT's cash flows and profits and eventually its stock prices. Given this, it is useful to compare the stock performance and operating efficiency of internally versus externally advised REITs.

Stock Performance

The evidence on the difference in stock performance between internally and externally advised REITs is strong and consistent. Using a sample of 42 firms, Cannon and Vogt (1995) report that over the 1987–92 period internally advised REITs outperform externally advised REITs. Capozza and Seguin (1998) report a similar finding. Using a sample of 75 firms, they find that, during the period from 1985 to 1992, internally advised REITs outperform externally advised REITs by more than 7%. This figure is considered very large, especially during the 1985–92 period, when the average returns from investing in stocks were not as high as they would be in the later 1990s.

Capozza and Seguin (1998) also investigate which factors contribute to the poor performance of internally advised REITs. They find a very interesting phenomenon in that externally advised REITs typically use more debt and pay higher interest rates on that debt than do the internally advised variety. They further report that the debt contracts of externally advised REITs are negotiated at rates exceeding the current yield on projects financed with the loan funds. Since advisors are normally compensated based on the size of a REIT's assets, they have an incentive to increase the asset base by issuing debt even if the interest rates of the debt are unfavorable and cannot be justified based on the cash flow generated from the property purchased using the debt. Capozza and Seguin's findings might underscore the consequences of self-dealing and captive arrangements that could be caused by external advisors.

Operating Performance

Ambrose and Linneman (2001) examine the financial and accounting differences between older, externally advised REITs and the internally advised REITs prevalent in the 1990s. Their sample consists of 139 equity REITs trading on either the NYSE or the American Stock Exchange between 1990 and 1996. Their study might be the most comprehensive investigation of the impact of differences in organizational structure using standard accounting and financial measures of REIT growth prospects, revenue and expense ratios, profitability ratios, and capital cost estimates.

Ambrose and Linneman's (2001) results are consistent with those of Capozza and Seguin (1998), who find that externally advised REITs consistently have higher financing expenses than the internally advised type. They also conduct a very comprehensive study to detect whether internally advised and externally advised REITs differ with respect to their cost of capital (such as weighted average cost of capital, return on capital, and economic value-added [EVA]). Their overall result on the weighted average cost of capital seems to be consistent with Capozza and Seguin's results, which show that internally advised REITs continue to outperform externally advised REITs.

The evidence on operating efficiency is mixed. Ambrose and Linneman's results indicate that internally advised REITs do have higher ratios of rental revenue to total revenue, lower payout ratios, and lower costs of capital; yet they found no significant differences in return on capital, return on book equity, or profit margins. Thus, it appears that after controlling for firm size and property-sector effects, any advantage enjoyed by internally advised REITs is minor.

Ambrose and Linneman (2001) also find that the leverage ratios of internally and externally advised REITs have converged during more recent periods. Capozza and Seguin (1998) note that, between 1985 and 1992, externally advised REITs consistently used more debt relative to internally advised REITs and they believe that this excess debt could be the reason for the underperformance of the stock. Thus, the shift in leverage ratios might indicate that externally advised REITs have altered their operating characteristics to remain competitive with internally advised REITs.

Finally, Ambrose and Linneman report that internally advised REITs have significantly higher betas than externally advised REITs. They believe that this could reflect the market's perception that the former are growth stocks, and that operating companies (internally advised REITs) are viewed as riskier than asset-holding companies (externally advised REITs). This finding is interesting in that it points out that the stock market may view internally and externally advised REITs as two different types of investments.

To summarize, while Ambrose and Linneman (2001) find that internally advised REITs can have some advantages in operating performance over externally advised REITs, those advantages have been disappearing in recent years. They believe that this is because externally advised REITs are transforming themselves to remain competitive with internally advised REITs.

Issues Complicated by Compensation Schemes

The compensation mechanism for advisors can further complicate the advisor-performance matter. A REIT can choose to compensate its advisors on either a *formula-based* or a *discretionary-based* compensation method (or a combination of both). A typical formula-based contract compensates a legally separated advisory firm by using certain indicators (such as book value, return on assets, or other factors representing operating efficiency) as the base in the formula. In most cases, formula-based REITs are externally advised.Discretionary contracts are salary based, and the advisor is treated as an in-house employee. Under the discretionary contract, the board of directors of the REIT also has the freedom to award bonuses to encourage performance.

Golec (1994) finds that when a REIT selects the formula-based compensation plan to award advisors, the agency problems mentioned in the previous section seem to be particularly serious. When compared with discretionary-based compensation plans, formula-based plans tend to strip cash from assets and to have both small stock appreciation and small premia in market-to-book values. These problems presumably can be attributed to the fact that external advisors tend to manage REITs in a way that maximizes their own compensation based on the formula. Note that this finding is also consistent with that of Capozza and Seguin (1998), who find that external REIT advisors could have the incentive to increase the use of loans (and, therefore, asset size) in order to maximize their own compensation.

These findings point out an important lesson. In an industry suffering from high agency costs, compensation design will be extremely important in determining the performance of a REIT. However, since Solt and Miller first pointed out the connection between compensation design and agency costs in 1985, there seems to have been little research on how to design a compensation contract to minimize the agency problem in the REIT industry. This is perhaps what researchers need to pay attention to in the future.

What Have We Learned?

Several conclusions can be drawn from the literature regarding the use of advisors for REITs. Among them, we know the following:

- There are two types of advisors for the REIT industry: internal advisors/managers and external advisors/managers.
- It is commonly agreed that external advisors are less likely to work to maximize the welfare of REIT stockholders. Instead, the advisors will have more incentive to maximize their own welfare.
- Internally advised REITs also have their own agency problems, although they are not as serious as those of externally advised REITs.
- Empirical evidence also indicates that the financial performance of the stock of internally advised REITs is, on average, better than that of externally advised REITs.
- Within the externally advised category, the financial performance of captive REITs is worse than that of non-captive REITs.
- Within the externally advised category, the financial performance of REITs that have more noticeable advisors is better than the performance of those with less noticeable advisors.
- The operating performance of internally advised REITs is, in general, slightly better than that of externally advised REITs. However, the margin has been disappearing in recent years.
- There is evidence that externally advised REITs, under market pressure, are transforming themselves in order to improve their performance.
- The compensation method is very important to advisor performance. The use of asset size as the base for compensation is, in general, not a good idea.

The overall evidence seems to indicate that it might be better for a REIT to use an internal (do-it-yourself) than an external (outsource) advisor.

What Is the Future Direction?

A natural question for a REIT owner to ask is whether he or she should use external or internal advisors. From the evidence presented in the previous section, the answer to this question is quite clear: The use of an internal advisor can reduce (although not eliminate) the agency problems prevailing in the REIT market. Under no circumstances are we able to identify conditions under which the use of an external advisor is an optimal decision.

Given this, the next question to ask is whether the internal-advisor mechanism should be "the" way for REITs to manage their properties. We guess the answer is not entirely affirmative. Although the use of internal advisors helps minimize (not eliminate) the agency problems existing within internally advised REITs, the structure may need to be revised again for future REITs.

The 1999 REIT Modernization Act provides a hint about the direction of future REIT management styles. This act allows a REIT to retain more capital (the payout ratio is reduced from 95 to 90% of taxable income) and also allows a REIT to create a new type of taxable subsidiary for operating businesses that are not involved in real estate rental activities. Given this, it is anticipated that REITs will more or less be like operating companies pursuing growth opportunities similar to other operating companies in the stock market, and it is likely that we will see a new type of REIT management contract in the near future.

However, one puzzle remains. Given the performance of the externally advised REITs and the well-known agency issues, *why do some REITs remain externally advised?* The only plausible answer to this question is that external advisors may be working to improve their own efficiency so that there will be no performance difference between using internal or external advisors (as suggested by Ambrose and Linneman 2001). Even if this is the case, the safer and better way to manage a REIT is still to use internal advisors. Why should we trust external advisors even if we believe they might be improving? This might be the most important question an investor needs to ask when he or she considers investing in an externally advised REIT.

NOTES

1. An article on REITS published in the *Journal of Financial Economics* in 1992 by two of the authors of this book and a third coauthor might be partially responsible for the cold REIT IPO market during the 1989–92 period. In the article, Wang, Chan, and Gau (1992) report that REIT IPOs are, on average, overpriced and that few institutional investors participate in REIT IPOs. After the circulation of the paper in 1989, no new REIT IPOs

took place until November 1991. (See chapter 9 for a detailed discussion on REIT security offerings.)

2. The information on internally and externally advised/managed REITs is obtained from various issues of NAREIT publications from the period 1974 to 2000. NAREIT began publishing information on UPREIT and internally/externally advised REITs after 1992. The type of information on managers and advisors contained in each issue varies over time. REIT publications stopped providing summary information on internally/externally managed REITs after 1997. Similarly, information on externally advised REITs is not explicitly provided in the 1993 and 1994 REIT publications. The sample of REITs used in tables 4.1 and 4.2, which includes both private and publicly traded REITs, is different from the sample reported in tables 3.1–3.3, which includes publicly traded REITs.

REFERENCES

Ambrose, Brent, and Peter Linneman. 2001. REIT organizational structure and operating characteristics. *Journal of Real Estate Research* 21: 146–62.

Cannon, Susanne, and Stephen Vogt. 1995. REITs and their management: An analysis of organizational structure, performance and management compensation. *Journal of Real Estate Research* 10:297–317.

Capozza, Dennis, and Paul Seguin. 2000. Debt, agency and management contracts in REITs: The external advisor puzzle. *Journal of Real Estate Finance and Economics* 20:91–116.

Friday, Swint, and G. Stacy Sirmans. 2000. Market pricing of agency costs in REITs. Florida State University. Working paper.

Golec, Joseph. 1994. Compensation policies and financial characteristics of real estate investment trusts. *Journal of Accounting and Economics* 17:177–205.

Howe, John, and James Shilling. 1990. REIT advisor performance. *AREUEA Journal* 18:479–99.

Hsieh, Cheng-Ho, and C. F. Sirmans. 1991. REITs as captive-financing affiliates: Impact on financial performance. *Journal of Real Estate Research* 6:179–89.

Linneman, Peter. 1997. Forces changing the real estate industry forever. *Wharton Real Estate Review* 1:1–12.

Reeder, Milton. 1992. Under new management: The meridian point REITs. *Real Estate Finance* 9:19–24.

Solt, Michael, and Norman Miller. 1985. Managerial incentives: Implications for the financial performance of real estate investment trusts. *AREUEA Journal* 13:404–23.

Sagalyn, Lynne. 1996. Conflicts of interest in the structure of REITs. *Real Estate Finance* 13:34–51.

Schulkin, Peter. 1971. Real estate investment trusts: A conflict of interests. *Financial Analyst Journal* 27:33–78.

Starkman, Dean. 2001. *Wall Street Journal* (January 16), p, A1.

Wang, Ko, Su Han Chan, and George Gau. 1992. Initial Public Offering of Equity Securities: Anomalous Evidence Using REITs. *Journal of Financial Economics* 31:381–410.

Wei, Peihwang, Cheng-Ho Hsieh, and C. F. Sirmans. 1995. Captive financing arrangements and information asymmetry: The case of REITs. *Real Estate Economics* 23:385–94.

5

REIT Economies of Scale

Does Size Matter?

Those who have been watching the development of Internet stocks closely will undoubtedly appreciate the benefit of size. After the establishment of thousands of Internet companies, we are now observing a wave of consolidations among them. It appears that, after the consolidations, there will be only a few dominant players (such as America Online) in the industry. Given this trend, one might wonder whether size could be important to the profitability and survivorship of REITs, as well.

This question is particularly relevant to the REIT industry now; given the significant and increasing merger activities in the REIT market during the mid-1990s and the explosive growth of large REIT initial public offerings in the 1993–96 period, it seems that players in the industry might believe that large REITs have certain advantages over small REITs. Is this true? The answer to this question is important because of its bearing on how REIT investors should select among REIT stocks, and on how managers of smaller REITs might want to reconsider their operating strategies.

While it might not be appropriate to use the example in the Internet industry to draw a conclusion about the REIT industry (since the operating characteristics of the two industries are totally different), it is quite clear that we can learn a lesson from the merger wave in the banking industry during the 1970–80 period. During those years, most people believed that in the future there would be only a few megabanks because of the potential savings in operating expenses and the increase in revenues due to economies of scale in large banks. While the economies-of- scale argument does make sense, the so-called few-megabanks phenomenon has never materialized. This casts at least some doubt on the economies-of-scale argument for large REITs.

In this chapter, we will review three important questions. First, should the size of a REIT be an important factor in determining its profitability? We will present arguments from both sides of the fence. Second, we will review the literature to see whether size has been a determinant of REIT returns in the past. Finally, if the average size of REITs should become larger in the future, will mergers and acquisitions be the tool to accomplish the goal? The information presented here will be useful both to investors who are looking for the right REIT stocks to invest in and to managers who are interested in learning about the growth strategies of REITs.

Arguments in Favor of Large REITs

The debate on the optimal size of REITs began to receive considerable attention after Linneman (1997) posited his famous *REIT-size hypothesis.* Linneman believes that large REITs enjoy significant advantages over smaller ones with respect to economies of scale in revenues, expenses, and capital. With these additional advantages, it is possible to see that, in a competitive market, large REITs will dominate the future REIT market.

In the scenario described by Linneman (1997), large REITs will become even larger (and eventually dominate the industry) and the total number of REITs in the stock market will be significantly reduced. This hypothesis has received some support. For example, Campbell, Ghosh, and Sirmans (2000) report that there were 85 merger transactions among REITs from 1994 to 1998. Given the number of REITs available in the stock market (see table 5.1), 85 merger transactions correlate with heavy merger and acquisition (M&A) activity.

While Linneman's argument is interesting, one might ponder why the projected large-REIT phenomenon has not yet occurred. Indeed, if large REITs enjoy economies of scale in revenues, expenses, and capital, then large REITs should already dominate the market since they have been enjoying similar advantages for a long time. Given this, the important question for us to ask is "Do large REITs really enjoy the benefit of economies of scale?" In addition, it would be interesting to see whether, on top of the possible benefits accruing to economies of scale, there are any other benefits that can be enjoyed by larger REITs.

Economies of Scale

It is reasonable to suspect that large REITs might have lower operating-expense ratios because they can allocate fixed expenses among more projects. It is also possible that large REITs might have a higher revenue ratio

Table 5.1 Comparison of the Size of REITs with That of Non-REIT Firms from Various Exchanges

Year (Dec 31)	Average Market Capitalization ($ '000)								
		Non-REIT Firms				REIT vs. Non-REIT Size (%)			
	REITs	All Exchanges	NYSE	AMEX	Nasdaq	All Exchanges	NYSE	AMEX	NASDAQ
1962	21,010	177,803	289,550	28,636	—	12	7	73	—
1963	20,637	207,970	336,736	31,123	—	10	6	66	—
1964	21,073	232,574	378,206	33,185	—	9	6	64	—
1965	33,138	259,096	420,615	35,344	—	13	8	94	—
1966	26,993	228,322	371,990	30,975	—	12	7	87	—
1967	32,926	288,384	468,403	48,488	—	11	7	68	—
1968	68,379	327,971	530,757	62,347	—	21	13	110	—
1969	64,702	279,374	465,777	44,265	—	23	14	146	—
1970	51,216	268,362	457,957	34,687	—	19	11	148	—
1971	62,575	298,534	508,334	40,535	—	21	12	154	—
1972	59,823	193,872	573,317	44,340	59,017	31	10	135	101
1973	37,290	164,873	452,371	31,100	52,158	23	8	120	71
1974	11,912	121,464	317,379	20,046	38,008	10	4	59	31
1975	13,239	171,819	432,323	26,806	68,989	8	3	49	19
1976	18,048	214,346	533,341	33,505	87,743	8	3	54	21
1977	20,399	207,008	500,356	34,472	87,957	10	4	59	23
1978	19,939	228,901	516,922	37,786	114,421	9	4	53	17

1979	25,499	267,009	609,708	64,961	121,447	10	4	39	21
1980	31,449	349,471	791,123	87,473	174,018	9	4	36	18
1981	32,113	298,890	732,103	76,550	140,416	11	4	42	23
1982	46,337	311,886	861,650	74,578	105,451	15	5	62	44
1983	58,615	320,653	1,028,072	96,780	78,605	18	6	61	75
1984	70,218	296,947	1,011,491	86,961	59,812	24	7	81	117
1985	74,824	367,897	1,257,993	107,140	77,065	20	6	70	97
1986	91,518	390,637	1,397,630	110,694	81,545	23	7	83	112
1987	79,941	365,447	1,332,156	103,074	71,850	22	6	78	111
1988	89,918	411,351	1,438,676	117,812	78,176	22	6	76	115
1989	94,854	514,614	1,744,598	144,281	93,325	18	5	66	102
1990	72,426	473,551	1,554,953	111,332	79,397	15	5	65	91
1991	92,910	624,609	1,905,324	138,029	129,542	15	5	67	72
1992	111,969	664,517	1,870,466	127,723	154,773	17	6	88	72
1993	177,075	691,827	1,910,539	146,925	173,663	26	9	121	102
1994	194,138	648,265	1,752,483	141,849	166,485	30	11	137	117
1995	252,195	849,894	2,260,795	177,401	235,381	30	11	142	107
1996	409,898	973,262	2,563,069	176,317	281,700	42	16	232	146
1997	630,108	1,258,379	3,279,230	201,310	346,339	50	19	313	182
1998	635,573	1,626,327	3,911,115	190,694	538,682	39	16	333	118
1999	611,895	2,154,363	4,539,533	169,193	1,075,903	28	13	362	57
2000	725,714	2,032,856	4,674,328	168,658	792,824	36	16	430	92
Average	133,141	506,752	1,281,574	88,138	191,886	20	8	116	78

Source: Authors' own calculations using the REIT sample described in the appendix and market capitalization data from the CRSP tapes.

because they can go after deals they might not have been able to get, had they been smaller. Finally, it may be that large REITs are able to secure financing more easily (or on better terms) than smaller REITs because of banks' perception of the increased security and business opportunities of large REITs. Given these possible advantages, it is reasonable to believe that scale economies exist for large REITs and that large REITs will have certain advantages over smaller ones.

Ambrose and Linneman (2001) provide evidence to support the argument for scale economies. In a comprehensive study, they report that larger REITs tend to have higher profit margins, higher rental-revenue ratios, and lower implied capitalization rates. They also find that large REITs have a significantly lower cost of capital than small REITs. Their results indicate that for every $1 billion increase in market capitalization, there is a 2.2% reduction in the capital costs of a REIT. In other words, their empirical result supports the economies-of-scale argument.

Bers and Springer (1998a,b) also present empirical evidence on the economies of scale for large REITs and their sources. They investigate several categories of cost sources: general and administrative expenses, management fees, operating expenses, and interest expenses. Using REIT data from 1992–96, they find that, overall, economies of scale exist for all cost categories except interest expenses. Not surprisingly, they report that general and administrative expenses and management fees demonstrate the largest economies of scale, whereas operating expenses show only a modest effect. Capozza and Seguin (1998) also find substantial economies of scale when they separated a REIT's general and administrative expenses into a "structural" and a "style" component. Their result suggests that a REIT might be able to enhance its value by lowering the structural component of its expenses (by expanding its size).

Bers and Springer (1998a,b) also find that scale economies differ among types of REITs. They find that externally managed, low-leverage, and well-diversified REITs might enjoy higher economies of scale. Mortgage REITs might benefit more than equity REITs, and REITs focused on special property types might enjoy more savings from scale economies than other equity REITs.

However, there are also challenges to the economies-of-scale argument. Among others, Vogel (1997) discusses some of the factors that may inhibit the future size of REITs. He points out that it is possible for economies of scale to decrease when firms grow beyond a certain size. Although the unit cost might decrease as the size of the REIT increases, it might actually begin to increase because the REIT becomes too large. In other words, it is possible that the cost function of REITs is not linear, but is in fact quadratic with respect to the size of the firm.

Taking this possibility into consideration, Yang (2001) examines the validity of cost functions of the REIT industry and the existence of scale economies. They use accounting data of equity REITs between 1992 and

1998 and find that the concave quadratic types of cost functions perform better than other types of cost functions, which implies that there is an optimal size for REITs in terms of cost savings. In other words, when the size of a REIT becomes particularly large (passing an optimal point), then *diseconomies of scale* set in. Furthermore, Ambrose et al. (2000) offer the most direct empirical evidence against the economies-of-scale argument. Using property-level data from 41 multifamily REITs, they find no evidence to support the scale-economies argument. They also note that simply being big will not help a REIT to create a niche market. This well-done research, along with further work on the subject by Green Street Advisors (a well-known advisor on REITs) and others, has put a serious dent in the argument that bigger is always better.

To summarize, the evidence supporting the economies-of-scale is mixed. Although it is generally agreed that there are cost savings when a REIT increases its size up to a certain level, the evidence supporting the establishment of mega-REITs is simply not there.

Other Benefits of Size

Rosenthal (1996) points out two other types of benefits that could be enjoyed by large REITs. First, he believes that large REITs have certain advantages over smaller ones because they can bid for bigger and more lucrative properties. He also believes that when a REIT can buy a whole portfolio of properties, it might be able to capitalize on the discount that would not be available if it bought only individual properties.

This argument, although intuitively appealing, has an inherent weakness. We know that banks can form syndicates to make loans, investors can form partnerships to invest in real estate, and hi-tech firms can form consortia to invest in specific projects. There is no reason that REITs could not form their own syndicate to invest in a portfolio of properties or in a particularly large property if they wish. Given this, we doubt that the ability to take on bigger projects is a sufficient reason for REITs to grow larger.

Rosenthal (1996) also argues that, by virtue of being big, REITs might find it easier to identify better investment opportunities because they have adequate resources to identify new market segments (an argument that assumes REITs do in fact expend a significant amount of their resources studying geographical and property markets.) Thus, large REITs may enjoy an informational advantage that enables them to enter the right market at the right time, with increased profitability as a result.

While this argument is intuitively appealing, it could not have been true back when REITs were required by law to hire external advisors to manage their properties. Since REITs did not deal with property acquisitions and management, the impact of economies of scale on their revenues and expenses should have been small. Even when applied to the later time when REITs were allowed to hire internal advisors, this argument still has its weaknesses. First, there is no empirical evidence that REITs spend a significant amount of resources studying different property markets. Second, if the study of property markets can increase the profitability of investments, then small REITs and property consultants can also do it, especially if they pool their resources. Given this, we believe that REITs should not expand their size just because of the perceived informational benefits.

Finally, Rosenthal (1996) argues that larger REITs attract more security analysts to follow their stocks, and that this increased scrutiny can reduce REITs' potential agency costs. We believe that this was a valid argument when the REIT market was totally neglected by institutional investors and financial analysts. (Financial analysts always follow the stocks in which institutional investors have interest.) Recently we have seen that there are more institutional investors in the REIT stock market than in the general stock market (and in the next chapter we will discuss their impact on REIT stock returns). Under this circumstance, it may not be necessary for a REIT to become large in order to attract the attention of institutional investors.

Arguments Against Large REITs

The argument against large REITs is based on the inherent communication difficulties among decision makers and the resulting loss of efficiency in operations. If an individual works in a small company, that individual might be able to communicate a new idea to the decision maker directly and thus make decisions quickly. However, when an individual works for a large company, the decision-making process is likely to go through several levels (e.g., the manager, the division head, and then the president) before the final decision is made. During the process, some information might be lost because the individual with the idea might never have the opportunity to talk directly to the person who will eventually make the decision.

We use figure 5.1 to illustrate this concept. Suppose that there are four small REITs specializing in apartment, single-family, office, and retail properties, respectively (see Case A). The president of each company has special knowledge about the property and can make decisions directly with the front people who manage the properties.

If we make the REITs bigger by combining two of them (apartment with single-family, and office with retail), as shown in Case B, we will have to create one more level in the decision-making hierarchy for the new REIT. We will now have three levels in the hierarchy: (1) one president, (2) two managers, and (3) the front people. Under this new structure, some decisions will need to go through two steps (instead of one) before they can reach the final decision maker. Clearly, we can already see some extra costs and inefficiencies in this structure when compared with the structure presented in Case A.

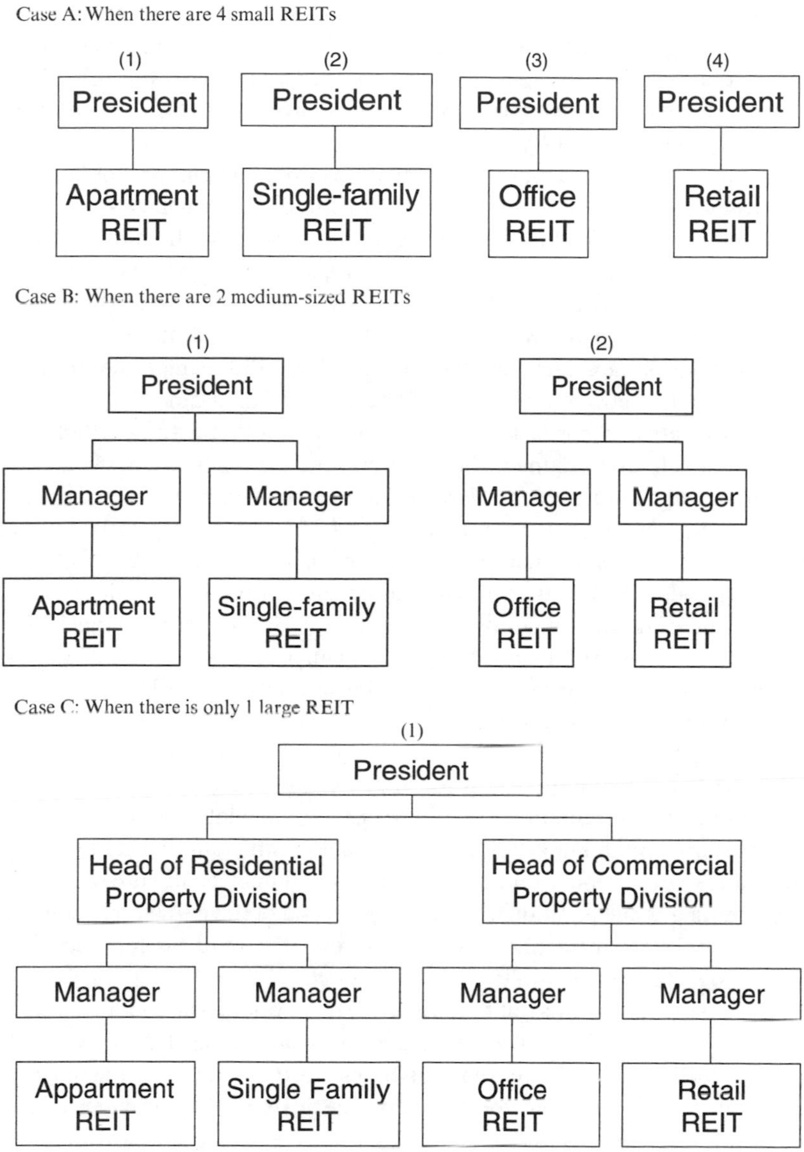

Figure 5.1 An Illustration of REIT Size and Firm Structure

Let us try to make the REIT even bigger. We now combine all the four REITs, as shown in Case C. Now we will have levels in the hierarchy: (1) one president, (2) two division heads, (3) four managers, and (4) the front people. Although some cost savings may be derived from the combination of REITs, there are also more positions created. In addition, some of the important decisions will have to be made at the president's level. That is, the information provided by the front people will reach the president via three steps. Furthermore, in Case A (when the REIT is small), the president needs to have knowledge about only one property type in order to perform his or her job satisfactorily.

In Case C, the president will now need to understand all property types (apartment, single-family, office, and retail) in order to make a sound decision. (You can guess the odds of finding one person with all these abilities.) Consequently, it is clear that there are some costs attached to large REITs. Given this structure, under a normal circumstance, large REITs cannot make decisions as quickly as small REITs can. In addition, when the outside environment changes dramatically, large REITs might not be able to adapt to the new environment as fast as small REITs can.

Salaries are another factor to consider, and another area in which the economies-of-scale argument breaks down as firm size increases past a certain point. Among others, Hardin (1998) reports that large size is a determinant in the executive compensation of REITs. In other words, as size increases, it is possible that the unit cost of salaries does not decrease because the salary level will take size into consideration. Under this circumstance, there should not be great savings in salaries for being a large REIT.

Presumably, one of the most important benefits of being a large REIT is the ability to buy a portfolio of properties at a lower cost. However, this might pose a problem for certain REITs with concentrated investments in a special property type or special geographical region. For those REITs, there will be limited opportunities to grow, and growth in size could be detrimental to their profitability. There is some anecdotal evidence to support this argument. For example, Fitch (1999) points out that some excellent REITs simply focus on their properties and manage them well rather than going after acquisitions. For investors who believe that real estate is still a local and specialized niche business that requires local market knowledge, then mega-REITs are clearly a bad choice.[1]

Mueller (1998) points out that, in order to maintain a certain profitability level as it grows, a REIT needs to find more properties that can provide profits similar to those from the properties it already holds. When a REIT is small, it need not hold too many properties and therefore can select among alternatives. Under this circumstance, it is likely that the REIT can choose properties with high returns. However, when a REIT becomes too large and cannot find many good investments, it might have to settle for less profitable ones. Mueller notes that the earnings-per-share growth rate of a REIT tends to slow down as the number of outstanding shares of the REIT increases (an increase that may mean the REIT will become larger). He also observes a sizeable price decline in the first half of 1988 in large REITs. His evidence clearly questions whether the bigger-is-better philosophy is justifiable.

Net Results of the Evidence

Given the fact that both sides of the size issue present convincing arguments, it appears that the validity of each argument can be evaluated only through empirical evidence. To do this, we will review two sets of literature. First, we will examine whether the size of a REIT affects its returns. Second, within the REIT industry, we will examine whether there is a difference in the financial performance between larger and smaller REITs.

Size and Stock Returns

It is well documented in the finance literature that small firms have abnormally high rates of return compared with large firms. Given this, there seems to be no reason for a REIT to seek to grow if it can earn high returns in the stock market by being small. To examine these issues, we will need to answer two questions: First, are REITs really small stocks when compared with other stocks in the market? If not, we needn't consider this issue any further. Second, does the small-firm effect prevailing in the general stock market also apply to the REIT stock market?

To see whether REIT stocks can be considered small stocks, we calculate the average annual size of REIT stocks and compare it to that of non-REIT stocks trading on the NYSE, Amex, and Nasdaq during the 1962–2000 period. To facilitate comparisons, we also calculate the percentage of REIT size when compared with that of non-REIT stocks in the market for each year under investigation.

The results are reported in table 5.1 and plotted in figure 5.2, from which it is clear that REIT stocks can be considered small when compared with stocks in the general market. While we observe a dramatic increase in REIT capitalization after 1993, the average size of the non-REIT stocks traded on the NYSE and Nasdaq continues to dominate the size of REITs. The differential is large. For example, during the sample period, the average size of REIT stocks is only about 20% of the size of all non-REIT stocks traded on all the exchanges during the 1962–2000 period. In 2000, the average size of REITs stocks was only 16% of the average size of non-REIT stocks traded on the NYSE.[2] Since stocks traded on the NYSE are, in general, the larger stocks in the market, we can safely conclude that REIT stocks are, indeed, small stocks.

Since REITs are small stocks, it is possible that the small-firm effect reported in the finance literature affects their stock returns. Thus, we need to determine whether there is a difference between the performances of small and large REITs. We can do this in two ways: by examining the stock performance of REITs, and by examining the relationship between the stock value and net asset values of the properties owned by the REITs.

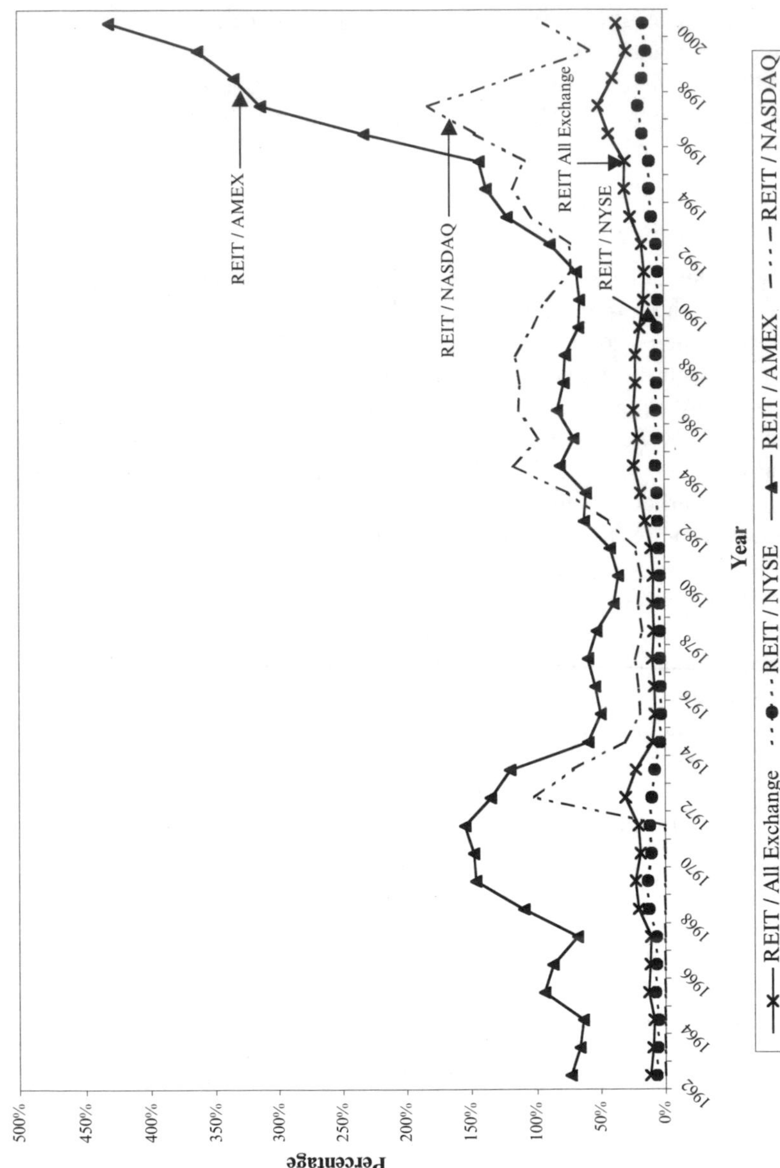

Figure 5.2 Size of REITs

Size and Stock Performance of REITs

Colwell and Park (1990) might have been the first to explicitly examine the impact of size on REIT stock returns. Their finding is interesting in that a reverse size effect exists in certain months other than January. This indicates that large REITs may earn higher returns than small REITs in certain months of the year. However, McIntosh, Liang, and Tompkins (1991) provide conflicting evidence on the issue. They examine the small-firm effect within the REIT industry using a larger sample than Colwell and Park and find that the small-firm effect exists in the REIT industry—that is, small REITs earn higher returns than large REITs.

Following Colwell and Park (1990) and McIntosh, Liang, and Tompkins (1991), many other studies have examined REIT stock returns using size as a pricing factor. However, since the objectives and methodologies vary significantly among the studies, their results also lack consistency.[3] We will cite only a more recent study conducted by Chen et al. (1998) that analyzes REIT stock returns using firm-specific variables (such as size and book-to-market ratios, macroeconomic variables, and different asset-pricing models. Their study finds that, regardless of the models used, size is always an important pricing factor for REIT stock returns. In other words, the observation that small REITs earn abnormally high returns still holds in their study.

What do we learn from all of these studies? The answer is that the evidence is not conclusive. However, even if we are not completely sure whether small REITs earn abnormally higher returns than large REITs, we can see that large REITs do not earn significantly higher returns than smaller ones. Given this, there seems to be no special advantages for a REIT to try to increase in size, at least not from the perspectives of REIT investors in the stock market.

Size and Net Asset Value of REITs

Capozza and Lee (1995) examine the relationship between size and REIT net asset value. Using data for equity REITs between 1985 and 1992, they find that small REITs trade at significant discounts to their net asset values, whereas large REITs trade at a premium over the values of their underlying commercial properties. They also report that large REITs are more highly leveraged than small REITs, whereas small REITs are more concentrated geographically.

Their evidence indicates that the stock market will pay a price higher than the REIT's underlying property value (the *net asset value*) if its size is large. If the REIT is small, then the stock market will pay less for the underlying property. This evidence provides very strong support to the economies-of-scale argument. The evidence basically tells the reader that investors in the stock market value large REITs more than small REITs and that larger REITs will be able to borrow more.

What Can We Conclude?

From the evidence presented so far, it appears that we cannot give a definite answer to the question of whether the stock market values the size of REITs, or even whether it likes or dislikes large REITs alone. However, if forced to answer these questions, we would probably say that size does not matter, and that, based on the evidence we have seen, the stock market seems to prefer small REITs to large ones.

The Future of Big Consolidations

According to Linneman (1997) the REIT industry is experiencing the beginning of a revolutionary consolidation of its structure and will eventually be dominated by a few very large REITs. Goodman (1998), a respected expert in the field, also believes that there is considerable room for the large to get larger, at least in still-fragmented markets such as apartment REITs. Will the predictions of Linneman and Goodman come true? Will some REITs become larger through consolidations?

To gain a better understanding of the size issue, we examine REIT merger activities. We know that one of the methods a REIT can use to grow is to merge with or to acquire other REITs. How does the stock market react to these merger activities? If the stock market does not value REIT mergers, it is highly unlikely that we will observe the large REIT phenomenon predicted by Linneman (1997) .

A fair way to address their prediction is to assess the market reaction to the announcement of REIT mergers. In other words, if investors in the stock market think that mergers among REITs are a good idea, they will tend to buy the stocks of those REITs involved in mergers and push the prices of those stocks upward. Similarly, if investors do not believe that the mergers are a good idea, the price of these stocks should decrease.

Empirical Evidence on REIT Mergers

Allen and Sirmans (1987) are the first to examine whether merger activities increase the value of REIT stocks. They argue that REIT mergers might be beneficial for the following reasons:

- *Tax benefits:* The net operating losses of one REIT can be used by another REIT if the two merge.[4]
- *Efficient management:* A merger can replace inefficient management or make better use of underutilized assets.

Allen and Sirmans (1987) find that when one REIT acquires another, the acquiring REIT experiences a significant wealth increase (meaning that its stock price increases) when it announces the merger. They also find that the amount of the increase is determined by whether the merger is between REITs with similar types of assets, which suggests that investors perceive management synergies in REIT mergers. Recently, Li, Elayan, and Meyer (2001) also report that the stock market reaction to REIT merger announcements is positive and significant. They believe, however, that the positive response is due to the fact that an acquisition can reduce the investor's tax liability.

McIntosh, Officer, and Born (1989) report similar evidence when they examine the stock price of target firms in REIT merger transactions. Elayan and Young (1994) examine the market reaction for full and partial acquisitions in the real estate industry. They find that target firms earn positive returns when REITs announce their acquisition decisions. Collectively, then, the evidence seems to support the notion that investors in the stock market value REIT merger activities.

However, it should be noted that Campbell, Ghosh, and Sirmans (2001) report a different result using a much larger and more recent (1994–98) REIT merger sample. Their result indicates that the market reaction to acquiring REITs is negative if the target firm is also a public company. Given this finding—which is the most recent and should be relied upon the most in forming an opinion—there is probably not much gain to a REIT's conducting merger activities.

Merging to Become Bigger?

What about the recent observations that REITs are merging in order to increase their size? Will this phenomenon continue in the future? Campbell, Ghosh, and Sirmans (1998) give a concise answer to this question. They point out that the REIT consolidation movement cannot happen unless three essential conditions are met:

- The perceived lower cost due to economies of scale and lower cost of capital must actually exist.
- The economies of scale must not decrease at a low ceiling size.
- Even if scale economies exist, the REIT must be able to handle the corporate control issues resulting from the merger.

It is clear that responses to these three conditions would vary according to the individual REIT. However, one can probably conclude that in the absence of dominant benefits from REIT mergers (discussed earlier), a big wave of consolidations among REITs is unlikely to happen.

This is particularly true given the special legal protection enjoyed by REIT managers against hostile takeovers. A routine provision in REIT charters, called the *excess share provision,* allows management to suspend the voting and dividend rights of certain investors. This could be a very effective takeover defense if management does not like a proposed merger deal or if management faces a hostile takeover.

We know that few firm managers would like to see their companies taken over by another firm, if only because they might lose their jobs, perks, and power as a result. Without the threat of a hostile takeover, it might be difficult for the managers of companies to negotiate seriously with one another. This indicates that there are extra hurdles to cross for REITs to merge. Perhaps the most interesting phenomenon pointed out by Campbell, Ghosh, and Sirmans (1998) is that there is a complete absence of successful hostile merger activities during their sample period. Since we know that hostile takeovers are common in the market for non-REIT firms, the absence of such activities in the REIT market indicates that their special legal protection is quite effective.

This evidence, together with the evidence that the investors put little value on REIT merger deals, tell us that there will be few consolidation activities in the future unless the regulations change.[5] Given this, we believe that if the average size of REITs does become larger, their growth will probably be due to internal growth rather than mergers.

What Have We Learned?

As an investor, should you favor large REIT stocks? As a REIT manager, should you grow the REIT using the merger as a tool? We can summarize the main points in the chapter to answer these questions.

- There are probably some benefits to REIT growth because of economies of scale.
- However, if a REIT becomes too big, the benefits of economies of scale will probably vanish.
- There is difficulty in communication among decision makers if a REIT becomes too big.
- There is evidence that real estate is a localized business, which works against the bigger-is-better philosophy for REITs.
- When compared with other stocks in the general stock market, REIT stocks are considered small in size.
- There is no conclusive evidence that the stocks of small REITs perform better than the stocks of large REITs.
- However, there is evidence that investors in the stock market may pay a higher price for the underlying assets of large REITs.
- There was a great deal of REIT merger activity in the mid-1990s.
- However, it seems that investors do not value REIT mergers that much.
- Given this, we probably will not observe the mega-REIT phenomenon

that has been proposed by some people in the industry. That is, we may not see a few REITs dominating the REIT market in the near future.

What Does the Future Hold for the Size of REITs?

The discussion in this chapter clearly indicates that there is no one answer to the question of optimal REIT size, and that sophisticated analysis is needed to understand the options. Moreover, the optimal size of a REIT differs according to the objectives, asset types, investment strategies, and management philosophy of each REIT. It is difficult for us to envision that a REIT specializing in a particular property type or limited to a small geographical region could benefit from economies of scale. However, for a REIT specializing in, for example, grade-A office buildings, we can clearly see the benefits of scale economies.

The evidence presented in the chapter tells a REIT manager that there is no fixed rule on the size of REITs. The manager should determine the size based on the REIT's objectives, opportunities, and constraints. However, one thing we are quite sure about is that there will not be many mega-REITs in the near future, as predicted by some experts in the field.

Although the finance literature indicates that there is a size effect in stock returns, the evidence for the small-firm effect in REIT stocks is inconclusive. When selecting REIT stocks, we suggest that investors should pay more attention to the fundamentals of a REIT than to its size.

NOTES

1. However, it should also be noted that the empirical evidence provided by Gyourko and Nelling (1996) and Ambrose et al. (2000) indicates that REITs do not benefit by geographical specialization. In other words, not all empirical evidence supports the notion that a larger REIT is more profitable. We will talk more about this issue in chapter 7.

2. The average size of REITs is similar to the average size of Nasdaq stocks during the period. (Nasdaq was considered to be the place for listing small stocks.)

3. There is evidence that the relation between REITs and small stocks may have gotten stronger in recent years (see Liang and McIntosh 1998 and Glascock, Lu, and So 2000). It may be that there continues to be enough small REITs that, even though the average capitalization has increased, they still behave like small stocks. Thus, even though the return variability of REITs relative to the market (i.e., the market risk) has declined, REITs continue to share a significant common relationship with small stocks. We will talk about the related studies when we discuss REIT stock performance in chapter 10.

4. It should be noted that in 1986 Congress enacted strict limits on the use of acquired net operating losses for tax purposes.

5. However, we also observe some instances of shareholder activism in the REIT industry. For example, the management of Malan Realty Investors and JDN Realty Corporation were changed because of shareholder dissatisfaction. We will address this issue in chapter 6.

REFERENCES

Allen, Paul, and C.T. Sirmans. 1987. An analysis of gains to acquiring firms shareholders: The special case of REITs. *Journal of Financial Economics* 18:175–84.

Ambrose, Brent, Steven Ehrlich, William Hughes, and Susan Wachter. 2000. REIT economies of scale: Fact or fiction? *Journal of Real Estate Finance and Economics* 20:211–24.

Ambrose, Brent, and Peter Linneman. 2001. REIT organizational structure and operating characteristics. *Journal of Real Estate Research* 21: 141–62.

Bers, Martina, and Thomas Springer. 1998a. Economies-of-scale for real estate investment trust. *Journal of Real Estate Research* 14:275–90.

———. 1998b. Sources of scale economies for REITs. *Real Estate Finance* 14 (Winter): 47–56.

Campbell, Robert D., Chinmoy Ghosh, and C. F. Sirmans. 1998. The great REIT consolidation: Fact or fancy? *Real Estate Finance* 15 (Summer): 45–54.

———. The information content of method of payment in mergers: Evidence from real estate investment trusts (REITs). *Real Estate Economics* 29:361–87.

Capozza, Dennis R., and S. Lee. 1995. Property types, size, and REIT value. *Journal of Real Estate Research* 10 (4): 363–80.

Capozza, Dennis R. and Paul J. Seguin. 1998. Managerial style and firm value. *Real Estate Economics* 26:131–50.

Chen, Su-Jane, Chenho Hsieh, Timothy Vines, and Shur-Nuaan Chiou. 1998. Macroeconomic variables, firm-specific variables and returns to REITs. *Journal of Real Estate Research* 16:269–77.

Colwell, Peter, and Hun Park. 1990. Seasonality and size effect: The case of real-estate-related investment. *Journal of Real Estate Finance and Economics* 3:251–59.

Elayan, Fayez A., and Philip J. Young. 1994. The value of control: Evidence from full and partial acquisitions in the real estate industry. *Journal of Real Estate Finance and Economics* 8:167–82.

Fitch, Stephane. 1999. REITlets. *Forbes* (June 14), pp. 352–55.

Glascock, John L., Chiuling Lu, and Raymond W. So. 2000. Further evidence on the integration of REIT, bond, and stock returns. *Journal of Real Estate Finance and Economics* 20:177–94.

Goodman, Jack. 1998. Making sense of real estate consolidation. *Real Estate Finance* 15:43–49.

Gyourko, Joseph, and Edward Nelling. 1996. Systematic risk and diversification in the equity market. *Real Estate Economics* 24:493–515.

Hardin, William. 1998. Executive compensation in EREITs: EREIT size is but one determinant. *Journal of Real Estate Research* 16:401–09.

Li, Jingyu, Fayez Elayan, and Thomas Meyer. 2001. Acquisitions by real estate investment trusts as a strategy for minimization of investor tax liability. *Journal of Economics and Finance* 25:115–34.

Liang, Youguo, and Willard McIntosh. 1998. REIT style and performance. *Journal of Real Estate Portfolio Management* 4:69–78.

Linneman, Peter. 1997. Forces changing the real estate industry forever. *Wharton Real Estate Review* 1:1–12.

McIntosh, Willard, Youguo Liang, and Daniel Tompkins. 1991. An examination of the small-firm effect within the REIT industry. *Journal of Real Estate Research* 6:9–17.

McIntosh, Willard, Dennis Officer, and Jeffrey Born. 1989. The wealth effects of merger activities: Further evidence from real estate investment trusts. *Journal of Real Estate Research* 4:141–55.

Mueller, Glenn. 1998. REIT size and earnings growth: Is bigger better, or a new challenge. *Journal of Real Estate Portfolio Management* 4:149–57.

Rosenthal, Mindy. Bigger REITs, better REITs. *Institutional Investor* 30 (February): 101.

Vogel, John. 1997. Why the new conventional wisdom about REITs is wrong. *Real Estate Finance* 14 (2): 7–12.

Yang, Shiawee. 2001. Is bigger better? Reexamining the scale economies of REITs. *Journal of Real Estate Portfolio Management* 7:67–78.

6

The Impact of Institutional Investors

Does It Matter Who Owns the Stocks?

You are a casual investor in the stock market who does not do much research on individual stocks. One day, two of your friends give you their suggestions on which stock you should buy. The first friend is a casual investor, just like you. The other friend is the head of the research division of a big pension fund. You know both friends are equally smart but you can take advice from only one of them. We guess that you will probably pick the stock recommended by the friend working for the pension fund. Why? You think this friend knows more about the stock he or she recommends.

However, your answer might be different if we changed the scenario slightly. Suppose that your "sophisticated" friend (who works for the pension fund) recommends that you buy stock in IBM and your less-informed friend (the casual investor) recommends that you buy stock in General Motors. We guess that you will probably have no preference between these two recommendations. Since both companies are so large and so many people follow their stocks, there is plenty of information about the companies. You might wonder how your sophisticated friend could know much more than your less sophisticated friend about those stocks.

Finally, let us talk about one extreme scenario. You are now looking at the initial public offerings (IPOs) of two new Internet companies. You know that neither company has any earnings or track record and that the products of both companies are basically the same. Your friend working for the pension fund tells you that his company will invest a lot in one of the companies, but he also admits that the pension fund knows no more about one company than the other.

In this scenario, if you definitely want to pick a stock from one of the two companies, which company will you pick? We guess that your choice will be the one with a high pension-fund investment. Why? Because even if the sophisticated investor (the pension fund) does not know much more about the company than the less sophisticated investor (the individual), it will be nice to have a pension fund to monitor the managers of the new company and to examine what the start-up is doing. You might wonder why the pension fund would expend effort to monitor the company. The answer is simple—it wants to protect its investment. As an individual investor, you can simply free-ride on the efforts of the pension fund.

These three examples illustrate the importance of having institutional investors involved in the stock market, especially in markets with thin stock-trading activity, less available information, and high agency costs that require monitoring efforts from shareholders of the company. The participation of institutional investors will be particularly relevant to deal with those inefficiencies. It is clear that the REIT market fits those descriptions, or at least that it did before 1990.

In this chapter, we will review the involvement of institutional investors in the REIT market. *We will also discuss some anomalous behavior of stocks in relation to the institutional holding level of REIT stocks.* From our analyses, we will be able to see how the increase in institutional investors in REIT stocks has transformed the market. With the monitoring ability offered by institutional investors, it is clear that the agency problems prevailing in the REIT stock market can be minimized. The trading activities of institutional investors will generate more information about the value of REIT stocks, which in turn will increase their liquidity and reduce their trading costs. Indeed, we believe that the increasing involvement of institutional investors is probably the most positive development for the REIT stock market.

The Roles of Institutional Investors

Institutional investors perform at least two functions for the stock market in general and a third for the REIT market in particular. The first of these functions is that, since institutional investors are constantly gathering pricing information about the stocks in the market, they probably act as price setters. Second, once institutional investors hold a large chunk of stocks in a particular company, they will worry more about the performance of that company and its management team. Since they have both the knowledge and the voting power, they will tend to monitor the investment and financing decisions of the firms in which they are heavily invested.

The third function is one that may be applicable to the REIT stock market alone. This function is to lend credibility to and bolster confidence in any unknown start-up companies (such as most REITs in the early period) they sponsor. The general public may generalize a well-known institutional investor's high-quality reputation onto a young REIT in which it invests. They may also believe that the REIT knows what it is doing because of help from the institutional investor. Given the above, it is safe to say that, while institutional-investor participation is important to all companies in the market, their attention is probably even more important for REITs.

Monitoring Management's Decisions

Monitoring power and the ability to influence management's decisions make institutional investors increasingly important in the stock market. As their ownership increases, institutions begin to abandon their traditional role as passive shareholders and become more active participants in the governance of the corporations in which they have purchased stocks. During the past decade, shareholder activism led by institutional investors has become an important characteristic of the financial market.

The trend of institutional-shareholder activism basically began in 1986. The Investor Responsibility Research Center reports that, between 1987 and 1994, public pensions sponsored 463 proxy proposals that sought changes in the corporate decisions of the firms in which they held stocks. Beginning in the early 1990s, institutional investors (especially the big public pension funds) began to target firms with relatively poor performance as the firms they would pay attention to. In other words, pension funds look closely at the performance of a firm and decide whether they should interfere with management's decisions. Under the scrutiny of institutional investors, firms with relatively poor performance will have something to worry about.

Gillan and Starks (2000) provide the most comprehensive study on the effectiveness of shareholder activism by institutional and individual investors. They examine 2,042 shareholder proposals submitted to 452 firms during the 1987–94 period. They find that proposals sponsored by active individual investors generate fewer total votes, whereas proposals sponsored by institutional investors (such as public pension funds) or coordinated groups of investors receive significantly more votes. Indeed, under the monitoring of institutional investors, there are incentives for management to perform better. In addition, the problems associated with conflicts of interest between management and shareholders can be reduced under the monitoring of institutional investors.

Practitioners in the REIT stock market have observed that the lack of monitoring and bargaining power enjoyed by institutional investors might affect REIT returns. For example, Wang (1992) notes that money managers normally charge approximately 20% less to institutional investors than to typical sponsors. It should be noted that the higher the fee a company needs to pay, the lower its profits will be.

Rudnitsky (1992) observed that Trammell Crow forgave $6.5 million in management fees for its Trammell Crow Equity Partner Fund (a real estate fund dominated by institutional investors) when the fund performed worse than expected. Trammell Crow, however, still collected management fees from its Trammell Crow Real Estate Investors REIT, even when the share price of the REIT dropped from $15 per share in 1986 to approximately $2 in 1991. It should be noted that most of the 2,900 stockholders of the REIT were individual investors. The difference between the treatment of the REIT and that of the real estate fund is probably due to the presence (or absence) of institutional investors.

Setting Stock Prices

A growing body of research in the finance literature documents interesting relationships between institutional investors' trading strategies and the movement of security prices. For example, Lakonishok, Shleifer, and Vishny (1992) find that institutional investors conduct positive-feedback trading in smaller stocks. Similarly, Chan and Lakonishok (1993, 1995) document that such institutional trades are associated with price pressures, although the average effect is small and varies by firm capitalization. Keim and Madhavan (1995) find that there is a significant relation between the buy-sell decision and past excess returns for certain types of institutional investors.

In addition, there is also evidence indicating that institutional investors lead the price movement of stocks. For example, Badrinath, Kale, and Noe (1995) document that the return on a portfolio of stocks with the highest level of institutional ownership leads the returns on portfolios of stocks with lower levels of institutional ownership. Nofsinger and Sias (1999) show a strong positive relation between annual changes in institutional ownership and returns, which suggests that either institutional investors engage in intrayear positive-feedback trading more than individual investors, or institutional investors' herding affects prices more than individual investors' herding does.

This evidence clearly shows that institutional investors contribute to price setting in the stock market. In addition, there is evidence that individual investors' performance is worse than the movement of the general stock market. For example, Barber and Odean (2000) examine the trading activities of 66,465 households during the 1991–96 period, finding that individual investors who trade actively tend to have below-market performance. This evidence shows at least that institutional investors might be considered more sophisticated traders than individuals.

It is well known in the REIT market that there are certain advantages to following the lead of institutional investors in the selection of stocks. For example, in an article teaching investors the right way to invest in REITs, Simonoff and Baig (1997) point out that investors should focus on REITs with high levels of institutional and insider ownership. Woolley (1998) points out that, while many investors are attracted to IPOs of mortgage REITs, sophisticated institutional investors hold back because they observe that the hard-to-value REIT stocks will tend to drop in price after their IPOs. (We might add that the empirical evidence proves that those institutional investors are correct in that assumption.)

The Reputation Effect

The reputation effect associated with institutional investors is an important factor in the REIT industry that warrants our attention. Recall that, in chapter 4, we talked about the relationship between the reputation of an advisor (or sponsor) and the stock performance of a REIT. We know that when a REIT is sponsored by a well-known institutional investor, such as a pension fund, it will perform better than a REIT whose sponsor is relatively unknown (such as an individual).

Indeed, in a market that is traditionally viewed as having thin trading and small stocks, the visibility of a famous institutional sponsor can truly help a REIT, which may have an easier time attracting the attention of financial analysts (and hence the attention of individual investors) and acquiring financing or properties because of its sponsor's connections.

The popular press also indicates that there is a *peer effect* among institutional investors. That is, institutional investors generally know each other and tend to buy the stocks of the REITs that are sponsored by their peers. Given this, in order to attract institutional investors to buy a REIT stock, it might pay for the REIT to find an institutional sponsor before its establishment. McMahan (1994) notes that after 1993 the management of most REIT IPOs held significant equity in their offerings and typically worked as a team long before the IPOs took place. It is quite clear that the peer effect contributed to the success of most of the REIT IPOs during the 1993–95 period.

It is also a common belief that institutional investors tend to invest in high-quality stocks. Malpezzi and Shilling (2000) confirm that although both REITs and institutional investors generally tilt their real estate holdings toward quality, the tilt is much more pronounced in the case of institutional investors. They also report that, holding quality constant, institutional investors prefer to invest in properties in locations where the share of local employment in business services, finance, insurance, real estate, and transportation is relatively high when compared to national averages. This evidence seems to indicate that the investments made by institutional investors are induced by the constraints of the *prudent-man rule*. That is, institutional investors tend to invest in safer and less speculative locations because they want to make sure that their investments are wise.

Institutional Investors in the REIT Market

At the time of this writing, there are no comprehensive studies that examine the institutional holding levels (i.e., percentage of stock owned by institutional investors) of all REIT stocks over time.[1] Some empirical studies have examined the institutional holding level of a small group of REITs during a specific sample period; however, the samples of these studies are typically small when compared to the number of REITs available in the market. This is probably due to the difficulty in gathering institutional holding data on REITs; many of these studies, in fact, hand-collected the institutional ownership data from the Standard and Poor's stock reports.

In order to discuss institutional involvement in the REIT stock market in a meaningful way, we needed institutional holding information over time for both REIT stocks and all other stocks in the stock market. Since we could not find such information in the existing literature, we had to collect it on our own, which required us to conduct our own research and decide how to gather a massive amount of data in an efficient way. Clearly, hand-collecting the data for all REITs over a long time period may not be economically feasible; fortunately, we found a fast and convenient way to obtain institutional data that we would like to share with the reader. We are firm believers that the presence of institutional investors is very important to the price and management of a REIT, and we hope that our readers, by knowing where and how to get this information, will be able to make better investment decisions when investing in REIT stocks.

Gathering Institutional Data

We used the *Spectrum 3:13(f) Institutional Stock Holdings Survey* published by Computer Directions Advisors (CDA) as our information source. This may well be the most comprehensive collection of institutional holding information available. Since the data are available on tape, we can extract a large amount in a very speedy and convenient way. The institutions in the *Spectrum* survey have combined equity assets exceeding $100 million and include banks, insurance companies, investment companies, investment advisors, pension funds, endowments, and foundations. All NYSE and Amex stocks are included in the survey, along with the majority of over-the-counter (OTC) stocks.

However, even with the *Spectrum* tapes, we still cannot find institutional holding information for some of the REITs identified in the appendix and have been unable to include them in our investigation of institutional holdings of REIT stocks. Since the *Spectrum* tapes only began to report institutional information after 1979 and information on REIT stocks became more complete after 1981, we limit our sample to the 1981–99 period. (We cannot include data after 1999 because the tapes have not been made available to us for the analysis.) In this chapter we will report the average percentage of institutional holdings, computed as the number of shares held by institutional investors divided by the total number of shares outstanding, for REIT stocks as well as for stocks in the general stock market during the 1981–99 period.

Institutional Holdings of REIT Stocks

Table 6.1 presents summary statistics on the distribution of institutional holdings for REIT stocks as well as for all other stocks during the 1981–99 period. From the table and figure 6.1, we can see a dramatic increase over the period in institutional participation in the REIT stock market. The mean institutional holding of REIT stocks traded in all exchanges is around 10% in 1981 and 39% in 1999. It should also be noted that the percentage of institutional holdings is basically an increasing function of time in the REIT stock market. On the other hand, the percentage of stocks with zero institutional holding decreases from about 11% in 1981 to 3% in 1999. Except for 1999, the 0% holding is basically a decreasing function of time in the REIT stock market. This evidence indicates that, during the sample period, institutional investors as a group became dominant players in the REIT stock market. If we believe that institutional investors are more informed than individual investors, then our evidence suggests that REIT markets should be more efficient in the recent years.

One might wonder whether the increase in institutional participation in the REIT market is due to the growth in institutional participation in the general stock market. The answer, however, is no. Table 6.1 allows us to compare the institutional holding level for all stocks in the market with that for REIT stocks. In 1981, the average institutional holding in the stock market is approximately 15%, an amount that grew to 31% in 1999. Although we can also see that more institutional investors participate in the general stock market over time, the rate of increase is much slower than that in the REIT market.

From figure 6.1 it is clear that before 1993 the institutional holding level in the general stock market is much higher than that in the REIT stock market. However, beginning in 1995 it is also clear that the institutional holding level in the REIT stock market is higher than that in the general market. This shows that institutional investors who had neglected REIT stocks in the past are now paying more attention to them (which is probably due to the creation of modern REITs after 1993). With this level of institutional participation, we have no doubt that the REIT stock market should become more efficient in the future.

We also wished to find out whether the percentage of institutional holdings differs among stock markets. Table 6.2 and figures 6.2–6.4 show the percentage of institutional holdings categorized by different markets. It is

Table 6.1 Institutional Holdings of REIT Stocks versus All Stocks

	Institutional Holdings									
	For REIT Stocks					For All Stocks				
	Mean (%)	Maximum (%)	Minimum (%)	Firms with Zero Holdings (%)	Number of Obs.	Mean (%)	Maximum (%)	Minimum (%)	Firms with Zero Holdings (%)	Number of Obs.
1981	10	84	0	11	115	15	93	0	12	4,304
1982	10	61	0	8	108	15	99	0	10	4,481
1983	10	68	0	7	109	17	99	0	7	4,790
1984	11	91	0	6	99	17	98	0	7	5,431
1985	12	82	0	4	107	19	96	0	7	5,436
1986	14	82	0	2	126	20	98	0	5	5,771
1987	15	89	0	3	141	20	98	0	5	6,112
1988	14	84	0	3	149	20	100	0	5	6,340
1989	15	81	0	2	145	21	100	0	4	6,200
1990	14	76	0	1	147	22	97	0	4	6,182
1991	15	75	0	1	136	23	99	0	3	6,102
1992	14	89	0	0	150	25	99	0	2	6,372
1993	19	76	0	0	166	26	100	0	1	6,695
1994	26	84	0	0	237	27	98	0	1	7,566
1995	31	96	0	0	233	28	100	0	1	7,722
1996	33	100	0	0	227	29	100	0	2	8,129
1997	38	99	0	0	212	30	100	0	2	8,424
1998	40	93	0	0	237	31	100	0	2	8,569
1999	39	93	0	3	220	31	100	0	1	8,071
1981–89	13	91	0	5	1,099	18	100	0	6	48,865
1990–99	29	100	0	1	1,965	27	100	0	2	73,832
1981–99	23	100	0	3	3,064	24	100	0	4	122,697

Source: Authors' own calculations using institutional-holdings data from *Spectrum 3:13(f) Institutional Stock Holdings Survey.*

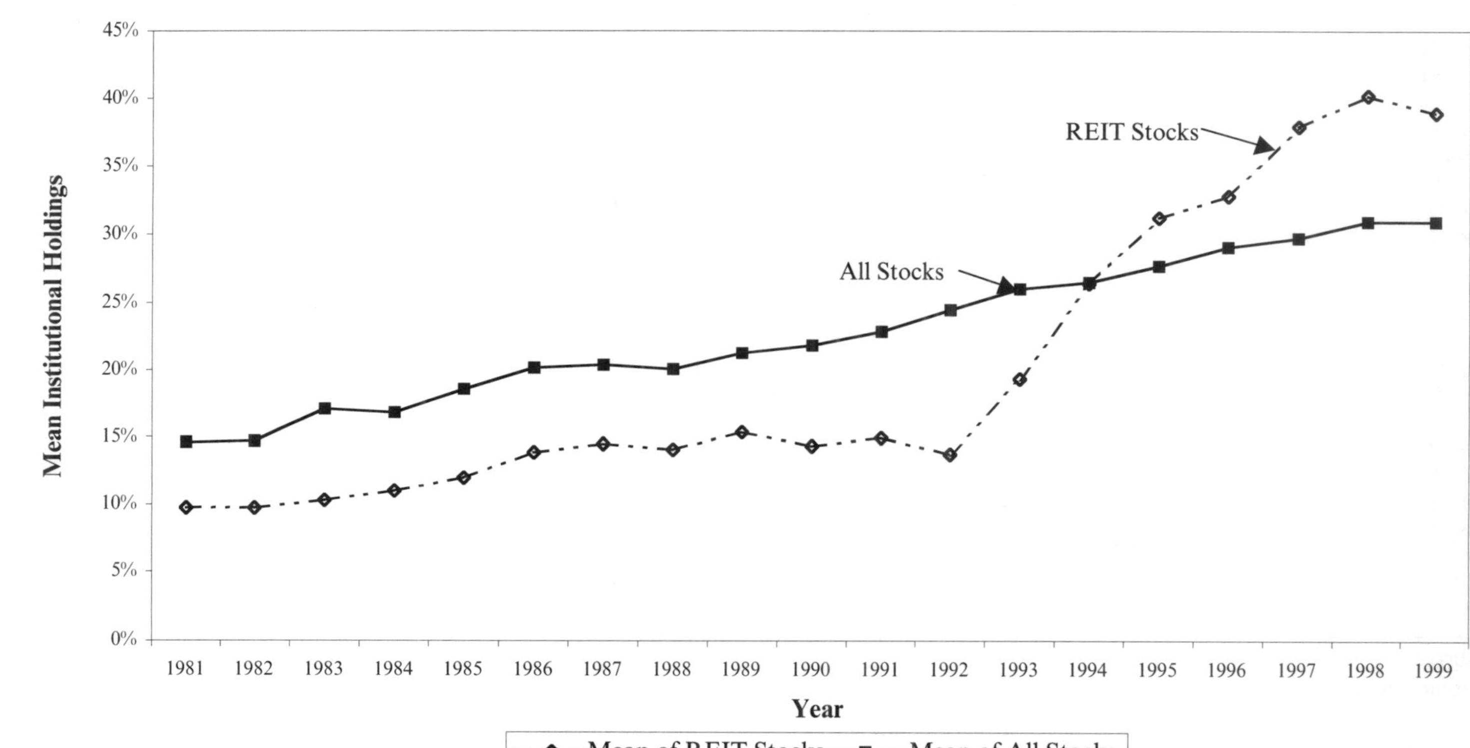

Figure 6.1 Institutional Holdings of REIT Stocks versus All Stocks

Table 6.2 Institutional Holdings of REIT Stocks versus All Stocks, by Market

	Mean Institutional Holdings (%)					
	NYSE		Amex		Nasdaq	
	REITs	All Stocks	REITs	All Stocks	REITs	All Stocks
1981	15	26	14	9	4	8
1982	16	26	10	10	5	8
1983	18	31	9	12	6	11
1984	19	32	10	12	7	11
1985	22	34	11	14	7	13
1986	22	36	13	16	8	14
1987	20	36	13	17	10	15
1988	19	35	10	16	11	15
1989	19	35	12	18	12	16
1990	19	36	10	18	10	17
1991	20	37	9	17	12	18
1992	20	37	7	17	11	20
1993	28	37	8	18	16	21
1994	37	38	9	17	16	22
1995	40	39	10	17	28	23
1996	42	41	10	18	22	25
1997	44	43	18	18	24	24
1998	46	44	20	19	25	25
1999	45	44	18	17	23	25
1981–89	19	32	11	14	8	12
1990–99	34	39	12	18	19	22
1981–99	27	36	12	16	13	17

Source: Authors' own calculations using institutional-holdings data from *Spectrum 3:13(f) Institutional Stock Holdings Survey.*

clear that institutional investors pay much more attention to REITs listed on the NYSE than to those listed on the other two markets. Table 6.2 reports that NYSE firms on average have a significantly higher percentage of institutional holdings than both Amex and Nasdaq firms during the period of analysis.

For REITs traded on the NYSE, the average percentage of institutional holdings is 15% in 1981 and 45% in 1999. The mean institutional holdings for REITs traded on Amex and NASDAQ are 14% and 4%, respectively, in 1981, and 18% and 23%, respectively, in 1999. We should note that, except on the Amex, the institutional holding level of REIT stocks exceeded that of the general stock market beginning in 1995. The institutional holding level of Amex stocks was higher than that of Nasdaq stocks until the late 1980s. From 1991 onward, the trend reverses and Amex firms show a significantly lower percentage of institutional holdings than NASDAQ

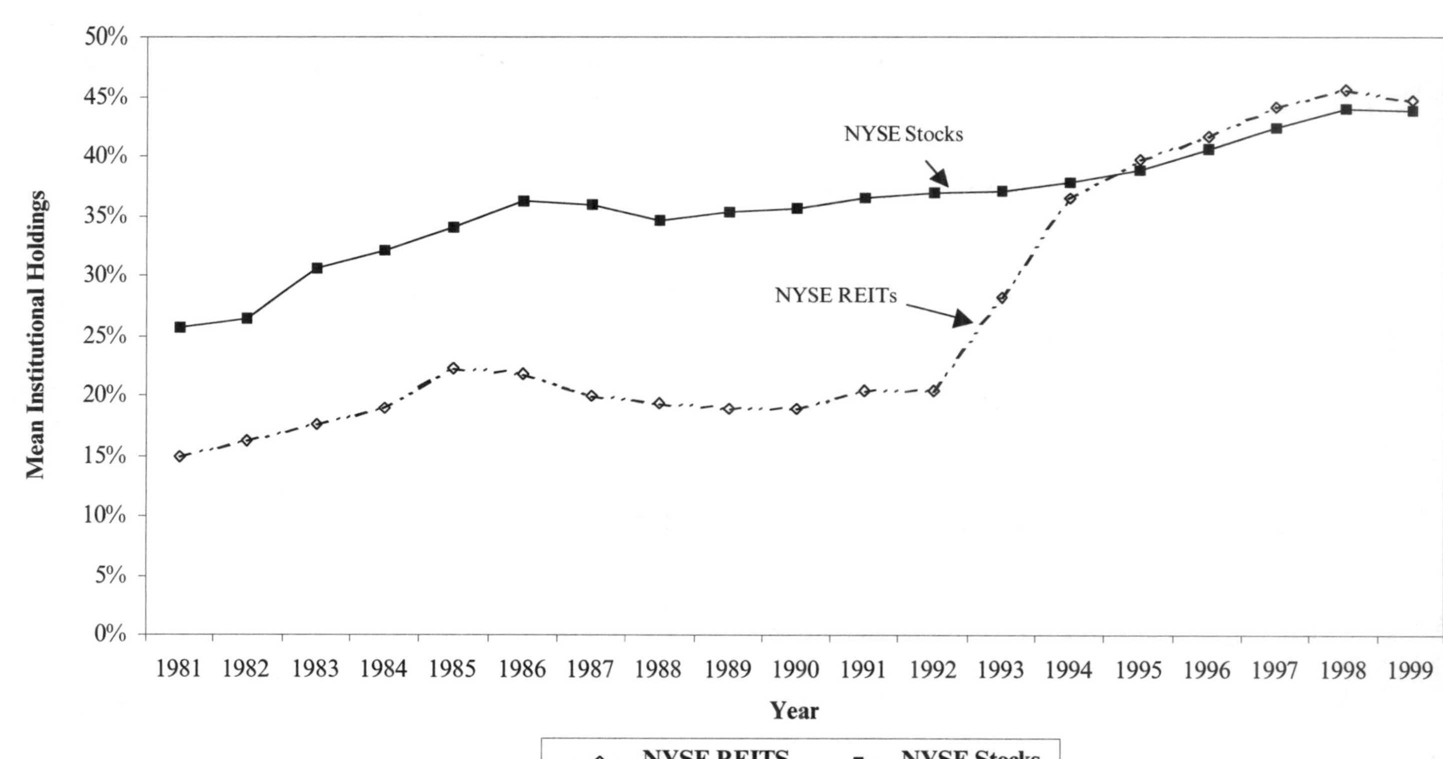

Figure 6.2 Institutional Holdings of NYSE REIT Stocks

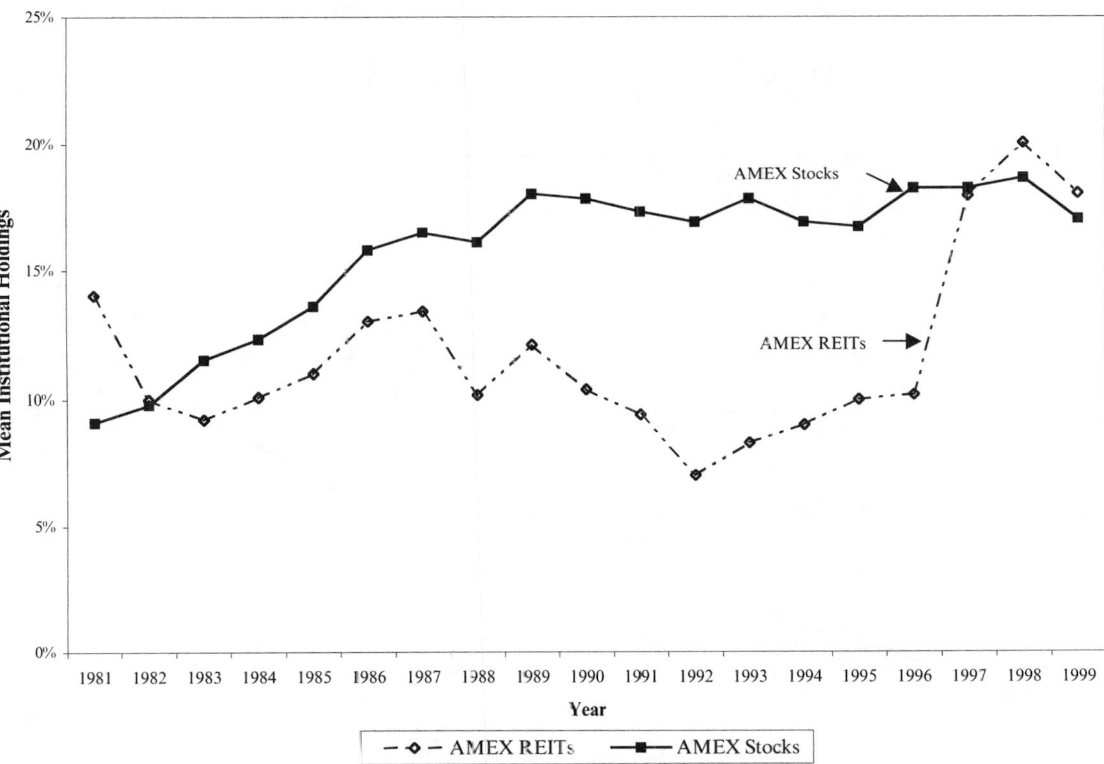

Figure 6.3 Institutional Holdings of Amex REIT Stocks

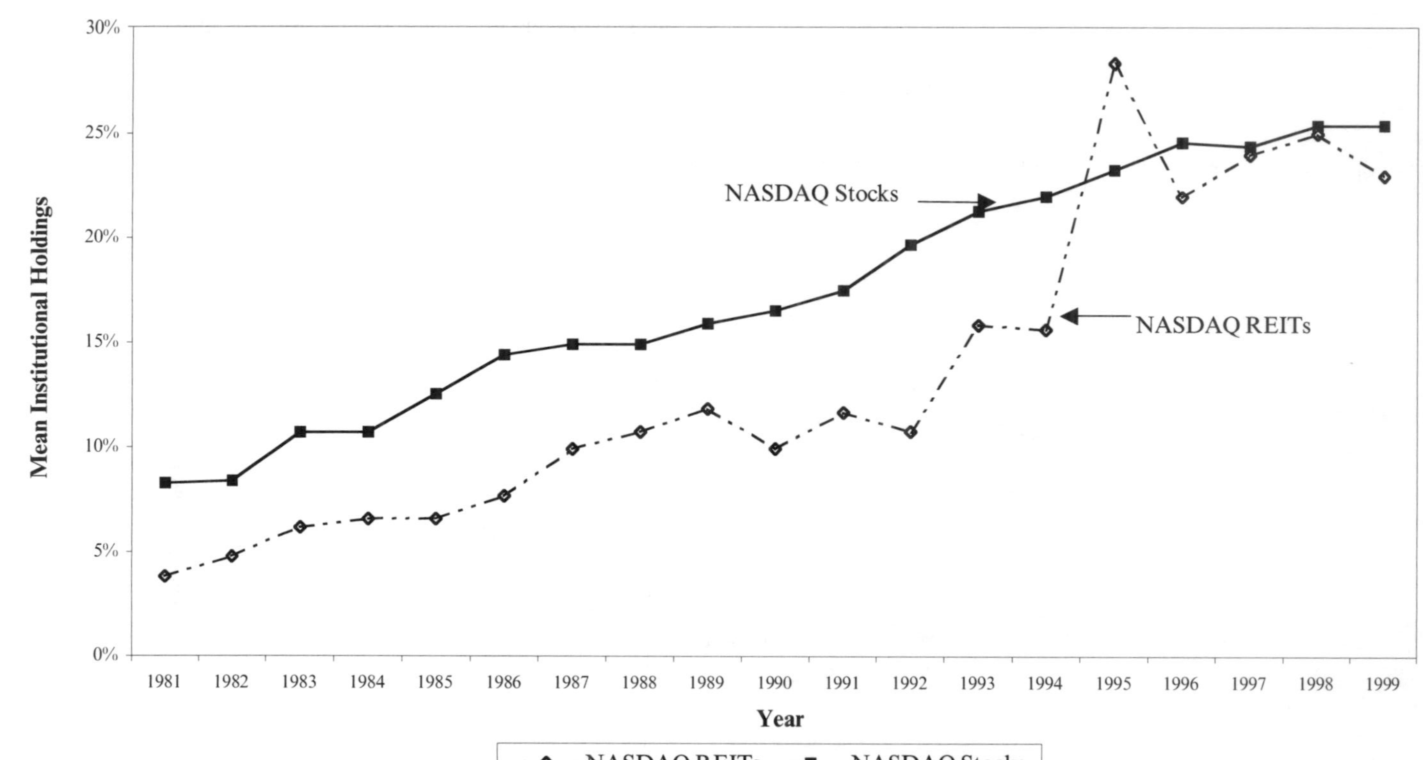

Figure 6.4 Institutional Holdings of Nasdaq REIT Stocks

firms. (This provides support for a CNN news report on March 12, 1998, that Amex has been eclipsed in recent years by Nasdaq.)

From 1981 to 1999, we note that institutional holdings in Nasdaq stocks show a substantial increase of 475% (from 4% in 1981 to 23% in 1999), while the increases for NYSE and Amex stocks are 200% (from 15% in 1981 to 45% in 1999) and 28% (from 14% in 1981 to 18% in 1999), respectively. Given this, although we see increases in all the three stock markets, the most dramatic growth in institutional participation seems to be in the Nasdaq market.

Table 6.3 reports the institutional holding level for equity REITs, mortgage REITs, hybrid REITs, infinite-life REITs, and finite-life REITs during the 1981–99 period. When REITs are partitioned by asset type, it is clear that institutional investors pay much more attention to equity REITs than to mortgage REITs. Figure 6.5 shows a significant increase in institutional investors in the equity-REIT market after 1993. This indicates that the main reason for institutional investors to participate in the REIT market is to have a claim on the cash flows of the underlying real properties the REITs own. When REITs are partitioned by the duration of the organization, it is also clear that institutional investors pay little attention to finite-life REITs. Figure 6.6 shows that the institutional holding level of infinite-life REITs is much higher than that of finite-life REITs. The gap in the holdings widens after 1993, indicating that institutional investors prefer to invest in REITs with growth potential.

A Note of Caution

It should be noted that the growing institutional interest in REITs that we have observed might be due to an increase in holdings from a relatively small group of institutional investors. For example, Chan, Leung, and Wang (1998) report that one institutional investor (Cohen & Steers Capital Management) held the amount of REIT stocks equivalent to the size of six average REITs. The top 20 institutional investors in the REIT stock market collectively held combined REIT stocks equivalent to the average size of 46 REITs at the end of 1995. It is difficult to say whether this is a good or bad pattern for the REIT market. We know that these 20 institutional investors will pay a great deal of attention to the REIT market; however, whether they will be able to provide the necessary monitoring function to the REIT stock market is another question we need to consider.

The encouraging news is that even if there are only a few institutional investors concentrating their investments in the REIT stock market, they do not concentrate their investment in only a few REIT stocks. Chan, Leung, and Wang (1998) report that, in 1995, each institutional investor (that participates in the REIT market) invests in an average of 10.67 REITs. In other words, most institutional investors, when they invest in the REIT market, hold a diversified REIT portfolio. In addition, in 1995, 4.2% of the

Table 6.3 Institutional Holdings by REIT Type and Duration

	Equity REIT		Mortgage REIT		Hybrid REIT		Infinite REIT		Finite REIT	
Year	Mean (%)	Number of Obs.	Mean (%)	Number of Obs.	Mean (%)	Number of Obs.	Mean (%)	Number of Obs.	Mean (%)	Number of Obs.
1981	11	53	10	15	9	47	10	114	0	1
1982	10	54	12	15	9	39	10	107	0	1
1983	11	52	11	13	9	44	11	107	0	2
1984	11	48	11	12	11	39	12	94	3	5
1985	14	54	10	14	12	39	13	94	6	13
1986	15	63	8	23	15	40	15	109	6	17
1987	15	81	11	23	16	37	16	119	7	22
1988	15	79	11	31	16	39	16	122	6	27
1989	16	79	10	30	18	36	17	121	6	24
1990	15	82	10	30	16	35	16	124	6	23
1991	17	79	9	29	16	28	17	110	5	26
1992	15	94	7	29	16	27	17	112	3	38
1993	23	111	8	30	18	25	24	123	4	43
1994	31	179	10	32	18	26	32	191	5	46
1995	37	179	9	30	16	24	36	195	7	38
1996	37	177	11	28	21	22	37	194	7	33
1997	42	169	18	25	27	18	40	197	19	15
1998	44	180	27	35	27	22	41	224	19	13
1999	43	177	23	30	20	13	40	209	18	11
1981–89	13	563	10	176	13	360	13	987	6	112
1990–99	34	1,427	13	298	19	240	32	1,679	7	286
1981–99	28	1,990	12	474	15	600	25	2,666	7	398

Source: Authors' own calculations using institutional-holdings data from *Spectrum 3:13(f) Institutional Stock Holdings Survey.*

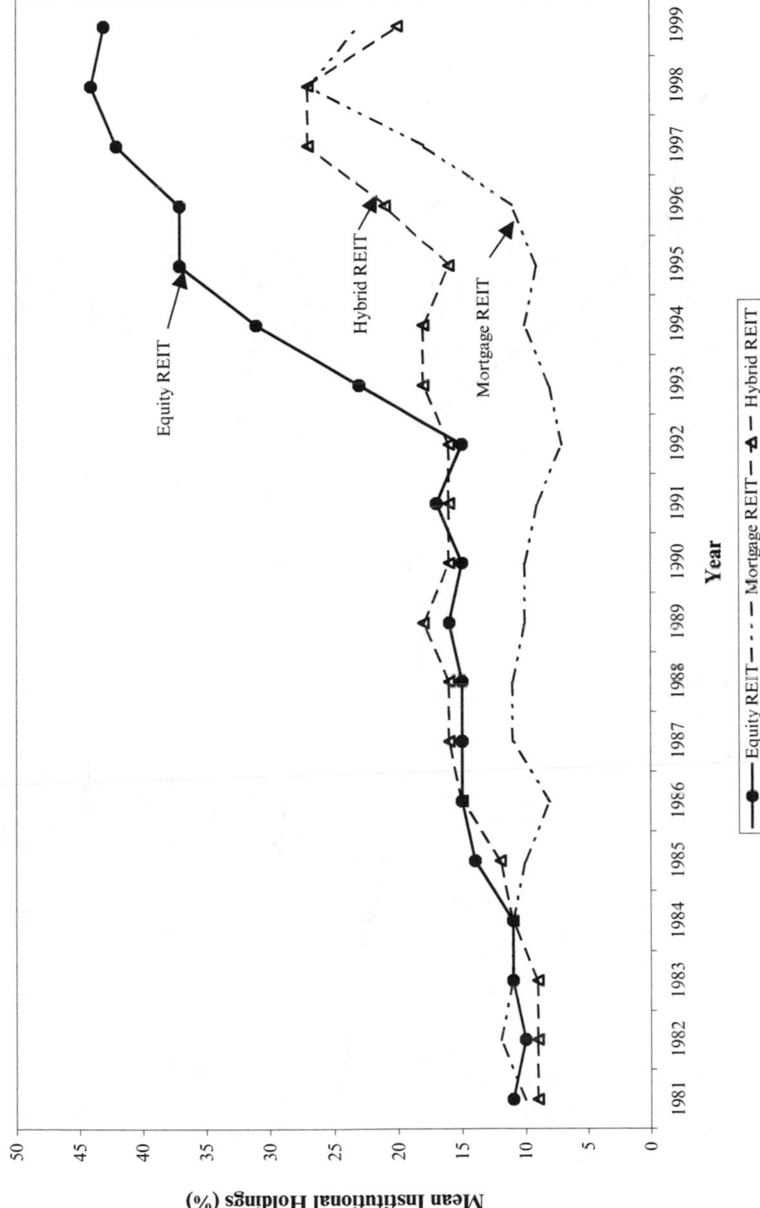

Figure 6.5 Institutional Holdings of REIT Type

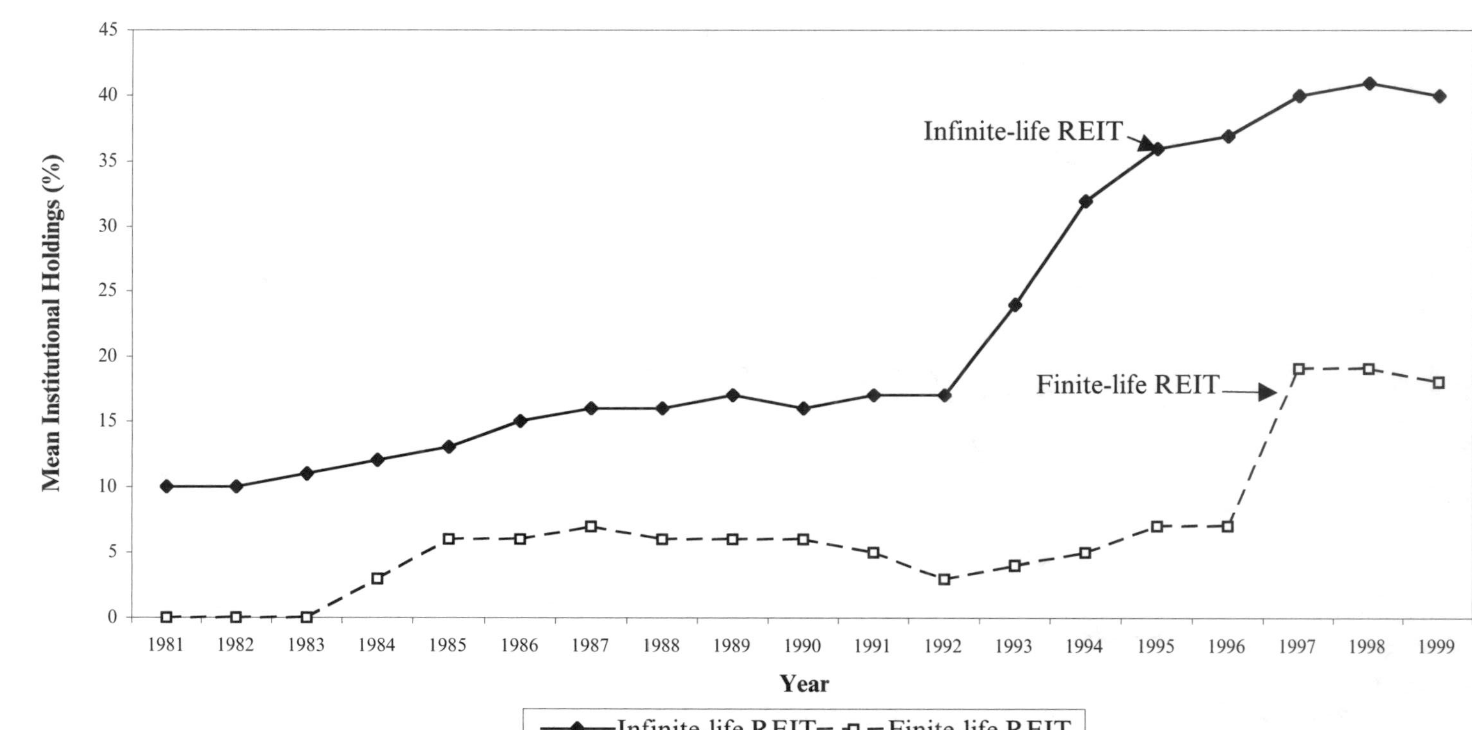

Figure 6.6 Institutional Holdings of by Finite-Life and Infinite-Life REITs

firms held by the 648 institutional investors surveyed were REITs. Given this, it is safe to say that institutional investors do not concentrate on only a few REIT stocks. We believe that this diversified investment strategy is healthy for the development of the REIT market.

To summarize, from our information from a large data set, we find that there has been a dramatic change in institutional interest in the REIT market. Before 1993, institutional investors did not pay much attention to REIT stocks. However, recent evidence indicates that they now pay more attention to REIT stocks than to other stocks in the market. The significant change in the levels of institutional ownership suggests that an examination of the relationship between institutional investors and price behavior in the stock market might yield some interesting lessons for investors. This is what we examine in the next section.

Stock Performance and Institutional Investors

So far we have provided only anecdotal evidence on the impact institutional investors have on REIT stocks. In this section, we summarize the results of several studies that explicitly examine REIT performance under different levels of institutional involvement. Those studies can be grouped under three topics: REIT IPOs, the Monday effect on REITs, and REIT general performance.

REIT Initial Public Offerings

Studies on REIT IPOs may provide the most direct empirical evidence of the reputation effect discussed earlier. It is common knowledge among experienced investors that IPO investors in the stock market earn a very high return on the first day of trading. That is, the stocks of IPO firms increased around 18%, on average, on the first trading day in the stock market during the 1970–2000 period. However, this significant price phenomenon does not apply to REIT IPOs. Wang, Chan, and Gau (1992) find that the IPOs of 87 REITs during the 1971–88 period were overpriced. This means that the stock price of the REITs dropped on the first day of trading.

Why should REIT stocks be overpriced? During the 1971–88 period, few institutional investors were involved in REIT IPOs, and it may be that the lack of institutional investors is the reason for this unique pricing behavior. Ling and Ryngaert (1997) find that REIT IPOs in the early 1990s were no longer overpriced (although the price still did not go up much) on the first trading day. Their finding corresponds with an increase in the number of institutional investors in the market during that period.

More importantly, Wang, Chan, and Gau (1992) find a positive relationship between the first-day return of REIT IPOs and the percentage of institutional investors holding the REIT IPO stocks. In other words, if there are more institutional investors participating in a REIT IPO, the stock price of the REIT will gain support when it is traded in the stock market. Although we cannot say that the level of institutional holdings is the only factor determining a REIT's market price on its first trading day, it is clear that the price of a REIT stock will gain support in the stock market if the IPO has more institutional participants. (Chapter 9 will discuss in greater detail the issues and evidence surrounding REIT IPO pricing.)

The Monday Effect

One of the most noticeable seasonal anomalies documented in the finance literature is the significantly negative average stock returns on Monday (the so-called *Monday effect*). This anomalous Monday return pattern is observed not only in U.S. and foreign stock markets, but also in debt markets. In a recent study, Chan, Leung, and Wang (2001) examine the relationship between the Monday returns for REITs and the level of institutional participation in REITs, and come up with quite interesting findings.

Chan, Leung, and Wang (2001) document that the well-known Monday effect also applied to REITs prior to 1990. However, they also find that this effect has disappeared in recent years. Their empirical evidence indicates that the average Monday return recently changed from negative to positive, and this change coincides with the increase in institutional investors in the stock market. In other words, the increase in institutional holdings in the REIT stock market effectively takes care of an anomalous return phenomenon in that market—or, put another way, the significantly negative Monday return is caused by those REIT stocks with relatively few institutional investors. (Thus, if you want to buy a REIT stock on a Monday morning [or a Friday afternoon], do not buy those with low institutional holdings.)

General Performance

The study by Wang et al. (1995) provides the most comprehensive evidence to date on the impact of institutional ownership on REIT stock performance. They find that institutional holdings of REIT stocks were significantly lower than the holdings of stocks in the general market during the 1970–89 period. They also report that REIT stocks with low levels of institutional holdings significantly underperformed the stock market during that period. (It should be noted that the REIT market is considered to be less informationally efficient when compared with the general stock market prior to 1990.)

An analysis of the risk-adjusted performance of REITs over three subperiods between 1979 and 1989 shows a strong positive correlation between performance and the number of security analysts following REITs, in addition to the correlation with the percentage of institutional holdings discussed previously. These results indicate that the performance of REIT stocks is positively affected by the flow of information about REITs to the market. These findings also imply that part of the superior performance of equity REIT stocks relative to mortgage REITs may be explained by the greater amount of information available about equity REITs. Larger REITs are also followed by more financial analysts and have a greater percentage of their shares owned by institutional investors. This may explain why larger REITs have a more stable long-run performance.[2]

Downs (1998) provides an interesting and comprehensive study on the effect of relaxing the five-or-fewer rule in the REIT industry. Recall that, to qualify as a REIT, the firm cannot have a combination of five shareholders owning more than 50% of the stocks of a firm. (We refer to this as the *5/50 rule.*) This rule might limit institutional investors' willingness to invest in REITs. However, the depressed real estate market in the early 1990s seems to have convinced Congress to relax this 5/50 rule in order to attract more institutional investors into the real estate (and REIT) market.

The REIT industry seems to have welcomed Congress's decision. Before the change in the tax laws, large institutional investors might have found it difficult to accumulate a significant position in individual REITs if the market capitalization of the REIT was too small. Relaxing the 5/50 rule seems to have addressed this problem. For example, Martin (1993) and Vincour (1994) posit that the change in the tax law would result in pension funds and other institutions increasing their investment activities in REIT securities.

Downs (1998) asks whether there is any value to attract institutional investors to the REIT market, and finds that the answer is yes. He documents an industry-wide creation and distribution of value caused by the increase in institutional investors (due to the change in the 5/50 rule) in the REIT stock market. His main conclusion is that institutional ownership contributes to REIT value. While the absolute level of institutional investors is not an important determinant of REIT returns, Downs finds that the absolute change in institutional ownership is contemporaneous with the risk-adjusted returns of REITs. This means that REITs experiencing an increase (or decrease) in institutional ownership will perform better (or worse) in terms of their stock performance during the period.

It is also interesting to note that Crain, Cudd, and Brown (2000) report that after the increase in the institutional ownership of REIT stocks, the unsystematic (or diversifiable) risk component of equity REIT stocks has been significantly reduced. This means that REIT stocks now move in tandem with the stocks in the general stock market. Their evidence seems to indicate that institutional investors affect both the return and risk dimensions of REIT stocks.

In a sense, although Downs's (1998) finding is similar to (although not exactly the same as) the result reported by Wang et al. (1995), his result reaffirms that institutional ownership is an important factor affecting REIT returns. Indeed, Downs's study is particularly relevant to the issue of the relation between institutional holdings and REIT returns because it utilizes a more recent sample period covering the time period in which there are increases in institutional holdings in the REIT market.

Relationship with Financial Analysts

Wang et al. (1995) also address the valuation of REIT stocks by examining the extent to which security analysts and institutional holdings of REIT stocks play a role in REITs' return performances. They show that, over the period 1979–89, the percentage of institutional holdings in REIT stocks increased significantly but represented only a fraction of total REIT ownership. Similarly, financial analysts and institutional investors showed greater interest in non-REIT stocks than in REIT stocks and more interest in equity REITs than in mortgage REITs. Wang et al. also report that before 1992 financial analysts paid very little attention to REIT stocks, which was probably due to the lack of institutional interest.[3]

Khoo, Hartzell, and Hoesli (1993) examine the decline in the risk of equity REITs and show that as the number of analysts following them increases, the risk (as measured by the variability of returns) declines. They believe that an increase in the amount of information about equity-REIT stocks is an important explanation for the secular decline in risk. Furthermore, the decline in risk is consistent with the evidence that the level of institutional interest and the number of analysts following REITs have increased. In other words, as investors become more familiar with REITs and how REITs operate, they perceive a decline in the risk of investing in REIT stocks.

Financial analysts exist because there are demands for their services. However, one can safely conclude that it is the large institutional investors (and not the small individual investors) who create the bulk of the demand for information provided by financial analysts. Hence it is natural for analysts to pay special attention to the stocks that institutional investors are interested in. The empirical evidence discussed previously seems to support this intuition. It seems reasonable to conclude that the increase in institutional investors in the REIT market led to the increase in financial analysts in the market. This increase, in turn, provides more information about REIT stocks to investors.

Other Kinds of Informed Investors

Institutional investors are not the only well-informed investors. Other insiders (such as the chairman of the board, managers, and members of the board of directors) must also have the ability to affect a REIT's performance. To make our story complete, we should also understand the relationship between insiders and REIT performance.

Friday, Sirmans, and Conover (1999) examine the relation between the level of insider ownership and the value of a REIT, using the market-to-book ratio as a proxy for REIT performance. In other words, if the market value of a REIT (as determined by its stock price) is much higher than its book value, then we can say that the REIT performs quite well. Friday, Sirmans, and Conover define *inside block holders* as officers and directors or insiders with other affiliations. They define *outside block holders* simply as outside directors who are block holders of the REIT.

Friday, Sirmans, and Conover (1999) find that low levels of insider ownership are associated with increased market-to-book ratios of equity REITs. This means that if equity-REIT insiders hold little of a REIT's stock, it will perform better and have a higher value. In other words, an increase in insider holding will decrease the market value of the REIT. The authors believe that when there are many insider-shareholders in the REIT, they can become entrenched and are able to expropriate outside shareholders' wealth. Their finding indicates that investors might want to avoid investing in REITs with a high percentage of insider ownership.

McIntosh et al. (1994) and Friday and Sirmans (1998) report a relationship between the composition of a REIT's board of directors and the value of the REIT. Specifically, they find that the value of a REIT is higher if there is more outside-director representation on the board. This finding suggests that outside directors can monitor a REIT's investment decisions more effectively than inside directors can. However, Friday and Sirmans also report that this observation holds only if the ratio of outside representation is less than 50% of the board. In other words, if there are too many outsiders on the board, they become less effective in monitoring the REIT's decisions.

What Have We Learned?

The intuitions behind all the arguments in this chapter are easy to understand, and the empirical evidence is straightforward and prompts no contradictory conclusions. Thus it is easy to summarize this chapter, as follows:

- Who owns stock is important in determining REIT value.
- Institutional investors monitor REIT management's decisions.
- Institutional investors know more about a REIT's value than individual investors.
- Institutional investors help a, REIT establish its reputation by participating in its establishment (as illustrated by the price movements of REIT IPOs).
- REIT stocks with more institutional investors perform better than those with fewer institutional investors.
- The presence of institutional investors helps the REIT stock market eliminate anomalous price movements, such as the negative Monday return.

- The increase in institutional investors (and hence in financial analysts) in the REIT market helps improve the flow of information.
- Although the REIT market lacked institutional investors prior to 1990, it now has more institutional investors than the general stock market.
- The increase in institutional investors will make the REIT stock market more transparent and efficient.
- An increase in insider holdings in a REIT will decrease its market value.
- The value of a REIT is higher if there is more outside-director representation on its board of directors.

The Future of Institutional Investment in REITs

The main conclusion we can draw from this chapter is that who owns the stock is important to a REIT's value and performance. If you are a small investor with little spare time to track the stock performance of a REIT or to monitor the investment decisions of its managers, why not take a free ride by following the actions of institutional investors? From the evidence presented in this chapter, it is clear that REIT stocks with high institutional holdings perform better in every respect than those with low institutional holdings. This advice was true in the past and holds up to now.

Will this advice still hold in the future? In other words, given that the level of institutional investment in the market is already so high, will the phenomena we discussed still hold with the passage of time? The answer is probably no, at least for a while. The percentage of REIT stocks held by institutional investors is high, but those stocks are concentrated in the hands of one small group of investors. In other words, we have yet to observe a diversified group of institutional investors in the REIT market. Moreover, there is a close association between the institutional investors and the managers of the REIT. Thus, although the situation is improving, we still suggest that small investors examine a REIT's ownership structure before writing a check.

NOTES

1. One exception is the study by Chan, Leung, and Wang (1998). Since the sample we used in this book significantly overlaps theirs, we will not discuss their study in detail.

2. Below, Kiely and McIntosh (1995) examine the impact of trading activity on REIT stock performance. They conclude that trading activity is not as important a determinant of REIT performance as the level of institutional ownership.

3. Downs and Guner (2000) also classify REITs as asset-specific, information-deficient firms.

REFERENCES

Badrinath, S. G., Jayant Kale, and Thomas Noe. 1995. Of shepherds, sheep, and the cross-autocorrelation in equity returns. *Review of Financial Studies* 2:401–30.

Barber, Brad, and Terrance Odean. 2000. Trading is hazardous to your wealth: The common stock investment performance of individual investors. *Journal of Finance* 55:773–806.

Below, Scott D., Joseph K. Kiely, and Willard McIntosh. 1995. An examination of informed traders and the market microstructure of real estate investment trusts. *Journal of Real Estate Research* 10:335–61.

Chan, Louis K. C., and Josef Lakonishok. 1993. Institutional trades and intraday stock price behavior. *Journal of Financial Economics* 33:173–99.

Chan, Louis K. C., and Josef Lakonishok. 1995. The behavior of stock prices around institutional trades. *Journal of Finance* 50:1147–74.

Chan, Louis K. C., and Josef Lakonishok. 1997. Institutional equity trading costs: NYSE versus Nasdaq. *Journal of Finance* 52:713–35.

Chan, Su Han, W. K. Leung, and Ko Wang. 1998. Institutional investment in REITs: Evidence and implications. *Journal of Real Estate Research* 16 (3): 357–74.

Chan, Su Han, W. K. Leung, and Ko Wang. 2001. Monday returns and institutional investors of REITs. University of Hong Kong. Working paper.

Cooper, Michael, David Downs, and Gary Patterson. 1999. Real estate securities and a filter-based, short-term trading strategy. *Journal of Real Estate Research* 18:313–33.

Crain, John, Mike Cudd, and Christopher Brown. 2000. The impact of the Revenue Reconciliation Act of 1993 and institutional ownership on the pricing structure of equity REITs. *Journal of Real Estate Research* 19:275–85.

Downs, David. 1998. The value in targeting institutional investors: Evidence from the five-or-fewer rule change. *Real Estate Economics* 26:613–49.

Downs, David, and Z. Nuray Guner. 2000. Investment analysis, price formation and neglected firms: Does real estate make a difference? *Real Estate Economics* 28:549–79.

Friday, Swint, and Stacy Sirmans. 1998. Board of director monitoring and firm value in REITs. *Journal of Real Estate Research* 16:411–27.

Friday, Swint, Stacy Sirmans, and Mitchell Conover. 1999. Ownership structure and the value of the firms: The case of REITs. *Journal of Real Estate Research* 17:71–90.

Gillan, Stuart, and Laura Starks. 2000. Corporate government proposals and shareholder activism: The role of institutional investors. *Journal of Financial Economics* 57:275–305.

Grinblatt, Mark, Sheridan Titman, and Russ Wermers. 1995. Momentum investment strategies, portfolio performance and herding: A study of mutual fund behavior. *American Economic Review* 85:1088–1105.

Keim, Donald, and Ananth Madhavan. 1995. Anatomy of the trading process: Empirical evidence on the behavior of institutional traders. *Journal of Financial Economics* 32:371–98.

Khoo, Terence, David Hartzell, and Martin Hoesli. 1992. An investigation of the change in real estate investment trust betas. *AREUEA Journal* 21:107–30.

Lakonishok, Josef, Andrei Shleifer, and Robert Vishny. 1992. The impact of institutional trading on stock prices. *Journal of Financial Economics* 32:23–43.

Ling, David, and M. Ryngaert. 1997. Valuation uncertainty, institutional involvement, and the underpricing of IPOs: The case of REITs. *Journal of Financial Economics* 43:433–56.

Malpezzi, Stephen, and James Shilling. 2000. Institutional investors tilt their real estate holdings toward quality, too. *Journal of Real Estate Finance and Economics* 21:113–40.

Martin, Ellen James. 1993. REITs' new pull on pensions. *Institutional Investor* 27 (November): 149.

McIntosh, Willard, Ronald Rogers, C. F. Sirmans, and Youguo Liang. 1994. Stock price and management changes: The case of REITs. *AREUEA Journal* 22:515–26.

McMahan, John. 1994. The long view: A perspective on the REIT market. *Real Estate Issues* 19:1–4.

Nofsinger, John, and Richard Sias. 1999. Herding and feedback trading by institutional and individual investors. *Journal of Finance* 54: 2263–95.

Rudnitsky, H. 1992. A tale of two funds. *Forbes* (January 6), p. 80.

Sias, Richard, and Laura Starks. 1995. The day-of-the-week anomaly: The role of institutional investors. *Financial Analysts Journal* 51:58–67.

Sias, Richard, and Laura Starks. 1997. Return autocorrelation and institutional investors. *Journal of Financial Economics* 46:103–31.

Simonoff, Evan, and Edward Baig. 1997. The right way to invest in REITs. *Business Week* (April 14), p. 110.

Vincour, Barry. 1994. With REIT market in slump, pension funds show interest in buying. *Barron's* (December 5), p. 46.

Wang, Ko, Su Han Chan, and George Gau. 1992. Initial public offerings of equity securities: Anomalous evidence using REITs. *Journal of Financial Economics* 31:381–410.

Wang, Ko, and John Erickson. 1997. The stock performance of securitized real estate and master limited partnerships. *Real Estate Economics* 25:295–319.

Wang, Ko, John Erickson, George Gau, and Su Han Chan. 1995. Market microstructure and real estate returns. *Real Estate Economics* 23: 85–100.

Wang, Ko, Yuming Li, and John Erickson. 1997. A new look at the Monday effect. *Journal of Finance* 52:2171–86.

Wang, P. 1992. Ways to fight high fund fees. *Money* 21 (July): 122–28.

Woolly, Suzanne. 1998. REIT for the bold. *Business Week* (June 22), pp. 209–10.

7

Diversification versus Focus

Do You Really Want All Your Eggs in One Basket?

In a room full of REIT managers, all that is needed to start a heated debate is for someone to say, "Should we concentrate or diversify our investments?" Indeed, all practitioners and academics alike have strong views on this issue and those on each side seem to have good theoretical justifications for the positions they hold. The best way to end the argument would seem to be the use of empirical evidence; yet, although there are some empirical studies on the issue, the results are mixed.

Intuitively, we all understand the benefits of using a diversification strategy: holding a diversified portfolio of properties reduces risk. On the other hand, even if REITs do not diversify, individual investors can still form diversified portfolios simply by purchasing shares in a number of REITs that specialize in different property types and/or geographical sectors. It would be easy to argue that, because REIT investors can diversify their portfolios on their own, they should not care whether a particular REIT is diversified or not. Yet if this is the case, why should REIT managers still care whether their REITs hold diversified portfolios or concentrate their investments?

Indeed, the question of adopting a diversified or focused investment strategy is more complicated than it seems at first glance. The simple answer that diversification stabilizes the income stream of a REIT or reduces its risk might not justify the increased costs due to the use of the diversification strategy. Stabilization of earnings and risk reduction are certainly beneficial to employees, suppliers, and customers, but their value is less certain from the standpoint of investors. Since investors can form portfolios to reduce risk at the personal level, a strategy must be able to increase cash flows to the REIT should it adopt a diversification strategy at the corporate level. In other words, for a REIT to adopt a diversification strategy, there must be other benefits in addition to risk reduction before the strategy can be of value to its investors.

Those of us in the finance field have all been taught that diversification provides benefits. However, recent empirical evidence in the finance literature shows that stocks of firms with focused business segments generally perform better than those of firms with diversified segments. Do the findings in the finance literature also apply to REITs? This chapter first summarizes the arguments we frequently hear from REIT managers and analysts, both for and against diversification and focused investment strategies. We then examine the rationales behind these arguments and discuss the conditions under which one strategy might be better than the other. Finally, we present our recommendation based on the theorectical arguments and the limited empirical evidence available in the field.

What the Industry People Say

Conventional wisdom in the REIT market has always been that REITs' portfolios should be diversified in both geographical location and property type in order to maintain steady income streams under different market conditions. This argument seems to have been quite popular until the early 1990s, at which time writers in both academia and the popular press began to cast doubt on whether the traditional wisdom still held under the current REIT market environment.

Indeed, a survey of the opinions of REIT experts in the industry indicates that there is little consensus on this issue. While we will not cite too many of the reports we read in the popular press, we can select a few representative ones to illustrate the differing views on the issue. For example, in support of the traditional wisdom (i.e., the diversification strategy), Avidon (1995), citing the opinions of many well-known REIT managers, points out that a key to success is to have a portfolio spread throughout numerous markets and made up of a diverse tenant base. On the other hand, Kistner (1996) specifically advises investors to buy REITs that concentrate in a special property type, although he suggests that the REITs might be diversified in terms of geographic location.

In an article on the right way to invest in REITs, Simonoff and Baig (1997) specifically recommend that investors make sure that they choose individual REITs that are diversified by property type and by geographic location. In the meantime, McMahan (1994) makes an interesting observation. He notes that virtually all new REIT initial public offerings after 1993 are more or less operating companies (in the UPREIT form) that are self-administrated and specialized by property type. He also observes that most REIT managers have spent their careers specializing in particular property types and have worked with other managers in teams for many years.

As the reader can see, these four articles illustrate four different views, ranging from favoring a complete diversification strategy (on both property type and geographical area) to arguing for an extremely focused strategy (on both property type and geographical area). Indeed, these four examples demonstrate the lack of consensus on this issue in the industry. To give the reader a broader perspective on the debate, we summarize the pros and cons of diversified and focused strategies using the results of a survey reported by Johnson (1999) and conducted by Intertec Marketing Research Department, using a sample of 85 REITs.

The first interesting point we can learn from the survey is that there is a consensus that the geographical scope of the REIT, the location of properties, and the type of property owned do affect REIT value, which has implications for the REIT's choice of investment strategy. When the REIT managers surveyed were asked about the advantages and disadvantages of having a focused strategy, most respondents mentioned the following advantages:

- A focused strategy provides better understanding of specialized markets.
- It reduces the number of markets a REIT needs to worry about.
- It allows both investors and managers to know the REIT better.
- It allows both investors and managers freedom from having to be an expert in all markets.
- It avoids increased management costs due to the need to take care of many property markets.

The disadvantages of a focused strategy often mentioned by the respondents are the following:

- Not having enough risk reduction.
- Not allowing better property diversity.
- Not offering customers multiple locations to satisfy their needs.
- Being more susceptible to regional market trends and economic swings.
- Having the possibility of large fluctuations in income streams.

The arguments from both sides make some intuitive sense. It might be time for us to examine what really has happened in the industry and to see whether the arguments make sense not only intuitively, but from the perspective of financial theory.

The Function of REIT Managers

Before we formally address this issue, we want to make it clear that it may be difficult to know whether a REIT is diversified or focused. Geltner and Kluger (1998) point out that REITs seldom have only one property type in their investment portfolios. Therefore, to say that a REIT is diversified based on the number of property types in its portfolio can be misleading. Indeed, if we used the number of property types as the classification means, most REITs could be classified as diversified.

Brent and Linneman (2001) use the percentages of investment in property types as their classification criterion. If a REIT has more than 75% of its assets concentrated in one property type, it can be classified as a REIT with a focused strategy. Brent and Linneman report that, in their sample, 72% of internally advised REITs and 84% of externally advised REITs are focused on a single property type. However, this classification system does have its problems. If a REIT has 75% of its assets in apartments and 5% in each of another five property types, the REIT will still incur the costs of overseeing the six different property types. Although the REIT can be classified as focused under this criterion, it is difficult to say that it has a focused investment strategy.

In recent years, the industry has begun to pay considerable attention to the investment strategies of REITs. This is evident from an examination of the information reported in various publications by the National Association of Real Estate Investment Trusts (NAREIT). Starting in early 1990, REIT publications began to list the investment portfolios of REITs and to classify REITs into different property types. The *Year 2000 NAREIT Statistical Digest* classifies REITs into eight different property categories: industrial/office, retail, residential, diversified, lodging/resorts, self-storage, health care, and specialty (timber properties, golf properties, entertainment properties, etc.) The inclusion of this information in NAREIT publications shows that REITs' investment strategies (focused or diversified) have become an important issue for their managers.

In addition to the market's dawning awareness of the issue in general, beginning in the early 1990s, equity REITs in particular began to focus their investment strategies on certain sectors of the real estate market. Table 7.1 summarizes the number of REITs under each property type as listed in various NAREIT publications from 1994 to 2000. In 1994, 48 REITs could be classified as the diversified type. The number of diversified REITs declined each year and was reduced to 20 by the year 2000. We also see a significant reduction in the number of REITs specializing in the self-storage property sector. (This was caused by the consolidation activities of the Public Storage Properties funds in the late 1990s.) That more REITs are concentrating their investments in the mainstream property sectors indicates an overall trend in the use of more focused investment strategies.

However, while it is true that the REIT industry appreciates the need to know the optimal investment strategy and that REITs are tending to pursue strategies that are more focused, it is not clear whether the pros and cons of each strategy have been thoroughly discussed yet. The remaining sections of this chapter will examine these pros and cons from a theoretical point of view, using the limited empirical evidence available in the field.

Table 7.1 REIT Investment Type During the 1994–2000 Period

	Number of REITs						
Property Type[a]	1994	1995	1996	1997	1998	1999	2000
Industrial/office							
Office	13	14	13	20	22	20	21
Industrial	12	12	9	13	13	14	10
Mixed	4	6	5	5	4	7	7
Retail							
Shopping centers	28	29	26	28	27	28	31
Regional malls	11	11	10	11	11	11	12
Freestanding						7	7
Outlet centers	7	6	6	6	6	3	
Other		1	1	2	2		
Residential							
Apartments	34	36	37	33	32	27	22
Manufactured homes	5	5	5	4	4	6	6
Diversified	48	37	29	27	26	24	20
Lodging and resorts	10	12	14	14	15	15	15
Self storage	21	20	13	7	7	5	4
Health care	12	12	12	12	12	13	13
Specialty							
Triple net lease	8	7	7	9	10	7	8
Other	3	3	3	2			
Mortgage backed	10	8	9	18	18	23	24
Total	226	219	199	211	209	210	200

Source: Various issues of publications by NAREIT (see appendix for details).

[a] Segment and subsegment.

To Diversify or Not to Diversify: The Pros and Cons

As we discussed at the beginning of this chapter, diversified-strategy advocates rely on the argument that REIT investors need to hold a diversified group of properties in order to achieve a certain level of risk reduction—even though a REIT does not need to be diversified because investors themselves can diversify their portfolios on their own. That is, even if every REIT followed a focused strategy, investors could still obtain the diversification benefit by simply investing in, say, ten REITs specializing in different property sectors.

Given this, if risk reduction is the only benefit REIT investors are looking for, there seems to be little need for a REIT to diversify its portfolio for the benefit of its investors. Yet, if so many REITs are using a diversification strategy, the traditional wisdom cannot be *completely* wrong. Is there any circumstance under which a diversified strategy might be better for the investors than a focused strategy would be? This question can be answered only by examining the pros and cons of each strategy.

Against the Diversification Strategy

The two cases illustrated in figure 7.1 provide strong evidence against the use of a diversification strategy. In Case A, we assume that there are four investor-groups (A, B, C, and D). There are also four identical REITs (1, 2, 3, and 4). All the REITs use a diversification strategy. Each REIT has a $400 million portfolio with one-fourth of its investment in apartment, office, retail, and industrial properties. In this scenario, each investor group invests in only one REIT. Since every REIT is diversified, each investor holds a diversified portfolio.

Now, let us look at the scenario presented in Case B. We also assume that there are four investor groups, A, B, C, and D. This time, however,

Case A: With Four Diversified REITs

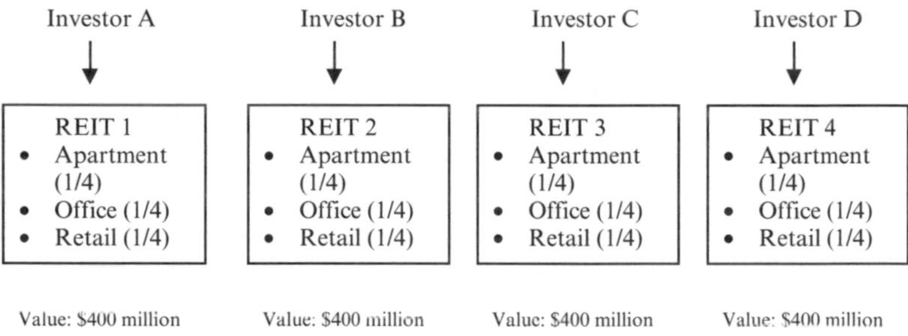

Case B: With Four Focused REITs

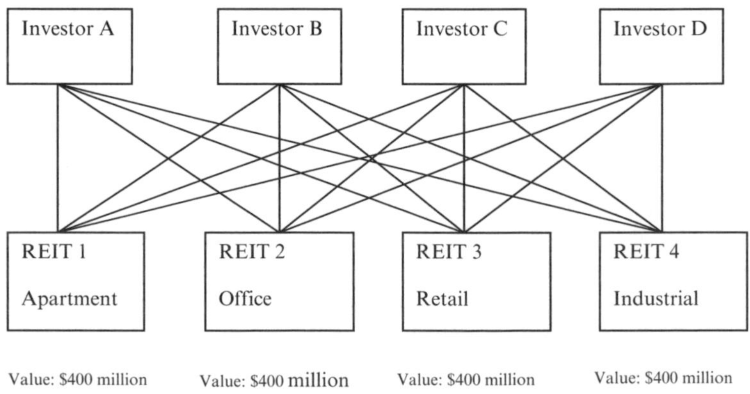

Figure 7.1 Illustration of Benefits from Diversification and Focus

there are four focused REITs (1, 2, 3, and 4) and each specializes in one property type (apartment, office, retail, or industrial). The reader can imagine a reshuffle among REIT assets. In other words, one can view REIT 1 as now having all the apartment properties previously owned by all the other REITs. REIT 2 now has the office properties previously owned by all the other REITs, and so on.

In Case A, when diversified REITs are available, an investor can simply invest in any of the diversified REITs to gain the risk-reduction benefit. In Case B, investors can achieve an identical risk-reduction benefit even though there are only four specialized REITs. To do this, each investor group will invest one-fourth of its wealth in each of the four focused REITs. If an investor adopts this strategy, then the payoff in Case B will be identical to the payoff in Case A under any circumstance. These two cases illustrate that it is unnecessary for a REIT to adopt a diversified strategy to achieve risk reduction for its investors. If the diversification strategy is at the same time costly, then these two cases provide evidence against the adoption of a diversification strategy.

Gyourko and Nelling (1996) investigate whether diversification across property types and geographical locations is important to REIT value. They find no evidence in support of the idea that such diversification actually results in meaningful diversification benefits. Since their evidence indicates that there may be no significant risk-reduction benefit, there is no need for REITs to diversify. Chen and Peiser (1999) also show that REITs that diversify by property type have a lower level of return after adjusting for total risk. Both these studies seems to indicate that diversification by property type does not help to improve a REIT's value.

For the Diversification Strategy

We have demonstrated that, since REIT investors can obtain identical payoffs under either scenario, it does not matter whether REITs are focused or diversified. The choice of investment strategy, therefore, seems to be irrelevant if the payoff is the only consideration—yet if this is so, why are there still heated debates on the issue? Clearly, there must be at least two sides to the story.

It should be noted that when a REIT uses a diversification strategy, the income streams at the corporate level will be more stable than if it adopts a focused strategy. In other words, depending on the performance of the underlying property sector, some REITs will perform very well while others will perform very poorly. From an investor's point of view, as long as the combined income stream from the four REITs illustrated in Case B is stable, it does not matter whether the individual income streams are stable. However, this might not be the case for the managers of the four REITs, who might not like to see too much fluctuation in the income streams of the individual REITs they manage. We say this for two reasons.

First, from a psychological and performance-evaluation point of view, a highly fluctuating income stream might give investors a bad feeling about the REIT. When a REIT adopts a focused strategy, it is more likely that it will have a particularly good or a particularly bad year when compared to the REIT industry average. When investors enjoy particularly good performance on their investments, they most likely will attribute that to their superior judgment of REIT stocks. When they experience very bad performance, however, they most likely will blame the REIT manager. In addition, if the returns of a REIT (such as the hotel REIT) vary too much over time, investors get the bad impression that the REIT's returns are difficult to predict. Given this, a REIT manager might be motivated to adopt a diversified strategy. This is especially true when a REIT's performance is benchmarked against the industry average, and when the manager is evaluated based on the performance of the REIT.

Second, the unstable income streams associated with the focused strategy might impose financial costs on the REIT. This is especially true when the REIT employs high leverage. For a REIT with a highly fluctuating income stream, lenders will certainly demand a higher interest rate to compensate for the additional risk. In the worst case, the fluctuations in the income stream could result in bankruptcy and its resultant costs. When the level of debt used by a REIT is high *and* the variability in the income stream is high, the probability of bankruptcy will likewise be high. If a REIT invested in assets that cannot be sold in a short period at a reasonable price (such as assets that are difficult to value or when the market for this type of asset is thin), then the REIT might want to use a diversification strategy to reduce the probability of bankruptcy and its very high associated costs.

The Verdict

From the previous discussions, it is clear that if a REIT manager is to adopt a diversified investment strategy, he or she cannot simply rely on the risk-reduction argument but must illustrate how the strategy will affect the bottom line (profits) and the value of the REIT.

Intuitively, an increase in focus should improve overall REIT returns because it allows management to concentrate its expertise and energy on one area of the real estate market instead of on multiple areas. This concentration of activities can at least allow the REIT to reduce its operating costs (if not increase its revenues). Indeed, according to the empirical evidence reported by Capozza and Lee (1995), diversified REITs have above-average expense ratios when compared with focused REITs. If we believe that focused REITs, on average, have lower operating costs than diversified REITs, then Case A and Case B in figure 7.1 provide a strong justification for the use of a focused investment strategy.

The other potential advantage of using a focused strategy is the information advantage, which has been argued to be significant for a REIT that focuses on a specific geographic market. A narrow market focus can allow an REIT to achieve the economies of scale resulting from information efficiencies, and therefore to can make better investment decisions. However, when Ambrose et al. (2000) conducted a detailed study to examine whether the information advantage exists for certain types of REITs, they found no empirical support for this type of claim, at least for the multifamily residential property market. Of course, we cannot draw general conclusions from this one study. We know only that for the special group of properties used in the study during the sampling period, the information advantage cannot be detected.

On the other hand, we know that under certain circumstances the diversification strategy can provide real benefits to REIT shareholders. For example, when a REIT adopts a focused investment strategy, the variability in its income stream will be larger than under the diversified strategy. This can be a problem if the REIT also uses a high level of debt or invests in assets that are difficult to value or sell at a reasonable price in a short period. The increase in bankruptcy costs arising from a focused strategy might force certain REITs to adopt a diversified strategy instead.

In summary, both the diversified and focused strategies make sense under certain conditions. However, since the condition for the use of a diversified strategy is the presence of a high debt level, it is more likely that a REIT will use a focused strategy because the average debt ratio is not very high in the REIT market. (See chapter 8 for detailed information on REIT debt ratios.)

Three Related Questions on the Diversification Issue

It is a common knowledge that returns differ significantly among different property markets. Given this, investors might also expect that the performance of equity-REIT stocks would differ by property type if there were a relationship between REIT stock returns and the return on assets. Does the REIT stock return reflect the value of its underlying properties? If a REIT specializes in office buildings, will its stock returns reflect the movements in the office-property market?

If there is a disconnect between the returns of the REIT and its underlying property type, then there is no need to worry about its investment strategy. If, however, the returns of a REIT are correlated with the assets it owns, then one might also wonder which property sector was the winner during past decades. Indeed, if the returns of all REITs, regardless of their property types, move concurrently with each other, then there is no need to discuss a diversified or focused strategy. In other words, if a REIT specializing in the office sector has a similar risk- and-return tradeoff relationship as a REIT specializing in the retail sector, then it does not matter whether the REIT adopts a diversified or a focused investment strategy.

Is REIT Type Correlated with the Property Market?

Mueller and Laposa (1996) address this important question. In an analysis of REIT performance by property type over three different time periods from 1976 to 1995, they find that REIT returns are related to the performance of the property sectors in which they operate. In other words, they observe that the stocks of REITs with investments in a similar property type have similar performance, although REITs with similar investments in the same geographical areas might have different performance results.

In a similar analysis of the performance of different REIT sectors during the period 1993–97, Chen and Peiser (1999) show that sector performance is related to the performance of the underlying property markets. However, it should also be noted that Myer and Webb (1994) do not find a positive relationship between retail real estate and REITs specializing in retail properties. However, since Myer and Webb's study covers only one property type, we will place more weight on the evidence from the other two studies and tentatively conclude that there is a relationship between a focused REIT and the property sector it focuses on.

Does Property Type Matter in Determining REIT Returns?

The most important finding reported by Mueller and Laposa (1996) is that REIT returns are different among property-type groups. Although the returns of REITs with different property types move very closely during the 1972–85 period, their returns diverge across property types after 1990. This conclusion makes sense intuitively. We know that, prior to 1990, there were not many focused REITs. REITs began to concentrate their investments in property sectors only after 1990.

However, using data during the 1989–98 period, Young (2000) finds that the equity REIT market is integrated and that property type is not an important factor in REIT stock movements. Thus, the evidence available in the field is mixed regarding whether the property type (or geographical concentration) of a REIT's investments is important to the value of its stock. Since Young's study is based on statistical inference, which makes it difficult to detect the difference in returns, we put more emphasis on the evidence from Mueller and Laposa (1996) to draw our conclusions on this issue.

Who are the Winners, and Should We Care?

Based on the study by Mueller and Laposa (1996), it is clear that retail and health care REITs performed better than other property types during the 1986–95 period. It is also clear that the volatility of hotel REITs is significantly higher than for all other REIT types. According to the evidence from this study, investors might want to buy health care REITs and avoid hotel

REITs. However, Chen and Peiser (1999) show that, during the 1993–97 period, REITs specializing in the office, industrial, and hotel sectors had the highest average monthly returns. Given this evidence, investors desiring higher returns might want to buy REITs specializing in office, industrial, and hotel markets. It is also clear that the winners reported by the two studies are not consistent.

We want to emphasize that you should not pay too much attention to who the past winners or losers are. In other words, we do not think it is a good idea for investors to select a property type based on its past performance. Investors who invest in Internet stocks will definitely tell you that to select a stock based on past performance could be unwise. There is no guarantee that a company can replicate past performance. Although we report the past winners and losers here, readers should not use this information as the sole basis to select property types for their investments.

Furthermore, Gyourko and Nelling (1996) investigate whether the selection of property type is reflected in a market-based measure of systematic risk (beta). They find that the higher return earned by some focused REITs compensates for a higher beta. That is, even if the return on a certain property type is high, this could be due to the high beta associated with the property type. This evidence also indicates that it might not be fruitful for investors to invest in REIT stocks based solely on the property type and geographical location of the properties owned by the REIT.

The New Evidence and a New Argument

From the discussion so far, it is clear that in order for a diversification strategy to work for a REIT it either must have a direct impact on the REIT's cash flows or it must allow investors to understand the REIT better (or more easily). At this moment, there are only two studies in the literature addressing this issue directly. Capozza and Seguin (1998, 1999) conducted them both.

In their 1998 study, Capozza and Seguin analyze the relationship between the value of a REIT and the factors related to the managerial style (such as a focused or diversified investment strategy) of the REIT. They report very interesting findings. First, they find that REITs with greater diversification are associated with higher operating expenses. However, the operating expense is higher only if the REIT has more property types in its portfolio, but not if the REIT invests in wider geographical regions. They also find that the increase in operating expenses due to the diversification strategy can be offset (at least partially) by higher revenues. In other words, the use of a focused or diversified strategy, according to the authors, should not have any effect on the REIT's bottom line. This would indicate that it actually does not matter whether a REIT adopts a diversification strategy or a focused strategy because investors will simply view those strategies as zero NPV (net present value) projects—that is, projects that result in no net gains to the investors. This is a new concept to the field.

A year later, Capozza and Seguin (1999) extended their analysis. This time, they found that REITs that increase their focus on a particular property sector and geographic location can increase the value of their stocks (relative to REITs that are diversified along the same lines). Interestingly, however, the increase in stock value from a focused strategy does not come about because diversification leads to poor management decisions or reduces cash flows. Rather, the increase in the value of the REIT stock comes from the increased liquidity provided by the increase in focus. This is true because, if a REIT holds a diversified portfolio, it will be more difficult for lenders and stockholders to value the REIT's holdings and, therefore, the liquidity of the REIT's stock is reduced.

Because lenders and shareholders will incur a higher cost to obtain information if a REIT uses a diversification strategy, they will rationally discount the value of the cash flows generated from the REIT. On the other hand, an increase in a REIT's investment focus makes it easier for investors to value those REITs. It is also easier for investors to project the future performance of a REIT if it is highly specialized by property type and geographic location. In other words, focus leads to greater liquidity, which results in a lower cost of raising funds and higher stock values. Capozza and Seguin's (1999) finding suggests that a REIT should adopt a focused strategy simply because it is more transparent and more attractive to investors.

Normally, we would rely on high-quality studies like the two by Capozza and Seguin when we make our recommendations. However, although these two studies were carefully done, they also have their limitations. Both studies use data between 1985 and 1992, so we cannot be sure that the results can be generalized to the new group of REITs that came out after 1993. We might need further empirical evidence that examines REITs from more recent years to reaffirm the findings.

What Have We Learned?

We can summarize the main points of this chapter as follows:

- Traditional wisdom in the REIT industry is that REITs should diversify their investments to reduce risk.
- However, finance theory tells us that REITs do not need to diversify because investors can diversify by themselves.
- If diversification involves costs, then it might pay to adopt a focused investment strategy. This line of thought seems to have gained momentum in the REIT market.

- However, if a REIT adopts a focused strategy it is subject to a higher probability of bankruptcy. Given this, REITs that have a high leverage ratio or assets that are difficult to value might want to use the diversification strategy.
- Higher operating expenses are associated with REITs that adopt a diversification strategy. However, it is likely that the increase in revenues due to the use of the diversification strategy can at least partially offset the cost. In the end, the bottom line (profits) could be the same regardless of whether a REIT uses a focused or a diversification strategy.
- There is a correlation between the performance of a property sector and the returns of the REIT specializing in that property sector.
- There is evidence that because investors and lenders must incur costs to gather information to evaluate a REIT, they might prefer REITs that use a focused investment strategy.

Conclusions

Obviously, considerable research must be done before we can have a more concrete understanding about the trade-off between focused and diversified investment strategies. We do know that a REIT should not use a diversification strategy just because of the perceived risk-reduction benefit, and that it should adopt this strategy if its debt level is high (indicating a high probability of bankruptcy) and/or the assets it owns are difficult to value and sell at a fair price (indicating a high liquidating cost when bankrupt). However, since we know that most REITs use quite low debt levels and since information on REITs has become more accessible recently, we predict that we will see more focused REITs in the future.

Nevertheless, even if a REIT would like to adopt a focused strategy, the limited market opportunities might not allow it to do so. This is especially true if the REIT is also adopting a growth strategy and is increasing its size over time. Capozza and Lee (1995) report that small REITs are those that are more concentrated geographically. This observation makes sense because small REITs do not need to find many investment opportunities. However, since there might be a need for large REITs to expand their market areas in order to obtain more investment opportunities, we might also see some REITs adopting a diversified investment strategy regardless of whether they prefer it.

It is advisable that if a REIT has to reach out to other property markets to find enough investment opportunities to support its growth, it should keep a significant portion of its holdings in its main line of business (a focused property type or geographical area). In other words, given all the available theoretical arguments and empirical evidence, we can safely say that it is not a good idea for a REIT to distribute its holdings evenly among several property types or geographical areas. We strongly recommend, therefore, that a REIT use some type of focused investment strategy in managing its portfolio.

REFERENCES

Ambrose, Brent, Steven Ehrlich, William Hughes, and Susan Wachter. 2000. REIT economies of scale: Fact or fiction? *Journal of Real Estate Finance and Economics* 20:2111–224.

Ambrose, Brent, and Peter Linneman. 2001. REIT organizational structure and operating characteristics. *Journal of Real Estate Research* 21: 141–62.

Avidon, Eric. 1995. REITs agree: Diversity = stability. *National Mortgage News* 20 (12): 18–19.

Capozza, Dennis R., and Sohan Lee. 1995. Property type, size and REIT value. *Journal of Real Estate Research* 10:363–79.

Capozza, Dennis R., and Paul J. Seguin. 1998. Managerial style and firm value. *Real Estate Economics* 26:131–50.

Capozza, Dennis R., and Paul J. Seguin. 1999. Focus, transparency, and value: The REIT evidence. *Real Estate Economics* 27:587–619.

Chen, Jun, and Richard Peiser. 1999. The risk and return characteristics of REITs, 1993–1997. *Real Estate Finance* 16 (1): 61–68.

Geltner, David, and B. Kluger. 1998. REIT-based pure-play portfolios: The case of property types. *Real Estate Economics* 26:581–612.

Gyourko, Joseph, and Edward Nelling. 1996. Systematic risk and diversification in the equity market. *Real Estate Economics* 24:493–515.

Johnson, Ben. 1999. Calling all REITs: What's the word on the street? *National Real Estate Investor* 41:87–96.

Kistner, William. 1996. Diversifying portfolios with equity real estate investment trusts. *Healthcare Financial Management* 50 (12): 78–79.

McMahan, John. 1994. The long view: A perspective on the REIT market. *Real Estate Issues* 19:1–4.

Mueller, Glen R., and Seven P. Laposa. 1996. REIT returns: A property-type perspective. *Real Estate Finance* 13:45+.

Myer, Neil, and James Webb. 1994. Retail stocks, retail REITs, and retail real Estate. *Journal of Real Estate Research* 9:65–84.

Simonoff, Evan, and Edward Baig. 1997. The right way to invest in REITs. *Business Week* (April 14), p. 110.

Young, Michael. 2000. REIT property-type sector integration. *Journal of Real Estate Research* 19:3–21.

8

Dividends and Debt Policies of REITs

They Pay Out More Than Is Required but Borrow Less Than Is Allowed

Traditional wisdom in the REIT market tells us that the most important impediment to a REIT's growth is the limitation on its ability to retain earnings. Currently, a REIT must pay out 90% of its taxable earnings as dividends. (This payout ratio was reduced from 95% as a result of the passage of the REIT Modernization Act of 1999.) Given this high payout ratio, it is reasonable to assume that, while retained earnings provide some funding for growth, the amount is relatively insignificant. Because internal funding is limited, REITs must look for external funds in order to grow.

Two sources of external funding can be used to support REIT growth: the issuance of debt securities and the issuance of new equity. The use of debt will increase the financial leverage of a REIT, which can improve its profitability when real estate markets are booming. However, higher levels of financial leverage are undesirable in declining markets because leverage magnifies losses as well as gains.

The advantage of internal sources of funding is that they are more stable and less costly than external sources. Since REITs are required to pay out a significant portion of their earnings as dividends, they should pay only the amount that can satisfy the regulatory constraint if they would like to conserve cash for future growth. This is especially true given the costliness of issuing both debt and equity securities.[1] If this is the case, then the 90% payout ratio and the earnings level should determine the REIT's dividend policy—in reality, however, this does not happen. REITs pay out significantly more dividends than required by law. We will explain why in this chapter.

Anyone who has purchased a house knows that one of the most important advantages of doing so is the tax shelter resulting from the borrowing of the mortgage. Standard finance and real estate textbooks add that the main advantage of borrowing in general is the tax shelter provided by the interest payments. However, REITs do not need to pay taxes at the corporate level, so we would not expect them to borrow as much as other tax-paying operations in the market. Yet our expectation is wrong—REITs borrow even more than tax-paying firms, although they borrow less than investors in the property market where the loan-to-value ratio is typically around 80%.

This chapter will first review the constraint on REIT dividend policies and show the actual dividend payout ratios of REITs during the past 20 years. We will provide five different theories on why this might be the case and explain the determinants of REIT dividend payments. We will then talk about the pros and cons of the use of debt and report the debt ratios carried by REITs during the past 20 years. We will examine the literature to find out the determinants for REITs to use debt and to provide evidence on whether investors prefer that REITs increase their debt ratios by issuing more debt securities.

Constraints on REITs' Dividend Policies

When a REIT pays dividends, it is essentially distributing its capital to its investors. Intuition tells us that if a REIT is also adopting an expansion policy, it will have incentives to minimize its dividends in order to conserve capital for future investments. Given the 90% required payout ratio, one would expect that a REIT's dividend payment should be determined by its earnings—that is, the dividend payment should be 90% of earnings so the REIT can conserve the remaining 10% for future use.

However, some literature in the finance field tells firm managers that it is important for them to maintain a stable (and increasing) dividend-payment stream. Otherwise, the stock market will penalize them by lowering the value of their firms' stocks. If a REIT is required to pay out 90% of its earnings, it will have trouble maintaining a stable dividend-payment stream because earnings fluctuate over time. If a REIT has to pay out nearly all its earnings it cannot reserve cash when times are good (during the high-earnings period) and use its cash reserves to make up the payments when times are bad (during the low-earnings period). In other words, the dividend level of a REIT should fluctuate with its earnings level if the 90% payout ratio is a real constraint. If investors are looking for stable dividend payments, then REITs may not be able to fulfil this need.

The finance literature also tells us that the manager of a firm can use dividend payments to signal to the stock market his or her belief about the future earnings of the firm. Since investors do not like fluctuating dividend payments, a manager will be unwilling to increase dividend payments if he or she does not believe the firm's future income will be able to sustain the increase in future dividends. By increasing the dividend payment the manager is, in fact, telling the stock market his or her belief that the future income stream of the firm will increase. Similarly, by lowering a firm's dividends, the manager conveys a negative signal about his or her belief of the firm's future earnings. Thus, if a REIT's dividend policy is truly set at the 90% level of its earnings, it is unclear what kind of signal it will send.

No One Seems to Care about the Constraint

Wang, Erickson, and Gau (1993) were the first to point out that REIT dividend policies cannot be constrained by the 95% taxable-income distribution requirement. They found that, during their sample period, REITs on average pay 165% of their taxable income. Bradley, Capozza, and Seguin (1998) also report that the dividend payouts in their sample are about twice the level of net income, on average.

The reason REITs can pay out a greater percentage of dividends than required by law is that their annual cash flows are normally higher than their taxable incomes. We know that the depreciation of a building is not a cash-flow item. Since REITs (especially equity REITs) primarily own properties in their portfolios, they are able to reduce their taxable income significantly because of the depreciation write-off. REITs under these circumstances should have the opportunity to set dividend policies that are not determined solely by tax regulations.

Table 8.1 and figure 8.1 provide direct evidence to support the observation made by Wang, Erickson, and Gau (1993). During the 1980–2000 period, the average ratio of cash dividends to net income was about 117%. If we exclude the 1980–84 period (during which many REITs lost their tax-qualified status) the ratio will be much higher. The conclusion is similar if we use pretax income as the base. The information provided in table 8.1 clearly demonstrates that REITs pay out more dividends than required by law.

Tables 8.2 and 8.3 report the dividend-payout ratio for different types of REITs (equity, mortgage, and hybrid) and for finite-life and infinite-life REITs. In general, we find that equity REITs pay out more dividends than mortgage REITs do, regardless of whether we use net income or pretax income as the base. Finite-life REITs also pay out more income as dividends than infinite-life REITs. This makes sense intuitively because finite-life REITs have no growth potential and therefore do not need to conserve cash for new investments.

The information provided in the literature as well as in our tables indicates that, because of non-cash expense items, a REIT can still have the flex-

Table 8.1 REIT Dividend-Payout Ratios

	Cash Dividend to Net Income		Cash Dividend to Pretax Income	
	Average (%)	Number of Obs.	Average (%)	Number of Obs.
1980	88	45	85	45
1981	96	58	90	57
1982	89	51	87	51
1983	87	49	85	49
1984	88	47	88	48
1985	102	53	99	54
1986	109	76	108	76
1987	123	81	125	82
1988	117	74	117	76
1989	124	68	122	70
1990	135	67	134	67
1991	137	71	133	71
1992	127	65	123	65
1993	126	100	120	101
1994	134	153	121	157
1995	138	158	124	164
1996	125	141	108	145
1997	125	153	107	162
1998	130	155	106	161
1999	130	160	113	163
2000	120	143	108	147
1980–1989	102		101	
1990–2000	130		118	
1980–2000	117		110	

Source: Authors' own calculations using the REIT sample described in the appendix and data from COMPUSTAT. The number of observations varies in each year depending on the availability of COMPUSTAT data. Values that are zero, negative, or in excess of 300% are excluded from the computation of the average ratio.

ibility to determine its dividend payout level, regardless of its asset type and duration. Moreover, a REIT's dividend policy can be affected by the fact that it does not need to pay taxes at the corporate level and that its organizational structure is more or less like that of a closed-end fund. In the next subsection, we examine the reason and motivation for a REIT to use a payout ratio that is much higher than that required by tax regulations.

Why REITs Pay Such High Dividends

Why would a REIT pay out greater dividends than they are legally required to? Why do they not simply pay out 90% of their taxable incomes and retain the remaining cash flow for future growth? In other words, REIT managers can let tax regulations decide the amount of dividends they should

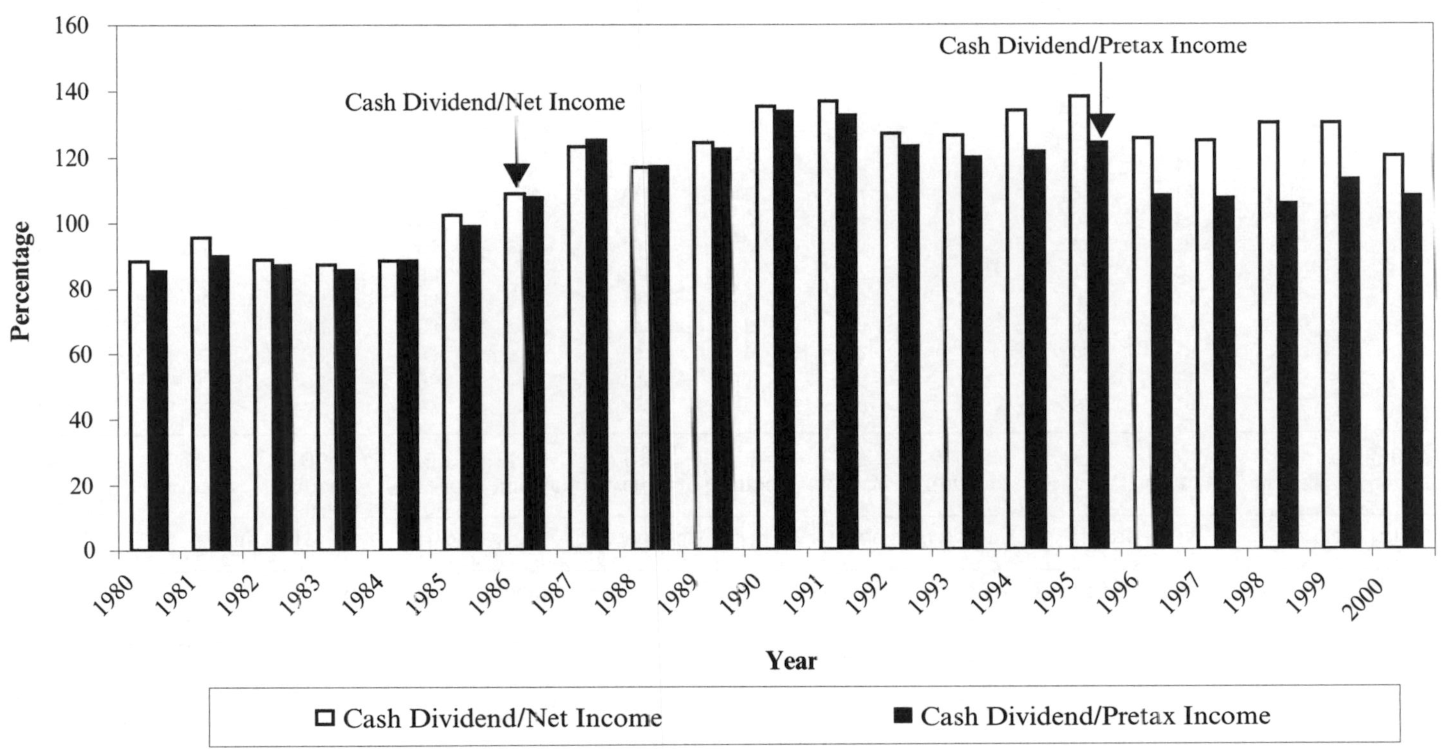

Figure 8.1 REIT Dividend Payout Ratios

Table 8.2 Dividend Payout Ratios by REIT Type

	Cash Dividend/Net Income						Cash Dividend/Pretax Income					
	Equity REITs		Hybrid REITs		Mortgage REITs		Equity REITs		Hybrid REITs		Mortgage REITs	
	Average (%)	Number of Obs.	Average (%)	Number of Obs.	Average (%)	Number of Obs.	Average (%)	Number of Obs.	Average (%)	Number of Obs.	Average (%)	Number of Obs.
1980	93	29	57	10	117	6	90	29	55	10	115	6
1981	92	36	96	11	106	11	85	35	91	11	105	11
1982	85	32	93	10	97	9	82	32	95	10	97	9
1983	86	29	83	12	101	8	83	29	82	12	100	8
1984	86	28	83	12	106	7	86	29	82	12	106	7
1985	110	32	86	10	96	11	107	32	79	11	96	11
1986	118	40	94	14	102	22	115	40	96	14	102	22
1987	130	45	102	14	122	22	134	46	102	14	121	22
1988	113	41	125	14	118	19	114	43	127	14	117	19
1989	130	36	124	11	115	21	130	37	119	12	111	21

1990	138	35	143	12	127	20	137	35	143	12	123	20
1991	139	43	143	8	131	20	137	43	133	8	123	20
1992	129	46	96	7	137	12	127	46	83	7	132	12
1993	129	81	130	8	106	11	122	81	118	8	107	12
1994	143	128	97	8	87	17	128	132	91	8	82	17
1995	141	134	139	8	114	16	126	140	130	8	108	16
1996	133	118	104	8	80	15	114	122	82	8	75	15
1997	128	128	117	10	100	15	109	137	107	10	90	15
1998	133	132	119	10	110	13	105	137	113	10	107	14
1999	130	133	120	10	139	17	112	137	98	18	136	17
2000	122	122	122	9	106	12	108	126	112	9	102	12
1980–1989	104		94		108		103		93		107	
1990–2000	133		121		112		120		110		108	
1980–2000	119		108		110		112		102		107	

Source: Authors' own calculations using the REIT sample described in the appendix and data from COMPUSTAT. The number of observations varies in each year depending on the availability of COMPUSTAT data. Values that are zero, negative, or in excess of 300% are excluded from the computation of the average ratio.

Table 8.3 Dividend Payout Ratios for Infinite-Life and Finite-Life REITs

	Cash Dividend/Net Income				Cash Dividend/Pretax Income			
	Infinite-Life REITs		Finite-Life REITs		Infinite-Life REITs		Finite-Life REITs	
	Average (%)	Number of Obs.	Average (%)	Number of Obs.	Average (%)	Number of Obs.	Average (%)	Number of Obs.
1980	88	45	—	0	85	45	—	0
1981	95	57	107	1	90	56	107	1
1982	88	50	145	1	86	50	145	1
1983	86	46	104	3	84	46	108	3
1984	87	44	106	3	87	45	113	3
1985	100	43	114	10	96	44	114	10
1986	105	57	120	19	103	57	120	19
1987	119	64	139	17	122	65	136	17
1988	116	58	120	16	115	58	124	18
1989	123	56	130	12	121	58	130	12
1990	130	51	153	16	127	51	153	16
1991	128	48	156	23	121	48	156	23
1992	122	43	138	22	118	43	133	22
1993	131	76	111	24	123	77	108	24
1994	139	130	104	23	125	134	102	23
1995	140	139	124	19	125	145	121	19
1996	128	130	92	11	110	134	88	11
1997	127	143	94	10	109	152	82	10
1998	131	149	99	6	106	155	88	6
1999	131	154	117	6	115	157	72	6
2000	120	147	135	6	107	191	124	7
1980–1989	101		121		99		122	
1990–2000	130		120		117		112	
1980–2000	116		120		108		116	

Source: Authors' own calculations using the REIT sample described in the appendix and data from COMPUSTAT. The number of observations varies in each year depending on the availability of COMPUSTAT data. Values that are zero, negative, or in excess of 300% are excluded from the computation of the average ratio.

pay and retain a significant amount of cash under their control to spend the way they like. From a review of the literature and stories in the popular press, we have found five reasons that might explain these dividend policies.

To Reduce Agency Costs

Wang, Erickson, and Gau (1993) specifically examine the relationship between dividend payout and the agency costs of REITs. It has been well documented that managers have incentives to invest in negative NPV (net present value) projects if their compensation is related to the size of the company (chapter 4 introduced the idea of REIT advisors' investing in projects that do not maximize the wealth of their stockholders).

Given this agency cost, Wang, Erickson, and Gau (1993) hypothesize that it might be better for REIT stockholders to force their managers to pay out most of their earnings as dividends. Under this circumstance, REIT managers will not be able to invest their companies' funds in any projects they happen to like. To be able to invest in any new properties, managers will have to issue new equity or debt securities. When a REIT issues securities, the capital market will take a close look at the projects the REIT intends to invest in. In other words, Wang, Erickson, and Gau argue that, although it involves additional issuance costs when a REIT pays out all its cash flow as dividends and simultaneously raises capital from the market, the additional monitoring function provided by the capital market can justify the cost.

Using data for the 1985–88 period, Wang, Erickson, and Gau find that the dividend policy of a REIT is affected by four factors: the type of REIT, the asset growth rate, the debt-to-asset ratio, and the return on assets (ROA). Equity REITs pay out significantly more dividends than mortgage REITs. This may be because equity REITs have more cash flows arising from the depreciation shelter and, therefore, should be able to pay out more dividends than required by tax regulations. In addition, REITs with high debt-to-asset ratios tend to pay out more dividends, probably because the use of debt increases their available cash flows. Furthermore, REITs with high asset-growth rates tend to pay lower dividends because they will have to retain more cash for future investments.

These three factors affecting REIT dividend policies are both simple and intuitively sound. The most interesting finding of Wang, Erickson, and Gau (1993) is that REIT managers pay out most of their cash flows when REITs perform poorly (i.e., when they have low ROA), perhaps because, when a REIT performs poorly, its stockholders would like their managers to seek new funds from the capital market, which can then monitor the new investments. When a REIT performs well, then the payout ratio can be lower and the managers can retain more internal capital for future investments. This evidence strongly suggests that dividend-payout ratios of REITs can be used to reduce agency conflicts between REIT managers and stockholders.

To Signal Private Information

Wang, Erickson, and Gau (1993) also test whether the dividend announcements of REITs convey information to the investors. Since managers have more information than investors about the REIT's future prospects, they can convey this information to the market by increasing (or decreasing) their dividend payments. In other words, if REIT managers believe that the future cash flows of their REITs will increase (or decrease), they can convey this information to the market by increasing (or decreasing) the dividend payments. REIT investors, upon observing this policy, will adjust the price of the REIT stock accordingly.

By examining 182 dividend announcements during the 1979–89 period, Wang, Erickson, and Gau (1993) find that they do convey information to the market. The stock price of a REIT, on average, increases after the REIT announces it will increase its dividends. The stock prices, on average, drop significantly if REIT managers announce that they will cut their dividends. In addition, the authors find that the information content of dividend announcements differs by REIT type. Since there is a high level of information asymmetry between REIT managers and investors in equity REITs, dividend announcements convey more information when they are announced by equity REITs than by mortgage REITs. The evidence strongly suggests that REIT managers can use their dividend policies as a tool to convey to investors their private information about a REIT's future cash-flow level.

To Signal the Volatility of Future Cash Flows

Bradley, Capozza, and Seguin (1998) examine the link between the cash-flow volatility of a REIT and its dividend-payout policy. They believe that there is a shareholder wealth penalty associated with cutting dividends, giving REIT managers an incentive to avoid such cuts. Therefore, REIT managers will rationally use a low dividend-payout ratio if they believe that the volatility of their future cash flows is high.

Indeed, the worst thing a manager could do is to cut dividends. It is a common belief that managers should maintain increasing dividend-payment streams to support the stock values of their REITs. We can cite the case of Weingarten Realty Investors as an example. Dowd (1993) attributes part of the reason for the company's remarkable price increase to the fact that the company consistently increased its dividends to stockholders by 5.25% per year. Obviously it may pay for a REIT manager to adopt a conservative dividend policy if he or she is unsure of the REIT's cash-flow prospects.

Using a sample of 75 REITs during the 1985–92 period, Bradley, Capozza, and Seguin (1998) confirm the finding of Wang, Erickson, and Gau (1993) that the market reacts negatively to REIT dividend-cut announcements. Given this evidence, it is obvious that REIT managers have an incentive to adopt a dividend policy that can avoid this cost. Bradley, Capozza, and Seguin further report that REITs with greater leverage, smaller asset bases, or undiversified asset bases offer lower dividend-payout rates when compared with other REITs.

We should note that it is reasonable to expect that the future cash-flow volatility of REITs with greater leverage, smaller asset bases, or undiversified asset bases should be high. Since the volatility of the future cash flow might be high, it is more difficult for REIT managers to maintain high dividend-payout ratios. In other words, Bradley, Capozza, and Seguin (1998) suggest that REIT managers should adopt conservative dividend policies based on their REITs' projected cash flows. By using low payout ratios, managers can make sure that, even if the anticipated future cash flows cannot be realized, they still do not need to cut future dividends and incur the negative penalty imposed by the stock market.

To Reduce Information Asymmetry

McDonald, Nixon, and Slawson (2000) examine the asymmetric information component of the bid-ask spread immediately prior to and following REIT dividend announcements during the 1995–96 period. The finance literature indicates that dealers tend to increase the bid-ask spreads of stocks they sell if they believe that the firm's managers know more about the stock than they do. The authors find that dividend announcements of equity REITs have significant information content that reduces the level of asymmetric information and hence reduces the bid-ask spread of the stocks for small REITs and equity REITs. They report that for small REITs and equity REITs, the asymmetric information cost is abnormally high on the day prior to dividend announcement and disappears afterward. Their evidence supports the notion that dividend policy can be used by REIT managers to convey information to REIT participants in the market.

Downs, Guner, and Patterson (2000) examine the relationship between a REIT's distribution policy and the asymmetry level of its information. Similar to McDonald, Nixon, and Slawson (2000), they also use the bid-ask spread of a REIT stock as a proxy for the asymmetric information level of the REIT. Their result also shows that REITs that choose to distribute more capital subsequently reduce the level of asymmetric information in the market.

Both studies indicate that it is healthy for REITs to use high dividend-payout ratios because they will convey information about the future prospects of the company to the market. Furthermore, with a high payout ratio the bid-ask spread of a REIT's stock will be narrowed, reducing investors' transaction costs and increasing their returns. This is perhaps the reason REITs have adopted such high dividend-payout ratios during the past 20 years.

To Attract Investors

Forest (1994) indicates that the high dividend yield of REITs is the main reason investors move into the REIT market, especially when the market faces high interest rates or when regulatory problems and competition put pressure on the dividend levels of utility companies. In other words, Forest assumes that there is a group of investors that is looking for high dividend payment stocks. To attract this group of investors, REITs should maintain very high payout ratios. Indeed, many articles in the popular press share a similar view and advocate high dividend payment as one of the main attractions of REIT stocks. (Following this line of reasoning, Forest advises investors to look for REITs with enough cash generated by operations to cover dividend payments.)

We know that investors should look at the total return (not the dividend yield) and the risk of the stock in making an investment decision. However, it is also possible that high-dividend stocks look particularly attractive when the dividend yields of all other stocks in the market are particularly low. In a period when there seems to be little potential for stocks to increase in value, high-dividend stocks will attract investors' attention. Although this type of argument seems to advocate market inefficiency, a REIT might have to adopt a high payout ratio if the manager believes that investors are looking for high dividend payments and if all other REITs are using high payout ratios.

Constraints on REIT Debt Policies

The finance literature tells us in simple terms that the use of debt is a tradeoff between an increase in tax shelter and an increase in potential bankruptcy costs. In other words, since the interest payment of debt is tax deductible, there is an incentive for investors to use as much debt as possible. Debt payment is a fixed obligation, however, and if a firm cannot meet this obligation, there is a consequence. When a firm cannot pay the interest on its debt, the lender can liquidate the firm and there will be foreclosure costs. We know that the probability that a firm cannot pay its interest payments increases when the firm uses more debt. Given this, the optimal capital structure simply seems to be a compromise between tax savings and potential liquidation costs.

However, it is more complicated than that for the REIT to make a decision on its capital structure. On the one hand, REITs do not need to pay taxes at the corporate level; following the traditional wisdom that the best use of debt is as a tax shelter, then, they seem to have no incentive to borrow. On the other hand, other types of investors do borrow heavily when investing in the property market. It is common for individual investors borrow at 75–80% of the property value from a bank. However, REITs cannot do this because the typical firms in the stock market will not use such a high debt ratio. Underwriters in the stock market simply will not underwrite debt instruments with a debt ratio of up to 80% of the firm's value.

Given this, it will be particularly difficult for REITs to select an appropriate debt level. On the one hand, REITs must compete with individual property-market investors who typically use very high debt ratios; on the other hand firms in the stock market do not use as high a debt ratio as firms do in the property market. REITs have to take this constraint into consideration because of competition from other firms in the same debt market. It appears that REITs are torn between the property market and the stock market in determining their debt policies.

Arguments Against the Use of Debt

Since the motivation of a firm to use debt is to obtain a tax shelter for the firm, there should be no advantage for REITs to use debt. Furthermore, Howe and Shilling (1988) point out that it is not a good idea for REITs to use debt because they will have to compete in the debt market with firms for which interest payments are tax deductible. Since tax-paying firms can enjoy tax savings, they can afford to pay a high interest rate on the debt. Non-tax-paying firms such as REITs will be at a comparative disadvantage because they have to pay the same interest rate despite not having tax savings.

The negative consequence (potential bankruptcy costs) of using debt is particularly relevant for REITs, for two reasons. First, real estate markets are cyclical. Periods of high growth followed by significant downturns are common. Second, most equity REITs typically have high levels of fixed operating costs (operating leverage) because much of their operating expenses are in the form of property taxes, utility costs, insurance premiums, ongoing maintenance expenses, and on-site management and administration costs. Piling financial leverage onto already high levels of operating leverage can significantly increase the impact of declining markets on earnings and cash flows.

These arguments naturally lead to the expectation that REITs will maintain a minimal debt level; empirical evidence, however, tells us that they do not. Many REITs do use debt, and their debt levels are no less than those used by industrial firms. Given this, there must be other reasons for REITs to use debt.

Argument for the Use of Debt

Jaffe (1991) points out several reasons REITs (and partnerships) can and should use leverage. The author first demonstrates that as long as REIT investors can borrow (and lend) at the same interest rate as the REIT, it does not matter whether the REIT or its investors use leverage. REIT investors can undo a REIT's leverage decision by lending their personal funds to the capital markets if they believe that the REIT is using too much debt. Alternatively, REIT investors can borrow from the capital markets if they believe that the REIT is using too little debt. Following Jaffe's argument, the disadvantage for REITs to use debt disappears and there is no reason that REITs should not use debt as far as tax considerations are concerned. Of course, Jaffe's argument holds if and only if REIT investors can borrow and lend at the same rate as the REIT—an assumption that might not hold in the real world.

Hamill (1993) extends Jaffe's analysis and shows that with non-recourse loans, a lower transaction cost could increase the value of a partnership (or a REIT) when it uses more leverage. Given Hamill's arguments, even if interest payments are not deductible at the corporate level, the REIT is still better off increasing its leverage as long as the debt is a non-recourse loan. However, Maris and Elayan (1991) find no correlation between the tax status of REIT investors and the leverage ratio of the REIT. This evidence does not support the arguments advanced by Jaffe (1991) and Hamill. Even so, Jaffe and Hamill demonstrate that it is fine for REITs to use debt even if they do not pay taxes at the corporate level.

Jaffe (1991) also observes that partnerships (and REITs) appear to be more highly levered than corporations (industrial firms). He attributes this to two possible causes. First, since both partnerships and REITs are small firms and small firms find the issuance costs of debt to be lower than the issuance costs of equity, there is an incentive for REITs to choose debt over equity. Second, it might be easier for REITs to borrow because of their underlying assets. Since real properties are viewed to have a high degree of debt capacity, it might be easier for REITs to obtain debt financing at more favorable rates than industrial firms could obtain with intangible assets.

A less commonly mentioned reason in the academic literature (although it is frequently mentioned in the popular press) is the *leverage effect.* If a REIT can earn, for example, a 10% return on its properties, then it has a great incentive to borrow if it can do so at an 8% interest rate. Under this circumstance, the more the REIT borrows, the higher its value. In other words, as long as the interest rate is lower than the ROA, the use of leverage increases the return to equity holders.

Table 8.4 and figure 8.2 demonstrate a positive leverage effect for REITs. Table 8.4 reports the gross profit margin, net profit margin, ROA, and return on equity (ROE) of REITs during the 1980–2000 period. It is clear that the gross and net profit margins of REITs are both quite high, at 46.6% and 22.6%, respectively. Although the ROA and the ROE are quite low (at 2.7 and 4.8%, respectively), we should understand that these two ratios are *accounting ratios.* That is, the cash used for the depreciation of the buildings is not included in calculating the returns. Even so, we should pay some attention to the relationship between the ROA and ROE of those REITs. When a REIT's ROE is significantly higher than its ROA, this means that the REIT is enjoying a positive leverage effect. That is, borrowing enhances the return of this REIT.

Table 8.5 reports the price-to-book and price-to-earnings ratios of REITs during the 1988–2000 period. As the reader can see, REITs enjoy quite high price-to-book ratios (averaging 1.6) and price-to-earnings ratios (averaging 19.3), meaning that, for every dollar in equity book value, the stock market will pay $1.6, on average. With this kind of price-to-book ratio, REITs have an incentive to use leverage to purchase properties. A price-to-earnings ratio at 19.3 is equivalent to about a 5% capitalization rate.

Table 8.4 REIT Profitability Ratios

	Gross Profit Margin[a]		Net Profit Margin[b]		Return on Asset[c]		Return on Equity[d]	
	Average (%)	Number of Obs.	Average (%)	Number of Obs.	Average (%)	Number of Obs.	Average (%)	Number of Obs.
1980	48.8	83	23.4	83	4.1	84	5.0	83
1981	42.8	92	15.8	92	3.3	93	9.6	93
1982	50.8	78	24.9	78	4.3	79	11.0	78
1983	47.6	77	33.2	75	0.4	77	3.0	77
1984	53.9	67	40.7	67	6.2	67	9.7	66
1985	54.1	77	43.6	75	8.9	78	5.5	77
1986	58.5	97	40.8	96	5.2	97	11.7	97
1987	58.1	102	32.7	102	4.1	102	9.3	101
1988	52.7	107	26.6	106	3.4	107	6.9	106
1989	43.4	109	14.0	106	0.3	108	–1.8	108
1990	38.0	104	8.0	102	–2.5	107	–5.7	106
1991	28.1	121	2.7	116	–0.7	123	–0.3	121
1992	20.2	127	1.3	124	–2.4	128	–7.7	127
1993	37.9	164	11.4	163	1.5	169	0.5	169
1994	39.9	212	19.6	210	1.7	213	5.4	213
1995	46.7	201	22.5	199	2.6	203	5.6	202
1996	48.3	188	24.9	188	2.8	189	4.9	189
1997	50.8	198	27.3	198	4.0	198	7.0	197
1998	52.6	210	23.1	209	3.0	210	4.1	209
1999	52.4	191	21.1	191	3.7	191	8.8	190
2000	52.2	186	17.0	186	3.7	187	8.3	186
1980–1989	51.1		29.6		4.0		7.0	
1990–2000	42.5		16.3		1.6		2.8	
1980–2000	46.6		22.6		2.7		4.8	

Source: Authors' own calculations, using the REIT sample described in the appendix and data from COMPUSTAT. The number of observations varies in each year depending on the availability of COMPUSTAT data. Ratios for firms that are in excess of 300% are excluded from the computation of the average ratio.

[a] Net sales minus cost of goods sold, divided by net sales.

[b] Income before extraordinary items divided by net sales.

[c] Income before extraordinary items divided by total assets.

[d] Income before extraordinary items divided by common equity.

This low capitalization rate will definitely give a REIT a great incentive to expand its asset base through borrowing.

Practices in the Field

In a study of REIT financing events (issuance of debt and equity securities) during the period 1965–92, Hsieh, Poon, and Wei (2000) compare the

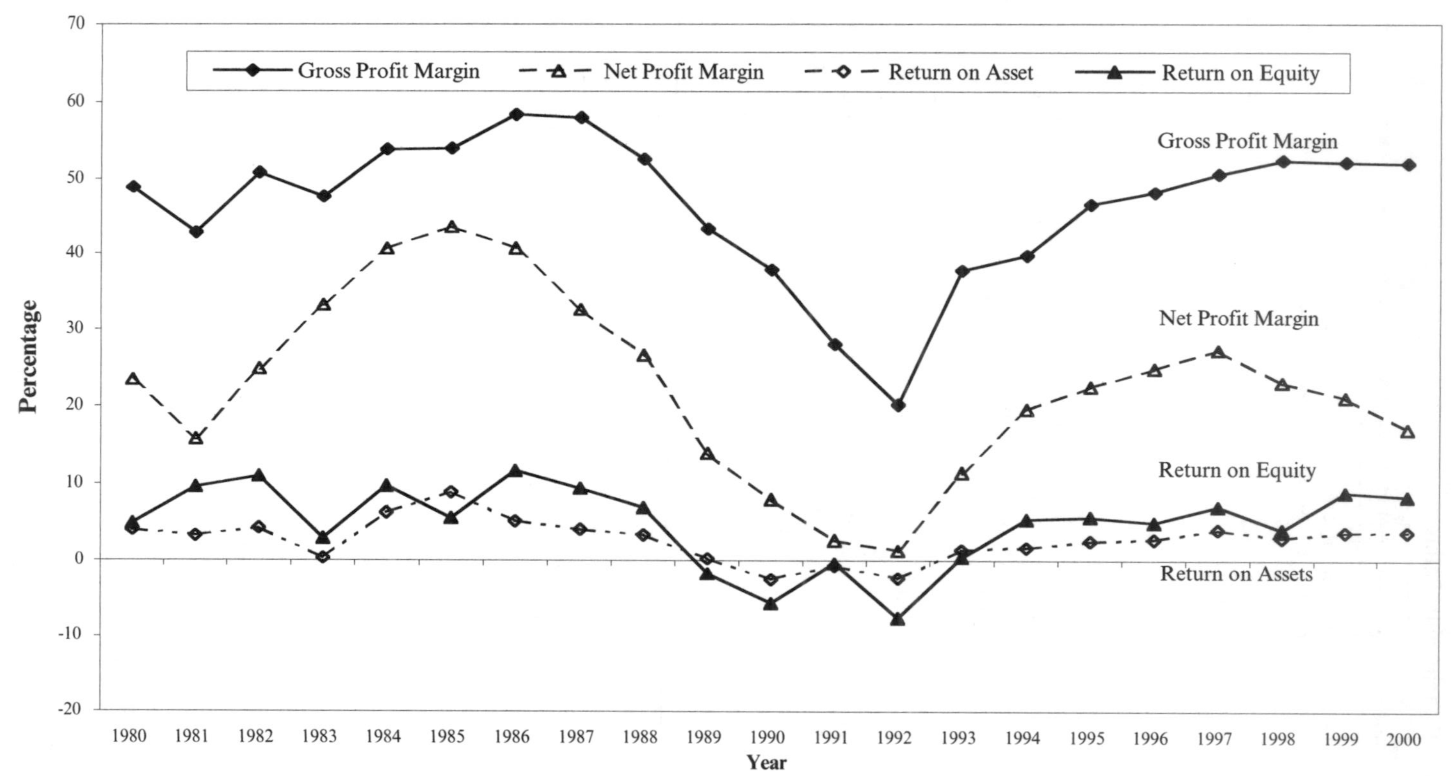

Figure 8.2 REIT Profitability Ratios

Table 8.5 REIT Market Value Ratios

	Price-to-Book[a]		Price-to-Earnings[b]	
	Average	Number of Obs.	Average	Number of Obs.
1980	—	0	—	0
1981	—	0	—	0
1982	—	0	—	0
1983	—	0	—	0
1984	—	0	—	0
1985	—	0	—	0
1986	—	0	—	0
1987	—	0	—	0
1988	1.5	6	11.1	5
1989	1.0	104	15.8	77
1990	0.7	107	11.5	71
1991	0.9	116	19.8	82
1992	1.2	129	19.8	77
1993	1.4	158	25.4	84
1994	1.6	217	25.3	159
1995	1.7	210	20.3	169
1996	2.9	187	23.3	159
1997	2.1	194	24.9	159
1998	1.9	209	18.0	165
1999	1.5	187	16.7	170
2000	1.9	186	18.6	164
1988–1993	1.1		17.2	
1994–2000	2.0		21.0	
1988–2000	1.6		19.3	

Source: Authors' own calculations using the REIT sample described in the appendix and data from COMPUSTAT. The number of observations varies in each year depending on the availability of COMPUSTAT data. Values that are zero or negative are excluded from the computation of the average ratio.

[a] Market value of common equity divided by book value of common equity.

[b] Closing price divided by earnings per share.

financing patterns of REITs with those of industrial firms. They find that, in terms of frequency, REITs use more short-term debt and common stock (65%) than long-term debt and convertible debt (35%) when financing their capital needs; but, when compared to tax-paying industrial corporations, REITs utilize less debt financing to fulfil their capital needs. Specifically, the authors find that only 53% of the financing events of REITs are debt financing, whereas for industrial firms the figure is 81%.However, even if REITs issue less debt when compared to the industrial firms, we should keep in mind that 53% of REIT financing decisions involves the use of debt.

Table 8.6 reports the ratios of long-term debt to total capital (book value); total debt to total capital (book value); long-term debt to total capitaliza-

Table 8.6 REIT Leverage Ratios

	Long-Term Debt to Total Capital[a]		Long-Term Debt to Total Market Capitalization[b]		Total Debt to Total Capital[a]		Total Debt to Total Market Capitalization[b]	
	Average (%)	Number of Obs.	Average (%)	Number of Obs.	Average (%)	Number of Obs.	Average (%)	Number of Obs.
1980	41	83	34	78	81	83	54	78
1981	37	93	32	91	62	92	47	91
1982	36	80	30	79	63	80	45	79
1983	34	77	26	76	54	76	37	76
1984	31	67	24	66	53	66	36	66
1985	28	78	21	76	47	76	30	76
1986	31	102	24	98	44	99	31	98
1987	34	104	29	103	49	103	37	103
1988	34	113	29	112	49	112	39	112
1989	34	109	32	107	49	108	41	107
1990	36	107	37	106	47	106	49	106
1991	31	127	27	122	41	120	38	122
1992	30	131	28	131	45	128	39	131
1993	32	175	28	175	41	172	35	175
1994	38	214	33	212	45	207	39	212
1995	39	203	32	204	45	198	38	204
1996	43	189	33	184	49	181	38	184
1997	41	203	33	200	48	194	39	200
1998	48	213	43	209	61	203	53	209
1999	48	196	46	192	61	189	56	192
2000	50	187	46	186	62	180	56	186
1980–1989	34		28		55		40	
1990–2000	40		35		50		44	
1980–2000	37		32		52		42	

Source: Authors' own calculations using the REIT sample described in the appendix and data from COMPUSTAT. The number of observations varies in each year depending on the availability of COMPUSTAT data. Ratios for firms that are negative or in excess of 300% are excluded from the computation of the average ratio.

[a] Total capital is the sum of long-term debt, preferred stock, minority interest, and common equity.

[b] Total market capitalization is the sum of total debt (long-term plus current), preferred stock, and the market value of common equity. The market value of common equity is the share price multiplied by the number of shares outstanding.

tion (market value); and total debt to total capitalization (market value) for all REITs during the 1980–2000 period. The average leverage ratios (based on long-term debt) during this period are 37% based on book value and 32% based on market value. It is clear that REITs also use a lot of short-term debt. The total debt to total capital ratio is 52%, indicating that 15% of the total book value of capital is supported by short-term financing. We also observe a trend in the use of debt. From the table, it is clear that the average debt ratio of REITs is higher after 1990 than before 1990, probably because the REIT industry has a higher percentage of companies with investment-grade ratings than many other industries in the stock market. This certainly makes it easier for REITs to borrow in the debt market.

Table 8.7 reports information similar to that in table 8.6 for all stocks traded on the NYSE, Amex, and Nasdaq markets during the same period. It should be noted that on both the book-value and the market-value basis,

Table 8.7 Leverage Ratios for All Publicly Traded Stocks

	Total Debt to Total Capital[a]		Total Debt to Total Market Capitalization[b]	
	Average (%)	Number of Obs.	Average (%)	Number of Obs.
1980	47	1,614	34	1,345
1981	45	1,648	33	1,499
1982	44	2,105	32	1,861
1983	43	2,300	26	2,014
1984	42	2,461	27	2,185
1985	44	2,723	26	2,329
1986	45	3,021	26	2,567
1987	44	3,265	27	2,823
1988	46	3,453	28	2,978
1989	49	3,622	28	3,116
1990	49	3,844	32	3,285
1991	46	4,136	28	3,500
1992	45	4,601	25	3,778
1993	43	5,428	22	4,486
1994	42	5,989	23	5,031
1995	44	6,942	23	5,816
1996	43	7,613	22	6,787
1997	43	7,984	22	7,425
1998	46	8,610	27	7,942
1999	46	9,245	27	8,720
2000	45	7,890	30	7,892
1980–1989	45		29	
1990–2000	45		26	
1980–2000	45		27	

Source: Authors' own calculations using all firms from COMPUSTAT. The number of observations varies in each year depending on the availability of COMPUSTAT data. Ratios for firms that are negative or in excess of 300% are excluded from the computation of the average ratio.

[a] Total capital is the sum of long-term debt, preferred stock, minority interest, and common equity.

[b] Total market capitalization is the sum of total debt (long-term plus current), preferred stock, and the market value of common equity. The market value of common equity is the share price multiplied by the number of shares outstanding.

REITs use much more debt than industrial firms do (52% vs. 45% on a book-value basis, and 42% vs. 27% on a market-value basis). Figure 8.3 plots the debt ratio of REITs and industrial firms during the period. The figure shows that the debt ratio of REITs, on a book-value basis, is consistently larger than that of the industrial firms. Tables 8.6 and 8.7 clearly demonstrate that REITs use more debt than industrial firms do.

Tables 8.8 and 8.9 report the debt ratios for different types of REITs (equity, mortgage, and hybrid) and for finite-life and infinite-life REITs. In general, we find that mortgage REITs use more debt than equity REITs do, regardless of whether we use book value or market value. The high leverage of mortgage REITs could imply that they are making profits from the difference between the short-term borrowing rate and the long-term lending rate—a very risky strategy by which to seek a profit. Infinite-life REITs also use more debt than finite-life REITs, which implies that REITs with growth potential might use more debt.

Before we discuss the debt policies of REITs, it might be useful to look at the capital decisions of investors in the property market first. After all, an equity REIT is simply a corporate entity that holds real properties. If we understand why investors want to borrow to purchase properties, we can transfer that knowledge to the corporate level to help us understand why REITs also want to borrow.

Evidence from the Real Estate Market

Gau and Wang (1990) study the capital structure decisions of the 1,243 property transactions over the 1971–85 period in Vancouver, Canada. Specifically, they identify five factors that affect investors decisions to use more debt in their investments. Some of those factors are related to the tax shelter, some are related to economic conditions, and some are related to market imperfections.

The authors first find that investors in properties with a large existing tax shelter from building depreciation tend to use less debt. This is true because, with a large existing tax shelter, the interest-payment deduction might not be needed. Under this circumstance, it is reasonable for investors in the properties to use less debt. They also find that corporate investors (with higher tax rates) tend to use more debt. This makes sense because a higher tax rate means a higher tax shelter, given the identical amount of interest deduction. Both findings confirm that the tax shelter is the main reason for investors to use debt to finance property acquisitions.

Gau and Wang (1990) also find that investors tend to borrow less when the interest rate is high, probably because lenders typically use a debt coverage ratio to determine the loan amount. A higher interest rate means a high debt payment, which in turn indicates a low loan-to-value ratio. The authors also report that a higher priced investment tends to use more debt.

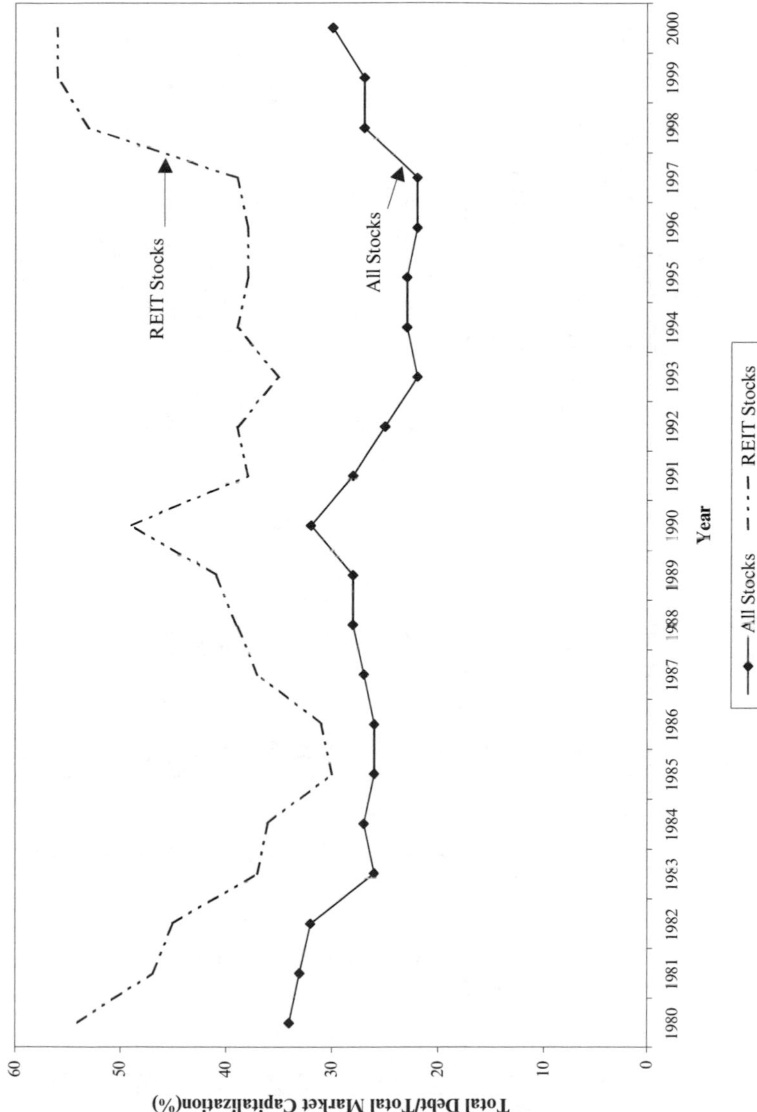

Figure 8.3 Comparing Leverage Ratios

Table 8.8 Leverage Ratios by REIT Type

	Total Debt to Total Capital[a]						Total Debt to Total Market Capitalization[b]					
	Equity REIT		Hybrid REIT		Mortgage REIT		Equity REIT		Hybrid REIT		Mortgage REIT	
	Average (%)	Number of Obs.	Average (%)	Number of Obs.	Average (%)	Number of Obs.	Average (%)	Number of Obs.	Average (%)	Number of Obs.	Average (%)	Number of Obs.
1980	65	40	90	36	131	7	50	38	59	33	58	7
1981	53	46	58	34	106	12	42	46	51	33	54	12
1982	56	43	54	25	106	12	41	42	47	25	52	12
1983	51	40	49	26	78	10	39	40	37	26	30	10
1984	47	39	44	18	98	9	37	39	33	18	36	9
1985	48	47	38	17	57	12	32	46	29	17	26	13
1986	43	57	39	18	48	24	31	55	27	18	35	25
1987	45	62	45	18	60	23	36	62	32	18	44	23
1988	45	65	43	20	62	27	37	65	30	19	50	28
1989	46	60	52	20	51	28	39	59	36	20	49	28
1990	48	60	35	20	54	26	49	59	39	20	56	27
1991	36	75	40	20	55	25	33	76	41	20	51	26

1992	39	83	35	19	72	26	37	85	36	20	48	26
1993	37	127	41	20	58	25	33	129	38	20	43	26
1994	47	166	35	18	40	23	39	167	37	19	41	26
1995	47	160	34	16	40	22	39	163	36	17	33	24
1996	48	150	48	12	55	19	38	153	35	12	38	19
1997	47	162	49	12	60	20	38	163	42	13	46	24
1998	56	166	74	13	92	24	50	166	50	13	70	30
1999	57	159	63	10	95	20	54	157	49	11	72	24
2000	60	154	57	9	91	18	54	154	54	11	72	22
1980–1989	50		51		80		38		38		43	
1990–2000	48		47		65		42		42		52	
1980–2000	49		49		72		40		40		48	

Source: Authors' own calculations using the REIT sample described in the appendix and data from COMPUSTAT. The number of observations varies in each year depending on the availability of COMPUSTAT data. Ratios for firms that are negative or in excess of 300% are excluded from the computation of the average ratio.

[a] Total capital is the sum of long-term debt, preferred stock, minority interest, and common equity.

[b] Total market capitalization is the sum of total debt (long-term plus current), preferred stock, and the market value of common equity. The market value of common equity is the share price multiplied by the number of shares outstanding.

Table 8.9 Leverage Ratios for Infinite-life REITs and Finite-life REITs

	Total Debt to Total Capital[a]				Total Debt to Total Capitalization[b]			
	Infinite-life REITs		Finite-life REITs		Infinite-life REITs		Finite-life REITs	
	Average (%)	Number of Obs.	Average (%)	Number of Obs.	Average (%)	Number of Obs.	Average (%)	Number of Obs.
1980	81	83	—	0	54	78	—	0
1981	62	91	16	1	47	90	18	1
1982	63	79	33	1	45	78	28	1
1983	55	72	35	4	38	72	23	4
1984	55	62	28	4	36	62	26	4
1985	51	63	30	13	33	64	20	12
1986	52	76	17	23	36	76	14	22
1987	57	81	20	22	42	81	20	22
1988	57	85	21	27	44	86	22	26
1989	57	83	23	25	45	82	28	25
1990	54	78	28	28	54	78	36	28
1991	55	82	11	38	49	83	16	39
1992	59	85	19	43	47	88	24	43
1993	48	129	18	43	38	132	24	43
1994	52	165	18	42	43	169	24	43
1995	52	163	17	35	42	168	18	36
1996	52	157	27	24	40	160	24	24
1997	49	181	38	13	39	186	41	14
1998	62	194	49	9	53	199	53	10
1999	62	181	41	8	56	184	44	8
2000	63	173	47	8	56	179	53	8
1980–89	59		25		42		22	
1990–2000	55		28		47		33	
1980–2000	57		27		45		28	

Source: Authors' own calculations using all firms from COMPUSTAT. The number of observations varies in each year depending on the availability of COMPUSTAT data. Ratios for firms that are negative or in excess of 300% are excluded from the computation of the average ratio.

[a] Total capital is the sum of long-term debt, preferred stock, minority interest, and common equity.

[b] Total market capitalization is the sum of total debt (long-term plus current), preferred stock, and the market value of common equity. The market value of common equity is the share price multiplied by the number of shares outstanding.

They interpret that this is caused by the constraint in the equity capital market. That is, if it is difficult for investors to obtain equity financing for large investments, they will have no choice but to borrow.

Finally, the authors find that the magnitude of bankruptcy costs and the likelihood of incurring those costs affect the capital decision. Investors tend to borrow less if they are not certain about the level of future cash flows. Indeed, bankruptcy costs—which are high and difficult to avoid once a loan is in default—might be the most important factor that prohibits investors from unlimited borrowing. Brown (2000) shows that the vast majority of nonperforming loans owned by mortgage REITs are foreclosed. The author examines the annual reports of 24 mortgage REITs during the 1989–91 period, finding that 421 commercial real estate loans (among a total of 1,289 owned by the REITs) were defaulted during the period. Of the 421 loans, 354 loans were foreclosed and only 31 obtained long-term extensions from the lenders. This evidence indicates that liquidation cost is a real concern when making capital structure decisions.

Evidence from the REIT Market

Using data drawn from 61 REITs during the 1981–87 period, Maris and Elayan (1990) identify four factors that affect a REIT's borrowing decisions. These factors are the *size* of the firm, the *growth rate* of the firm, the *uncertainty level* about the cash flow, and the *income derived* from mortgages. They also find that these factors have different impacts on the borrowing decisions of equity and mortgage REITs.

The authors find that equity REITs with high growth rates tend to use less debt and that those with high uncertainty about their future cash flows or that are large in size tend to use more debt. The result indicates that high-growth REITs tend to use equity to finance their investments and that, therefore, their debt ratios are lower than those of low-growth REITs. This result also shows that larger REITs tend to use more debt. However, it is not clear why equity REITs with higher levels of uncertainty in their cash flows tend to use more debt. This is inconsistent with the intuition that the potential bankruptcy costs will reduce the leverage ratio of REITs with high uncertainty about their future cash flows.

Maris and Elayan (1990) find that mortgage REITs with high growth rates and larger sizes tend to use more debt. However, mortgage REITs with high uncertainty about their future cash flows tend to use less debt. Clearly, this result is different from that for equity REITs, and the authors cannot explain the phenomenon. Given the evidence presented by the authors, we can conclude only that larger REITs (regardless of being of the equity or mortgage type) tend to use more debt.

In addition, Ghosh, Nag, and Sirmans (1997) argue that REIT managers' financing decisions can be influenced by their perception of the changes in the real estate market. Managers of REITs that performed well tend to raise more funds using equity financing if they believe that the property sector in which the REIT specializes is hot. Hence, REITs specializing in a particular property market tend to use more debt financing when the underlying property market does not perform well.

Is There a Consensus View in the Market?

The finance literature indicates that there should be an optimal capital structure for firms. However, the literature also tells us that optimal ratios should differ for firms with different characteristics. In other words, a high leverage ratio might be interpreted as a good financial policy for one particular firm but not for another. This makes it is very difficult to determine whether the stock market prefers REITs to use a high (or low) leverage ratio.

The only way we can obtain any evidence on the optimal debt level is to examine the market's reaction when a firm changes its capital structure. That is, we can observe whether the price of the stock increases or decreases when a firm issues new debt to judge what the stock market prefers the firm to do. We will summarize the empirical result on this issue for both industrial firms and REITs.

Market Reaction to Announcements by Industrial Firms

The evidence on the market response to seasoned debt issues, so far, is more or less mixed depending on the nature and purpose of the debt issue. In general, the older studies on debt-for-equity swaps by industrial firms show that leverage-increasing issues (in which debt is substituted for equity) result in stock price increases whereas leverage-decreasing issues along with unexpected decreases in cash flows result in stock price decreases. This result is consistent with corporate tax shield benefits and with the use of debt to signal favorable information about the firm's existing and future projects.

More recent studies on this issue, however, present a different picture. Eckbo (1986) finds no significant effects on stock prices on the announcements of straight debt issues but a negative stock price effect for convertible debt issues. (The latter is similar to the evidence on stock issuance announcements.) Akhigbe, Easterwood, and Pettit (1997) further show that the motivation behind debt issues plays a role in determining the price reaction. They find no significant reaction when debt issues are motivated by an unexpected increase in capital expenditures or an expected refinancing of existing debt, but a negative and significant price reaction when the debt issue is motivated by an unexpected shortfall in cash flow.

In summary, the finance literature indicates in general that market participants might not interpret the issuance of new debt securities as either good or bad news. However, unless investors interpret that the firm is borrowing because it is in trouble they will not react to the change in a firm's leverage ratio. It seems that, from the investors' point of view, the increase in other related costs (such as bankruptcy costs) can offset the increase in the tax shelter resulting from an increase in leverage. Does the same pattern hold for REITs? We know that REITs, because of their tax-exempt status, will be unable to utilize the additional tax shelter provided by the interest deduction. Does this mean the market interprets REITs' debt policies differently?

Market Reactions to REIT Announcements

Unlike the typical industrial firm, REITs (which are tax exempt) have no tax-based motivation to use debt. For REITs (with a marginal tax rate of zero), the net tax gain to debt usage is unambiguously negative (or non-positive). Therefore, based on the tax-based motivation, one would expect investors to react negatively to debt offerings by REITs. However, if investors interpret the issuance of debt as signaling favorable information about the REIT, they are inclined to react positively to the debt offerings. Hence, announcements of debt issuance may trigger either a positive or negative stock price reaction.

We will now review three studies that provide empirical evidence on the announcement effects of debt offerings by REITs. Howe and Shilling (1988) study the market response to 73 debt-offering announcements by NYSE- or Amex-listed REITs during the 1970–85 period. Contrary to prior evidence on industrial-firm debt offerings, they find a significant and positive market response to debt announcements by REITs, most of which occurs in response to short-term debt announcements. The authors propose that their finding supports the use of short-term debt as a positive signaling mechanism. In addition, Allen and Rutherford (1992) also find a positive stock price response when tax-paying real estate corporations issue long-term debt securities.

Using a larger sample of 116 seasoned debt offers by equity REITs from the 1991–97 period, Nag, Ghosh, and Sirmans (1999) also find a positive and significant reaction to announcements of debt offers, thus corroborating the earlier Howe and Shilling (1988) evidence. In addition, they find that price changes are significantly positively related to the amount of debt issued and significantly negatively related to apartment- and mall-property types.

Contrary to the previous two studies, Hsieh, Poon, and Wei (2000), analyzing 100 straight-debt (long-term and short-term) financing announcements by REITs in the 1965–92 period, find no significant stock price responses to the announcements of debt issuance. The non-positive response to long-term debt offerings is similar to that for tax-paying industrial corporations. In addition, the authors also examine the stock price response to 31 convertible debt offerings, finding negative and significant price reactions similar to those found in studies of industrial corporations. In other words, different from the studies done by Howe and Shilling (1988) and Nag, Ghosh, and Sirmans (1999), Hsieh, Poon, and Wei find that the market's reactions to REITs' debt offerings do not differ from those of industrial firms.

Although it is puzzling why different studies examining similar samples draw different conclusions, we at least know from the empirical evidence that the stock market might not object to the idea that REITs use debt to finance their growth. (This is probably why the debt level of REITs is higher than that of industrial firms, as reported in our tables.) It is also interesting to note that the stock market reacts to a REIT's debt policy differently from the way it reacts to industrial firms' debt policies.

What Have We Learned?

We have discussed the fact that REITs pay out more dividends than required by law, and that REITs borrow less than their competitors in the property market but more than their peers in the stock market. The regulations governing REIT payout levels and the fact that they do not need to pay income tax, however, make it difficult to understand their dividend policies and debt structures. From this chapter, then, we learn the following:

- A REIT's dividend policy is not constrained by the payout ratio set by tax regulations. REITs pay out significantly more dividends than the regulations require.
- REIT investors prefer REITs to pay out more dividends because they would like to see REITs obtain external funds in order to grow. When REITs pay out more, the stock and debt markets tend to monitor managers' investment decisions and hence minimize the agency problems prevailing in the market. However, investors (or at least institutional investors) might prefer REITs to reserve more earnings to finance growth in the recent period because of the difficulty in raising capital from the equity market.
- An increase (or decrease) in a REIT's dividend payment signals information about the its future earnings to the stock market, which reacts by increasing (or decreasing) the stock price of the REIT. The use of a high payout ratio also enables investors in the stock market to understand the REIT more thoroughly.
- Equity REITs, REITs with high volatility in earnings, REITs with poor performance, and high-growth REITs typically pay out lower dividends.
- It is possible that investors buy REIT stocks because of their high payout ratios. Those REITs that do not use high payout ratios could be penalized by investors.
- REITs have significantly lower debt ratios than investors do in the property market, but they use more debt than other firms do in the stock market.
- Empirical evidence indicates that there is a positive leverage effect in the REIT market. That is, the use of debt increases the returns to equity investors.
- Larger REITs tend to use more debt than smaller REITs do.

- The stock market does not seem to object to the idea that REITs use debt to finance their growth. There is evidence that the stock market reacts positively when a REIT issues debt securities.

Conclusions

We now know that REITs pay out more dividends than required by the tax regulations, and we know the reasons that they adopt their dividend policies. However, the comprehensibility of those reasons does not make the practice an accepted one. To pay out most of a REIT's internal funds and then to use external funds to facilitate the company's growth is a very costly practice. The issuance cost of debt or equity securities can be saved if the REIT is allowed to retain most of its earnings to support its growth. From a pure financing point of view, REITs are better served by paying out only the levels of dividends required by tax regulations. This issue will be more important in the future, as more REITs adopt growth strategies and actively issue securities in the stock and debt markets. A review of (and a revision in) REIT dividend policy might be necessary to make it easier for future REITs to adopt growth strategies. These may not be easy tasks—whatever the REITs choose to do, the stock market has to know about (and agree with) the policy first.

It might be possible that REITs will have to increase their current debt ratios. This is especially true if they have difficulty issuing equity securities. Investors in the property market can borrow as much as 80% of the property values and still have their investments viewed as prudent by banks and regulators. Given what has happened in the property market, there is no reason that stock market participants should object to REITs' use of high leverage ratios. When the stock market understands REITs better than it currently does, we anticipate that REIT debt ratios will increase. This could, in turn, provide the capital required for REITs to sustain the rapid growth they have experienced in recent years.

NOTES

1. The alternative to debt financing is equity financing, which we will discuss in the next chapter.

REFERENCES

Akhigbe, A., J. C. Easterwood, and R. R. Pettit. 1997. Wealth effects of corporate debt issues: The impact of issuer motivations. *Financial Management* 26:32–47.

Allen, Marcus, and Ronald Rutherford. 1992. The impact of financing decisions on the security returns of real estate corporations. *Journal of Real Estate Finance and Economics* 5:393–400.

Bradley, Michael, Dennis Capozza, and Paul Seguin. 1998. Dividend policy and cash flow uncertainty. *Real Estate Economics* 26:555–80.

Brown, David. 2000. Liquidity and liquidation: Evidence from real estate trusts. *Journal of Finance* 55:469–85.

Dowd, Michael. 1993. How in the world can REIT stocks sell at a five percent yield? *Real Estate Finance* 10:13+.

Downs, David, Nuray Guner, and Gary Patterson. 2000. Capital distribution policy and information asymmetry: A real estate market perspective. *Journal of Real Estate Finance and Economics* 21:235–50.

Eckbo, B. E. 1986. Valuation effects of corporate debt offerings. *Journal of Financial Economics* 15:119–51.

Forest, Anderson. 1994. Now, dividend hunters are stalking REITs. *Business Week* (June 6), pp. 120–21.

Gau, George, and Ko Wang. 1990. Capital structure decisions in real estate investment." *AREUEA Journal* 18:501–21.

Ghosh, Chinmoy, Raja Nag, and C.F. Sirmans. 1997. Is there a window of opportunity? Stock market performance of REITs around secondary equity offerings. *Real Estate Finance* 13:175–92.

Hamill, James. 1993. A note on taxes and the capital structure of partnership, REITs, and related entities. *Journal of Real Estate Research* 8:279–86.

Howe, John, and James Shilling. 1988. Capital structure theory and REIT security offerings. *Journal of Finance* 43:983–93.

Hsieh, Chengho, Percy Poon, and Peihwang Wei. 2000. An analysis of REIT financing decision. Louisiana State University at Shreveport. Working paper.

Jaffe, Jeffrey. 1991. Taxes and the capital structure of partnerships, REITs, and related entities. *Journal of Finance* 46:401–07.

Maris, Brian, and Fayez Elayan. 1990. Capital structure and the cost of capital for untaxed firms: The case of REITs. *AREUEA Journal* 18:22–39.

Maris, Brian, and Fayez Elayan. 1991. A test for tax-induced investor clienteles in REITs. *Journal of Real Estate Research* 6:169–68.

McDonald, Cynthia G., Terry D. Nixon, and V. Carlos Slawson. 2000. The changing asymmetric information component of REIT spreads: A study of anticipated announcements. *Journal of Real Estate Finance and Economics* 20:195–200.

Nag, Raja, Chinmoy Ghosh, and C. F. Sirmans. 1999. An analysis of seasoned equity offerings by equity REITs, 1991 to 1995. *Journal of Real Estate Finance and Economics* 19:175–93.

Wang, Ko, John Erickson, and George Gau. 1993. Dividend policies and dividend announcement effects for real estate investment trusts. *Real Estate Economics* 21:185–201.

9

REIT Security Offerings

Are They Different from Other Securities?

Investors in initial public offerings (IPOs) of common stocks in the United States earned, on average, about an 18% return on the first day of trading during the 1970–2000 period. Recent examples from the Internet industry show an even higher price jump on the first day—as high as 697.5% for VA Linux, which went public in December 1999. However, if you are an investor in the REIT IPO market, do not get too excited when you are allocated some REIT IPO shares. The average price increase of these shares on the first trading day was only 0.21% during the 1970–2000 period.

The finance literature forewarns investors in the IPO market about the large but not sustainable price increase on the first day of trading, a significant portion of the abnormally high return may be lost over the 200 days following the IPO. For the IPOs of industrial firms, the gains on the first trading day will be reduced if examined in relation to a longer holding period. Unfortunately, REITs do not enjoy the significant first-day price increase, and the performance of their stocks after their IPOs is quite poor when compared with other stocks in the market. This means that investors in the REIT IPO market earn inferior returns if we look at a longer holding period.

Why should REIT IPOs perform so poorly and differently from industrial firm IPOs? Is their performance due to their fund-like organizational structure or to their holdings in real properties and mortgages? Is it possible that investors in the REIT IPO market are different from those in industrial firm IPOs? In other words, we are interested in finding out why REIT IPOs behave so differently. Our findings should be particularly important to investors in the IPO markets (for both REIT and non-REIT stocks).

In addition, as pointed out in chapter 8, a REIT's tax-exempt status requires it to pay out 90% of its taxable income to shareholders as dividends. Because of this high dividend-payout requirement and the capital-intensive nature of the real estate business, REITs must go constantly to the market to raise funds for growth or expansion. They can do this by issuing either debt or equity securities. We discussed the implications of issuing debt securities in chapter 8; in this chapter, we will discuss the market reaction to the secondary offerings made by REITs.

We first examine some of the features of REIT IPOs that might make investors value them differently from the IPOs of industrial firms. We then summarize the empirical evidence on how REIT IPOs perform both on the first day of trading and in the longer run. Finally, we present evidence on investor response to secondary offerings of REIT securities.

What Is Unique about REIT IPOs?

Wang, Chan, and Gau (1992) indicate three possible reasons for REIT IPOs to behave differently from industrial firm IPOs. First, the uncertainty regarding the value of REITs is higher than that for industrial firms. Second, there were many uninformed investors in the REIT market when compared to the general stock market during their period of study (1971–88). Third, REIT IPOs should behave more like mutual fund IPO than like industrial firm IPOs.

Uncertainty about the Value of the Properties

Both academics and practitioners in the REIT market suspect that the uncertainty about the value of real estate stocks is greater than that for stocks of most industrial firms with operating assets. For example, Palmon and Seidler (1978) and Hite, Owers, and Rogers (1987) report that real estate companies complain that the stock market underestimates their "real value" more often than it underestimates the real value of industrial firms. They also point out that several real estate firms have liquidated some or all of their real estate assets because they believe their stock prices do not reflect the underlying property value.[1]

Firstenberg, Ross, and Zisler (1988) point out that the complexity of information flows in the real estate market is due to the fact that it is not an auction market offering divisible shares in every property. Since the underlying property value of a REIT is difficult to obtain, it will be difficult for REIT IPO investors to ascertain the value of the REIT. In addition, Titman and Warga (1986) examine the risk and performance of mortgage and equity REITs and conclude that "because of the very high volatility of these investment trusts, it is very difficult to obtain an accurate measure of performance using any of the performance measures" (428). Their evidence points out the difficulty in valuing REITs.

Given the evidence, it seems that REIT IPOs are, on average, associated with a greater level of valuation uncertainty than industrial firm IPOs. However, the finance literature tells us that greater uncertainty should lead us to expect REIT IPOs to be, on average, significantly underpriced. That is, REIT IPO investors should earn an even higher first-day return than investors buying industrial firm IPOs. Apparently, the prediction offered by the finance literature is different from what actually happens in market. In fact, some of the more sophisticated investors are aware of this strange phenomenon and try to avoid buying REIT stocks at the IPO stage. For example, some very successful real estate stock funds attribute their success to a strategy of avoiding stocks of newer REITs until after their prices have dropped to attractive levels (*Wall Street Journal,* July 30, 1986, p. 21). Kenneth Campbell of Audit Investment, Inc., said, "If I can buy acceptable property at 10 percent to 20 percent discount, why should I pay full price?" (*Wall Street Journal,* June 25, 1985, p. 63).

The Buyers of REIT IPOs

The popular press has noted that prior to 1993 there was a lack of institutional interest in investing in REIT IPOs (see, e.g., *Barron's,* August 29, 1988, p. 44, and *Business Week,* February 26, 1990, p. 89). This means that investors in REIT IPOs at that time were mostly individuals. While it is difficult to get information on the number of investors in an IPO, we do have data from one investment fund. The REIT IPO prospectus of VMS Mortgage Investment Fund reports that four REIT IPOs of affiliated companies issued shares totaling $475 million to 33,600 investors (approximately $14,000 per investor). This evidence together with the evidence reported in chapter 6 indicates that individual investors may have dominated the REIT IPO market in the 1980s and early 1990s.

Individual investors are often considered to be less sophisticated than institutional investors. If the REIT IPO market is dominated by individual investors, it is possible that the underwriters of REIT IPOs will be able to charge investors the highest price they can to sell the shares, which they can do with an aggressive selling strategy. We can also observe this type of strategy in the mutual fund market. For example, Weiss (1989) documents that close-end fund shares are not bought *by* investors; instead, those shares are aggressively sold *to* investors.

The Fund-Like Organizational Structure

It is fair to say that a traditional REIT is similar to a closed-end fund, except that a REIT invests in real properties and mortgage related assets whereas a mutual fund invests in stocks and bonds. Mutual fund IPOs are neither underpriced nor overpriced; thus the IPO price of a mutual fund is very similar to the price of the mutual fund stock on the first trading day. With REITs having a fund-like structure, should we expect their IPOs to behave like those of closed-end fund shares? To answer this, we may need to compare the type of assets owned by a REIT with those owned by a closed-end fund.

REITs invest in infrequently traded real estate assets (properties and mortgages) and there is much uncertainty regarding their values, especially when compared with a mutual fund's investing in stocks with observable market values. Although sometimes a REIT's prospective investments are specified at the time of its IPO, the underlying assets generally have an uncertain market value because no price information is generated on the properties and mortgages by the real estate or capital markets at the time of the IPO. Given this valuation uncertainty, there is no strong support that REIT IPO pricing behavior should be similar to that of close-end fund stocks.

However, Chan, Stohs, and Wang (2001), analyzing the IPOs of real estate operating firms in Hong Kong and their non–real estate counterparts, find a significant underpricing of 16% and 19% on the first trading day for real estate–related IPOs and non–real estate IPOs, respectively. Similarly, in the United Kingdom, the level of underpricing for property company IPOs is found to be similar to that of all other firm IPOs (see Gerlich, Levis, and Venmore-Rowland 1995). The similarity of the IPO pricing of real estate firms and non–real estate firms in both the United Kingdom and Hong Kong suggests that the underlying assets of these firms do not cause a difference in the valuation of the IPOs. This finding implies that the large difference in IPO pricing observed for REITs versus operating firms in the United States may be attributable more to the organizational structure and management strategy of REITs than to the underlying real estate assets they hold.

Empirical Evidence on REIT IPOs

With the understanding that there are reasons for REIT IPOs to behave differently from industrial firm IPOs, we now turn to the academic evidence concerning the characteristics of the REIT IPO market and the initial performance of REIT IPOs. In our discussion we also compare the evidence for REITs with that for industrial firm IPOs.

Data Collection

At this moment, we cannot find a study that provides comprehensive evidence on REIT IPOs using data spanning the period 1970–2000. To accomplish this, we gather our own sample consisting of all initial public offerings of equity by REITs from 1970 to 2000 listed in various publications of the National Association of Real Estate Investment Trusts, Inc. (NAREIT). Note that there was no REIT IPO activity in 2000–2001 (as of June 30).

Initial offering prices and characteristics for the sample REITs are obtained from NAREIT publications and other sources, such as the Securities and Exchange Commission's *Registered Offerings Statistics* tape, the *Wall Street Journal,* the *Dow Jones News Retrieval Service Database, Lexis-Nexis Database, Standard and Poor's Stock Reports, Securities Data Company's* new issues database, *Investment Dealer's Digest,* the *Directory of Corporate Financing,* and the *Corporate Finance Sourcebook.* We also obtain IPO prospectuses (from Disclosure Info Centers) for those IPOs offered on a best-efforts basis and for those offerings that cannot be verified from at least two sources.

For each REIT, we use the CRSP database as well as the *Standard and Poor's Daily Stock Price Record* for NYSE, Amex, and over-the-counter (OTC) firms to obtain aftermarket price data for the first trading day and for the 200 subsequent trading days. The first day's price is taken to be the closing transaction price (NYSE, Amex, and Nasdaq national market stocks) or the bid price (OTC stocks) on the first day of public trading, which is the first day for which transaction volume is noted. REITs without aftermarket price data from these sources and those that are offered through a stock exchange or a stock distribution by the issuing firm are deleted from the initial sample. The final sample consists of 261 REIT IPOs with offering dates spanning the 1970–2000 period.

IPO Activities

Table 9.1 compares the volume, gross proceeds, and average initial-day return of REIT IPOs to those of industrial firm (non-REIT) IPOs during the 1970–2000 period. The data for non-REIT firms is based on an updated version (as of April 16, 2001) of Ibbotson, Sindelar, and Ritter's (1994) table and is available on Jay Ritter's website (http://bear.cba.ufl.edu/ritter). Figures 9.1 and 9.2 provide a visual comparison of the average gross proceeds and the percentage of IPOs in each year. What we observe from the table and the figures is that although both REITs and non-REIT firms exhibit similar offering trends, the fluctuation in volume is more substantial for REITs than for the non-REIT firms. There are five years (1974–78) with virtually no IPO activity in the REIT market (note that it was a rather cold period for non-REIT IPOs in general). We also observe low REIT IPO activity during the 1999–2001 period. For REITs, IPO activity was prominent in four periods: 1971–73, 1985–88, 1993–94, and 1997–98.[2]

Most noticeable is the 1993 and 1994 REIT IPO frenzy in response to institutional appetites for securitized real estate. The financial press noted that the relatively low yields on equities and fixed-income investments in

Table 9.1 Annual Summary of Initial Public Offerings for REITs and Non-REIT Firms (1970–2000)

	REITs			Non-REITs		
	Number of Offerings	Average Gross Proceeds ($millions)	Average Initial-Day Return (%)	Number of Offerings	Average Gross Proceeds ($millions)	Average Initial-Day Return (%)
1970	1	61	–0.63	358	2	–0.70
1971	6	30	3.00	391	4	21.20
1972	10	17	–4.55	562	5	7.50
1973	6	10	–7.32	105	3	–17.80
1974	0	—	—	9	6	–7.00
1975	0	—	—	14	19	–1.90
1976	0	—	—	35	7	2.90
1977	0	—	—	35	4	21.00
1978	0	—	—	50	5	25.70
1979	1	10	–2.44	81	5	24.60
1980	1	30	–5.83	238	6	49.40
1981	1	50	0.00	438	7	16.80
1982	3	72	5.67	198	7	20.30
1983	2	34	0.00	848	16	20.80
1984	6	40	–1.42	516	8	11.50
1985	28	97	–2.41	507	21	12.40
1986	16	57	–4.52	953	18	10.00

1987	6	90	−3.89	630	22	10.40
1988	12	80	−3.50	223	20	9.80
1989	3	167	−14.17	210	27	12.60
1990	3	117	−24.58	172	28	14.50
1991	3	69	−0.25	365	44	14.70
1992	6	146	1.24	513	45	12.50
1993	45	188	3.19	665	46	15.20
1994	44	150	1.47	567	34	13.40
1995	7	132	1.98	571	52	20.50
1996	7	162	−0.16	831	52	17.00
1997	25	249	7.91	603	56	13.20
1998	17	132	1.23	357	98	20.20
1999	2	146	1.27	543	121	66.70
2000	0	—	—	449	148	55.50
2001	0	—	—	n.a.	n.a.	n.a.
1970–1979	24	20	−3.10	1,640	4	9.00
1980–1989	78	80	−3.14	4,761	16	15.30
1990–2000	159	172	2.36	5,636	65	23.80
1970–2000	261	130	0.21	12,037	37	18.48

Source: For data on the REIT sample, refer to the appendix. For data on non-REIT firms, see Jay R. Ritter's website (http://bear.cba.ufl.edu/ritter) as of April 16, 2001. The data for REITs include best- efforts offerings while the data for non-REIT firms in 1988–2000 exclude best-efforts offerings.

Note: Initial returns are computed as the percentage return from the offering price to the end-of-the-first-day bid or transaction price, without adjusting for market movements. The number of REIT IPOs reported in year 2001 is as of October 31.

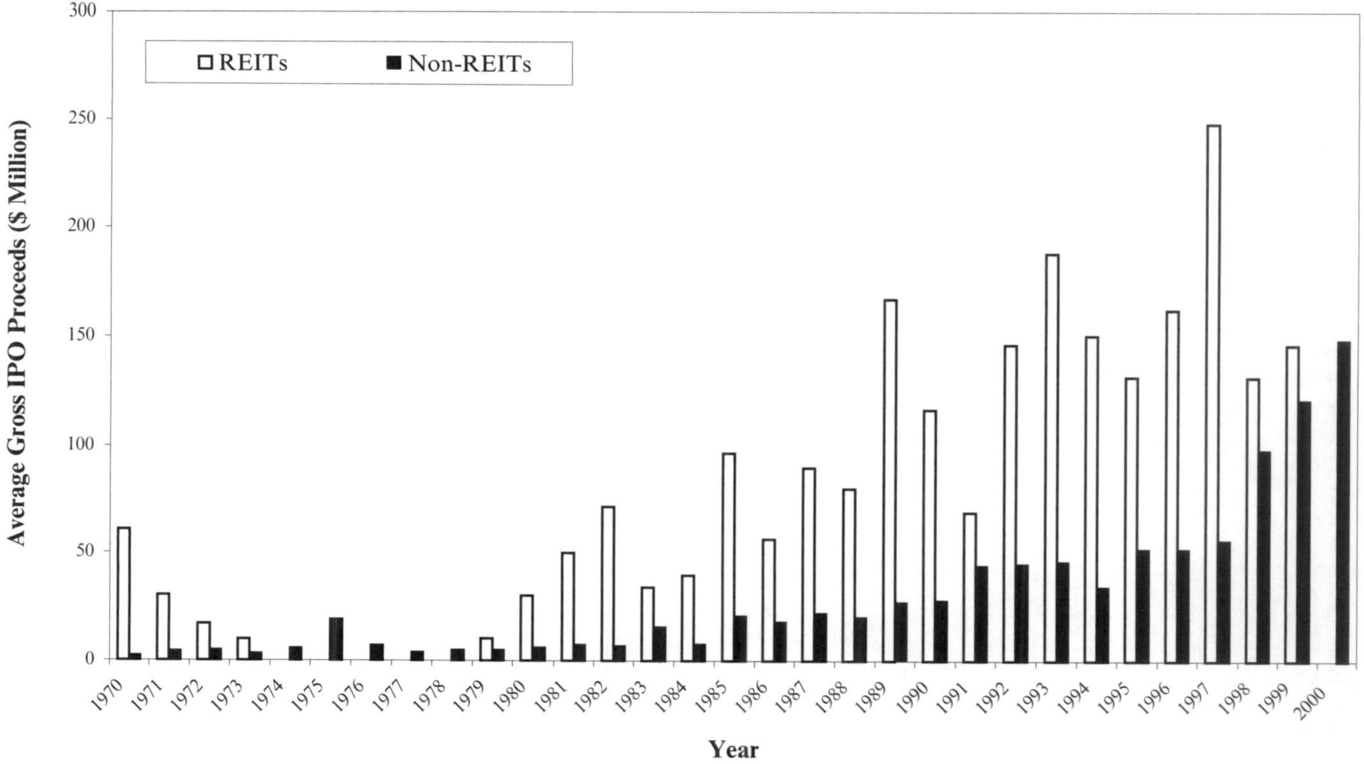

Figure 9.1 Average Gross IPO Proceeds

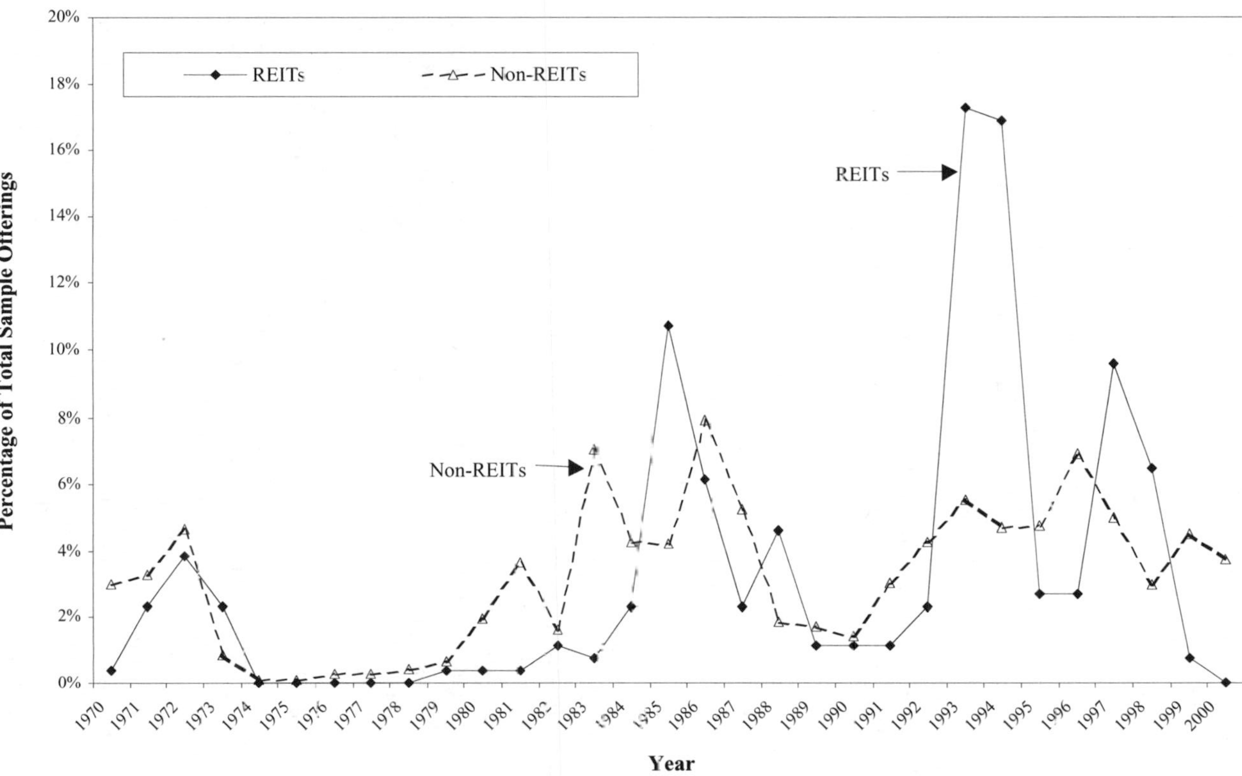

Figure 9.2 Percentage of REIT and Non-REIT Offerings

the early 1990s increased the attractiveness of real estate securities. A *Business Week* article by Woolley (1993) quoted Anthony Downs, a Brookings Institution senior fellow, as saying, "These people are so eager to buy yield, they're creating excess demand, which is leading to a supply to meet that demand." The article also noted that the net assets in the seven real estate funds tracked by Morningstar, Inc. swelled almost 200%, from $259 million at the end of 1992 to $764 million in September 1993.

In 1997, heightened investor interest in REIT stocks returned. NAREIT president and chief executive officer Steven Wechsler attributed this capital-raising success to investors' recognition of the growth prospects of REITs (*PR Newswire,* January 22, 1998). It could also be that a number of investors were looking at REITs as a safer haven, given the volatile stock market conditions in 1997.

However, the number of REIT offerings dropped in 1999 to two (a fall of 88% from the previous year) while the number of non-REIT stock offerings increased by about 52% from the previous year. This could be due, in part, to investors' fearing a slower economy because of rising interest rates, and in part to investors' fascination with growth stocks such as Internet and technology stocks. In mid-2000, with the crash in technology issues, the REIT sector again became popular with investors looking for high cash-dividend yields in a volatile stock market. However, as of October 2001 there were still no new REIT IPOs on the market. A press article noted that this could be due to low REIT stock prices' making it costly for REITs to raise capital through stock offerings. Instead, REITs resorted to using joint ventures (partnering with an institutional or outside developers) to raise equity dollars through sources other than public capital markets (*Los Angeles Times,* May 30, 2000).

Our data in table 9.1 also show that the total proceeds of REIT-industry initial offerings represent a significant share of the total initial offerings in the stock market. Between 1970 and 2000, 261 REITs alone raised a total of about $34 billion from initial public equity offerings (excluding private placements) while 12,037 IPOs of non-REIT industrial firms raised approximately $449 billion. The total dollar amount raised by the 261 REIT IPOs is therefore about 7% of the total amount raised by all IPOs (including REITs and non-REIT firms). As table 9.1 shows, the average of gross IPO proceeds for REITs is about $130 million over the 1970–2000 period. This amount is more than three times the $37 million reported for non-REIT industrial-firm IPOs.

The evidence so far indicates that REITs use IPOs more frequently than other firms in the stock market. Except for the 1999–2000 period, REIT IPO activities move closely with the stock market. They raise more funds when the IPO markets are hot and less when the markets are cold. When REITs raise equity using IPOs, the size of their offerings is significantly larger than those of industrial firm IPOs. This shows that real estate is truly a capital-intensive business. With these observations in mind, we are ready to examine the price performance of REIT IPOs.

Pricing of REIT IPOs

It is well documented in the finance literature that investors in IPOs, on average, earn large returns of around 18% on the first trading day. The underpricing result, however, does not apply to special types of firms such as close-end mutual funds and master limited partnerships (MLPs). For example, Muscarella (1988) and Michaely and Shaw (1994) find that MLP IPOs, which have limited institutional ownership, are less underpriced than operating company IPOs. Muscarella further finds significant average price declines of –0.53% and –0.19% for eight hotel/motel MLPs and eight oil/gas MLPs, respectively. Weiss (1989) and Peavy (1990) also do not find significant underpricing for close-end fund IPOs. (Peavy attributes the insignificant initial-day return to the lack of uncertainty about the underlying value of the funds' assets.)

Wang, Chan, and Gau (1992) are the first to report the anomalous pricing of REIT IPOs. They show that, unlike operating company IPOs, REIT IPOs suffered a significant 2.82% percent price decline on the first trading day during the 1971–98 period. Ling and Ryngaert (1997) extend Wang, Chan, and Gau's study to the post-1990 period, finding that equity REIT IPOs in the 1991–94 period are no longer overpriced but appreciate by 3.6% on the first trading day. Given Ling and Ryngaert's evidence, there seems to be a need to analyze the performance of REIT IPOs after 1994 to see if the trend continues.

Table 9.1 shows the average initial-day return for REIT and non-REIT IPOs in each year and each subperiod during the 1970–2000 period. It is clear from the table that REIT IPOs are slightly overpriced before 1990 and then slightly underpriced in the post-1990 period. These findings conform to the results of both Wang, Chan, and Gau (1992) and Ling and Ryngaert (1997). However, if we consider the whole 1970–2000 period, we find no significant over- or underpricing of REIT IPOs (mean return = 0.21%). Moreover, the average initial-day return for REITs throughout the period is still substantially below that for non-REIT firms (mean return = 18.48%).

A number of studies on non-REIT IPOs have found that the degree of underpricing is cyclical.[3] Do the initial-day returns for REIT IPOs behave the same way? Figure 9.3 shows the relationship between the volume of REIT IPOs and the average initial-day return for REITs during the 1970–2000 period, while Figure 9.4 compares the average initial-day return for REIT IPOs with that for non-REIT IPOs. Although there are certain periods in the pre-1990 period in which we witness a temporary boom in REIT IPO offerings, the issues are still overpriced in all except two years. Furthermore, there is no observable pattern in the relationship between the average

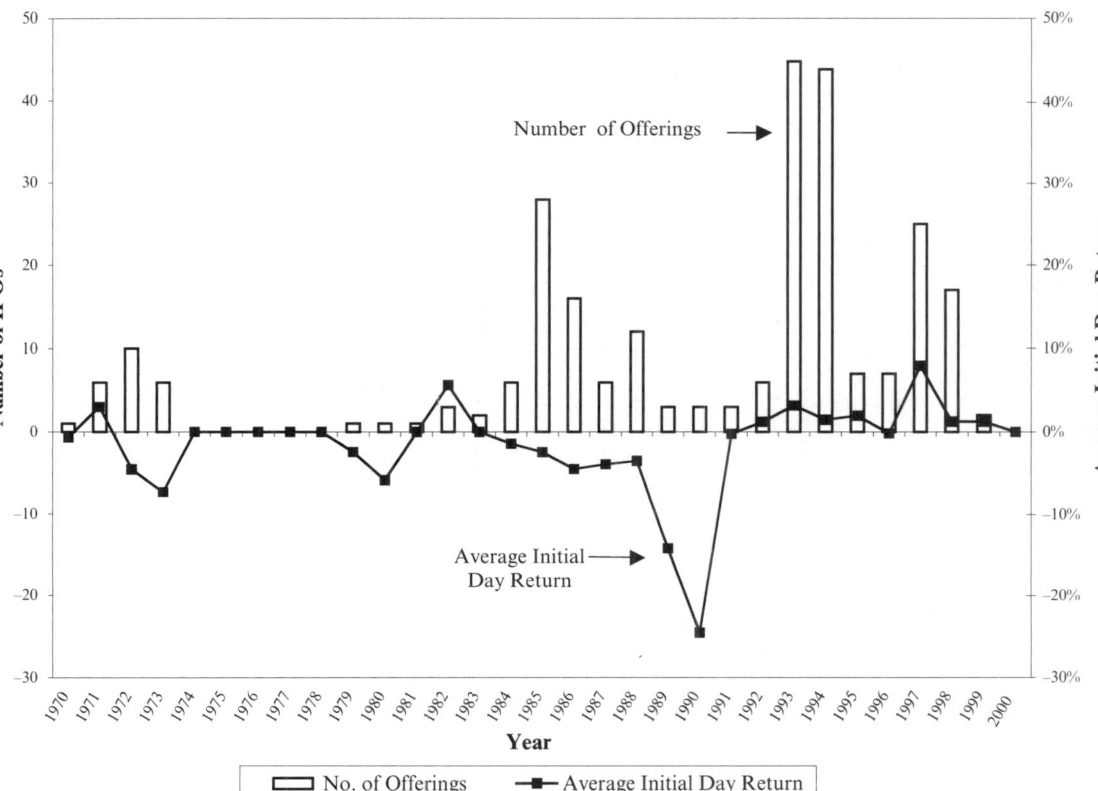

Figure 9.3 Number of REIT Initial Public Offerings

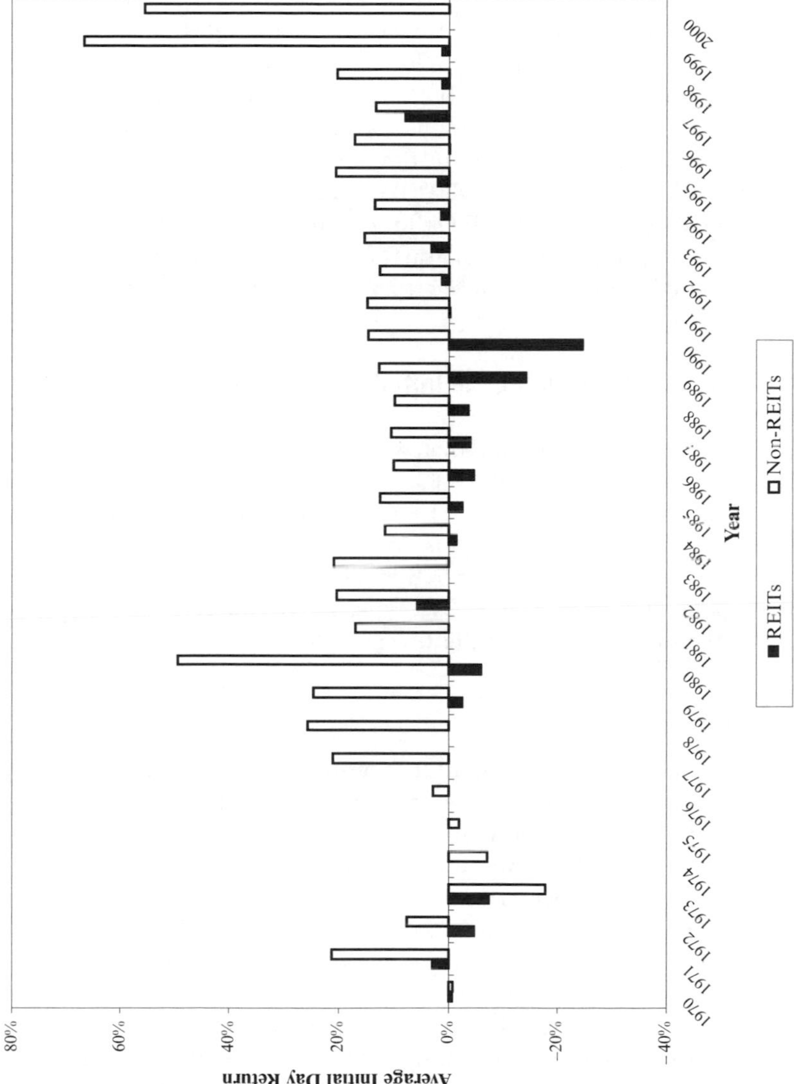

Figure 9.4 Average Initial Day Return

level of overpricing of REIT IPOs and the volume of new issues. Over the same period, overpricing is exhibited in only four years in the early 1970s for industrial firm IPOs. Therefore, we see no evidence from the figures that greater REIT IPS underpricing is associated with a hot issue market and no distinct cyclical pattern of overpricing.

However, the most important question is not whether REIT IPOs are, on average, under- or overpriced. Table 9.1 clearly demonstrates that REIT IPOs perform much worse than industrial firm IPOs. If an investor buys a REIT IPO, he or she can expect to earn a 0.21% return on the first day of trading. However, if the investor buys an industrial firm IPO, he or she can expect an 18.48% return on the first trading day. Given this, the most important question to ask is who would buy REIT IPOs? Investors are obviously much better off buying industrial firm IPOs. Indeed, the initial-day return differences between REIT and industrial firm IPOs are large and persistent over a long time period. Why haven't investors learned from their past experience?

Factors Determining the Initial-Day Return

Wang, Chan, and Gau (1992) find that, while the average first-day return of REITs is negative during the 1971–88 period, there is a large variation in first-trading-day returns among REIT IPOs. Although the authors find that the overpricing result of REIT IPOs is invariant to the offer price and issue size, they also report that the distribution method, stock exchange, underwriter reputation, investor type, asset type, and firm duration are important in determining whether a REIT IPO is under- or overpriced.

Underwriter and Stock Listing

Wang, Chan, and Gau (1992) report that prestigious underwriters, on average, are associated with less overpriced REIT IPOs during the 1971–88 period. In other words, underwriters with good reputations do not overprice the REIT IPOs they underwrite. Only those underwriters without reputations to maintain overprice the IPOs they underwrite. Ling and Ryngaert (1997) report that the variance in the initial-day returns of REIT IPOs is higher if the IPOs are underwritten by less prestigious underwriters. Wang, Chan, and Gau also document that REIT IPOs traded over the counter are more overpriced than REITs traded on the NYSE and Amex. Moreover, the listing requirements are more stringent for the NYSE than for Nasdaq, so stocks listed on the former are more closely scrutinized in the IPO stage than those on the latter.

This evidence gives a strong indication that the overpricing of some of the REIT IPOs could be due to inefficiency in the market. Those underwriters who do not need to worry about their reputations might dump REIT shares onto the market as long as they can find demand for them. In other words, the REIT IPO market may not provide the necessary monitoring function to ensure that investors fully understand the value of each issue. The fact that most REIT IPO overpricing occurred on Nasdaq, where it is easier for a firm to list its stock, gives support to this inefficiency argument. However, even if an underwriter would want to dump REIT IPO stocks in the market, someone has to be willing to buy the stocks before a transaction can occur. Who the buyers of REIT IPOs are becomes an important issue for us to examine.

Institutional Investors

Table 9.2 compares the institutional holdings of REIT IPOs with those of non-REIT IPOs. We can see a significant increase in institutional participation in the REIT IPO market from the pre-1990 period to the post-1990 period. In the pre-1990 period, institutional investors, on average, held only about 7% of the common shares of newly traded REITs in the first quarter following the IPO. The average holding increased to about 9% by the end of the second quarter following the IPO. In the 1990–99 period, the average institutional holding was around 39% in the first quarter of the IPO and around 47% in the second quarter of the IPO.

Wang, Chan, and Gau (1992) show that the REIT IPOs with higher institutional holdings are not overpriced, suggesting that institutional investors do not overpay. Ling and Ryngaert (1997) further find that REIT IPOs issued between 1991 and 1994 are significantly underpriced if more than 30% percent of the IPO stocks are bought by institutional investors. In general, the evidence on institutional participation in REIT IPOs in the pre-1990 period is similar to Weiss's (1989) finding that few institutional investors are interested in close-end fund IPOs. Weiss documents, using a sample of 64 close-end funds, that the average proportion of equity owned by institutional investors at the end of the first quarter following the IPOs is only 3.5%.

Wang, Chan, and Gau (1992) also show that, on average, institutional investors participate more in issues that are larger, that are distributed under firm commitment contracts, and that are underwritten by prestigious underwriters. They also seem to invest more in the traditional type of REIT (infinite-life) and in those with more observable assets (equity REITs and fully or partially specified REITs). There is little institutional participation in best-efforts REIT IPOs. These results also hold for data drawn from the 1970–99 period.

The Distribution Method

Table 9.3 shows that, between 1970 and 2000, approximately 14.5% of the REIT IPOs were made on a best-efforts basis. This percentage does not deviate too much from that reported for industrial firm IPOs (see Ritter 1987

Table 9.2 Comparison of Institutional Holdings among REIT IPOs, All REITs and All Stocks (1970–2000)

	Number of Initial Public Offerings	Average Initial-day Return (%)	Average Institutional Holdings (%)			
			First Quarter of IPO	Second Quarter of IPO	For All REITs	For All Publicly Traded Stocks
1970	1	−0.63	n.a.	n.a.	n.a.	n.a.
1971	6	3.00	n.a.	n.a.	n.a.	n.a.
1972	10	−4.55	n.a.	n.a.	n.a.	n.a.
1973	6	−7.32	n.a.	n.a.	n.a.	n.a.
1974	—	—	—	—	n.a.	n.a.
1975	—	—	—	—	n.a.	n.a.
1976	—	—	—	—	n.a.	n.a.
1977	—	—	—	—	n.a.	n.a.
1978	—	—	—	—	n.a.	n.a.
1979	1	−2.44	n.a.	n.a.	n.a.	n.a.
1980	1	−5.83	0.10	0.30	n.a.	n.a.
1981	1	0.00	5.00	11.00	9.74	14.60
1982	3	5.67	6.00	7.68	9.75	14.70
1983	2	0.00	0.00	0.00	10.31	17.10
1984	6	−1.42	12.67	2.58	11.01	16.80
1985	28	−2.41	12.06	14.30	12.59	18.60

1986	16	−4.52	1.43	7.18	13.94	20.20
1987	6	−3.89	9.51	14.84	14.50	20.40
1988	12	−3.50	2.29	2.04	14.06	20.10
1989	3	−14.17	0.11	0.13	15.36	21.30
1990	3	−24.58	0.00	0.00	14.37	21.90
1991	3	−0.25	10.28	11.28	15.04	22.90
1992	6	1.24	29.50	38.33	13.77	24.50
1993	45	3.19	41.29	50.91	19.43	26.00
1994	44	1.47	36.85	45.90	26.40	26.50
1995	7	1.98	38.59	47.39	31.27	27.70
1996	7	−0.16	49.90	44.49	32.89	29.10
1997	25	7.91	44.28	50.74	38.49	29.80
1998	17	1.23	45.95	54.83	40.33	31.00
1999	2	1.27	33.38	39.41	38.76	31.20
2000	0	—	—	—	n.a.	n.a.
1970–1979	24	−3.10	—	—	—	—
1980–1989	78	−3.14	6.98	8.71	12.62	18.50
1990–1999	159	2.36	39.38	47.15	28.89	27.48
1970–1999	261	0.21	26.08	31.33	23.04	23.91

Source: Authors' own computations. For data on institutional holdings, *Spectrum 3:13(f) Institutional Stock Holdings Survey* published by Computer Directions Advisors, Inc.

Table 9.3 Average Initial-Day Return and Institutional Holdings of REIT IPOs, by Distribution Method (1970–2000)

	Firm Commitment			Best Efforts		
	Average Initial-Day Return (%)	Average Institutional Holdings (%)[a]	Number of Offerings	Average Initial-Day Return (%)	Average Institutional Holdings (%)[a]	Number of Offerings
1970	–0.63	n.a.	1	—	—	0
1971	3.00	n.a.	6	—	—	0
1972	–4.55	n.a.	10	—	—	0
1973	–7.32	n.a.	6	—	—	0
1974	—	—	0	—	—	0
1975	—	—	0	—	—	0
1976	—	—	0	—	—	0
1977	—	—	0	—	—	0
1978	—	—	0	—	—	0
1979	–2.44	n.a.	1	—	—	0
1980	–5.83	0.10	1	—	—	0
1981	0.00	5.00	1	—	—	0
1982	0.00	9.00	1	8.50	4.50	2
1983	5.00	0.00	1	–5.00	0.00	1
1984	–1.42	12.67	6	—	—	0

1985	−1.08	14.75	22	−7.29	0.26	6
1986	−0.73	2.18	10	−10.84	0.17	6
1987	−4.58	14.26	4	−2.50	0.00	2
1988	0.53	2.49	8	−11.56	1.95	4
1989	—	—	0	−14.17	0.11	3
1990	—	—	0	−24.58	0.00	3
1991	−0.25	10.28	3	—	—	0
1992	1.24	29.50	6	—	—	0
1993	3.19	41.29	45	—	—	0
1994	3.49	40.63	40	−18.75	0.00	4
1995	1.98	38.59	7	—	—	0
1996	1.06	49.90	6	−7.50	n.a.	1
1997	7.91	44.28	25	—	—	0
1998	1.99	45.95	16	−10.94	n.a.	1
1999	1.27	33.38	2	—	—	0
2000	—	—	0	—	—	0
1970–2000	1.81	32.76	228	−10.84	0.64	33

Source: Authors' own computations based on the sample described in the appendix. For data on institutional holdings, *Spectrum 3:13(f) Institutional Stock Holdings Survey*, published by Computer Directions Advisers, Inc.

[a] First quarter of IPO.

and Johnson and Miller 1988). The table also shows that IPOs exhibit the greatest overpricing level when best-efforts contracts are used. The mean initial-day return of the best-efforts IPOs is around –10.84%, whereas that for firm-commitment IPOs is 1.81%.

This result contrasts with Ritter's (1987) and Chalk and Peavy's (1987) findings that the level of underpricing, on average, is greater for industrial firm IPOs using best-efforts contracts. Note that in the REIT market, there are many fewer institutional investors in best-efforts IPOs than in firm-commitment IPOs. This probably explains the overpricing result for best-efforts REIT IPOs. Again, since only those REIT IPOs that cannot attract the attention of the main players in the market use best-efforts contracts, overpriced REIT IPOs tend to be those that are neglected by the stock market and that are aggressively sold to individual investors.

Valuation Uncertainty

Table 9.4 presents the initial-day returns and average institutional holdings of REIT IPOs, classified by asset type. During the 1970–2000 period, whereas equity REITs are slightly underpriced by 1.2%, mortgage REITs are slightly overpriced with an initial-day return of –0.78%. The initial-day return of hybrid REITs is –6.72%, but because the sample is relatively small (eight firms), we will not devote much attention to this type of REIT. It is interesting to note that the institutional holdings in equity REITs are much higher than that in mortgage REITs, although institutional participation in mortgage REITs has increased quite significantly in recent years.

Prior to 1993, some of the REIT IPOs do not specify the properties they will acquire. For REITs with unspecified property portfolios, investors should have more uncertainty regarding the underlying portfolio of the trust and the management's investment strategy. Wang, Chan, and Gau (1992) examine the IPO pricing of REITs that do not specify the properties they intend to acquire with the IPO proceeds at the offering stage. For the 70 identified IPOs during their sample period (1971–88), 36 fully or partially specify their holdings and 34 do not. The authors find that unspecified REIT IPOs, on average, are more overpriced than fully or partially specified IPOs. This evidence also indicates that uncertainty about a REIT's value might lead to the overpricing of its IPOs.

Fund Duration

Wang, Chan, and Gau (1992) also analyze the average initial-day return of finite-life versus infinite-life REITs. These REITs are used as proxies to measure investor uncertainty over whether the REIT's share price will reflect its underlying asset value. The finance literature tells us that the stock value of a close-end mutual fund might be less than the value of the stocks the fund owns, because investors worry that they cannot freely sell the

Table 9.4 Average Initial-Day Return and Institutional Holdings of REIT IPOs, by Asset Type (1970–2000)

	Equity REITs			Hybrid REITs			Mortgage REITs		
	Average Initial-Day Return (%)	Average Institutional Holdings (%)[a]	Number of Offerings	Average Initial-Day Return (%)	Average Institutional Holdings (%)[a]	Number of Offerings	Average Initial-Day Return (%)	Average Institutional Holdings (%)[a]	Number of Offerings
1970	—	—	0	—	—	0	−0.63	n.a.	1
1971	7.87	n.a.	3	—	—	0	−0.63	n.a.	1
1972	−20.32	n.a.	2	—	—	0	−0.88	n.a.	2
1973	—	—	0	—	—	0	—	—	0
1974	—	—	0	—	—	0	—	—	0
1975	—	—	0	—	—	0	—	—	0
1976	—	—	0	—	—	0	—	—	0
1977	—	—	0	—	—	0	—	—	0
1978	—	—	0	—	—	0	—	—	0
1979	−2.44	n.a.	1	—	—	0	—	—	0
1980	−5.83	0.10	1	—	—	0	—	—	0
1981	—	—	0	—	—	0	0.00	5.00	1
1982	0.00	9.00	1	—	—	0	8.50	4.50	2
1983	0.00	0.00	2	—	—	0	—	—	0
1984	−1.60	17.00	3	−2.50	8.00	1	−0.63	8.50	2
1985	−2.19	14.19	16	−1.25	16.00	1	−2.84	8.27	11
1986	−6.95	2.29	8	1.25	0.00	1	−2.56	0.64	7
1987	−4.58	13.01	4	—	—	0	−2.50	2.50	2
1988	−15.00	3.50	2	−0.63	5.50	2	−1.34	1.03	8

(*continued*)

Table 9.4 *Continued*

	Equity REITs			Hybrid REITs			Mortgage REITs		
	Average Initial-Day Return (%)	Average Institutional Holdings (%)[a]	Number of Offerings	Average Initial-Day Return (%)	Average Institutional Holdings (%)[a]	Number of Offerings	Average Initial-Day Return (%)	Average Institutional Holdings (%)[a]	Number of Offerings
1989	—	—	0	−20.00	0.04	1	−11.25	0.15	2
1990	−20.00	0.00	1	−30.00	0.00	1	−23.75	0.00	1
1991	−0.25	10.28	3	—	—	0	—	—	0
1992	3.04	32.67	3	0.00	35.00	1	−0.84	22.00	2
1993	3.42	43.71	42	—	—	0	0.00	7.33	3
1994	1.47	36.85	44	—	—	0	—	—	0
1995	0.67	40.10	5	—	—	0	5.24	34.83	2
1996	−0.16	49.90	7	—	—	0	—	—	0
1997	7.92	44.65	18	—	—	0	7.87	43.33	7
1998	4.47	54.03	8	—	—	0	−1.64	38.88	9
1999	1.27	33.38	2	—	—	0	—	—	0
2000	—	—	0	—	—	0	—	—	0
1970–2000	1.20	34.14	176	−6.72	8.76	8	−0.78	15.74	63

Source: Authors' own computations based on the sample described in the appendix. For data on institutional holdings, *Spectrum 3:13(f) Institutional Stock Holdings Survey* , published by Computer Directions Advisors, Inc.

[a] First quarter

stocks owned by the mutual fund when they think they should. Thus the inability of investors to control the mutual fund's decisions penalizes the fund's value.

Finite-life REITs (with a plan to liquidate their holdings at some specified future date) are designed to ensure that their shares will eventually be liquidated at a price close to asset value. If investors worry that the fund-like structure of REITs might impose a cost on shareholders, then they should worry less about finite-life REITs, which will sell all their properties at some particular point in time.

Contrary to our expectation, table 9.5 reports that the initial-day return of the 41 finite-life REITs during the 1970–2000 period is –9.03%. This evidence seems to indicate that the pricing behavior of REIT IPOs cannot be explained by their fund-like structure. Again, we can see from the table that the level of institutional participation in the two types of REIT has something to do with their IPO pricing. There is much more institutional participation in infinite-life REITs than in the finite-life variety. The lack of attention from the main players in the REIT stock market, again, probably explains the large magnitude of overpricing of finite-life REIT IPOs.

The Changing Nature of REITs: Pre- and Post-1990

Table 9.1 clearly indicates that the explosion in REIT security offerings did not occur until after 1992. We also know that the 102 REIT IPOs in the 1970 to 1989 period are significantly overpriced (also see Wang, Chan, and Gau 1992) whereas the 159 REIT IPOs in the 1990s are significantly underpriced (also see Ling and Ryngaert 1997). What are the reasons behind the explosive growth and the change in the pricing strategy of REIT IPOs?

Ling and Ryngaert (1997) attribute the initial-day underpricing of recent REIT IPOs to greater valuation uncertainty due to changes in the characteristics of post-1990 REITs and to greater institutional involvement in the recent REIT IPO market. Specifically, the explosive growth may be tied to changes in the organizational and ownership structure of REITs in the post-1990 period. These factors made it necessary for REITs to underprice their IPOs to ensure that individual investors would continue to participate in the REIT IPO market.

Changes in Organizational Structure

As noted in chapter 2, prior to the Tax Reform Act of 1986 REITs were precluded from managing their own properties. Most of the early REITs employed advisory firms to determine their management and investment policies. In the post-1990 period, however, REITs have become increasingly like fully integrated operating companies pursuing the goals of strategic advantage and long-term profitability. The umbrella partnership

Table 9.5 Average Initial-Day Return and Institutional Holdings of REIT IPOs, by Duration (1970–2000)

	Infinite-Life REITs			Finite-Life REITs		
	Average Initial-Day Return (%)	Average Institutional Holdings (%)[a]	Number of Offerings	Average Initial-Day Return (%)	Average Institutional Holdings (%)[a]	Number of Offerings
1970	−0.63	n.a.	1	—	—	0
1971	3.00	n.a.	6	—	—	0
1972	−4.55	n.a.	10	—	—	0
1973	−7.32	n.a.	6	—	—	0
1974	—	—	0	—	—	0
1975	—	—	0	—	—	0
1976	—	—	0	—	—	0
1977	—	—	0	—	—	0
1978	—	—	0	—	—	0
1979	−2.44	n.a.	1	—	—	0
1980	−5.83	0.10	1	—	—	0
1981	0.00	5.00	1	—	—	0
1982	5.67	6.00	3	—	—	0
1983	5.00	0.00	1	−5.00	0.00	1
1984	−1.21	13.60	5	−2.50	8.00	1

1985	−1.13	18.23	15	−3.90	4.36	13
1986	−2.48	2.39	9	−7.14	0.19	7
1987	−4.58	14.26	4	−2.50	0.00	2
1988	0.00	2.40	7	−8.40	2.16	5
1989	—	—	0	−14.17	0.11	3
1990	—	—	0	−24.58	0.00	3
1991	−1.88	12.00	2	3.00	6.85	1
1992	1.83	34.40	5	−1.67	5.00	1
1993	3.27	42.20	44	0.00	1.00	1
1994	4.02	39.61	41	−33.33	0.00	3
1995	1.98	38.59	7	—	—	0
1996	−0.16	49.90	7	—	—	0
1997	7.91	44.28	25	—	—	0
1998	1.23	45.95	17	—	—	0
1999	1.27	33.38	2	—	—	0
2000	—	—	0	—	—	0
1970–2000	1.94	34.24	220	−9.03	2.19	41

Source: Authors' own computations based on the sample described in the appendix. For data on institutional holdings, *Spectrum 3:13(f) Institutional Stock Holdings Survey* , published by Computer Directions Advisors, Inc.

[a] First quarter.

REIT (UPREIT) structure, which essentially combines the investment features of a partnership with REIT ownership (see chapter 3 for details on this structure), represents a new breed of REITs.[4] These newer REITs are managed internally rather than externally, which helps align the interests of management and shareholders and brings the REIT structure closer to that of an operating firm. As Ling and Ryngaert (1997) argue, this restructuring leads to more ex ante uncertainty about the firm's value when compared to pre-1990 REITs.

Since REITs can be viewed as operating companies after 1990, it is reasonable to argue that their IPO pricing strategy during that time should resemble that of industrial firm IPOs; if this were the case we would expect to see a change in the pricing behavior of REIT IPOs in the 1990s, which is indeed what we have observed in the real world. However, while this argument makes some sense, it cannot explain why the average initial-day return of REIT IPOs is only 2.36% during the 1990–2000 period, whereas the initial-day return of industrial firm IPOs during the same period is a much higher 23.80%.

Ownership of REIT Shares

The ownership of REIT shares has also shifted over time. Many more institutional investors hold REIT stocks in the post-1990 period than they held in the pre-1990 period (see chapter 6 for detailed information). It is also reasonable to suspect that the underpricing result observed in the post-1990 period is attributable to the increased presence of institutional investors in the REIT IPO market.

Again, however, we doubt that this is the case—that the increase in institutional investors in the REIT IPO market actually solved all the market's problems. During the 1990s, in terms of percentage of stock ownership, institutional investors bought more REIT IPO stocks than industrial firm IPO stocks. However, during that period, the initial-day return of REIT IPOs (2.36%) is still much lower than that of industrial firm IPOs (23.80%). Clearly the increase in institutional ownership in the REIT IPO market is not a complete explanation for the difference in REIT versus industrial firm IPO behavior.

The Lesson We Learned

As we have discussed, investors in the REIT IPO market during the 1970–89 period suffered losses. No one can find a reason to explain why REIT IPOs before 1990 could be sold at a premium over their first-day trading prices while industrial IPOs had to sell at a big discount to attract buyers. The only possible reason identified by Wang, Chan, and Gau (1992) is that the REIT IPO market was inefficient and that REIT IPOs were aggressively sold to uninformed investors who lacked a clear idea about the value of the shares of REIT IPOs.

After Wang, Chan, and Gau circulated their initial findings in early 1989, the REIT IPO market became inactive for two years—there were no new REIT IPOs in 1989 and 1990. (The issues listed in table 9.1 for 1989 and 1990 are best-efforts contracts, which were issued in 1987 and 1988 and subsequently completed in 1989 and 1990). After two years of stagnation, the industry came up with a new breed of REIT, which led to an explosion of REIT IPOs and greater institutional participation over the next couple of years. The REIT IPO market was hot and players in the industry were happy. Martin (1997) notes that during this period many pension-plan sponsors were excitedly adding REIT shares to their portfolios, and investors were paying as much as 20–40% above the values of many REIT properties. For example, Spieker Properties, a REIT that excelled at finding bargain properties before they hit the market, commanded a 20–40% premium over the value of the office towers and industrial buildings it owned in the San Francisco area.

While some participants in the market believed that this new breed of REITs could solve all the problems the industry faced, reality now indicates otherwise. The REIT IPO market has slowed down significantly since 1999. Judging from this evidence, it is clear that the change in organizational structure and the participation of institutional investors did not solve the problems.

Indeed, we have further concerns as to whether this new type of REIT can be the solution in the longer run. We believe, judging from the empirical evidence presented in table 9.1, that the REIT IPO problem (i.e., low initial-day returns to investors) has not been solved by the introduction of the new type of REIT. During the 1970–79 period, the average initial-day return of REIT IPOs and industrial firm IPOs was –3.10% and 9.00%, respectively. This represents a spread of 12.10% between returns on REIT IPOs and industrial firm IPOs. This spread was 18.44% during the 1980–89 period and 21.44% during the 1990–2000 period. It is clear that, while the change in organizational structure and the increase in institutional participation alter the initial-day returns of REIT IPOs from negative to positive, the average return of REIT IPOs is still far below that of industrial firm IPOs. In other words, in terms of the magnitude of initial-day returns, we cannot see any improvement if an investor chooses a REIT IPO over an industrial firm IPO. (In fact, the situation seems to be the worst in the 1990–2000 period.)

At this moment, we still do not recommend that our readers invest in REIT IPOs. If an investor is interested in the IPO market, he or she should invest in the IPOs of industrial firms, where the return is much higher than that for REIT IPOs. We would also like to know whether the problem of REIT IPOs will continue in the future. The answer could be a no. We observe that whenever there is a change in the law governing REITs, there will be an increase in IPO activities following the change. It is quite possible that the next explosion of IPO activities will be around 2004. At that time, because of the REIT Modernization Act that goes into effect in 2001, more REITs will resemble operating companies more closely and another new breed of REITs might emerge to attract investors to the REIT market.

We believe that the increasing presence of informed institutional investors in the REIT market together with the availability of more databases, both about REITs and their underlying assets, may help mitigate the information asymmetry between the REITs and their investors. We believe that once investors know more about REIT IPOs, these IPOs should behave just like those of industrial firms. This means that REITs will have to offer IPO stocks at lower prices (i.e., underprice the stocks) in order to attract investors to their market. Until this happens, we can offer only one piece of advice to the reader: If you cannot obtain the same return in the REIT IPO market as in the industrial firm IPO market, you should buy REIT stocks only after they have been listed in the stock market for a period of time.

Price Performance Following IPOs

The finance literature tells us that IPO firms have poor aftermarket performance compared with other firms. Specifically, the gains from the first day of trading are lost in subsequent price declines over a 100–250 trading-day period after the IPO. These studies indicate that, regardless of whether the initial-day return is significantly positive (as for industrial firm IPOs) or insignificant (as for mutual funds), the new issues, on average, underperform the market in the long run.

Wang, Chan, and Gau (1992) show that the stock performance of REIT IPOs over days 2 to 190 is consistent with the performance reported for industrial firm IPOs. They find that REIT stocks substantially underperform the market during the first 190 trading days after the IPO, and that best-efforts IPOs substantially underperform the market to a greater degree than firm-commitment IPOs do. Ling and Ryngaert (1997), however, find that REIT IPOs issued during the 1991–94 period did not underperform seasoned equity REITs in the first 100 trading days after issue.

Figure 9.5 plots the cumulative return performance of the first 200 trading days following the IPOs of 261 REITs. As we can easily see from the graph, investors would not have done very well if they had invested in all of the 261 REIT IPOs. They would have earned only about a 3% return over the first 200 trading days. However, if investors had invested the same amount of money in a market index (which consists of all stocks traded on the NYSE, Amex, and Nasdaq), they could have earned approximately a 17% return.[5] Apparently, investing in REIT IPOs is not a good idea, given the low initial-day return and the non-stellar return performance over the first 200 days of trading.[6]

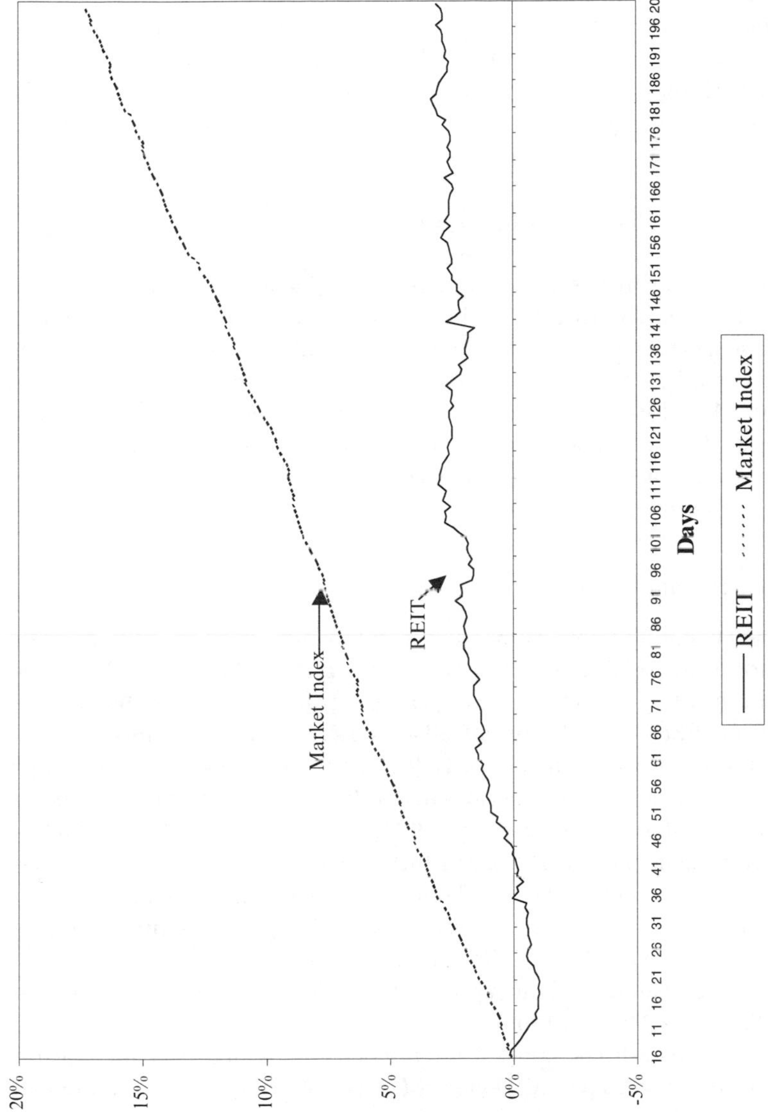

Figure 9.5 Long-run Performance of REIT IPO

However, Shelor and Anderson (1998) find a positive side to REIT IPOs when they examine changes in REIT operating performance following an initial public offering. They observe an enhancement in the value of the underlying assets of the REIT following an IPO. Unlike previous analyses of industrial firms, the authors find that REITs experience significant increases in their return on assets (ROA) and selected measures of financial performance. However, it is a mystery why the improvement in ROA does not translate into an improvement in stock price. A more detailed examination of this issue is required before we can provide a comprehensive answer.

Secondary Offerings of REIT Securities

As mentioned in previous chapters, REITs have to engage in constant capital-raising activities due to their high dividend payouts and the capital-intensive nature of real estate. Having gone public and gained access to the capital market, they will have to return to it periodically for additional capital. We already discussed how the stock market values a REIT's debt-offering decision in chapter 8. In this chapter, while still discussing REIT debt-offering activities, we pay special attention to a REIT's *secondary equity offerings (SEOs),* to which we now turn.

Secondary-Offering Activities

Table 9.6 and figure 9.6 show the secondary offerings of equity and debt securities by REITs during the 1982–2000 period. Similar to REIT IPOs, REIT secondary offerings also surged during most of the post-1990 period; yet when REIT IPO activity slowed after 1994 (dropping from 44 in 1994 to 0 in 2000, as shown in table 9.1), REITs still raised a significant amount of funds from secondary offerings of equity and debt. The total number of secondary offerings increased from 97 in 1994 to a peak of 457 in 1998 (as shown in table 9.6). REIT analyst Bill Sibley of SNL Securities observes that "the REIT IPO market was booming in 1993 and 1994. Now that the market has been saturated, investors are pouring equity into secondary offerings by established public companies. Investors are no longer interested in companies without a proven track record" (*Mortgage-Backed Securities Letter,* May 13, 1996).

As we can see from figure 9.6, REIT debt offerings increased dramatically during the 1995–99 period. Donohue (1999) noted that during the 1995–97 period, REITs with strong performance managed to secure good credit ratings and then entered the public debt markets. Many of those REITs shifted entirely to unsecured corporate debt, substantially increasing their financing flexibility. Prior to that, a REIT's access to debt was primarily through mortgages on single properties or pools of properties. Based on figures published by NAREIT, the number of unsecured debt offerings and the

Table 9.6 Secondary Offerings of Equity and Debt Securities by REITs (1982–2001)

	Secondary Equity[a]		Secondary Debt[b]	
	Number of Offerings	Total Capital Raised ($ millions)	Number of Offerings	Total Capital Raised ($ millions)
1982	5	115	1	5.0
1983	15	438	4	150
1984	8	173	4	1,125
1985	17	413	13	1,066
1986	17	624	26	2,841
1987	15	733	23	1,562
1988	13	785	11	910
1989	15	722	8	644
1990	8	389	6	494
1991	20	786	7	694
1992	24	1,055	25	4,541
1993	50	3,856	41	5,135
1994	52	3,945	47	3,600
1995	92	7,268	94	4,233
1996	139	11,201	80	5,081
1997	292	26,378	145	12,597
1998	297	19,354	160	17,774
1999	100	6,444	103	10,477
2000	42	2,834	72	7,542
2001[c]	60	4,515	36	8,170

Source: Data from various issues of *Statistical Digest,* published by NAREIT, and NAREIT's website, http://www.nareit.com.

[a]Includes common share offerings and preferred share offerings.

[b]Includes unsecured debt offerings and secured debt offerings.

[c]As of October 31, 2001.

total capital they raised exceeded that of mortgage-backed debt during the 1994–99 period.

In a study of REIT financing events during the 1965–92 period, Hsieh, Poon, and Wei (2000) compare the financing patterns of REITs with those of industrial firms. They find that, in terms of frequency, REITs use more short-term debt and common stock than long-term debt and convertible debt when they raise capital. In addition, when compared to taxpaying industrial corporations, REITs use less debt financing for capital needs. In other words, they find that common stock financing appears to be much more common among REITs than among industrial firms.

Indeed, table 9.6 and figure 9.6 clearly demonstrate this pattern. We can see that REITs used more equity financing and raised more funds in the equity market than in the debt market during the 1994–98 period, during

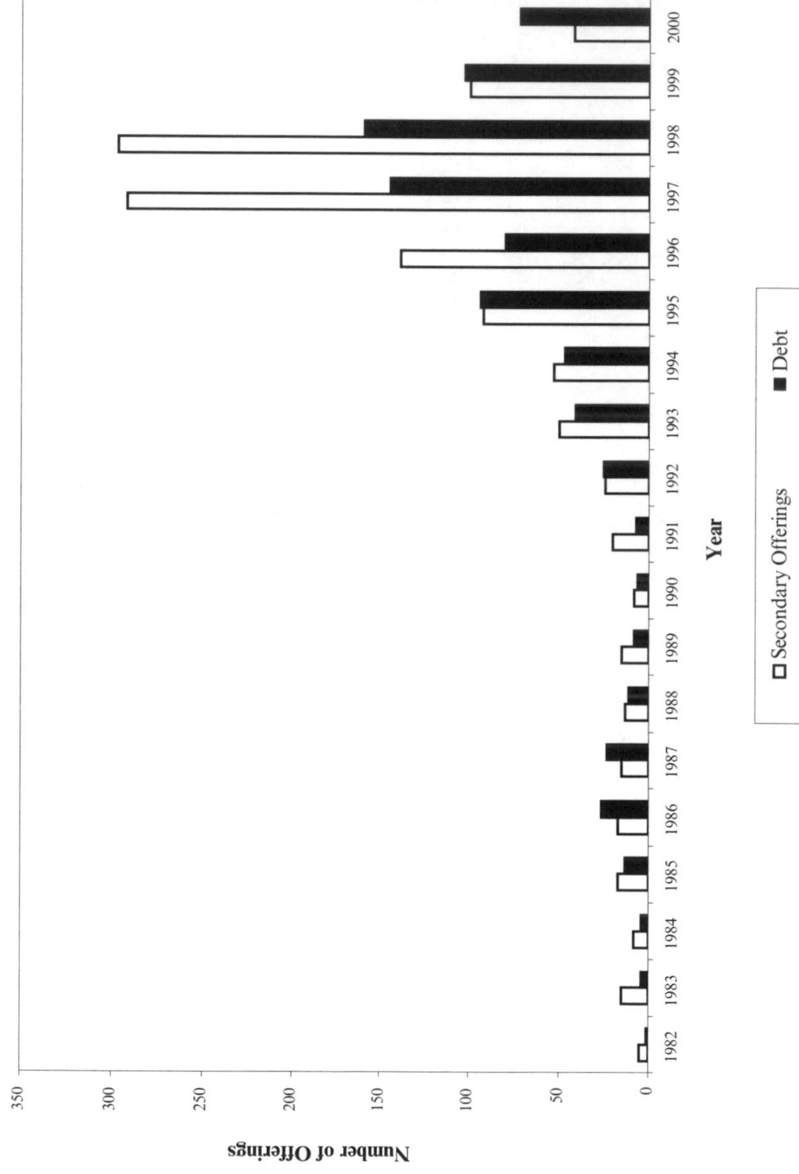

Figure 9.6 Secondary Equity and Debt Offerings

which time new REITs also flooded the market. Given the fact that their debt capacity is incompletely utilized, REITs have the potential, as we suggest in chapter 8, to raise more funds from the debt market to facilitate their future growth. Note that in 1999 and 2000, REITs raised more funds from the debt market than they did from the equity market. This is a trend to which we might want to pay more attention.

A comparison between tables 9.1 and 9.6 indicates that REITs relied more on the secondary equity market than on their IPOs for their equity capital needs after 1994. For example, in 1997, REITs raised a total of $26.4 billion from SEOs, but only $6.3 billion from IPOs. We also observe that REITs were able to raise a significant amount of funds from SEOs in 1999, when the REIT IPO market was cooling down. Since more information is available on seasoned REITs, this evidence supports what we stated previously: that investors might desire more information on REIT IPOs before they are willing to participate in the market.

Performance of REIT SEOs

Numerous studies in the finance literature show that the stock market, in general, responds negatively to seasoned equity offerings by taxpaying industrial firms. One possible explanation is that a new security sale conveys negative information about the issuing firms' expected cash flows from operations. Alternatively, investors presume that the managers of the firm would authorize new equity sales only if they believed that the firm's stock was overvalued. (Rationally, managers would not approve additional equity offerings when the market price of the firm's stock was lower than management's assessment of its value.) Consequently, investors discount the stock values of firms announcing equity offerings. The evidence from the literature also suggests that firms with higher potential information disparity between management and the market about the value of existing assets or the firm's future prospects tend to suffer larger negative stock price effects.

Do investors react similarly to REIT SEOs? Studies that examine the issuance of seasoned equity by REITs do, in fact, find evidence similar to that for industrial firms. Specifically, these studies, which examine REIT SEOs over various time periods, document that investors respond negatively to REIT SEO announcements.[7] However, although the equity-offering announcements by REITs seem to convey negative information to the market, the drop in stock prices for REITs is smaller in magnitude than that experienced by industrial firms. This is probably because REITs have to come to the market more frequently for capital, thus making their security offerings more predictable than those of an industrial firm. Interestingly, the price response to REIT SEOs is similar to that reported by Allen and Rutherford (1992) for taxpaying real estate corporations.

Which Types of REITs Should Use SEOs?

Do the specific characteristics of REITs affect the stock market's reaction to SEOs? A study by Ghosh et al. (1999) addresses this question. They find that investors react more negatively to REIT SEOs when the issue amount is larger and when the SEOs are filed by larger-sized REITs or by REITs with greater inside/managerial ownership. The negative reaction, however, is mitigated for REITs that use established and reputable underwriters for their SEOs. REIT structure (UPREIT or traditional) and REIT property type (apartments, malls, offices, and miscellaneous) do not seem to affect the stock price reaction to REIT SEOs. Ghosh, Nag, and Sirmans (2000) also report that REIT SEOs are more underpriced if REITs have a higher percentage of institutional owners or are underwritten by less prestigious underwriters.

In addition, Hsieh, Poon, and Wei (2000) document that the higher the stock price of the REIT prior to the announcement of the SEO, the more unfavorable are the investors' reactions to the announcement. This makes sense because investors tend to presume that managers believe their REIT stocks are overpriced and that they want to issue more stocks to exploit this situation. Ghosh, Nag, and Sirmans (1997) also analyze the stock price performance of REITs prior to and after they announce SEOs, finding that the issuing REITs significantly outperform other REITs in the market. This also makes sense because REIT managers would be likely to time their stock issues to coincide with the REITs' good performance and growth prospects.

To summarize, once investors perceive that REIT management is issuing new equity to exploit a hot market situation (wherein the market is excessively confident about the REIT's future), the investors will reassess the issuing REIT's current value by reducing its share price. They may respond differently if they believe that the REIT is issuing more equity for a good cause, such as funding profitable investments that would increase the REIT's value. However, unless outside investors have the same information as managers, it will be difficult for the investors to know whether the equity offering is for a good cause. Under this circumstance, the use of a reputable underwriter will help reduce the information disparity because investors are likely to trust the underwriter to do all the due-diligence work related to the equity issue.

Link between IPOs and SEOs

So far, the empirical evidence that analyzes the link between the IPO underpricing and subsequent seasoned equity offerings by industrial firms has been inconclusive. A recent study by Ghosh, Nag, and Sirmans (2000) provides evidence on the relationship between REIT IPOs and SEOs using a sample of equity REITs that make both an IPO and a subsequent SEO in the 1992–96 period. They find the following:

- REITs that underprice IPOs more are likely to sell seasoned equity sooner.
- A greater IPO underpricing results in a larger joint amount of capital raised through an IPO-SEO pair.
- REITs that underprice IPOs underprice SEOs as well.
- IPO underpricing does not mitigate the valuation loss associated with first SEOs.

In other words, the evidence implies that REITs that underprice their IPOs might want to return to the market sooner to capitalize on the favorable information they revealed to the market through their IPOs. Since investors will still have a good taste in their mouths, so to speak, from their experience with their IPO investments, they will be partial to SEOs by the same REITs. Those REITs also tend to issue the first seasoned equity in larger sizes in the hope to recover the loss incurred at the IPO.

The lesson to be learned here is that REIT managers might want to think carefully about their pricing strategies for equity security. Investors, unless they have reason to believe otherwise, tend to lower the stock price of a REIT when the REIT issues new equity. To price a REIT stock low at the IPO stage will tend to give investors a good taste and hence more confidence in the REIT stock. If this experience will enable investors to think positively about the REIT SEOs, then it might pay for the REIT to take a hit at the IPO stage and recoup the loss at the SEO stage. Regardless of whether REIT managers believes in this strategy, the evidence indicates that they should consider their equity-raising activities (for both IPOs and SEOs) in a comprehensive way to maximize the total benefits from issuing securities.

What Have We Learned?

- Before 1990, if you invested in REIT IPOs, you could expect to see a price drop of about 3.1% on the first day of trading.
- However, post-1990 REIT IPOs are different from pre-1990 REIT IPOs. We see a small price increase of about 2.4% on the first trading day.
- If we consider all REIT IPOs issued during the 1970–2000 period, the price increase on the first trading day is only 0.2% percent, whereas that for industrial firm IPOs during the same period is 18.5%.
- Although the average return of REIT IPOs turned positive during the 1990–2000 period, the first-trading-day return was still far below that of industrial firm IPOs. Judging from this angle, neither the change in REITs' organizational structure nor the presence of more institutional investors in the REIT market actually helped boost the performance of REIT IPOs.
- Who buys and who sells REIT IPOs is important to their performance. REIT IPOs with more institutional investors and underwritten by more prestigious investment banks tend to perform better than other REIT IPOs.

- Investors should try to avoid REIT IPOs issued by finite-life REITs or those issued on best-efforts contracts, although there were only a few such offerings after 1993.
- Experience tells us that REIT IPO activities peak when there is a change in laws affecting REIT organizational structure. Given this, it appears that the next surge of REIT IPOs could be around 2003, after the REIT Modernization Act takes effect in 2001.
- Investors react unfavorably to REIT SEOs. Empirical evidence indicates that REIT managers could develop a strategy for the pricing of REIT IPOs in connection with the planned SEOs to minimize the costs of raising equity capital.

Conclusions

We expect that REIT IPOs will gradually behave more like industrial firm IPOs. The increased presence of institutional investors in the REIT stock market together with the better use of technology have led to more data and higher quality research about real estate firms in the post-1990s. These changes (more informed investors, more information, and more liquidity) will help mitigate the information asymmetry surrounding REIT value.

In addition, new REITs are becoming more like operating firms; thus the fund-like structure of older REITs will become less of a concern in the future. With these changes, we believe that investing in REIT IPOs will be similar to investing in industrial firm IPOs in the near future. However, before this happens, we suggest that investors try to avoid purchasing REIT stocks in the IPO market.

The evidence on the IPOs of real estate firms in Hong Kong provides support for our prediction. We know that the price performance of Hong Kong real estate IPOs is the same as that of the IPOs of non–real estate firms. This could be due to three factors: (a) The Hong Kong popular press pays much more attention to real estate firms than to other types of firms; (b) large investors invest in real estate firms in Hong Kong; and (c) Hong Kong real estate firms are operational in nature. We believe that once REITs begin to exhibit characteristics similar to those of Hong Kong real estate firms, the difference in return performance between REIT IPOs and non-REIT IPOs should disappear.

NOTES

1. Similar arguments proffered by practitioners can be found in, for example, the *Wall Street Journal* (January 17, 1990) and the New York Institute of Finance's publication on REITs (1988, 18).
2. Wang, Chan, and Gau (1992) report that for periods prior to 1970, the

volume of REIT-industry IPOs is relatively high in the 1969–70 period (54 IPOs, with total proceeds of $2.3 billion) and relatively low in the 1961–68 period (74 IPOs, with $0.2 billion in total proceeds).

3. See, for example, Ibbotson and Jaffe (1975) and Ibbotson, Sindelar, and Ritter (1988).

4. Ghosh, Nag, and Sirmans (1997) note in their study that between 1992 and 1995, 70% of new REITs were formed under the UPREIT structure, whereas 80% of the REITs in existence prior to 1993 had the traditional structure. In chapter 2, we also note that in 1993 and 1994, 67% and 89%, respectively, of all new equity REIT capital was raised through IPOs using the UPREIT vehicle.

5. The market index is an equally weighted index constructed by the Center for Research in Security Prices (CRSP) at the University of Chicago, using all NYSE, Amex, and Nasdaq firms.

6. However, in a recent working paper, Hyland, Buttimer, and Sanders (2001) report that REIT IPOs generate positive abnormal returns during the 1990s, but not in the 1980s. This means that although REIT IPOs underperform the general stock market, they perform well after adjusting for their risk level.

7. Howe and Shilling (1988) examine the stock price reaction to the 27 equity-offering announcements made by NYSE- or Amex-listed REITs during the 1970–85 period. Ghosh et al. (1999) examine the filing announcements of 100 seasoned equity offerings by equity REITs in the 1991–95 period. Hsieh, Poon, and Wei (2000) study the stock price reaction to 57 common stock offerings by REITs over the 1965–92 period.

REFERENCES

Allen, Marcus T., and Ronald C. Rutherford. 1992. The impact of financing decisions on the security returns of real estate corporations. *Journal of Real Estate Finance and Economics* 5:393–400.

Chalk, Andrew J., and John W. Peavy. 1987. Initial public offerings: Daily returns, offering types, and the price effect. *Financial Analysts Journal* 43:65–69.

Chan, Su Han, Mark Stohs, and Ko Wang. 2001. Are real estate IPOs a different species? Evidence from Hong Kong IPOs. *Journal of Real Estate Research* 21:201–20.

Donohue, Ron M. 1999. Capital markets and the modern REIT era. *Real Estate Issues* 24 (2): 25–29.

Firstenberg, Paul M., Stephen A. Ross, and Randall C. Zisler. 1988. Real estate: The whole story. *Journal of Portfolio Management* 14:22–34.

Gerbich, M., M. Levis, and P. Venmore-Rowland. 1995. Property initial public offerings: Regulations, costs, and price reactions. *Journal of Property Finance* 6 (1): 38–54.

Ghosh, Chinmoy, Raja Nag, and C. F. Sirmans. 1997. Is there a window of opportunity? Stock market performance of REITs around secondary equity offerings. *Real Estate Finance* 13 (4): 23–30.

Ghosh, Chinmoy, Raja Nag, and C. F. Sirmans. 1999. An analysis of seasoned equity offerings by equity REITs (1991–95). *Journal of Real Estate Finance and Economics* 19 (3): 175–92.

Ghosh, Chinmoy, Raja Nag, and C. F. Sirmans. 2000a. The pricing of seasoned equity offerings: Evidence from REITs. *Real Estate Economics* 28:363–84.

Ghosh, Chinmoy, Raja Nag, and C. F. Sirmans. 2000b. A test of the signaling value of IPO underpricing with REIT IPO-SEO pairs. *Journal of Real Estate Finance and Economics* 20 (2): 137–54.

Hite, Gailen L., James E. Owers, and Ronald C. Rogers. 1987. The market for interfirm asset sales: Partial sell-offs and total liquidations. *Journal of Financial Economics* 18:229–52.

Howe, John S., and James D. Shilling. 1988. Capital structure theory and REIT security offerings. *Journal of Finance* 43:983–93.

Hsieh, Chengho, Percy S. Poon, and Peihwang Wei. 2000. An analysis of REIT financing decisions. Louisiana State University–Shreveport. Working paper.

Hyland, David, Richard Buttimer, and Anthony Sanders. 2001. The long-run performance of REIT IPOs. Ohio State University. Working paper.

Ibbotson, Roger G., and Jeffrey F. Jaffe. "Hot Issue" Markets. *Journal of Finance* 30:1027–42.

Ibbotson, Roger G., Jody L. Sindelar, and Jay R. Ritter. 1988. Initial public offerings. *Journal of Applied Corporate Finance* 1:37–45.

Ibbotson, Roger G., Jody L. Sindelar, and Jay R. Ritter. 1994. The market's problems with the pricing of initial public offerings. *Journal of Applied Corporate Finance* 7:66–74.

Johnson, James M., and Robert E. Miller. 1988. Investment banker prestige and the underpricing of initial public offerings. *Financial Management* 17:19–29.

Ling, David C., and Michael Ryngaert. 1997. Valuation uncertainty, institutional involvement, and the underpricing of IPOs: The case of REITs. *Journal of Financial Economics* 43 (3): 433–56.

Martin, Ellen James. 1997. REIT values. *Institutional Investor* 31 (May): 145–46.

Michaely, Roni, and W. Shaw. 1994. The pricing of initial public offerings: Tests of adverse selection and signaling theories. *Review of Financial Studies* 7:279–319.

Muscarella, Chris J. 1988. Price performance of the initial public offerings of master limited partnership units. *Financial Review* 23:513–21.

New York Institute of Finance (NYIF). 1988. *Real estate investment trusts: The low-risk, high-yield, asset-growth opportunity.* New York: NYIF.

Palmon, Dan, and Lee J. Seidler. 1978. Current value reporting of real estate companies and a possible example of market inefficiency. *The Accounting Review* 53:766–90.

Peavy, John W. 1990. Returns on initial public offerings of closed-end funds. *Review of Financial Studies* 3:695–708.

Ritter, Jay R. 1987. The costs of going public. *Journal of Financial Economics* 19:269–81.

Shelor, Roger M., and Dwight C. Anderson. 1998. The financial performance of REITs following initial public offerings. *Journal of Real Estate Research* 16:375–87.

Titman, Sheridan, and Arthur Warga. 1986. Risk and the performance of real estate investment trusts: A multiple index approach. *AREUEA Journal* 14:414–31.

Wang, Ko, Su Han Chan, and George W. Gau. 1992. Initial public offerings of equity securities: Anomalous evidence using REITs. *Journal of Financial Economics* 31:381–410.

Weiss, Kathleen A. 1989. The post-offering price performance of closed-end funds. *Financial Management* 18:57–67.

Woolley, Suzanne. 1993. REITs: Boom today, gloom tomorrow? *Business Week* (November 29), p. 116.

10

The Performance of REIT Stocks

Are REIT Stocks Really Different from Other Stocks in the Market?

As we have discussed in previous chapters, REIT stocks can be viewed as a form of securitized real estate representing claims on real property or mortgages. Given this, investors who are considering REITs as possible investment opportunities should ask two closely related questions. First, to what extent do REIT stocks reflect the returns to their underlying real estate assets? This issue is important because if REIT returns do not reflect the returns to their underlying assets, investors cannot use them as a convenient way to add a real estate component to their portfolios.

The second question the investor should ask is related to the pricing of REIT stocks. Because the pricing methods (and models) in property markets might be different from those in the stock market, it is important for investors to ask what the appropriate pricing model for REIT stocks might be—that is, whether we should price REITs as properties or as stocks. This question is important because in order for investors to pursue effective portfolio-diversification strategies, they need to be aware of the factors that affect the risk and return performance of REIT stocks.

The price movement of REIT stocks is probably related to that of the general stock market, as evidenced by the fact that REIT stock prices, just like those of all other stocks, change on a continuous basis. However, the prices in property markets do not change on a continuous basis, indicating that there are differences in the pricing behavior of REIT stocks listed on stock exchanges and that of real properties available in property markets. The extent to which the general movement in the stock market can affect REIT stocks is an issue that investors need to pay attention to.

Indeed, if the pricing models used in the property market and the REIT stock market are similar, it is likely that the movement of their returns will also be highly correlated. Under this circumstance, the diversification benefits in owning both real properties and REIT stocks simultaneously will be reduced. This means that investors should find out whether it is a good strategy to invest in REIT stocks instead of investing directly in real property. This chapter addresses these subjects.

REIT Stocks and Unsecuritized Real Estate

Intuition suggests that there ought to be a positive relationship between the stock returns of a company and the overall movement of the stock market. If this relationship holds true for operating companies, it is also likely to be true for REITs. However, intuition also suggests that the value of a REIT should be determined by the value of its properties. Both types of intuition make sense, but the question is, what is the dominant factor determining REIT returns?

Common Factors

There are at least three common influences underlying the returns to REIT stocks and real estate. First, since valuations in both markets are determined by the discounted value of their expected cash flows, then changes in interest rates ought to affect both real estate values and REIT stocks along with other stocks in a similar fashion.

Second, the level of real economic activity will affect REIT cash flows, corporate earnings, and the cash flows to real estate in the same way, all other things being equal. In other words, when bad news hit the stock market, it must also hit the REIT stock market (although the degree of impact might be different).

Third, equity REITs own real estate, and, in spite of the restrictions on the purchase and sale of REIT assets, the underlying real estate does affect the value of REITs. This argument also applies to some extent to non–real estate corporations and their stocks because most corporations own real estate.

Unique Factors

There are significant differences in the institutional characteristics of the REIT stock market and the unsecuritized real estate property market. These differences arise from the nature of the markets in which these types of assets are traded. For example, REIT stocks are traded in traditional auction markets in which a large number of buyers and sellers continuously trade securities based on the information flow about the security's value. Moreover, the value of a REIT's stock reflects the contribution made by the management of its properties rather than simply the returns to passively managed properties.

Real estate markets, on the other hand, are not auction markets. Real estate assets are traded infrequently and real estate values can be determined by periodic appraisals based on a property's characteristics and the current and historical sale values of properties with similar characteristics. Appraisal values are determined with an eye toward past values, and appraisal errors tend to persist until eventually corrected by time. As a result, there is a strong tendency for appraisal values to be smoothed. Also, information about real estate is generally more costly to obtain and, therefore, is less readily available.[1]

Is There a General Consensus?

The result is that an equity REIT's stock returns may differ from the returns to its underlying assets, especially when the value of its properties are difficult to determine (or can be estimated using appraisal-based data only). Thus, at first glance, while it would appear that there should be a relationship between the economic processes generating returns to REIT stocks and unsecuritized real estate, it is not clear what the relationship is or how reliable it is. Although our discussion applies primarily to equity REITs, the main points should also apply to mortgage REITs because their assets are typically claims on underlying real property.

Studies lack consensus on the issue of whether the REIT stock market and the real estate property market are integrated. Strictly speaking, the two markets are said to be integrated if their risk premiums are the same (or at least similar). Essentially, this means that there are important risk factors common to both markets. Furthermore, if the two markets are integrated, there should not be a significant difference in the predictability of their returns. We will review available empirical evidence to address this issue.

Evidence for Integration

Some researchers find either that REIT pricing is very similar to that of other stocks or that there is no evidence of market segmentation, suggesting that the two markets are integrated (see, e.g., Li and Wang 1995). However, the apparent lack of a relationship between the returns to REITs and real estate does not necessarily prove that the two markets are not integrated. It is possible that they are integrated but that such integration cannot be detected due to differences in the valuation parameters used in exchange-traded asset markets and the real estate market (see Giliberto and Mengden 1996).

Indeed, while it is difficult to find a contemporaneous relationship between the returns to unsecuritized and securitized real estate, there is evidence that the returns to the former lag behind those to the latter by as much as one to two years. This indicates an intertemporal relationship between REIT returns and the returns to real estate. This lag between real estate stock prices and appraisal values is explained by the ability of the stock market to incorporate information about real estate fundamentals much more rapidly than appraisal-based real estate prices can. These findings could suggest that the market for REIT stocks and the market for unsecuritized real estate share similar fundamentals.[2]

Evidence for Partial or No Integration

There is also evidence of a special real estate risk-factor premium affecting REIT returns and evidence that the capitalization rate (discount rate) used for valuing unsecuritized real estate does affect the returns to equity REITs (see Liu and Mei 1992; Mei and Lee 1994; Liao and Mei 1998). It is important to note that there is a relationship between the capitalization rate and REIT returns. If the capitalization rate employed to value real property affects the returns to equity REITs, then it provides strong evidence that REIT stock returns can be partially affected by the movement of property values in the property market. (However, whether the capitalization rate is a proxy for a general pricing factor is another issue that requires more attention from researchers.)

It should be noted that recent work by Clayton and MacKinnon (2000) also supports the view that the variability of equity REIT returns is affected not only by real estate markets but also by the stock market. Their research provides evidence that the REIT stock market may not be fully integrated with the general stock market. Finally, some researchers believe that the property market and the REIT market are not correlated. For example, Myer and Webb (1994) find a contemporaneous relationship between retail stocks and retail REITs but find no evidence of a positive relationship between the performance of retail real estate and retail REITs. Scott (1990) and Goetzman and Ibbotson (1990) find that REIT returns do not reflect the fundamentals of their underlying real estate but frequently diverge from them, and that there is no relationship between the returns to securitized versus unsecuritized real estate.

Is There a Compromise?

Although the evidence is obviously mixed, the conclusion that there is some basic relationship between the markets for unsecuritized and securitized real estate is a reasonable one, at least over the long run. If this is the case, then what could contribute to the difference in the findings on the issue? From the analysis of the empirical evidence, we find that while the risk-return characteristics of REIT stocks may have been more like non–real estate stocks in the past, in recent years REIT stocks have behaved more like unsecuritized real estate.[3] The difference in the sample periods probably explains a small portion of the differences in the findings among these studies

However, we should make it clear that whether REIT stocks are integrated with the stock market should not affect an investor's decision to include them in his or her portfolio. Even with the same pricing factors, REIT stocks can be used to reduce the risk of the investor's portfolio if they have lower betas than the average stock in the market. However, we should also point out that the question of whether investors should use REIT stocks as substitutes for real property in their portfolios is more difficult to answer. The evidence suggests that REIT stocks by themselves may not be sufficient to provide a strong real estate component to the investor's portfolio. If an investor is interested in establishing a portfolio that mimics the return behavior of the real estate markets, it might be best for the investor to include some direct real estate investments as well. (Table 10.1 summarizes the main points made by the studies highlighted in this section.)

The Risk and Return Characteristics of REITs

From the previous discussion, it is clear that there are certain advantages to including REIT stocks in a portfolio because REITs do possess certain unique characteristics. The next and most natural question to ask is whether, as a general group, REIT stocks are good investments. If an investor concentrated on investing only in REIT stocks, would the investor be able to outperform the general stock market?

REIT Stocks versus the Stock Market

The question of whether REIT stocks have outperformed the stock market is a difficult one to answer. As with most stocks, the returns on REIT securities have fluctuated significantly over time, and the empirical evidence indicates that REITs performed differently over different periods of time against the stock market (as measured by the returns to various stock- and bond-market indices). However, it is fair to say that, on a risk-adjusted basis, REIT stocks do not outperform the average non-REIT stock.

The General Trend of the Evidence

Early research on the long-run performance of REITs from the 1960s through the early 1980s generally concludes that the return performance of REITs is about the same as that of the general stock market. The studies by Smith and Schulman (1976) and Smith (1980) reach this conclusion

Table 10.1 Summary of Studies Addressing the Integration between the REIT Stock Market and the Real Estate Market

Author(s) of Study	Sample Period	Issues Addressed Regarding the Integration Hypothesis	Authors' Results and Our Interpretation of the Results as they Apply to Integration Hypothesis
Clayton and MacKinnon (2000)	Jan. 1993–Dec. 1998	The relative importance of a real estate market factor in explaining the variability of REIT returns.	While large stocks have accounted for an increasing proportion of the total variability of REIT stock returns over time, examination of subperiods indicates that in recent years large stocks have become less important and the real estate market more important in explaining the variability of the returns to REIT stocks.
Glascock, Lu, and So (2000)	Jan. 1972–Dec. 1996	Cointegration between REITs and unsecuritized real estate markets and the relationship between REIT stocks and other stocks and bonds.	Securitized and unsecuritized real estate markets are not cointegrated for the entire sample period, but since 1992–93 there has been cointegration between REITs and other stocks. They share common factors and pricing structures, and REITs behave more like small stocks.
Ling and Naranjo (1999)	1st quarter 1978–4th quarter 1994	Integration between the market for commercial real estate and the stock market.	Markets for exchange-traded real estate, including REITs, are integrated with non–real estate stocks.
Chaudhry, Myer, and Webb (1999)	Jan. 1978–Feb. 1996	Integration between markets for commercial real estate and markets for stocks, bonds, and T-bills (financial asset markets).	Financial asset markets and real estate markets are cointegrated. Stocks tend to have an inverse long-run relation ship with real estate. No cointegration between real estate markets by property type or geographical location.
Lieblich, Pagliari, and Webb (1998)	1st quarter 1978–4th quarter 1995	Relation between the long-run performance of REITs and the performance of underlying real properties.	Weak long-run statistical relationship between the total returns to securitized and unsecuritized real estate assets. No short-run relationship between returns to REITs and unsecuritized real estate.
Ghosh, Miles, and Sirmans (1996)	Jan. 1985–June 1996	Similarities between the market for REIT stocks and the market for non–real estate stocks.	REIT stocks have become less comparable to average stocks in recent periods. They act even less like small stocks and behave more like unsecuritized real estate.

(continued)

Table 10.1 *Continued*

Author(s) of Study	Sample Period	Issues Addressed Regarding the Integration Hypothesis	Authors' Results and Our Interpretation of the Results as they Apply to Integration Hypothesis
Giliberto and Mengden (1996)	March 1978–Dec. 1994	Effects of differences in market-valuation parameters as an explanation of the differences between performance of public real estate (REITs) and private real estate.	REIT stock return behavior and the return behavior of private real estate are very similar after adjusting for differences in valuation parameters used in the two markets.
Li and Wang (1995)	Jan. 1971–Dec. 1991	Predictability of returns to REIT stocks relative to the predictability of returns to other stocks, and the integration of real estate market with the general stock market.	Pricing in the real estate and stock markets is very similar. Returns to REITs are no more predictable than returns to the stock market, suggesting that the two markets are integrated.
Mei and Lee (1994)	1st quarter 1978–4th quarter 1989	Existence of real estate risk premium in addition to bond- and stock- market risk premiums in REIT returns, and the use of a more general pricing model to detect market segmentation between the REIT stock market and the real estate market.	A systematic real estate risk premium exists in REIT pricing in addition to a stock- and a bond-market factor. Market segmentation disappears after considering other factors that affect REIT returns. This implies that unsecuritized real estate assets can be treated like exchange-traded assets in evaluating their potential using the mean-variance efficient frontier analysis.
Myer and Webb (1994)	1st quarter 1983–4th quarter 1991	Relationship between retail REITs, retail real estate, and retail stocks resulting from overage rent provisions in their lease agreements.	A positive contemporaneous relationship exists between retail REIT returns and real estate stock returns supporting a fundamental relationship between them. There is only weak evidence of a relationship between retail REITs and real estate, and no evidence of a relationship between real estate returns and retail REITs.
Myer and Webb (1993)	1st quarter 1978–1st quarter 1990	Comparison of the distribution of equity REIT returns to those of common stocks and unsecuritized real estate.	Returns to REITs are similar to the returns to commercial real estate after accounting for the lag in returns relative to equity REIT returns, indicating a significant intertemporal relationship between the return series.

Liu and Mei (1992)	Dec. 1971–Dec. 1989	Predictability of equity REIT returns and the relationship between the market for equity REIT stocks and bond and stock markets.	Excess returns on REITs are more predictable than those on stocks and bonds. Conditions in the real estate markets as reflected by capitalization rates appear to influence the returns to both equity REITs and small stocks. Equity REITs are a hybrid of unsecuritized real estate and small-cap stocks and do not resemble bonds.
Ambrose, Ancel, and Griffiths (1992)	July 1962–Dec. 1990	Integration of REIT stock market with market for other stocks.	The REIT stock market is integrated with general stock market over the long run. However, REITs may not be a good proxy for the returns to unsecuritized real estate because of their stock-like characteristics.
Gyourko and Keim (1992)	1st quarter 1978–4th quarter 1990	Relationship between returns to equity REITs and appraisal-based returns to unsecuritized real estate.	Lagged REIT returns predict appraisal-based unsecuritized real estate returns, implying that factors affecting risk and return in real estate markets are reflected in REIT stocks and that the markets are related.
Liu et al. (1990)	2nd quarter 1978–3rd quarter 1986	Existence of integation or segmentation between commercial real estate markets and stock market.	The commercial real estate market is segmented from the stock market due to indirect barriers such as cost and differences in availability of information.
Giliberto (1990)	1st quarter 1978–4th quarter 1989	Relationship between equity REIT returns and returns to unsecuritized real estate.	After removing the effects of the stock and bond markets on the performance of equity REITs, there is a strong positive correlation between REIT returns and returns to unsecuritized real estate. This suggests the existence of common factors affecting returns to both types of assets.
Scott (1990)	Various sample periods	Impact of real estate market fundamentals on the prices of equity REIT stocks.	Equity REIT stock prices do not always track real estate market fundamentals. Therefore, REIT prices may not serve as reliable indicators of fundamental values for real estate.
Goetzman and Ibbotson (1990)	Various sample periods	Relationship between unsecuritized real estate performance and the performance of other asset classes in relation to portfolio-diversification strategies.	Real estate returns have little correlation with returns to stocks and bonds and are driven by different economic forces. Therefore, real estate provides a good alternative for portfolio diversification strategies.

even though REIT stocks declined significantly in 1973–74 period as a result of excessive leverage, poor investments, rising costs and interest rates, and a declining stock market.

However, more recent studies indicate that the performance of REIT stocks is less impressive than was previously believed. These studies report that REIT stocks either underperform the stock market (on a risk-adjusted basis) or perform no better than the stock market.[4] For example, Sanders (1998) compares the risk-adjusted return performance of REITs, as measured by the NAREIT index with and without health-care REITs, against a number of benchmarks, including the S&P 500 index, the Wilshire index, and various other stock- and bond-market indices. He reports that, over the period from 1978 to 1996, equity REITs have generally performed no better than the stock market indices in terms of their risk-adjusted excess returns.

Performance by Subperiod

REIT performance relative to the stock market has varied significantly for different subperiods. For example, Sanders (1998) finds that, during the period of January 1978 to December 1986, equity REITs outperformed the stock market indices, while for the period January 1987 through October 1990, equity REITs earned risk-adjusted excess returns below the stock market. For the more recent period from November 1990 through June 1996, REITs outperformed the S&P 500 index but did no better than the Wilshire index. Part of the reason for the latter result is that the S&P 500 does not contain small stocks whereas the Wilshire index does. Since most REITs were small stocks and small stocks typically outperform large stocks, it is not surprising that the NAREIT index has outperformed the large-stock S&P 500 index.

Han and Liang (1995) find similar performance results for the period 1970–93. They show that REITs performed no better or somewhat more poorly than a broad stock market index over this period but that this performance was better in some subperiods and worse in others. They also find that the performance of larger REITs tends to be more stable than that of smaller REITs. The latter result is undoubtedly due to the fact that portfolios of larger REITs tend to be more diversified than those of smaller REITs in terms of the number of properties held.

In a 2001 research report, Kenneth Rosen specifically analyzed REIT performance during the 1993–2000 period. He reports that on both the risk and the return spectrums, the stock performance of REITs (mean return = 10.79% and standard deviation = 17.16%) falls below the S&P 500 (mean return = 14.72% and standard deviation = 18.02%). Since REITs traditionally have a low beta, the lower return could be justifiable. In other words, while Clayton and Mckinnon (2000) report that REIT liquidity increased during the 1993–96 period and Downs et al. (2001) report that market commentaries on publicly traded real estate have a greater impact on prices after the REIT boom, there is no evidence in the literature that the stock performance of modern REITs in the 1993–2000 period is significantly different from (or better than) the performance of traditional REITs. This could be a surprise (and unwelcome evidence) for those who push modern REITs as a totally different species from traditional REITs.

Overall REIT Performance

In summary, the evidence indicates that over the long run, portfolios of REITs have not outperformed the stock market. However, during specific time periods, their risk-adjusted returns have been significantly higher or lower than the returns to the stock market. This unstable return performance is consistent with the strong cyclical behavior of property markets, although the stock market cycles of REITs tend to precede cycles in property markets. There is no evidence that, as a group, modern REITs perform differently from traditional REITs. Table 10.2 presents a summary of selected research on the question of the long-term performance of REITs.

REITs and Asset Type

It is very clear that there is a significant difference in the long-run performance of REITs based on asset type. Almost all academic research on the subject finds that of the three types of REITs classified by general asset category, equity REITs have outperformed mortgage REITs in terms of their risk-adjusted excess returns (at least since the early 1970s).[5] It is likely that the long-run underperformance of mortgage REITs is due to their tendency to use significantly more financial leverage, and as a result of their past failure, the REIT industry in recent years has been largely dominated by equity REITs, not only in number but also in market capitalization.

Research also indicates that equity REITs consistently have less market risk than mortgage or hybrid REITs, even though the performance of equity REITs has been superior. It is also argued that there has been a decline in the total risk of REITs over time.[6] One possible explanation for this result is that the rise in the number of analysts following equity REITs along with increased institutional ownership of equity REIT stocks has increased the amount of information available to investors. Khoo, Hartzell, and Hoesli (1993) and Below, Keily, and McIntosh (1996) believe that such information availability can improve investor monitoring of equity REITs and reduce investment uncertainty about them. This increase in information might tie REIT stock values more closely to the performance of their underlying assets, and might also reduce the risk of investing in REIT stocks.[7]

Table 10.2 Summary of Selected Studies Focusing on the Performance of REITs

Author(s) of Study	Sample Period	Purpose of Study	Authors' Results and Our Interpretation of the Results As They Apply to REIT Performance
Chen and Peiser (1999)	Aug. 1993–July 1997	Examines the risk and return performance of new REITs versus those of REITs created prior to 1993.	Over the sample period, REITs underperformed the stock market (S&P 500 and S&P 400 mid-cap indexes) on a nominal return basis and performed no better than stocks on a risk-adjusted basis. New and old REITs performed about the same, although new REITs had less systematic risk.
Wang and Erickson (1997)	March 1981–Dec. 1991	Examines the performance of MLPs relative to that of REITs.	REITs and real estate MLPs have similar performance but both underperformed the market on a risk-adjusted basis over the entire sample period. This suggests that differences in organizational structure are not the reason for the underperformance of these types of real estate securities, and that the market does not systematically undervalue real estate assets.
Sanders (1998)	Jan. 1978–June 1996	Examines the historical performance of REIT returns relative to those for other portfolios of assets in order to better explain the factors influencing this performance.	Over the entire sample period, REITs performed slightly worse or no better than stock market indices on a risk-adjusted basis. However, this performance varies over time. REITs outperform long-term government and long-term corporate bonds.
Han and Liang (1995)	Jan. 1970–Dec. 1993	Examines three issues: whether REITs performed differently from common stocks, whether REIT performance varies significantly over time, and whether REIT performance is sensitive to the time period and choice of performance benchmarks.	REIT portfolios performed slightly worse or no better than a passively managed portfolio of common stocks on a risk-adjusted basis. Equity REITs tend to perform better than mortgage REITs. Generally, REIT performance is not stable over time.
Glascock and Hughes (1995)	Jan. 1972–Dec. 1991	Examines the risk and return performance of a standardized set of REITs from NAREIT.	REITs underperformed the market on a nominal basis and performed no better than the market on a risk-adjusted basis. Also, REITs have lower systematic risk, with equity REITs having the lowest systematic risk.

Martin and Cook (1991)	Jan. 1980–March 1990	Compares the returns of closed-end (CEM) funds with those of equity REITs and FREITs and publicly traded partnerships (PTLPs) and determines the impact of TRA 1986 on their relative performance using a generalized stochastic dominance model of performance.	Investors prefer CEMs to individual REITS, FREITS, and PTLPs. When combined into portfolios, REITs, FREITs, and PTLPs dominated CEMs for the period 1980–85. For the post-TRA period, 1986–91 CEMs dominated REITs. REITs generally are found to be more risky than CEMs, and TRA 86 is found to have negative impact on REIT performance.
Howe and Shilling (1990)	Jan. 1973–Dec. 1987	Provides evidence on the performance of REITs by advisor type.	REITs generally performed worse than or no better than the market portfolio. However, the performance of REITs differs by advisor type. In addition, performance is affected by REIT size.
Sagalyn (1990)	3rd quarter 1973–4th quarter 1987	Examines the return performance of survivor samples of REITs and real estate companies (REOCs) relative to the stock market over different segments of the business cycle as measured by growth of real GNP.	Survivor REITs had higher and less volatile returns relative to the stock market due to higher returns, lower volatility, and lower systematic risk in periods of high growth of real GNP. Only equity REITs had significant risk-adjusted performance during periods of both high and low growth of GNP. The market offers no premium for active real estate management exhibited by the performance of REOCs over that of survivor REITs.
Chan, Hendershott, and Sanders (1990)	Jan. 1973–Dec. 1987	Examines the monthly returns on equity REITs traded on major exchanges rather than using appraisal-based returns to estimate the risk and return characteristics of REITs.	Equity REITs do not offer superior risk-adjusted returns to the stock market, although they have significantly less systematic risk.
Goebel and Kim (1989)	Jan. 1984–Dec. 1987	Analyzes the investment performance of REITs and finite life REITs (FREITs) and their relative diversification potential.	Returns to both REITs and FREITs underperformed the market. Systematic risk of both types of trusts is lower than that of the market but the reduction in risk may not be warranted by the reduction in returns.

(*continued*)

Table 10.2 *Continued*

Author(s) of Study	Sample Period	Purpose of Study	Authors' Results and Our Interpretation of the Results As They Apply to REIT Performance
Kuhle, Walther, and Wurtzebach (1986)	Jan. 1973–Dec. 1985	Updates the performance evaluation of REIT stocks and determine if REITs outperformed common stocks.	REIT risk-adjusted performance exceeded that of common stocks as measured by the S&P 500 in 10 of the 13 years of the sample period. However, risk-adjusted returns and standard deviations declined after 1980, suggesting an increase in the stability of REIT performance.
Titman and Warga (1986)	Jan. 1973–Dec. 1982	Examines the risk-adjusted performance of a sample of REITs using both a single factor and multiple factor pricing model.	No evidence that REITs outperformed the market on a risk-adjusted basis. Mortgage REITs have greater market risk than equity REITs.
Zerbst and Cambon (1984)	Various periods	Compares the historical performance of real estate assets with the performance of other asset classes.	Real estate returns are comparable to those of other assets while risk is lower. However, REITs are also more volatile relative to the returns to other assets.
Burns and Epley (1982)	1st quarter 1970–4th quarter 1979	Demonstrates that the historical performance of equity REIT stocks over the sample period would have produced a more efficient set if included in a portfolio of common stocks.	Equity REITs had the highest average quarterly return relative to mortgage and hybrid REITs and also the lowest volatility of returns, while mortgage REITs had the lowest returns and greatest risk. Investors would have improved the performance of a stock portfolio by including equity REITs.
Smith (1980)	Jan. 1965–Dec. 1977	Compares the performance of equity REITs with that of common stocks as represented by CEMs.	Over the entire sample period, equity REITs performed slightly better or about the same as CEM funds on a risk-adjusted basis but equity REITs were also less risky than common stocks.
Smith and Schulman (1976)	Jan. 1963–Dec. 1974	Compares the performance of equity REITs with that of common stocks as represented by CEMs.	Over the entire sample period, equity REITs underperformed the market due to their poor performance in 1974. Excluding 1974, equity REITs appeared to do about as well as or no better than common stocks on both a risk-adjusted and nominal-return basis.

Market Factors Affecting REIT Stocks

Investors need to know which market factors explain REIT returns to assess fully how REIT stocks fit into a mixed asset portfolio. Academic research on the issue suggests several market-related factors; in general, it is agreed that the most important ones are variations in the returns to the stock and bond markets and changes in interest rates and unexpected inflation. There is also evidence that REIT returns are affected by a unique real estate factor, as well.

Researchers have consistently shown that there are relationships between REIT returns and the returns of stocks and bonds.[8] In particular, Sanders (1998) suggests that REIT return behavior can best be described in terms of the behavior of a mixed-asset portfolio of stocks and bonds. He shows that REIT stock return behavior is more directly related to high-risk corporate bonds and small stocks than to other indices of portfolio returns.

The finding that REIT stocks behave like small stocks is not surprising. Chan, Hendershott, and Sanders (1990), Han and Liang (1995), Peterson and Hsieh (1997), and Oppenheimer and Grissom (1998) all report that the return behavior of REITs (especially equity REITs) is similar to that of a portfolio of small stocks. However, it should be noted that this finding might reflect the relatively small market capitalization of most REITs prior to the early 1990s. There is no evidence yet on whether the small-firm factor continued to exist in the late 1990s.

In addition, similar to returns to publicly traded non-REIT operating companies, REIT returns appear to be negatively related to their market-to-book value, a traditional measure of relative valuation among investors. That is, holding everything else constant, those REITs with low market-to-book values have higher returns. This is important evidence that further links the valuation of REIT stocks to the valuation of common stocks.[9] The most surprising market factor identified in the real estate literature is reported by Mei and Lee (1994). They find evidence that in addition to the traditional bond- and stock-market factors, a real estate market factor might affect REIT returns.

To summarize the results from this subsection, it would appear that a significant component of REIT stock market returns is systematically related to the returns to both the stock and bond markets. Some part of the variability of REIT returns is also affected by a REIT's market-to-book value and its stock market capitalization (size), and these pricing factors are common to both REITs and other stocks in the market. Furthermore, there is some evidence to indicate that there is a special real estate factor for the pricing of REIT stocks. If these findings are correct, they suggest that REIT stocks can be viewed as a type of hybrid security representing a combination of stocks, bonds, and real estate. Table 10.3 summarizes some of the studies surveying the market factors affecting REIT stock returns.

Table 10.3 Summary of Selected Studies on Market Factors Affecting REIT Stock Returns

Author(s) of Study	Sample Period	Issues Addressed Regarding the Risk and Return Characteristics of REITs	Authors' Results and Our Interpretation of the Results as They Apply to the Risk and Return Characteristics of REITs
Chandrashekaran (1999)	Jan. 1975–Dec. 1996	Determination of the portfolio-diversification benefits of REITs in a mixed asset portfolio (asset allocation), based on their past risk-return characteristics.	The covariability of REIT returns with stocks, bonds, and other macroeconomic variables changes over time, increasing with a decline in a REIT index and decreasing with an increase in the index. This suggests that timing the allocation of a mixed asset portfolio by increasing the investment in REITs can improve the risk-return characteristics of the investor's portfolio.
Oppenheimer and Grissom (1998)	Jan. 1989–Dec. 1994	Examines whether REIT return behavior is different than that of stocks or bonds in order to determine whether REITs provide a reduction in the firm-specific (non-market) risk of a portfolio.	The stock market has greater influence on REIT stock prices than on treasury securities. Among stocks, small-capitalization stocks have the greatest influence, suggesting that REITs behave more like small stocks (and to some extent longer-term bonds) and implying they may have little firm-specific risk-reduction potential in mixed-asset portfolios.
Geltner and Rodriquez (1997)	Jan. 1975–Dec. 1993 and various other sample periods	Examines the appropriateness of REITs for pension fund portfolios as a real estate investment vehicle that can provide diversification relative to direct investments in real property.	In the long run, there is a relatively high correlation between the returns to public and private real estate; the lag between the returns means that there should be an investment horizon of at least five years. REITs are most useful in pension fund portfolios when the target return is high.
Peterson and Hsieh (1997)	July 1976–Dec. 1992	Examines the factors explaining REITs returns and differences in the risk-return characteristics of equity and mortgage REITs.	Equity REIT returns are significantly influenced by stock market returns, size, and market-to-book (MTB) value (low MTB value leads to higher returns). Mortgage REIT returns are also influenced by interest rate factors. Mortgage REITS consistently underperform equity REITs.

Sanders (1998)	Jan. 1978–June 1996	The historical performance of REIT returns relative to those of other portfolios of assets in order to explain the factors influencing this performance.	REIT returns behave more like a portfolio of stocks and bonds; in particular, REITs behave more like small stocks and high yield corporate bonds. REIT returns have become less correlated with other investment vehicles. Equity REIT returns are even more sensitive to the ratio of MTB value, with a low MTB leading to higher returns. REITs are a unique type of stock.
Ghosh, Miles, and Sirmans (1996)	Jan. 1985–June 1996	Similarities between the market for REIT stocks and the market for non–real estate stocks.	The correlation of REIT stock returns with the stock market has declined over time, as has the total risk of REIT stocks. REIT stocks have become less comparable to the average stock in the market in recent years and behave more like unsecuritized real estate. This suggests that REITs may provide more diversification benefits to a mixed asset portfolio.
Liang, McIntosh, and Webb (1995)	Jan. 1973–Dec. 1989	The relationship between the risk of REITs relative to stock market and interest rate behavior.	REIT returns are significantly influenced by the stock market. The bond market has only a relatively small impact on equity REITs but a significant impact on mortgage and hybrid REITs. Market risk has declined significantly over the sample period and for equity REITs is lower and more stable over time than for mortgage and hybrid REITs.
Mueller, Pauley, and Morrill (1994)	Jan. 1976–June 1993	The performance and diversification effects of adding REITs to a mixed asset portfolio.	Including REITs in a mixed asset portfolio of stocks and bonds results in improved risk-return characteristics of the portfolio in all time periods, especially during rebounds in real estate markets. REITs should generally not be included in portfolios during downturns in real estate markets.
Khoo, Hartzell, and Hoesli (1993)	Jan. 1970–Dec. 1989	The change in the market risk of equity REITs over time.	There has been a significant decline in the market risk of equity REITs. This has resulted from the increase in the amount of information investors have about REITs because of the increase in the number of security analysts following them.

(*continued*)

Table 10.3 *Continued*

Author(s) of Study	Sample Period	Issues Addressed Regarding the Risk and Return Characteristics of REITs	Authors' Results and Our Interpretation of the Results as They Apply to the Risk and Return Characteristics of REITs
Chan, Hendershott, and Sanders (1990)	Jan. 1973–Dec. 1987	The relative riskiness of real estate returns using equity REIT stock market returns in a multifactor model.	Three factors drive both real estate and stock market returns: changes in market risk, the term structure of interest rates, and unexpected inflation. In addition, the discount on closed-end funds also affects equity REIT returns. The effects of market risk and term structure constitute about 60% of the impact on corporate stock returns, implying that REITs are less risky that other stocks.
Kuhle (1987)	Sept. 1980–Aug. 1985	The portfolio-diversification benefits of adding REITs to a common stock portfolio.	In a portfolio of common stocks and equity and mortgage REITs, risk reduction is greater for common stocks than for REITs as the number of assets increases. The risk-reduction benefits of adding equity REITs to a common stock portfolio are greater than those of adding mortgage REITs.
Titman and Warga (1986)	Jan. 1973–Dec. 1982	The risk-adjusted performance of a sample of REITs using both a single-factor and a multiple factor pricing model.	The stock market significantly influences REIT returns, and the bond market also influences mortgage REIT returns in the later part of the sample period. Mortgage REITs have greater market risk than equity REITs.

Interest Rates and Stock Factors

Because of their high dividend-payout ratios, REITs traditionally offer relatively stable cash flow streams that resemble the cash flows from fixed-rate bonds rather than those from stocks. The investor might, therefore, expect that both equity and mortgage REIT returns may be more sensitive than those of the average stock to changes in interest rates. That is, REIT returns would decline more than the average stock when interest rates increase. This would be particularly true for returns to mortgage REITs, which own debt securities such as residential mortgage loans and mortgage-backed securities.

Sanders (1998) finds that REIT returns tend to be sensitive to changes in interest rates. However, how sensitive they are depends on the rate used as a proxy for the movement of the interest rates. In general, the literature seems to agree that, other than the effect of the stock market, interest rate changes may explain most of the variation in REIT returns.

There is also plenty of evidence indicating that equity REITs tend to be less sensitive to variations in interest rates than mortgage REITs. Chen and Tzang (1988) use the duration concept to explain this phenomenon. (*Duration* is a measure of the interest rate sensitivity of an asset as determined by the average time to maturity of the asset's cash flows.) For mortgage REITs, an increase in interest rates will lower the market value of the debt instruments that mortgage REITs own. Because the cash flows to equity REITs come primarily from property leases, which are renewed on a more frequent basis, the average duration of cash flows from real property investments is shorter than that from mortgage securities. Therefore, equity REITs are less sensitive than mortgage REITs to changes in interest rates. In this regard, Allen, Madura, and Springer (2001) report that the differences in asset structure, financial leverage, management strategy, and degree of specification of REIT portfolios could affect their sensitivity to interest rates and market risk.

There is also evidence indicating that the interest rate sensitivity of REITs may have declined in recent years. This is explained in part by the popularity of adjustable-rate mortgages in the 1980s. Because this type of mortgage has a shorter duration, it has less interest rate risk and therefore reduces the interest rate sensitivity of mortgage REITs.

Consistent with this last point, Mueller and Pauley (1995) show that the response of REIT stock prices to changing interest rates is likely to be different in different interest rate environments. During periods of rising interest rates, REIT prices generally tend to decline; during periods of falling rates, they tend to rise. However, falling rates tend to affect REIT prices more than rising rates. For example, during the early 1970s, rising rates had a more significant negative impact on REIT stock prices than in other periods because REITs carried more debt during this period (see Mueller and Pauley 1995). Swanson, Theis, and Casey (2002) also report a structural shift during the 1990s that made REITs more sensitive to credit risk.

To summarize, both equity and mortgage REITs are sensitive to changes in interest rates, although equity REITs are less so than mortgage REITs. The interest sensitivity of mortgage REITs appears to have declined in recent years. Furthermore, the interest sensitivity of REITs over time depends on whether interest rates are rising or falling and how much debt REITs are using.

Inflation-Hedging and Diversification Benefits

Given the conclusion that, on a risk-adjusted basis, REIT stocks do not outperform the general stock market, one might wonder what the benefits are to the average investor to including REIT stocks in an investment portfolio. One potential benefit is that it appears, based on media reports, that real estate is a good hedge against inflation and offers diversification benefits. Are these popular beliefs true, and if so, are they reasons to invest in REIT stocks? This subsection addresses these questions.

Inflation-Hedging Potential

It is a commonly believed that real estate provides investors with some protection against inflation because property prices tend to be highly correlated with increases in the general price level. (This belief is backed up by the fact that the property-rent level is a significant part of the Consumer Price Index.) There is evidence in the literature indicating that real estate is, indeed, a good inflation hedge. For example, Hartzell, Hekman, and Miles (1987) report that, in the past, real estate has been an excellent hedge against both expected and unexpected inflation.[10] However, most of the studies on the inflation-hedging ability of real estate use appraisal-based data, and researchers who believe transactions-based data (such as REIT returns data) give more accurate results have debated these results.

Gyourko and Linneman (1988), Rubens, Bond, and Webb (1989), and Bond and Seiler (1998), however, use transactions data and still find that real estate is a good hedge against expected inflation. At the same time, they also find that certain types of real estate (such as residential real estate) provide much better inflation protection than others. This suggests that not all real properties are perfect hedges against inflation. Consequently, a natural question to ask is whether equity REITs are also inflation hedges.

The empirical evidence on this question is mixed, although in general we agree that REITs do not provide the same level of inflation protection as real estate. It appears that whether one believes REITs are or are not a good inflation hedge depends on the type of inflation (expected or unexpected), the type of REIT investment (equity REITs or mortgage REITs), and the length of the investor's holding period.

Gyourko and Linneman (1988) and Park, Mullineaux, and Chew (1990) provide evidence that REITs are *perverse inflation hedges* because their returns are negatively correlated with inflation. This is particularly true for unexpected inflation. On the other hand, Goebel and Kim (1989) and Chan, Hendershott, and Sanders (1990) suggest that REITs provide some hedging ability against expected inflation, but not against unexpected inflation. Furthermore, Chatrath and Liang (1998) and Murphy and Kleinman (1989) find that in the short run, REITs are poor inflation hedges against both permanent and temporary components of inflation. Over longer periods of time, on the other hand, they find weak evidence that REITs do provide some inflation protection. Finally, Glascock, Lu, and So (2002) report that the observed negative relationship between REIT returns and inflation is in fact a manifestation of the effect of changes in monetary policies.

These results indicate that overall REITs are probably not good inflation hedges in the short run and may even be perverse inflation hedges, especially against unexpected inflation. This is true for both equity REITs and mortgage REITs, even though equity REIT stocks are claims on real property assets. Over longer holding periods, however, it is not entirely clear what effect inflation has on REIT returns, although in general there is evidence to indicate that REITs can hedge against expected inflation. (See table 10.4 for a summary of selected research evidence on the inflation-hedging effectiveness of REITs.)

Diversification Potential

Does the inclusion of REIT stocks in a mixed asset portfolio provide diversification benefits? Based on the available empirical evidence on the stock movement of REITs, the answer should be yes. Most studies show that REIT correlation with the stock market is generally quite low. However, it is also generally agreed that equity REITs do not provide a direct substitute for unsecuritized real estate in a mixed asset portfolio. Indeed, since the price movement of equity REITs is also affected by the general movement of the stock market, equity REITs cannot be perfect substitutes for unsecuritized real estate because their risk and return characteristics are not the same.

Rosen (2001) indicates that during the 1993–2000 period the correlation coefficient between REITs and unsecuritized real estate is about –0.016 and between REITs and the S&P 500 is about 0.202. The evidence shows that the stock movements of the traditional REITs are similar to those of the modern REITs created in the 1990s.

Is there direct evidence that adding equity REITs to a mixed asset portfolio (a portfolio of stocks and bonds) improves the portfolio's risk and return characteristics? A number of researchers have looked at this issue and have found significant benefits to adding REITs to the investor's portfolio. In particular, the earliest evidence finds that including REITs in a mixed

Table 10.4 Summary of Selected Studies on the Inflation-Hedging Effectiveness and Diversification Benefits of REITs

Author(s) of Study	Sample Period	Issues Addressed Regarding the Inflation-Hedging Effectiveness of REITs or Real Estate	Authors' Results and Our Interpretation of the Results as they Apply to the Inflation-Hedging Characteristics of REITs or Real Estate
Chatrath and Liang (1998)	Jan. 1972–Dec. 1995	The inflation-hedging effectiveness of REITs over the short run and long run.	REITs are not good inflation hedges in the short run. There is weak evidence of a positive relationship between REIT returns and inflation over the long run.
Larsen and McQueen (1995)	Jan. 1972–Aug.1992	Equity REITs as a proxy for the inflation-hedging effectiveness of real estate in comparison to that of gold and gold stocks.	REITs are poor inflation hedges against expected inflation, especially against unexpected inflation. Investing in an asset representing a claim on real assets does not by itself insure that the investor is protected against inflation.
Yobaccio, Rubens, and Ketcham (1994)	Jan. 1972–Dec. 1992	The inflation-hedging effectiveness of REITs.	REITs offer poor protection against actual, expected, or unexpected inflation. Their poorest performance comes from unexpected inflation. At best, these results indicate that real estate acts as a partial hedge against expected inflation and a perverse hedge against unexpected inflation.
Chan, Hendershott, and Sanders (1990)	Jan. 1973–Dec. 1987	The impact of expected and unexpected inflation on REIT returns.	REIT returns are not affected by expected inflation. However, they are consistently and significantly lowered by unexpected inflation over the entire sample period and all three subperiods.

Park, Mullineaux, and Chew (1990)	Jan. 1972–Dec. 1986	The inflation-hedging effectiveness of REITs using two different measures of expected inflation.	REIT stocks in general behave as perverse inflation hedges against both expected and unexpected inflation using the T-bill rate as the measure of expected inflation. Using the Livingston Survey data to measure expected inflation, REITs are found to be a partial hedge against expected inflation but a perverse hedge against unexpected inflation.
Murphy and Kleinman (1989)	1972–85	The relationship between equity REIT returns and expected and unexpected inflation.	Equity REIT returns are negatively correlated with both expected and unexpected inflation over monthly holding periods. Over annual holding periods, there is no significant relation between REIT returns and either type of inflation.
Goebel and Kim (1989)	Jan. 1984–Dec. 1987	The effectiveness of REIT and FREIT stocks against inflation.	Both types of REIT have little ability to hedge against total inflation. They provide a good hedge against expected inflation but no inflation hedging ability against unexpected inflation.
Gyourko and Linneman (1988)	Feb. 1972–Dec. 1986 and various other sample periods	The hedging effectiveness of REIT stocks against total inflation and against expected and unexpected inflation.	REITs are found to provide partial protection against expected inflation but they are perverse hedges against unexpected inflation. This is particularly true of mortgage REITs.
Hartzell, Hekman, and Miles (1987)	4th quarter 1973–3rd quarter 1983	The inflation-hedging effectiveness of a diversified portfolio of real estate using data on properties from a large commingled real estate fund.	Real estate assets are found to provide a complete hedge against expected inflation over the sample period with larger properties providing greater inflation protection.

Note: Unexpected inflation is the difference between actual inflation and expected inflation.

asset portfolio of stocks and bonds significantly improved the performance of the portfolio during the 1970s and for the first half of the 1980s. Also, the greatest improvement came from adding equity REITs (as opposed to mortgage REITs) to a mixed asset portfolio (see, e.g., Burns and Epley 1982; Kuhle 1987).

In an analysis of the diversification benefits of public and private real estate for pension funds, Geltner and Rodriquez (1997) show that there are significant benefits to adding REITs to an efficient portfolio as the investor's return target rises. That is, more aggressive investors should increase the percentage of their portfolio devoted to REITs and other stocks and decrease the percentage devoted to private real estate and bonds. This is due to the higher average mean returns associated with REITs. Nevertheless, their data also indicate that for reasonable portfolio-return targets of 30% or less, REITs never make up more than 9% of the total portfolio.

Mueller, Pauley, and Morrill (1994) find that, over the period 1976–93, adding equity REITs to long-term portfolios with intermediate levels of risk improved portfolio efficiency for specific return targets, particularly during rebounds in real estate markets. This would indicate that there might be benefits to following a more dynamic diversification strategy. This is particularly true if the market risk of REITs changes over time. However, Ghosh, Miles, and Sirmans (1996) suggest that after considering the higher transaction costs of investing in REITs, the benefits of adding them to a portfolio may be diminished, if not eliminated.

Chandrashekaran (1999) studies the dynamic diversification benefits of REITs and finds that the variability and covariability of REIT returns with the general stock and bond markets are lower (or higher) when the REIT index is rising (or falling). This would indicate that investors should allocate more of their portfolio to REITs after an upward move in the REIT market and less after a downward move when the asset allocation benefits of REIT stocks are lower.

In summary, the discussion in this subsection suggests that, over the long term, REITs provide diversification benefits in the mixed asset portfolios of investors, probably as a result of their high and stable dividend payouts. Furthermore, there is some evidence indicating that investors may wish to consider timing their portfolio-diversification strategies and avoid purchasing REITs in declining markets. Thus, for portfolio-diversification purposes, REIT stocks do matter. For a summary of the results of selected research addressing these issues, see table 10.4.

Other Forms of Securitized Real Estate

The alternative forms of securitized real estate are the stocks of *real estate operating companies (REOCs)*, *master limited partnerships (MLPs)* holding real estate, and *commingled real estate funds (CREFs)*. Although the shares of REOCs trade in the stock market, they are different from REITs because they are not pass-through vehicles and lack the tax advantages of REITs. Also, REOCs actively manage their assets whereas REITs have not managed their properties, until recently, in any significant sense.

A *CREF* is a type of unit trust that operates a diversified portfolio of income-producing properties for pension fund investors. In this respect, CREFs are similar to open-end mutual funds because the investor cannot buy or sell a CREF's shares in the stock market and must redeem them directly from the CREF subject to the cash flow constraints of the fund. *Real estate MLPs* are similar to REITs in the sense that their shares (units) are traded on stock exchanges, and they do not pay taxes at the corporate level. Thus, real estate MLPs continue to have a tax status similar to REITs.

Relative Performance When Compared to CREFs

Studies in the literature indicate that CREFs might perform better than REITs and that the relative performance of CREFs and REITs depends on the type of properties held. Miles and McCue (1982) compare the performance of equity REITs and CREFs over the early and mid-1970s. They find that while the overall performance is similar, there are significant differences in the performance of specific property types held in their portfolios. They also report that the mean returns are higher for REITs concentrating in the hotel, resort, and residential sectors of the real estate market but lower for those in the industrial, office, and retail sectors, with the biggest differences occurring between the industrial and residential sectors.

Zerbst and Cambon (1984) compare the results of prior studies on the relative performance of real estate, REITs, and CREFs over the late 1960s through the mid-1970s. They find that REITs not only earn lower average returns over this time period but also have significantly higher risk. Similarly, Brueggeman, Chen, and Thibodeau (1984, 1992) report that the risk-adjusted performance of CREFs is superior to that of the stock and bond markets, at least over the period 1972–91. This is largely due to the lower level of total risk reported for CREFs. They also find that CREFs have superior risk-reduction benefits for the investor's portfolio and that they are more effective hedges against anticipated inflation, especially when compared with bonds.

One possible explanation for the superior performance of CREFs is that investors in CREFs are primarily institutional investors who are better able to determine the fund's potential based on its asset investments. Another explanation is that CREFs tend to invest in larger real estate projects. This explanation might make some sense because Miles and Esty (1982) and Fletcher (1993) report that the most important factor affecting CREF returns is the size of the investment made.

Nevertheless, it should be noted that the conclusion on CREF returns is based on either appraisal value or unit share value. (See Lai and Wang

1998 for a comprehensive discussion about the appraisal-smoothing hypothesis.) Both values are imperfect proxies for the true returns derived from the stock market. The use of unit share values in computing CREF returns might reduce the variance of the return series but does not help much because there is no real market for CREF units. Although there is no definite evidence, it is possible that the data problem may be responsible for at least part of the higher risk-adjusted returns to CREFs reported in the literature.

In addition, it should be noted that most of the studies cited in this subsection only cover periods in the 1970s and the 1980s. There is no academic literature examining CREF performance in the 1990s. However, Rosen (2001) does provide some related information. He concludes that the average return (10.79%) for modern REITs during the 1993–2000 period exceeds that of private real estate (9.14%). In addition, word on the street also indicates that the performance of CREFs in the 1990s was not as good as in the 1970s and early 1980s. Given this fact and the problem with the data (use of appraisal values), the reader must exercise caution when interpreting the results of the cited studies.

Relative Performance When Compared to REOCs

Gyourko and Keim (1992) report that, during the 1975–90 period, the performance of REOCs is not unlike that of equity REITs, given their respective levels of risk. Although they do not make a direct comparison of the relative performance of REOCs versus REITs, they do show that the returns to REOCs are highly correlated with the returns to equity REITs and the stock and bond markets.

In a direct comparison of the performance of REITs and REOCs, Sagalyn (1990) shows that the risk-adjusted performance of REITs exceeds that of commercial real estate and homebuilder REOCs during most of the 1970s and 1980s. Since one of the differences between REOCs and REITs is that the former actively manages its assets, Sagalyn indicates that these results may suggest that the market did not pay a premium for active management of real estate, at least through the 1980s.

Relative Performance When Compared to Real Estate MLPs

Wang and Erickson (1997) provide evidence on the relative performance of REITs and other types of securitized real estate for the period 1981–91. For this period, they show that REIT performance is similar to that of a portfolio of real estate MLPs and to the stock market in general. Because MLPs are operating companies that hold portfolios of real estate assets and do not pay taxes at the corporate level, the similar performance of REITs and MLPs indicates that it is unlikely that REIT performance is affected by the closed-end fund discount phenomenon. However, given this performance result, it is unclear why REITs became the dominant vehicle for holding real estate in the 1980s while real estate MLPs began to fall out of investors' favor.

The Verdict

In summary, it would appear that as a class of securitized real estate, REITs generally perform no worse than other types of real estate assets that trade on stock exchanges, after adjusting for risk. This would indicate that the stock market does not pay much attention to the organizational structure of securitized real estate. If this is true, REITs—which are now attracting more attention from both institutional and individual investors than REOCs and real estate MLPs—might be the dominant vehicle for holding real estate in the future.

On the other hand, there is evidence that CREFs may perform better than REIT stocks, although, again, there may be a reason. CREF units do not trade on exchanges and do not have much liquidity. The added liquidity risk of CREFs might justify their higher returns relative to REITs. In addition, CREFs may have an upward bias associated with their risk-adjusted returns because these returns are computed using appraisal values, not transaction data. Given this, it is difficult to say whether investing in CREFs is a better choice than investing in REITs.

REITs As Growth Stocks

While REITs are fully capable of growth, they cannot be growth stocks (and should not be viewed as such) both because of their high dividend-payout requirement and the restrictions on their ability to buy and sell their assets. Given this, and in spite of the significant growth of many REITs during the stock market boom of the 1990s, REIT stocks are more similar to income stocks than to growth stocks.

Limitations on Growth

Intuition tells us that, without the ability to retain earnings, growing through property acquisitions requires significant access to capital markets. However, as Wang, Erickson, and Gau (1995) point out, every time a REIT goes to the capital market for funds, the market looks closely at its performance. Mueller (1998) also indicates that, even with access to capital, a REIT must be able to maintain a consistent spread between its return on investment and its cost of capital (or find consistently profitable investments) should its managers decide to adopt a growth strategy.

Downs (1998) points out that the growth of real estate markets is significantly limited by the growth rate of the population and property obsolescence. Together, these sources of increased demand cannot generate a growth rate for the individual REIT of more than 4–5% per year unless the REIT increases its market share. Downs (1998) believes that this is why the natural growth rate of REITs is considerably less than the 15–20% annual growth that typically defines growth companies in the stock market.

Nevertheless, although REITs are not growth stocks, the market tends to pay a premium for growth. Thus REITs must still pursue strategies that generate some growth potential like other stocks in the market in order to continue to be attractive investments. This is especially true when one sector of the market (such as Internet and technology stocks in the 1990s) is attracting the attention of investors.

REITs as Income Stocks

The data reported in table 10.5 and figure 10.1 indicate that when we decompose REIT holding-period returns into price-appreciation and dividend components, the dividend component of the total return is much more stable and frequently larger than the capital gains component. This is further evidence that REIT stocks are more appropriately characterized as income stocks rather than growth stocks (see Liang 2000).

Be Wary of REITs with no Growth Potential

Although we believe that REITs should be classified as income stocks, we want to point out that investors should avoid REITs without any growth potential. This conclusion comes from an analysis of the performance of *self-liquidating finite-life REITs (FREITs)* conducted by Goebel and Kim (1989). FREITs are REITs that have a defined termination date at which time they liquidate their assets, although it is possible that a FREIT could liquidate its assets at an even earlier date if real estate market conditions warranted it.

FREITs were originally created to overcome the problem of the discount of a REIT's share value to its net asset value (the so called *closed-end fund discount phenomenon*) and to make it a more attractive investment vehicle by increasing the probability that investors would realize a capital gain upon termination. However, the benefits of FREITs do not compensate for their investment performance. Goebel and Kim (1989) analyze the investment performance of REITs and FREITs and find that FREITs significantly underperform the market on a risk-adjusted basis. This result is undoubtedly due to FREITs' limited growth potential.

However, because the study conducted by Goebel and Kim (1989) uses a small sample period and may be out of date, we decided to track the stock performance of FREITs over a more recent period to determine whether there is any reason to change our assessment of FREIT stock performance.

Table 10.5 REIT Total Return, Dividend, and Capital Gain Components During the 1963–2000 Period (%)

Year-End	Annual Total Return	Dividend Component	Capital Gain Component
1963	–2.58	2.88	–5.32
1964	26.25	3.57	21.99
1965	14.52	6.17	7.89
1966	–12.79	6.84	–18.50
1967	25.56	7.20	17.40
1968	65.99	6.16	56.81
1969	9.13	5.00	4.01
1970	8.07	8.27	–0.20
1971	29.46	7.71	20.37
1972	14.67	8.25	5.94
1973	–29.63	9.16	–35.71
1974	–66.89	10.55	–70.35
1975	21.70	4.92	16.06
1976	56.11	3.72	50.70
1977	36.11	3.57	31.54
1978	13.33	3.80	9.17
1979	43.67	4.54	37.61
1980	33.69	5.19	27.22
1981	7.61	6.69	0.93
1982	28.39	6.57	20.57
1983	32.82	6.51	24.82
1984	12.68	10.25	2.23
1985	13.32	7.05	5.93
1986	12.45	7.84	4.31
1987	–12.42	9.31	–20.06
1988	10.40	9.73	0.61
1989	–7.46	9.22	–15.39
1990	–24.39	9.96	–31.47
1991	26.87	8.20	17.35
1992	12.65	7.84	4.44
1993	39.18	6.29	31.15
1994	2.67	7.30	–4.36
1995	21.69	8.07	12.71
1996	37.30	8.18	27.13
1997	24.55	8.22	15.19
1998	–14.25	7.51	–20.30
1999	–2.39	9.53	–10.95
2000	15.96	11.78	4.18

Source: Authors' own calculations based on the REIT sample described in the appendix.

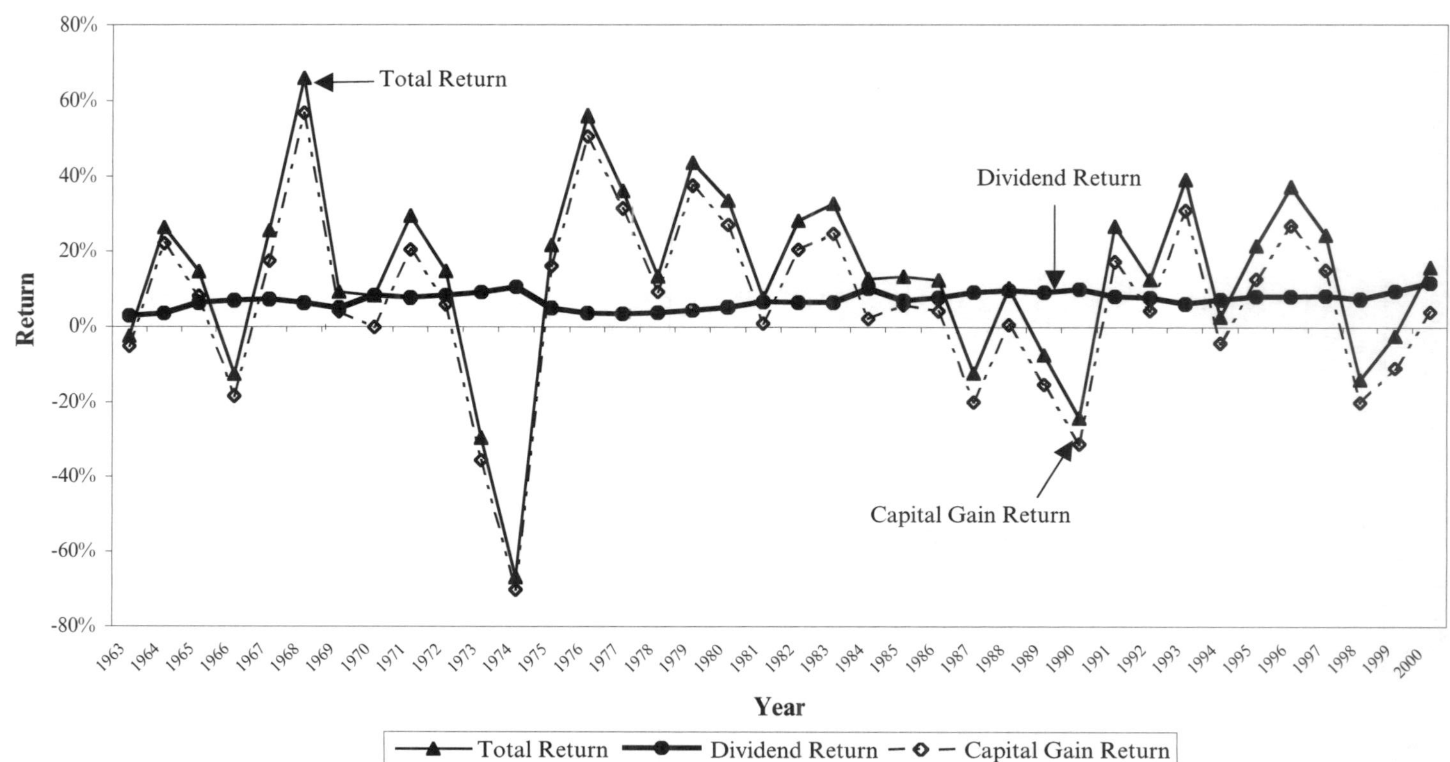

Figure 10.1 REIT Total Returns, Dividends, and Capital Gains Components

Table 10.6 Comparison of the Return Performance of Infinite-Life REITs and Finite-Life REITs

	Infinite-Life REIT		Finite-Life REIT	
Year-End	Mean Total Annual Return (%)	Return Index	Mean Total Annual Return (%)	Return Index
1980	—	100.00	—	100.00
1981	7.60	107.60	6.39	106.39
1982	28.55	138.32	28.81	137.03
1983	33.30	184.39	17.67	161.25
1984	13.71	209.67	0.55	162.14
1985	15.55	242.28	2.69	166.50
1986	18.61	287.37	−5.79	156.87
1987	−9.25	260.79	−21.55	123.06
1988	11.65	291.17	6.70	131.31
1989	−6.31	272.81	−11.27	116.50
1990	−20.95	215.66	−34.52	76.29
1991	32.55	285.87	13.97	86.95
1992	8.73	310.81	19.47	103.88
1993	33.45	414.79	53.23	159.18
1994	0.29	416.00	11.39	177.32
1995	20.53	501.42	25.33	222.23
1996	36.06	682.22	41.26	313.92
1997	23.64	843.49	31.87	413.95
1998	−14.87	718.04	−6.74	386.05
1999	−2.77	698.13	5.09	405.68
2000	16.14	810.81	11.31	451.56
Average	12.51		9.79	

Source: Authors' own calculations based on the REIT sample described in the appendix.

Note: Computations of the return series begins in 1981 because finite-life REITs were not traded until late 1980.

Table 10.6 summarizes the average annual returns of REITs and FREITs over the period from 1981 to 2000. (The first FREIT began trading after 1980.) It is clear from the evidence in the table that the stock returns of finite-life REITs are inferior to those of non-finite-life REITs.

Figure 10.2 charts the relative performance for a $100 investment in a non-finite-life REIT and a $100 investment in an FREIT since 1981. It can be seen that $100 invested in 1981 would have grown to $811 in 2000 if the money had been invested in non-finite-life REITs. However, the same $100 would have grown to $452 in 2000 if it had been invested in FREIT stocks. This confirms the results reported by Goebel and Kim (1989) that REIT investors should avoid REIT stocks that do not have any growth potential, such as finite-life REITs.

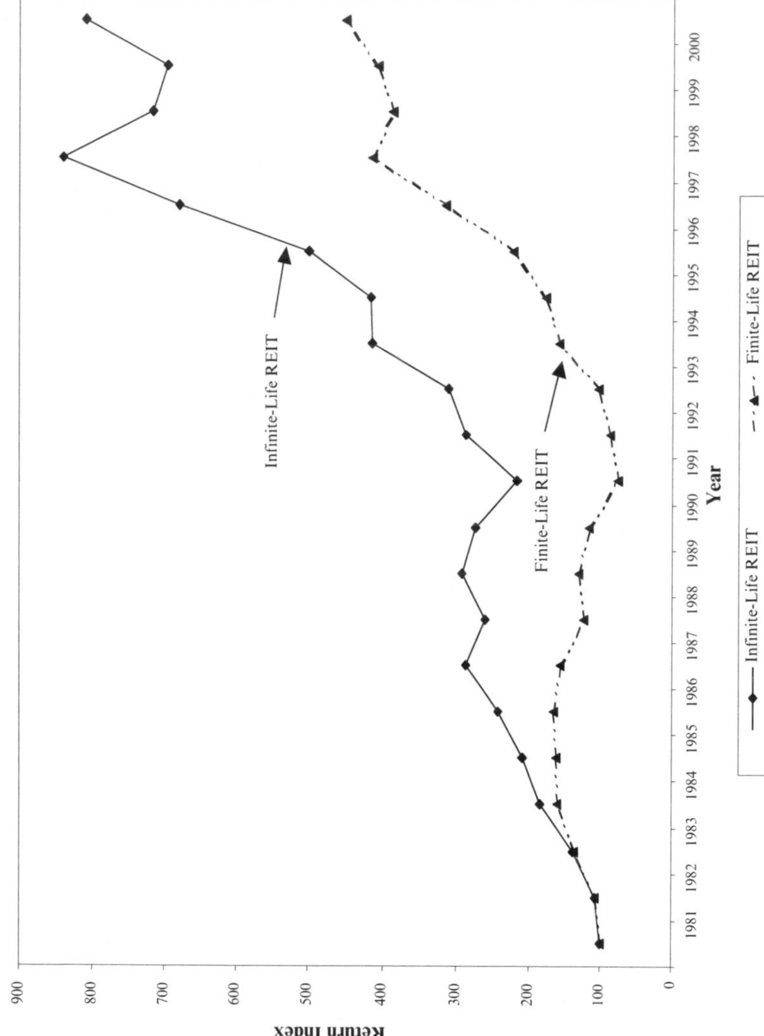

Figure 10.2 Annual Return Index for Infinite-Life and Finite-Life REITs

What Can We Say about Growth?

We know that REITs, by design, should not be high-growth stocks. However, empirical evidence also indicates that the absence of growth potential is not likely to be favorable for REITs. Given this, we might ask whether there are some strategies that REITs could pursue to improve their growth potential within their organizational limitations. Unfortunately, there is little research at this point defining what an optimal growth policy for REITs might be and how they might be achieved. Researchers may want to pay more attention to this topic in the future.

As far as we can see, growth is inevitable for REITs. As REITs gain more control over their operations, there may be potential benefits from scale economies associated with growth, at least up to a certain size. There are also competitive benefits from having a greater market share. Nevertheless, because of the regulatory constraints (tax regulations) limiting their ability to retain earnings, REITs will continue to be viewed mainly as income stocks in the foreseeable future. We also believe that those REITs that completely neglect growth are likely to be penalized by the stock market.

What Have We Learned?

Although there is conflicting evidence, the academic literature generally seems to agree on several important findings about REIT stock performance. These findings are the following:

- Over the long run, REIT stock performance is comparable to that of the stock market as a whole after adjusting for risk.
- Overall, REIT stock performance appears to be comparable to that of other types of securitized real estate on a risk-adjusted basis.
- Considering all REITs, it is quite clear that equity REIT performance has been superior to that of mortgage REITs and hybrid REITs. It is also evident that REITs with finite lives perform much worse than ordinary REITs.
- Over shorter periods of time, REITs as a group have both outperformed and underperformed the stock market. There is no evidence to indicate that the stock performance of modern REITs during the 1993–2000 period is significantly different from (or better than) the stock performance of traditional REITs in the pre-1990 period.
- REIT stocks appear to have better performance when the rate of inflation is relatively low and when interest rates are falling. This area might deserve more attention from real estate researchers.
- There has been a significant declining trend in the market risk of REITs. This reduction in market risk is consistent with the evidence that the flow of information about REITs has improved as REIT market capi-

talization has increased and the percentage ownership of REIT stocks by institutional investors has increased.
- Although REITs are not perfect substitutes for unsecuritized real estate in an investor's portfolio, they are, nevertheless, important additions to a portfolio.
- Small investors are likely to find REITs useful additions to their portfolios mainly because they offer a more stable income component.

Conclusions

It is fair to say that REITs cannot be characterized as growth companies. Although some REITs have tried to adopt growth strategies, they generally have been successful only in periods when real estate markets are rebounding. Given the historical performance of REITs, it is difficult to believe that investors are likely to make big profits in them in the short run even though in certain periods they have done quite well.

REITs are best viewed by investors as long-term investments. They have consistently provided high and stable dividend payments over the last 40 years. This stable payout policy has significantly reduced the variation in REIT returns, which has, in turn, provided stability to investor portfolios. Given this, investors who are looking for a steady income stream and a low-risk investment portfolio should not neglect REIT stocks.

However, for individual and institutional investors who are looking for ways to increase the real estate exposure of their portfolios, it is unclear whether they can achieve this goal by investing in REIT stocks. Although there is recent evidence that REIT stock price movements are correlated with price movements in underlying real estate property markets, it is not clear whether an investor can effectively use REIT stocks as a direct substitute for investments in real estate property markets.

Since it is difficult to predict the future, we cannot provide a simple forecast of how REIT stocks will perform. Nevertheless, it is clear that as REITs become more like operating companies due to changes in the regulations governing them, we can predict that REIT returns will become more correlated with those of the general stock market. In other words, the market risk of REITs will probably increase, not decrease, in the future.

As more institutional investors come into the REIT market and more REITs adopt the UPREIT type of structure, the agency issues and the information asymmetry problems that REITs have faced in the past will be reduced. Given this, the downside risk of investing in REITs will also be significantly reduced. Considering all the factors, we believe that we are less likely to see the extremely poor performance of certain types of REITs (such as FREITs) or REIT IPOs that occurred in the 1970s and 1980s. Rather, the changes in the REIT stock market that have occurred in the last decade suggest that this might be a good time to take a closer look at REIT stocks. It will be interesting to examine REIT performance ten years from now, when the analysis will be based on the stock performance of new REITs with newly adopted structures and larger sizes. It is quite likely that the performance results might be different from those we report here.

NOTES

1. See Ibbotson and Seigel (1984), Firstenburg, Ross, and Zisler (1988), Lusht (1988), Giliberto (1988), Roulac (1988), and Geltner (1989) for a discussion of these issues.

2. See Giliberto (1990), Gyourko and Keim (1992, 1993), Lieblich, Pagliari, and Webb (1998), and Geltner and Rodriquez (1998) for a discussion of these issues.

3. See Liu, Hartzell, Greig, and Grissom (1990) for the first type of evidence and Ghosh, Miles, and Sirmans (1996) and Clayton and MacKinnon (2000) for the second type of evidence.

4. See, for example, Goebel and Kim (1989), Howe and Shilling (1990), Chan, Hendershott, and Sanders (1990), Martin and Cook (1991), Glascock and Hughes (1995), Wang et al. (1995), Wang and Erickson (1997), and Chen and Peiser (1999) for this evidence.

5. See, for example, Kuhle, Walther, and Wurtzebach (1986), Han and Liang (1995), Sanders (1998), and Peterson and Hsieh (1997) for evidence on this issue.

6. See Gyourko and Keim (1992), Khoo, Hartzell, and Hoesli (1993), Liang, MacIntosh, and Webb (1995), Ghosh, Miles, and Sirmans (1996), Sanders (1998), Chandrashekaran (1999), Chen and Peiser (1999), and Liang (2000) for the first type of evidence and Chen and Peiser (1999) for the second type of evidence.

7. For an alternative view of the relationship between equity REIT stock prices and their underlying fundamentals and a discussion of the effects of institutional trading on REIT stock market liquidity, see Graff and Young (1997).

8. See, for example, Titman and Warga (1986), Chan, Hendershott, and Sanders (1990), Gyourko and Keim (1992), Liang, McIntosh, and Webb (1995), Sanders (1998), Oppenheimer and Grissom (1998), and Liang and McIntosh (1998) for this evidence.

9. See Sanders (1998) and Peterson and Hsieh (1997) for this evidence, and see Chen et al. (1998) for somewhat different evidence on this issue.

10. The actual rate of inflation has two components: an expected inflation component and an unexpected inflation component. *Expected inflation* is the component investors build into the rates of return they require on their investments. *Unexpected inflation* is the difference between actual and expected inflation and may be either positive or negative, depending on whether investor expectations of inflation are lower than or greater than the actual rate of inflation.

REFERENCES

Allen, Marcus T., Jeff Madura, and Thomas Springer. 2001. REIT characteristics and the sensitivity of REIT returns. *Journal of Real Estate and Economics* 21:141–52.

Ambrose, Brent W., Esther Ancel, and Mark D. Griffiths. 1992. The fractal structure of real estate investment trust returns: The search for evidence of market segmentation and nonlinear dependency. *Journal of the American of Real Estate and Urban Economics Association Journal* 20:25–54.

Below, Scott D., Joseph K. Keily, and Willard McIntosh. 1996. REIT pricing efficiency: Should investors still be concerned? *Journal of Real Estate Research* 12:397–412.

Bond, Michael T., and Michael J. Seiler. 1998. Real estate returns and inflation: An added variable approach. *Journal of Real Estate Research* 15:327–38.

Brueggeman, W. B., A. H. Chen, and T. G. Thibodeau. 1984. Real estate investment funds: Performance and portfolio considerations. *AREUEA Journal* 12:333–54.

Brueggeman, W. B., A. H. Chen, and T.G . Thibodeau. 1992. Some additional evidence on the performance of commingled real estate investment funds: 1972–1991. *Journal of Real Estate Research* 7:433–48.

Burns, William L., and Donal R. Epley. 1982. The performance of portfolios of REITs + stocks. *Journal of Portfolio Management* 8:37–42.

Chan, K. C., Patrick Hendershott, and Anthony B. Sanders. 1990. Risk and return on real estate: Evidence from equity REITs. *AREUEA Journal* 18:431–52.

Chandraskeharan, Vinod. 1999. Time-series properties and diversification benefits of REIT returns. *Journal of Real Estate Research* 17:91–111.

Chaudry, Mukesh K., F. C. Neil Myer, and James R. Webb. 1999. Stationarity and cointegration in systems with real estate and financial assets. *Journal of Real Estate Finance and Economics* 18:339–49.

Chatrath, Arjun, and Youguo Liang. 1998. REITs and inflation: A long-run perspective. *Journal of Real Estate Research* 16:311–25.

Chen, Su-Jane, Chengho Hsieh, Timothy W. Vines, and Shur-Nuaan Chiou. 1998. Microeconomic variables, firm-specific variables, and returns to REITs. *Journal of Real Estate Research* 16:269–77.

Chen, K. C., and Daniel D. Tzang. 1988. Interest-rate sensitivity of real estate investment trusts. *Journal of Real Estate Research* 3:13–22.

Chen, Jun, and Richard Peiser. 1999. The risk and return characteristics of REITs, 1993–1997. *Real Estate Finance* 16:61–68.

Clayton, Jim, and Greg MacKinnon. 2000a. What drives equity REIT returns? The relative influences of bond, stock, and real estate factors. Working paper.

Clayton, Jim, and Greg MacKinnon. 2000b. Measuring and explaining changes in REIT liquidity: Moving beyond the bid-ask spread. *Real Estate Economics* 28:89–115.

Downs, Anthony. 1998. REIT shares: Are they growth or income stocks? *National Real Estate Investor* 40:32–34+.

Downs, David, Z. Nuray Guner, David J. Hartzell, and Michael A. Torres. 2001. *Why do REIT prices change?* The information content of Barron's "The ground floor." *Journal of Real Estate Finance and Economics* 22:63–80.

Firstenburg Paul M., Stephen A. Ross, and Randall C. Zisler. 1988. Real estate: The whole story. *Journal of Portfolio Management* 14:22–34.

Fletcher, Stuart. 1993. Portfolio consideration in commingled real estate funds. *Journal of Real Estate Research* 8:171–87.

Geltner, David. 1989. Estimating real estate's systematic risk from aggregate level appraisal-based returns. *AREUEA Journal* 17:463–81.

Geltner, David, and Joe Rodriquez. 1997. Public and private real estate: Performance implications for asset allocation. In *Real estate investment trusts,* ed. Richard T. Garrigan and John F. C. Parsons, 371–409. New York: McGraw-Hill.

Ghosh, Chinmoy, Mike Miles, and C. F. Sirmans. 1996. Are REITs stocks? *Real Estate Finance* 13:46–53.

Giliberto, Michael S. 1988. A note on the use of appraisal data in indexes of performance measurement. *AREUEA Journal* 16:77–83.

Giliberto, Michael S. 1990. Equity real estate investment trusts and real estate returns. *Journal of Real Estate Research* 5:259–63.

Giliberto, Michael S., and Anne Mengden. 1996. REITs and real estate: Two markets reexamined. *Real Estate Finance* 13:56–60.

Glascock, John L. 1991. Market conditions, risk, and real estate portfolio returns: Some empirical evidence. *Journal of Real Estate Finance and Economics* 4:367–73.

Glascock, John L., and William T. Hughes Jr. 1995. NAREIT identified exchange listed REITs and their performance characteristics: 1972–1991. *Journal of Real Estate Literature* 3:63–83.

Glascock, John L., Chiuling Lu, and Raymond W. So. 2000. Further evidence on the integration of REIT, bond, and stock returns. *Journal of Real Estate Finance and Economics* 20:177–94.

Glascock, John L., Chiuling Lu, and Raymond W. So. 2002. REIT returns and inflation: Perverse or reverse causality effects? *Journal of Real Estate Finance and Economics* 24, (2002), forthcoming.

Goebel, Paul R., and Kee S. Kim. 1989. Performance evaluation of finite-life real estate investment trusts. *Journal of Real Estate Research* 4:57–69.

Goetzman, William N., and Roger G. Ibbotson. 1990. The performance of real estate as an asset class. *Journal of Applied Corporate Finance* 3:65–76.

Goldstein, Michael A., and Edward F. Nelling. 1999. REIT return behavior in advancing and declining stock markets. *Real Estate Finance* 15:68–77.

Graff, Richard A., and Michael S. Young. 1997. Institutional impact on equity REIT performance. *Real Estate Finance* 14:31–39.

Gyourko, Joseph, and Donald B. Keim. 1992. What does the stock market tell us about real estate returns. *Journal of the American Real Estate and Urban Economics Association* 20:457–85.

Gyourko, Joseph, and Donald B. Keim. 1993. Risk and return in real estate: Evidence from a real estate stock index. *Financial Analysts Journal* 19:39–46.

Gyourko, Joseph, and Peter Linneman. 1988. Owner-occupied homes, income-producing properties, and REITs as inflation hedges: Empirical findings. *Journal of Real Estate Finance and Economics* 1:347–72.

Hartzell, David, John S. Hekman, and Mike E. Miles. 1987. Real estate returns and inflation. *AREUEA Journal* 15:617–37.

Han, Jun, and Youguo Liang. 1995. The historical performance of real estate investment trusts. *Journal of Real Estate Research* 10: 235–63.

Howe, James S., and James D. Shilling. 1990. REIT advisor performance. *AREUEA Journal* 18:479–500.

Ibbotson, Rodger G., and Laurence B. Siegel. 1984. Real estate returns: A comparison with other investments. *AREUEA Journal* 12:219–42.

Khoo, Terence, David Hartzell, and Martin Hoesli. 1993. An investigation of the change in real estate investment trust betas. *AREUEA Journal* 21:107–30.

Kuhle, James L., Carl H. Walther, and Charles H. Wurtzebach. 1986. The financial performance of real estate investment trusts. *Journal of Real Estate Research* 1:67–75.

Kuhle, James L. 1987. Portfolio diversification and return benefits-common stock vs. real estate investment trusts (REITs). *Journal of Real Estate Research* 2:1–9.

Lai, Tsong-Yue, and Ko Wang. 1998. Appraisal smoothing: The other side of the story. *Real Estate Economics* 26:511–35.

Larsen, Alan B., and Grant R. McQueen. 1995. REITs, real estate, and inflation: Lessons from the gold market. *Journal of Real Estate Finance and Economics* 10:285–97.

Li, Yuming, and Ko Wang. 1995. The predictability of REIT returns and market segmentation. *Journal of Real Estate Research* 10:471–82.

Liang, Youguo. 2000. REIT correlation with stock indices. *Prudential Real Estate Investors Research Notes,* 1–3.

Liang, Youguo, and Willard McIntosh. REIT style and performance. *Journal of Real Estate Portfolio Management* 4:69–78.

Liang, Youguo, Willard McIntosh, and James R. Webb. 1995. Intertemporal changes in the riskiness of REITs. *Journal of Real Estate Research* 10:427–43.

Liao, Hsien-hsing, and Jianpig Mei. 1998. Risk characteristics of real estate related securities: An extension of Liu and Mei. *Journal of Real Estate Research* 16:279–90.

Lieblich, Frederich, Joseph L. Pagliari Jr., and James R. Webb. 1998. The historical behavior of REIT returns: A real estate perspective. In *Real estate investment trusts,* ed. Richard T. Garrigan and John F. C. Parsons, 306–38. New York: McGraw-Hill.

Ling, David C., and Andy Naranjo. 1999. The integration of commercial real estate markets and the stock markets. *Real Estate Economics* 27:483–515.

Liu, Crocker H., David J. Hartzell, Wylie Greig, and Terry V. Grissom. 1990. The integration of the real estate market and the stock market: Some preliminary evidence. *Journal of Real Estate Finance and Economics* 3:261–82.

Liu, Crocker, and Jianping Mei. 1992. The predictability of returns on equity REITs and their co-movement with other assets. *Journal of Real Estate Finance and Economics* 5:401–18.

Lusht, Kenneth M. 1988. The real estate pricing puzzle. *AREUEA Journal* 16:95–104.

Martin, John D., and Douglas O. Cook. 1991. A comparison of the recent performance of publicly traded real property portfolios and common stock. *AREUEA Journal* 19:184–212.

Mei, Jianping, and Ahyee Lee. 1994. Is there a real estate factor premium? *Journal of Real Estate Finance and Economics* 9:113–26.

Miles, Mike, and Arthur Esty. 1982. How well do commingled real estate funds perform? *Journal of Portfolio Management* 8:62–68.

Miles, Mike, and Tom McCue. 1982. Historic returns and institutional real estate portfolios. *AREUEA Journal* 70:184–99.

Mueller, Glenn R. 1998. REIT size and earnings growth: Is bigger better or a new challenge? *Journal of Real Estate Portfolio Management* 4:149–57.

Mueller, Glenn R., Keith R. Pauley, and William K. Morrill Jr. 1994. Should REITs be included in a mixed-asset portfolio? *Real Estate Finance* 11:23–28.

Mueller, Glenn R., and Keith R. Pauley. 1995. The effect of interest-rate movements on real estate investment trusts. *Journal of Real Estate Research* 10:319–25.

Murphy, J. Austin, and Robert T. Kleinman. 1989. The inflation-hedging characteristics of equity REITs: An empirical study. *Quarterly Review of Economics and Business* 29:95–101.

Myer, F. C. Neil, and James R. Webb. 1993. Return properties of equity REITs, common stocks, and commercial real estate: A comparison. *Journal of Real Estate Research* 8:87–106.

Myer, F. C. Neil, and James R. Webb. 1994. Retail stocks, retail REITs, and retail real estate. *Journal of Real Estate Research* 9:65–83.

Nelling, Edward F., James M. Mahoney, Terry L. Hildebrand, and Michael A. Goldstein. Real estate investment trusts, small stocks, and bid-ask spreads. *Real Estate Economics* 23:45–63.

Oppenheimer, Peter, and Terry Grissom. 1998. Frequency space correlation between REITs and capital market indices. *Journal of Real Estate Research* 16:291–309.

Park, Jeong Y., Donald J. Mullineaux, and It-Keong Chew. 1990. Are REITs inflation hedges? *Journal of Real Estate Finance and Economics* 3: 91–103.

Peterson, James D., and Cheng-Ho Hsieh. 1997. Do common risk factors in the returns on stocks and bonds explain returns on REITs. *Real Estate Economics* 25:321–45.

Rosen, Kenneth. 2001. Real estate investment trusts (REIT): A safe haven in volatile financial markets. Lend Lease Rosen. Research report, April. Berkeley, CA.

Roulac, Stephen E. 1988. How to value real estate securities. *Journal of Portfolio Management* 14:35–39.

Rubens, Jack H., Michael T. Bond, and James R. Webb. 1989. The inflation-hedging effectiveness of real estate. *Journal of Real Estate Research* 4:45–55.

Sagalyn, Lynne B. 1990. Real estate risk and the business cycle: Evidence from security markets. *Journal of Real Estate Research* 5:204–19.

Sanders, Anthony B. 1998. The historical behavior of REIT returns. In *Real estate investment trusts,* ed. Richard T. Garrigan and John F.C. Parsons, 227–305. New York: McGraw-Hill.

Scott, Louis O. Do prices reflect market fundamental in real estate markets? *Journal of Real Estate Finance and Economics* 3:5–23.

Smith, Keith V., and David Shulman. 1976. The performance of equity real estate investment trusts. *Financial Analysts Journal* 32:61–66.

Smith, Keith V. 1980. Historical returns of real estate equity portfolios. *The investment manager's handbook,* ed. Sumner Levine, 426–42. Homewood, Ill.: Dow Jones-Irwin.

Swanson, Zane, John Theis, and K. Michael Casey. 2002. REIT risk premium sensitivity and interest rates. *The Journal of Real Estate Finance and Economics* 24, forthcoming.

Titman, Sheridan, and Arthur Warga. 1986. Risk and the performance of real estate investment trusts: A multiple index approach. *AREUEA Journal* 14:414–31.

Wang, Ko, and John Erickson. 1997. The stock performance of securitized real estate and master limited partnerships. *Real Estate Economics* 25:295–319.

Wang, Ko, John Erickson, George Gau, and Su Han Chan. 1995. Market microstructure and real estate returns. *Real Estate Economics* 23:85–100.

Yobaccio, Elizabeth, Jack H. Rubens, and David C. Ketcham. 1994. The inflation-hedging properties of risk assets: The case of REITs. *Journal of Real Estate Research* 10:279–95.

Zerbst, Robert H. and Barbara R. Cambon. 1984. Real estate: Historical returns and risks. *Journal of Portfolio Management* 10:5–20.

11

The Predictability of the REIT Stock Market

If I Knew How to Beat the Market, Would I Tell You?

The idea that security prices might follow consistent, predictable patterns that would lead to profitable stock-trading strategies is one that has fascinated investors since securities exchanges were first invented. An investor can become very rich very quickly if he or she is able to earn an above-average profit consistently by simply using public information and a self-devised profitable trading strategy. Indeed, to devise a profitable trading strategy is the dream of every investor, including REIT investors.

However, can this dream come true? If REIT stocks are already priced on average to reflect all information that might be useful to investors, then by definition, any trading strategies based on the same set of information will simply not work. We call this *market efficiency.* In an efficient market, no above-average profit can be consistently earned by using any type of trading strategy. If you believe that the REIT market is efficient, the obvious implication is that REIT investors are better off with a buy-and-hold strategy than with an active trading strategy.

The concept of market efficiency has drawn considerable debate in the finance literature. It might be a topic on which we will never achieve consensus because no one can really exhaust all the possibilities to prove it.[1] However, because there are differences in the information available about different subgroups of stocks, we believe that it may be more realistic to think of market efficiency as a matter of degree rather than as an immutable characteristic of stock markets in general. Clearly, investors are more likely to be able to earn above-average profits if less information is available in the market about the stocks or if fewer informed investors trade the stocks on a regular basis; the reason for this is obvious.

Given this, investors need to be aware of the answers to the following questions when investing in REIT stocks: First, are there any reasons to believe that the REIT stock market may not be efficient? Second, if there are reasons to believe the REIT market is less efficient than the general stock market, can investors profit from the inefficiencies that may exist? These are the questions we address in this chapter.

Possible Reasons for REIT Stock Market Inefficiency

We can identify two reasons that the REIT stock market might be less efficient than the stock market as a whole. First, the finance literature tells us that the price behavior of small stocks is different from that of other stocks in the market. This inefficiency has generally been attributed either to the absence of information about small stocks or to other institutional characteristics of the market for them.

Historically, the behavior of REIT stock returns has been most similar to that of small stocks. As a general rule of the thumb, *small-capitalization (small-cap) stocks* are typically those with a market capitalization of less than $500 million. *Mid-cap stocks* have a market capitalization of approximately $500 million to $3 billion, while *large-cap stocks* have market values over $3 billion. If one compares these definitions to the market capitalization of REITs, it is clear that REITs have typically been small-cap stocks over most of their history. For example, the average equity-market capitalization of all REITs in 1962 was $21 million (see appendix table A.1). This value rose to $93 million in 1991 and reached a maximum of $636 million in 1998. It was not until after mid-1997 that the average equity-market capitalization of REITs moved beyond the small-cap limit of $500 million.

Since institutional investors have relatively little interest in small-cap stocks, securities analysts are much less likely to follow them. Without financial analysts to provide information and institutional investors to digest and trade on this information, the stock market will find it difficult to determine the true value of REIT stocks. Because of the lack of information about REITs there have been relatively fewer investors trading REIT stocks until recently. Consequently, there may be more potential opportunities for investors to consistently earn above-average profits trading REIT stocks if they are willing to study the market more carefully than other investors in the marketplace.

Second, the information on the value of the properties owned by REITs can be difficult to obtain. We know that on the balance sheet, real estate property values are determined by real estate appraisal methods or by their historical acquisition costs adjusted for depreciation. Neither method may fully reflect the true value of the properties. When a REIT holds a diversified portfolio, the valuation of the REIT can be even more difficult. Since real estate markets tend to be separated geographically into smaller local markets, one would have to investigate each and every property market to determine the value of a REIT's holdings—and the meager information available on real estate assets is often unavailable to the investing public. It is obvious that financial analysts will not spend their time doing this. If an individual investor is willing to spend the time to conduct research on a REIT, he or she is unlikely to share the information with others.

Roulac (1988) finds it difficult and expensive to evaluate equity REIT properties, and therefore, the value of their stocks. These valuation difficulties lead Scott (1990) to point out that REIT stock prices may not always reflect the true values of their underlying properties. This is the case even if we consider that REITs might trade at a discount to their net asset values. Given these valuation difficulties, investors who have a better understanding of the true value of the properties might perform better than other investors in the REIT market.

Evidence of REIT-Return Predictability

In order for any investor to profit from a particular trading strategy, the movement of REIT stock prices must be somewhat predictable. If the REIT stock market is efficient, these prices should follow a reasonably random pattern. This means that today's stock prices will not be significantly correlated with past stock prices or past economic variables. On the other hand, if some investors can use today's information (on REIT stock prices and relevant economic variables) to predict tomorrow's prices, they will be able to develop a trading strategy to profit from the predictability of REIT returns.

What is the evidence on the predictability of REIT returns? Initially, Liu and Mei (1992) document that the excess return on equity REITs is more predictable than that of other stocks in the market. They identify three variables that can be used to predict equity REIT returns: the month of January, the treasury-bill (T-bill) rate, and the capitalization rate on real estate (which measures the influence of real estate market conditions on equity REIT returns). Because of the variability in the risk premiums demanded by REIT investors, they suggest that there may be benefits for investors to use market-timing strategies to trade REIT stocks. Mei and Liu (1994) extend these results to include mortgage REITs as well as equity REITs and other real estate stocks. Liao and Mei (1998) also support the results that the returns on real estate–related securities are more predictable than the returns on small stocks and suggest that market timing could be useful to REIT investors.

Cooper, Downs, and Patterson (2000) and Nelling and Gyourko (1998) provide evidence that equity REIT returns are predictable, based on past returns. Of most interest here is that Nelling and Gyourko find that equity REIT return predictability essentially disappears as REITs become larger in terms of market capitalization. For example, in examining the predictability of returns to mid-cap stocks, they find no evidence of significant predictability based on past stock returns. The disappearance of return predictability for larger capitalization REITs may be due, in part, to their greater liquidity because they are more actively traded than smaller REIT stocks, resulting in more efficient pricing. Thus it would appear, based on this evidence, that inefficiency in the REIT stock market might be most closely associated with smaller rather than larger REITs.

However, Li and Wang (1995) find that REIT returns are no more predictable than the returns on other stocks. Karolyi and Sanders (1998) also find that REIT returns are predictable but that most of the predictability is due to the variation in risk premiums investors demand on REIT stocks. That is, after correcting for the risk premium, REIT stocks are no more predictable than other stocks in the market. Ultimately, then, the evidence is mixed, and we cannot be certain of the predictability of REIT returns at this time, which brings us to the next section.

Trading Strategies Based on Predictability

It is not important to the investor whether REIT returns are predictable. Rather, the important question to the investor is whether he or she can develop trading strategies based on this return predictability to earn above-average profits. Many studies in the literature examine the potential profitability of specific trading strategies based on REIT return predictability; as you may have gathered by now, it is unclear whether trading REIT stocks on an active basis can result in above-average profits. We now discuss some of these studies and their findings.

Bharati and Gupta (1992) compare the performance of two different kinds of trading portfolios: those that include different combinations of large stocks, actively traded REITs, and (in some cases) T-bills, versus passive portfolios of alternative combinations of the same assets. They find that in the presence of large transaction costs the active strategy still outperforms a passive trading strategy for quarterly investment periods. They conclude that there is some support for an active trading strategy even in the presence of transaction costs.

Mei and Liu (1994) provide similar evidence, finding that investors would earn above-average profits if they bought REITs when the excess returns in the real estate market were expected to rise and sold them when excess returns were expected to fall. They find moderate evidence that active strategies of investing in real estate stocks, including equity and mortgage REITs, earn higher excess returns relative to a buy-and-hold portfolio combining the same stocks, bonds, and the S&P 500 stock index.

Is it possible that investors could use information on economic policies to earn abnormal profits trading REIT stocks? Darrat and Glascock (1989, 1993) examine this issue by analyzing the role of economic policy variables on the returns to REIT stocks. They find that changes in the monetary base and changes in the returns to the stock market affect the returns to real estate stocks with a significant lag of one to two months. The most plausible explanation for their results, they suggest, is that the transaction costs from acting on information about the impact of fiscal policy on real estate stock returns are greater than the revenue that investors could earn. Given this evidence, it is unlikely that investors can use economic policy variables to earn above-average profits.

The most important study on REIT market efficiency is probably the one by Ling, Naranjo, and Ryngaert (2000). They examine the excess-return performance of five active trading strategies involving differing combinations of REITs, large stocks, small-cap stocks, and T-bills based on prior information about various macroeconomic and firm-specific variables along with prior REIT excess returns. Unlike previous studies that provide evidence that the REIT market might not be efficient, Ling, Naranjo, and Ryngaert find that over the entire period of their study (from 1980 to 1996), actively buying and selling REIT stocks does not outperform a buy-and-hold strategy. These results are important, especially because they cover the most recent period through 1996 and thus incorporate many of the significant changes that occurred in the REIT stock market during the 1990s.

It is clear that, although active trading strategies based on variables that appear to predict REIT returns may be useful in helping investors to earn above-average profits, there may be no above-average profitability associated with such strategies (at least in recent years). While these results may be discouraging for those investors who believe that above-average profits can be earned by actively trading REITs using a particular trading strategy, we are quite sure that the empirical evidence on this issue will not end here. Somehow, some day, some individual will come up with a trading strategy that he or she thinks will work.

Trading Strategies Based on Stock Price Reversals

Among others, Mei and Gao (1995), Graff and Young (1977), and Nelling and Gyourko (1998) have shown that REIT stocks exhibit significant price reversals. Moreover, Cooper, Downs, and Patterson (1999) suggest that this type of price behavior may be due to the investor-overreaction effect similar to that described by DeBondt and Thaler (1985) for the general stock market. What is most interesting about such pricing behavior is that it allows REIT investors to follow a contrarian strategy for picking specific REIT stocks based on past pricing behavior. That is, the investor should buy REIT stocks that have performed poorly in the past and sell (or sell short) REIT stocks that have performed well in the past. This type of unusual pricing behavior allows the investor to identify individual stocks that might lead to above-average profits.

In terms of assessing whether the REIT stock market is efficient, Mei and Gao (1995) point out that it is logical to assume that the market will be less efficient for shorter investment holding periods than over longer periods. This makes sense because shorter time periods allow investors less time to digest new information upon which to base their investment decisions. Consequently, market inefficiencies are more likely to be observed over shorter investment holding periods simply because there is less information available and less time to evaluate and act upon the information that is known about REIT stocks.

Given this, Mei and Gao (1995) look for the existence of a profitable trading strategy using short-term price reversals and short-term investor holding periods. They find that there are significant returns before transaction costs associated with various investment horizons and that these returns increase with the length of the investment horizon out to one year. On the other hand, they also find that the profitability of this strategy declines over the three decades they examine (1962–90) with the smallest profits occurring in the 1980s. More important, they also find that their trading strategy is not profitable for even moderate levels of transaction costs over any investment horizon up to one year. Similar conclusions are reached by Nelling and Gyourko (1998) over the period they examine covering the first half of the 1990s.

However, there is more recent and more encouraging evidence of the profitability of actively trading REIT stocks based on price reversals. Cooper, Downs, and Patterson (1999) examine whether it is possible to make above-average profits from actively trading REIT stocks using a filter rule and the contrarian approach of buying loser portfolios or selling-short winner portfolios. A *filter rule* can be thought of as a simple rule that tells the investor when to buy or sell stocks based on past price movements; for example, "Sell a stock if its price has risen by 10% and buy a stock if its price has fallen by 5%."

Before considering transaction costs, the authors find that their active filter strategies generate much higher returns than a buy-and-hold portfolio. Even after considering reasonable transactions costs, their moderate to extreme filter rules appear to be profitable based on the round-trip trading costs associated with online stock trading. One possible explanation the authors offer is based on the evidence that cash flow is more important in determining real estate returns relative to other stocks. If cash flow is more difficult to predict over a short investing period, REIT stock prices may be more susceptible to investor overreaction than other stocks. The results of this study are dramatic, particularly since the evidence runs through 1995 and incorporates many of the post-1990 REIT market changes.

To summarize, although the evidence on the profitability of trading strategies based on REIT stock price reversals is clearly mixed, it suggests that the REIT stock market is likely to be efficient after consideration of transaction costs and risk. On the other hand, the evidence for market timing using contrarian trading strategies based on short-term trading periods and moderate to extreme filter rules clearly indicates some possibility for earning above-average profits.

However, when a researcher presents the public with a profitable trading strategy, the natural question to ask is "So why not use the trading rule to make money in the REIT stock market instead of just reporting the strategy?" Of course, if the trading rule works, the researcher should make a lot of money trading REIT stocks; but once it is widely reported and everyone else begins to use it, we can be sure it will no longer work. Nevertheless, Cooper, Downs, and Patterson's 1999 work tells us it is possible to develop a trading rule for REIT stocks and profit from using it. In other words, investors who wish to employ active trading strategies might still be able to find opportunities in the REIT stock market. Table 11.1 summarizes the important research results discussed so far in this chapter.

Momentum Trading in REITs

The opposite of the contrarian trading strategy is *momentum trading*. It is well documented that the momentum effect exists in the U.S. stock market as well as in the international stock markets (see Jegadeesh and Titman 1993, 2001). The finance literature also finds reliable evidence that past winning (losing) stocks are more likely to be winners (losers) over a short (say, six-month) holding period. Given this, an investor who believes in momentum investment strategies should buy stocks that are past winners and sell those that are past losers.

Chui and Wei (2001) examine whether the momentum strategy works in the REIT stock market. They find that this strategy generates a profit of 0.76% per month from REIT stocks during the 1982–97 period. A profit of 0.61% is obtained from common stocks over the same period. They attribute the more pronounced momentum effect in REIT stocks to the fact that REITs are less liquid and smaller in size than common stocks.

Most interestingly, the authors also find that during the pre-1990 period the momentum effect in REITs is very weak. However, the profit derived from momentum-based trading becomes much stronger after 1990. They believe that the difference in the returns from using a momentum strategy is probably caused by the increase in valuation uncertainty associated with REITs. Indeed, when compared with the pre-1990 period, there should be more valuation uncertainty surrounding REITs after 1990 due to significant changes in REITs' organizational structures, ownership structures,

Table 11.1 Summary of Selected Studies Addressing the Existence of Profitable Trading Strategies for REIT Stocks

Author(s)	Sample Period	Issues Addressed Applying to the Profitability of Trading Strategies	Results and Our Interpretation of Them as They Apply to the Profitability of REIT Stock-Trading Strategies
Ling, Naranjo, and Ryngaert (2000)	Jan. 1980–Dec. 1996	Comparative performance of a passive REIT portfolio and five actively traded portfolios mixing REITs with T-bills, the S&P 500, and small stocks using REIT return predictability as the basis for the active strategies.	After adjusting for transaction costs and risk, the active trading strategies involving REITs and T-bills have a similar performance for the period 1980–1989. Over the entire sample period and during the period of the 1990s the active strategies underperformed the buy-and-hold REIT portfolio.
Cooper, Downs, and Patterson (1999)	Jan.1973–Dec. 1995	Performance of REITs using filter rules based on more extreme price movements resulting from investor overreaction to news about REIT stocks for different holding periods.	Considering transaction costs, the contrarian investment strategy examined yields significant abnormal profits after controlling for factors that would bias the results. These results occur not only for weekly trading periods but also for longer investment periods up to one year.
Nelling and Gyourko (1998)	Jan.1975–Dec. 1998	Predictability of returns on equity REITs and the performance of a contrarian strategy designed to take advantage of the negative monthly correlation of REIT returns.	Monthly returns on equity REITs are predictable, particularly for the periods 1975–84 and 1993–95. This predictability disappears for larger mid-cap stocks. Average monthly returns from a strategy of buying underperforming stocks and selling overperforming stocks are not large enough to cover transaction costs and make the strategy profitable.
Mei and Gao (1995)	July 2, 1962–Dec. 31, 1990	Usefulness of the predictability of returns to exchange-traded REITs and other real estate stocks in an arbitrage- trading strategy designed to profit from price reversals in real estate stocks.	While there are profits associated with a trading strategy based on the significant price reversals observed, after considering moderate levels of trading costs these profits disappear. The REIT stock market is probably economically efficient, although the results provide useful trading rules for longer-term real estate security fund managers.
Mei and Liu (1994)	Jan. 1971–April 1989	Performance of market timing for active trading strategies based on the predictability of REITs and other real estate security returns.	Active-trading strategies using market timing based on the predictability of real estate security returns outperform passive schemes on either a risk-adjusted or unadjusted basis. This is true for mortgage and equity REITs as well as other real estate securities relative to portfolios of stocks and government bonds.

and business strategies. Given this evidence, it appears that momentum trading is likely to continue to be a viable strategy because the valuation of REITs is becoming increasingly complicated.[2]

What Have We Learned?

This chapter asks whether investors should pursue strategies of actively trading REIT stocks based on the assumption that the REIT stock market is inefficient. The answer to this question can be briefly summarized in the following points:

- If REIT stock returns are predictable, investors might be able to consistently earn above-average profits even after consideration of transaction costs and risks.
- Although it is clear that REIT returns are somewhat predictable, it is not clear whether they are more predictable than other stocks in the market.
- There is no evidence to indicate that REIT investors using trading strategies based on economic variables are able to earn above-average profits after deducting transaction costs.
- There is limited evidence that in the past investors have been able to earn significant profits using a contrarian strategy of buying (and selling) REIT stocks. However, it is unclear whether this strategy will continue to work in the future.
- There is also evidence that a momentum trading strategy has been able to earn REIT investors excess profits after 1990, although this strategy did not work for the period before 1990.
- Intuitively, the use of a trading rule should not generate an above-average return because other investors are likely to discover it and compete away any profits. However, we cannot exclude the possibility that such a trading rule exists for REIT investors.

Conclusions

The empirical results documented by research on REIT stock market efficiency are more or less consistent with those on the efficiency of the general stock market. Although it is possible that the REIT market is less efficient than the stock market in general, it is unlikely that REIT investors could earn above-average profits by following certain trading strategies. It is intuitively clear that if reasonably simple and profitable trading strategies based on public information did exist, it is likely (although not certain) that other investors would have discovered them as well and acted upon this information. In the process it is likely that such competition would have eliminated any above-average profits.

Even if it is proven that certain trading rules can be profitable based on historical data, REIT investors should be careful when applying those rules. There is no guarantee that the trading rules that worked in the past will work in the future. Finally, we suggest that REIT investors pay little attention to published trading rules. If those rules really worked, the researcher would have used them to make money for him- or herself rather than publishing them.[3]

NOTES

1. See Fama (1991) and Haugen (1995, 1999) for the evidence for and against market efficiency.

2. However, it should be noted that Buttimer, Hyland, and Sanders (2001) point out in their recent working paper that REIT returns in the 1990s are entirely a function of REIT IPO returns. After controlling for REIT IPO returns, they find that REIT returns are not sensitive to momentum factors.

3. Professor Jianping Mei, who reviewed this chapter for the authors, casually pointed out a possibility that researchers might not have either the required capital or the risk tolerance to capitalize on the opportunity. Although we do not think that academicians are being paid so badly, we cannot rule out this possibility.

REFERENCES

Bharati, Takesh, and Manoj Gupta. 1992. Asset allocation and predictability of real estate returns. *Journal of Real Estate Research* 7 (4): 469–84.

Buttimer, Richard, David Hyland, and Anthony Sanders. 2001. IPOs and mutual fund returns. Ohio State University. Working paper.

Cooper, Michael, David H. Downs, and Gary A. Patterson. 1999. Real estate securities and a filter-based, short-term trading strategy. *Journal of Real Estate Research* 18 (2): 313–33.

Cooper, Michael, David H. Downs, and Gary A. Patterson. 2000. Asymmetric information and the predictability of real estate returns. *Journal of Real Estate Finance and Economics* 20 (2): 225–44.

Chui, C. W., and K. C. Wei. 2001. Investor overconfidence, valuation uncertainty, and momentum in REITs. Hong Kong University of Science and Technology. Working paper.

Darrat, Ali F., and John L. Glascock. 1989. Real estate returns, money, and fiscal deficits: Is the real estate market efficient? *Journal of Real Estate Finance and Economics* 2:197–208.

Darrat, Ali F., and John L. Glascock. 1993. On real estate market efficiency. *Journal of Real Estate Finance and Economics* 7 (1): 55–72.

DeBondt, W., and R. Thaler. 1985. Does the stock market overreact? *Journal of Finance* 40 (3): 793–805.

Fama, Eugene F. 1991. Efficient capital Markets: II. *Journal of Finance* 46 (5): 1575–1618.

Graff, Richard A., and Michael S. Young. 1997. Institutional impact on equity REIT performance. *Real Estate Finance* 14 (3): 31–39.

Haugen, Robert A. 1995. *The new finance: The case against efficient markets.* Englewood Cliffs, N.J.: Prentice Hall.

Haugen, Robert A. 1999. *The inefficient stockmarket: What pays off and why.* Englewood Cliffs, N.J.: Prentice Hall.

Jegadeesh, Narasimhan, and Sheridan Titman. 1993. Returns to buying winners and selling losers: Implications for stock market efficiency. *Journal of Finance* 48:65–91.

Jegadeesh, Narasimhan, and Sheridan Titman. 2001. Profitability of momentum strategies: An evaluation of alternative explanations. *Journal of Finance* 56:699–720.

Karolyi, Andrew G., and Anthony B. Sanders. 1998. The variation of economic risk premiums in real estate returns. *Journal of Real Estate Finance and Economics* 17 (3): 245–62.

Li, Yuming, and Ko Wang. 1995. The predictability of REIT returns and market segmentation. *Journal of Real Estate Research* 10 (4): 471–82.

Liao, Hsien-hsing, and Jianping Mei. 1992. Risk characteristics of real estate related securities: An extension of Liu and Mei (1992). *Journal of Real Estate Research* 16 (3): 279–90.

Ling, David C., Andy Naranjo, and Michael D. Ryngaert. 2000. The predictability of equity REIT returns: Time variation and economic significance. *Journal of Real Estate Finance and Economics* 20 (2): 117–36.

Liu, Crocker, and Jianping Mei. 1992. The predictability of returns on equity REITs and their co-movement with other assets. *Journal of Real Estate Finance and Economics* 5 (4): 401–18.

Mei, Jianping, and Crocker Liu. 1994. The predictability of real estate returns and market timing. *Journal of Real Estate Finance and Economics* 8 (2): 115–35.

Mei, Jianping, and Bin Gao. 1995. Price reversal, transaction costs, and arbitrage profits in the real estate securities market. *Journal of Real Estate Finance and Economics* 11:153–65.

Nelling, Edward, and Joseph Gyourko. 1998. The predictability of equity REIT returns. *Journal of Real Estate Research* 16 (3): 251–68.

Roulac, Stephen E. 1988. How to value real estate securities. *Journal of Portfolio Management* 14 (Spring): 35–39.

Scott, Louis O. 1990. Do prices reflect market fundamentals in real estate markets? *Journal of Real estate Finance and Economics* 3 (1): 5–23.

12

The Future of REITs

REITs Are Here to Stay—Because They Will Continue to Evolve

The REIT concept that was first introduced to public investors in the early 1960s has changed significantly over the past 40 years. During this period of evolution, REIT managers have become more seasoned and REITs themselves have become more structured. Security analysts and pension fund managers are paying more attention to REITs as their capitalization and trading volume have grown. These changes have caused Wall Street to recognize REITs as an increasingly important asset class that warrants greater attention.

Nevertheless, investors must be confident that the REIT industry will grow and prosper if REITs are to remain attractive long-term investment vehicles. In the past, many different forms of ownership structures for holding real estate investments existed in both the private and public capital markets. Mueller and Anikeeff (2001) point out that the most popular investment vehicles in the 1960s, 1970s, 1980s, and 1990s have been mortgage REITs, real estate limited partnerships (RELPs), real estate operating companies (REOCs), and equity REITs, respectively. It is clear that in the last 40 years, real estate developers and investors have tried many different structures as they searched for the optimal one for holding and investing in real assets. How can we be sure that the REIT concept will not lose favor in the near future?

A simple statistic points to the fact that there is tremendous potential for the increased securitization of real estate assets. Today in the United States it is estimated that REITs account for only a relatively small proportion, roughly 10%, of the total real estate assets owned by institutional investors. This suggests potential for the growth of the REIT industry in the future—but will the current REIT structure be the vehicle that is used for this growth? And if so, what changes to REITs might we anticipate in the future?

In this chapter, we predict that REITs are here to stay. We believe that although the current REIT format may change in the future, its use as an important investment vehicle for holding real estate will continue. We then discuss a number of changes that are likely to affect the growth and prosperity of the REIT industry. These changes are not merely predictions—to varying degrees, they are already underway.

Why REITs Will Always Stay with Us

Based on our observation of the performance of REIT stocks over the past 40 years, we believe the REIT concept will continue to thrive. While we cannot say that the stock performance of REITs over the past 40 years is superior to that of other stocks in the market, we can safely say that there is a clear demand for REIT stocks by investors; and as long as there is demand for REIT stocks, REITs will stay with us.

REITs' high dividend-payout ratios and zero corporate income taxes create the demand for their stocks. When the stock market is hot, both REITs and other stocks are all in demand. When the stock market is cold or volatile, however, REITs with their high cash-dividend yields will be preferred by investors who are looking for safer havens and steady cash flows. Indeed, when the stock market is cold (that is, when stock prices are falling), some investors might be unwilling to sell their stocks. In this situation, REITs are vehicles that will be able to provide stable investment income.

The reason REITs are able to generate a stable income stream is quite simple. The income of an equity REIT typically comes from the rental income of the properties it owns. Since rental income is normally secured by long-term leases, REIT cash flows will not be affected by the performance of the stock market, at least in the short run. The debt payments on the mortgages owned by mortgage REITs should be fixed if the underlying mortgages are fixed rate instruments. Under this circumstance, regardless of stock market fluctuations, the scheduled income of mortgage REITs should also be quite stable. Since REITs will pay out most of their taxable income, this high dividend payment together with the steady income stream will be a stable force for investors in a volatile market. For this reason, there will always be a demand for REIT stocks.

It might be fair to say that the current wave of increased investor interest in REITs is part of a shift from technology and Internet stocks to safe stocks. At the 2000 annual shareholders' meeting of Kilroy Realty, the managers noted that Kilroy's stock had jumped from its March 14, 2000 price of $19.75 to $22.94 at the end of May. In the same period, the tech-dominated Nasdaq composite index plummeted 32%. This example demonstrates that when the overall stock market is down, REIT stocks are more likely to look attractive to investors.

In addition, REITs are also favored by investors when interest rates are low. When investors realize that a REIT will provide, say, an 8–10% dividend yield while the interest rate is only perhaps 5%, investors will have considerable incentive to switch from fixed income securities to REITs. By doing so, they will be better off as long as the prices of REIT stocks do not drop.

Given this, investors could find REIT stocks attractive when interest rates are low, when the stock market is performing poorly, or when the stock market is volatile. How about when the stock market is performing well? We believe that REITs will also be in demand when the stock market is moving up. For diversification purposes, there is a need to find an easy way for investors to invest in real estate. Since the price for individual commercial properties is very high, it is typically difficult for small investors to come up with the required funds to invest directly in them. Furthermore, individual investors may not have the required expertise to select properties for investment, and even for those who do, the search costs may be too high.

We know that investors need to establish diversified portfolios and that a truly diversified portfolio must include real estate. Given this, there must be some convenient way for investors to hold real properties. With their tax advantage, REITs should have a competitive edge over other types of organizational forms in this arena. As a result, we believe we should see REITs flourish as long as Congress does not take away their tax advantages.

However, although we argue that REITs will remain as investment vehicles, the changing environment will force them to evolve. Again, since one of the main reasons for investing in REITs is the tax benefit, it is likely the majority of the changes will come hand-in-hand with changes in the tax laws. In the next five sections, we briefly discuss what the likely changes will be for REITs over the next couple of years.

Operating Company versus Mutual Funds

It is important to note that stocks of firms from many industries are traded in the market; however, only the real estate industry uses the fund-like organizational structure of the REIT. In other words, all other firms in the stock market are operating companies, whereas traditional REITs behave more like passive investment vehicles. Although it might be argued that closed-end mutual funds traded in the stock market are also passive vehicles, we should note that the underlying assets of a mutual fund are the stocks of operating companies. Unlike traditional REITs, stock mutual funds do not hire advisors to manage the companies they own. Thus, it is fair to say that the assets owned by stock mutual funds are still actively managed by operating companies. Traditional REITs, however, are purely passive investment vehicles and their assets are not internally managed.

Why do traditional REITs use this out-of-favor, fund-like structure to hold their assets? The answer is quite simple: This structure is required by law and is the price a firm has to pay if it wants to qualify as a REIT. If REITs were given the choice of becoming operating companies without affecting their eligibility to receive tax benefits, it is quite likely that many would become operating firms; once the tax laws governing REITs become less constraining, we should see this taking place. Indeed, given what we have observed, we believe that the next generation of REITs will be more like operating companies than they currently are.

If the intention of Congress in establishing REITs was to encourage investment in real estate by individuals, then there was no need to restrict REITs from becoming operating companies. The high dividend-payout ratio ensures that the primary function of REITs will be that of a passive investment vehicle. The passage of the REIT Simplification Act of 1997 (REITSA) and, more recently, the REIT Modernization Act of 1999 (RMA) demonstrate that the switch, although gradual, from a fund-like structure to an operating company is a possible direction for future REITs.

Prior to the Tax Relief Act of 1986, REITs could provide their tenants with customary services only by contracting with an independent third party. REITs could also invest in the non-voting stock (preferred stocks) of third-party subsidiaries (TPSs) that provided services to REIT tenants. However, since REITs cannot control TPSs, there is a potential conflict of interest as well as a loss of revenue that might otherwise have been earned by the REIT.

REITSA made it possible for REITs to provide a small number of services that were not customary as long as the income earned from such services did not exceed 1% of the property's gross income. This reduced the possibility that traditionally qualified income earned by a REIT would be disqualified by the IRS on the grounds that the REIT was earning other income through the provision of impermissible services. Nevertheless, REITs still lacked the necessary flexibility to effectively pursue alternative sources of income from the provision of unrelated services without using a TPS.

The RMA significantly improved this situation. The RMA allows REITs to own a controlling interest in the stock of a taxable REIT subsidiary (TRS) as long as this ownership is not greater than 20% of the REIT's assets. However, the flexibility that the RMA gives to a REIT to control ancillary businesses through a TRS also has a cost, and that is that a REIT must pay taxes on the income earned through a TRS. This might seem to be a drawback at first, but we should understand that the use of a TRS is simply an option. When REITs believe that they will be able to take advantage of new investment opportunities, they are likely to use a TRS. Otherwise, they still have the option to use the traditional approach and retain their tax exemption.

The trend is clear. REITs will become more like operating firms in the future. The stock market is also embracing this idea. In October 2001, Standard and Poor's announced that it will include several REITs in its S&P 500, S&P MidCap400, and S&P SmallCap600 indices, citing the fact that REITs have become operating companies as the major reason for this move. In the future, REITs will actively manage their own properties and will become more involved in real estate–related businesses based on their own individual strengths, the types of holdings, and the tax situations of the new businesses into which they enter. What kind of businesses will be more suitable for the new generation of REITs to pursue? The next subsection will discuss this issue.

Non–Real Estate Products

Because of the nature of their businesses, REITs—particularly equity REITs—have traditionally had access to significant amounts of information about their tenants' needs. This information, coupled with their existing tenant business relations, creates a ready market for the variety of products that REITs are uniquely positioned to supply as middlemen. REITs could conceivably provide certain goods and services at a lower cost to their customers than direct third-party suppliers can. These services range from traditional laundry and cable television services to the possibility of credit card services, telecommunications and computer services, utility services, mortgage brokerage services, title insurance services, and Internet access and other web-based services. To list a few examples, BRE Properties has invested in the provision of high-speed Internet services to its tenants. Summit Properties, Inc., has invested in an Internet vendor that allows builders and vendors to obtain supplies directly off the Internet. CarrAmerica has invested in a start-up technology that is the primary provider of telecommunications services to CarrAmerica's tenants. CenterPoint Properties has partnered with another company to consolidate their tenants' buying power to purchase telecommunications services, computer products, and utilities. CenterPoint also intends to provide their tenants with online rent-paying services, maintenance services, and accounting services.

REITs have also been forming cooperative arrangements to purchase electricity for their tenants to reduce the cost of electricity services. Some REITs employ vertical portals whereby they contract with a set of providers to obtain office products, office furniture, computers, and Internet services. Other REITs are providing more specialized services such as concierge and travel services. All of these activities not only provide a REIT's tenants with the products they need but, in providing these products in a more convenient fashion and at a lower cost, they improve the REIT's ability to retain its tenants while at the same time enhancing its revenues.[1]

Furthermore, it will be no surprise if REITs become involved in the property development and commercial banking businesses. In any case, REITs will be the buyers of the properties sold by developers or the buyers of the loans to the development. There is no reason that REITs cannot share some of the development profits with the developer by becoming an equity partner or by providing the required development loans for the project they intend to buy at the development stage. Development companies, on the other hand, should be happy to partner with REITs because by doing so they can be assured that the development projects will be sold at a reasonable profit without much risk.

Those REITs that know the specific needs of their tenants will be best suited to adopt this development strategy. Since they know the needs of their tenants, they can identify their demands, and then create the best product to satisfy these demands by partnering with developers. Given this, the involvement of REITs in the development business seems to be a win-win situation. Some REITs seem to be moving in this direction. For example, we note that in 2000, Spieker Properties had approximately $500 million in developments under construction, and Kilroy had approximately $600 million in developments in its portfolio.

However, in spite of the benefits that many of these non-real-estate-related activities convey to REIT clients, there is a concern that these activities will lead REITs to stray too far from their traditional real estate operations and they could find themselves dependent upon revenue sources from markets about which they have little expertise. This would make them vulnerable to adverse changes in these markets as well as expose them to a whole new set of competitors.

This concern, however, could be misplaced. Clearly, for REITs to stray too far from their original purpose (real estate investment) would not only expose them to new competitive pressures, but would likely raise significant questions about the logic of the tax benefits they currently receive. For example, it is speculated that McDonalds might spin off its vast property holdings into a REIT to take advantage of this new tax regulation (*Kiplinger's Personal Finance Magazine,* August 2001, 31). Clearly, an incident like this will soon attract the IRS's attention. However, as long as REITs use their TRS investments primarily to provide needed services and products to their tenants rather than undertaking entirely new businesses, they will have an edge over their competitors in conducting these businesses. Also, they will not arouse the attention of the IRS over whether they should continue to enjoy a special tax status. This means that future REITs should not stray too far from their real estate investment businesses and should use the TRS only to improve their competitive edge and to increase their revenues.

The Changes Ahead

It is clear that in the future REITs will not only make their own investment decisions and manage their own properties but will engage in the business of providing services and products to their tenants, suppliers, and customers as well. However, we might ask what the best ways are for REITs to deliver these new products and run new businesses. This might require some creative thinking.

Use of Alliances and Joint Ventures

Should a REIT start a new TRS to conduct the non-core real estate or real estate development businesses they intend to engage in? Our answer is definitely no. By forming a new firm to conduct this business, a REIT is, in fact, moving into a new and potentially unfamiliar area. Although it might be possible for a REIT to establish subsidiaries if the new business is profitable, we should also remember that investors choose REITs because of their real estate holdings and tax benefits—not their unrelated subsidiary businesses.

More important, we are skeptical of the wisdom of REITs' competing against specialists in other industries. While there is no doubt in our mind that REITs can make some profitable deals because they have business relationships with their tenants and know their needs, it is doubtful that the volume of the business resulting from this special relationship could support an independent firm. If it cannot, the newly established firm will need to compete with other firms in the field for survival.

Should REITs be providing tenants with services? Of course they should, as long as it is profitable, but they should be using strategic alliances or revenue-sharing arrangements and leaving it at that. In other words, a REIT should capitalize on the information advantage and business relationship it has with its tenants and suppliers, but it should leave the details of the non-core businesses to the experts in those particular fields. How? By forming a strategic alliance. In other words, the REIT could take a small equity stake in a strong company in the business it wants to join. The REIT will contribute information and its business relationships to the alliance while its partner firm takes care of all other aspects of the business.

Chan et al. (1997) demonstrate that strategic alliances create value for firms. Their empirical evidence indicates that the stock market seems to like this type of arrangement and responds favorably to firms' announcing the adoption of the alliance strategy. We know that, under an alliance or joint-venture arrangement, both parties will be able to contribute their expertise to the venture and need not take unnecessary risks. In addition, it will be easy to disband the joint venture at a low cost should the initial idea work out. Given this, we believe that a sensible way for REITs to explore investment opportunities in non-core real estate businesses is to avoid establishing their own subsidiaries. Instead, REITs should use strategic partners to minimize their risks and maximize their potential gains.

Increased Use of Technology

It is generally agreed that much of the significant increase in the productivity of business in the United States over the last decade is due to the successful adaptation of computer and new telecommunications technology to the needs of business. This is, of course, also true for REITs. However, compared with other industries, REITs were somewhat slow at first to adopt many of these new technologies. Apparently, once REITs become more like operating companies, this trend will change significantly. This is particularly true in the areas of accounting, leasing, and property management. In addition, technology will also be used to identify the needs of clients and provide them with a variety of revenue-enhancing services.

A growing number of REITs have recently adopted Internet technologies to consolidate their purchases of supplies and their maintenance and repair services. This has the benefit of reducing the costs of such services. Indeed, some REITs are investing directly in software technology designed to enhance their operations and earn additional income. Others are moving much farther in this direction by investing directly in technology companies in order to have more control over the provision of these products to their tenants.

The areas in which REITs are most active in using technology are the selling and leasing of their properties by listing them on Internet sites, providing services to their tenants via websites, and enhancing investor relations. These changes are crucial to improving customer relations and retaining current tenants, finding new customers, improving facilities management, reducing the costs of providing services to tenants, and disseminating information to investors.

Thus, REITs are beginning to adopt new technologies, albeit somewhat belatedly. Once REITs become more like operating companies, they will have to adopt new technologies in order to compete in the marketplace. These changes are underway and, because REITs now see the significant benefits that the use of new technologies can bring, we expect to see more of them in the future. In fact one should not be surprised to see the REIT industry become among the most technologically advanced in the marketplace.

Going Private and Increasing Debt Usage

We should remember that a REIT could choose to be a private (not publicly traded) company and still enjoy its current tax benefits. Given this, it is clear that tax benefits are not the motivation for a REIT to go public—so why do they? The increase in liquidity and the availability of public funds are the two main reasons, although there are associated costs. Moreover, since the price of REIT assets (the stock value of the publicly held REIT) is determined by a collection of investors in the capital market, this price may not reflect the fundamental value of the REIT's assets. A privately held REIT has less worry about this problem.

We anticipate that once the operating environment becomes more complicated and REITs become more operational in nature, some of them will elect to become private. Investors in capital markets will judge the value of a REIT not only by the assets it holds, but also by its organizational structure, management style, and growth strategy. Those REITs that hold a collection of good properties but lack an effective corporate strategy are likely to find their stocks prices penalized by the market. For these REITs, it may pay to stay private to capitalize on the true value of their properties.

In addition, REITs traditionally borrow much less than the 70–80% loan-to-value ratio commonly observed in the private real estate market, because financial analysts in the capital market are accustomed to analyzing firms with less than a 50% debt ratio and will not recommend that REITs carry a debt ratio above the norm. For this reason, if there are too many REITs competing for public equity funds at one time, it might be better for some to go private. Once a REIT does go private, the traditional private capital (both debt and equity) in the property market might be available to it, although it is conceivable that this capital might be more expensive than that available in public capital markets. A trade-off between availability and capital cost is likely to be something REITs (especially those traditional fund-like REITs) will have to consider seriously when making their decisions in the future.

Globalization of the REIT Concept

In the last few years we have observed that a small number of domestic REITs have begun to operate in real estate markets abroad. Will this trend continue? Our answer is definitely yes, since we see no reasons that would prohibit a REIT from investing in foreign properties. We can see added risks (such as foreign exchange rate risk) and difficulties for REITs investing abroad, but we also believe that such investments are likely to be profitable if made under the right circumstances. Indeed, if firms in other industries find it profitable to invest in foreign countries, why should REITs not do the same?

In addition, it is worth asking whether domestic REITs will face challenges from the foreign REITs. This issue might receive increasing attention in the near future as more and more countries are establishing their own REIT industries. We know that there are several big real estate markets outside the United States, and many of them offer very attractive returns on their real estate investments. (For example, except in the past few years, most of the wealthiest individuals in Asia have tied their wealth to real estate.) Sooner or later, there will be incentives for U.S. investors to take a serious look at foreign real estate markets. In the past, it has been difficult for U.S. investors to do so because there has been no convenient, low-cost conduit for this type of investment. However, once foreign countries begin to establish their own REITs, we anticipate that this trend will change.

Domestic REITs Investing Abroad

There are potentially a number of advantages for domestic REITs to venture into overseas real estate markets. First, under the right circumstances and using the right combination of domestic and foreign expertise, it is possible for REITs to purchase properties at significantly lower prices than may be available in the United States. This could happen because property cycles in overseas markets do not necessarily move in tandem with those in the United States; therefore, when U.S. property prices are high, investment opportunities abroad may be significantly more attractive, especially if exchange rates are also favorable to U.S. investments.

Second, investing abroad will allow REITs to establish their names and their expertise in new markets, which will, in turn, widen their brand identity. In moving portions of their portfolios into overseas properties, REITs will also be able to expand their investment horizons while obtaining expertise in foreign property markets. This expertise can be used to make even more profitable investments at a future time (e.g., when the foreign property market cycle is in a downswing). In addition, investing abroad can give a REIT the opportunity to extend its service and other product relationships with existing clients who have global business interests—and, of course, a global presence also increases the opportunity REITs have to expand their client rosters. For investors wishing to hold truly diversified portfolios, REITs with international holdings will more likely attract their attention.[2]

Third, the real estate expertise that U.S. REITs have gained over the years may be particularly valuable in those countries where such expertise is lacking. Partnering with foreign property companies could allow these REITs to obtain significant scale economies through the introduction of operating efficiencies, while also reducing the risk they might otherwise face. Even though there are relatively few U.S. REITs with active property investments abroad, this may change in the future as others follow in the search of new investment opportunities.[3]

Nevertheless, there are real hurdles that REITs must overcome before seeking opportunities abroad. Aside from exchange rate risks, which can be hedged to a significant degree, there are information risks in foreign markets. These markets often are significantly less transparent than domestic real estate markets. To some extent, this risk can be overcome by partnering with knowledgeable real estate companies in countries with similar markets.

Indeed, an important rule that most REITs follow when investing abroad is to seek out knowledgeable partners who understand the local customs and the regulations governing real estate markets. Naturally, these partners should also have the business experience and political connections necessary to identify and complete profitable transactions. The cultural and legal similarities between the U.S. and European real estate markets is a major reason most REITs that have investments abroad have focused these investments in Europe.

Some countries, especially those characterized by social instability, may represent a significant political risk for a REIT even when it engages a local partner. There is also the disadvantage that REIT income derived from foreign property investments is unlikely to be tax exempt. REITs generally pay taxes on at least a portion of their income to their host governments.

These potential hurdles notwithstanding, it is clear that we can expect the migration of at least some part of U.S. REIT operations abroad to continue (although this migration will be limited as long as the income from a REIT's foreign operations is not tax exempt). As capital markets become increasingly global, however, and to the extent that markets abroad become increasingly free of excessive foreign regulations, U.S. REITs will find profitable investment opportunities in overseas markets.

Adoption of the REIT Concept Abroad

Another way in which REITs might increase their global presence is through the adoption of the U.S. REIT concept (or a similar form of organization) by foreign governments. Clearly, the potential benefits associated with the securitization of real estate, such as the increased liquidity and the more efficient allocation of real estate capital, appeal to property investors abroad as well as to U.S. investors. How rapidly the foreign adoption of the U.S. REIT concept will occur will depend on a number factors, primarily the extent to which public policymakers in these countries view the REIT concept as a way to reinvigorate their real estate markets.

Currently, there are a significant number of countries with listed property trust markets, although these markets vary in their size and liquidity. However, unlike the REIT concept in the United States, many of the existing foreign trusts are taxed at the corporate level.[4] Will this situation improve? We think not. Without a sufficient number of property owners who find public markets essential to their development pushing the REIT format, there will be little incentive for governments to introduce tax incentives to encourage the development of tax-favored REITs.

One could argue that since it may be difficult for foreign countries to offer the generous tax breaks similar to those provided in the United States, these countries might find it difficult to develop a REIT market. Although this argument has its merits, it may not hold in reality once we look at the total picture. We know that the United Kingdom has well-established property companies paying the same corporate tax (31%) as other companies. If investors only looked at the tax benefit, the U.K. market would be dominated by limited partners who offer more generous tax breaks than property companies can. Clearly, property companies in the United Kingdom can survive without the lower tax rates. Judging from the U.K. experience and if the current trend continues, we expect that even without a tax benefit similar to that of U.S. REITs, the REIT concept will likely spread throughout the world in the not too distant future.

However, given the entrepreneurial climate that characterizes foreign real estate investments in many non-U.S. countries, especially in Asia, the investment and earnings retention constraints characterizing the U.S. REIT format may not be attractive to foreign real estate companies.[5] Because of this, we anticipate that the future REIT concept adopted by foreign countries will be different from the U.S. REIT concept not only in terms of tax treatment but also in terms of management style. We also expect that the REIT concept adopted abroad will differ from country to country.

The best developed securitized real estate markets (for REITs and property trusts) outside the United States are in Europe. Newell, Ling, and Hwa (2001) report that in 1997 there were 12 REITs or property trusts in the Netherlands. Maurer and Sebastian (2002) summarize quite well the history and current development of real estate securities in France (20 firms), Germany (38 firms), Switzerland (11 firms), and the United Kingdom (39 firms). For the 1980–98 period, they report that the average monthly returns of the real estate securities were 0.78%, 0.93%, 0.62%, and 1.14% for France, Germany, Switzerland, and United Kingdom, respectively. Sahi and Lee (2000) identify 48 U.K. property company IPOs during the 1986–95 period.

From the evidence presented in the above three studies, it is clear that there are securitized real estate markets outside the United States, although their sizes are not comparable to those in the U.S. REIT market at this moment. It is also clear that there has been significant growth in securitized real estate companies in recent years in a number of European countries. In addition, there are significant activities in Australia and Africa as well. As of 1995, Newell, Ling, and Hwa (2001) were able to find 50 property trusts and REITs in Australia, 12 in New Zealand, and 17 in South Africa.

Our prediction is that the next boom of REIT markets will be in Asia. In recent years, several Asian countries have been exploring the possibility of using REITs as a way to revitalize their real estate markets. Malaysia may be the first Asian country to establish a property trust. According to Newell, Ling, and Hwa (2001), the first property trust in Malaysia was established in 1989 and since then the total number of listed property trusts has grown from one to four by 1997. By comparison, Singapore is much more advanced in the development of mortgage-backed securities (MBSs). Ong, Ooi, and Sing (2000) report that during the 1986–98 period, 19 mortgage-backed securities were issued in Singapore. They also report that the Monetary Authority of Singapore issued regulatory guidelines for the setting up of property trusts on May 14, 1999. This could pave the way for Singapore to establish a REIT market in the future.

In this regard, Australia's Lend Lease Corporation announced in October 2000 that it plans to set up a REIT in Singapore in the following year or so (*Business Times Singapore,* October 19, 2000, p. 2). The group proposed to tie up with CapitaLand to launch what may be the first REIT in Singapore, which will have an initial portfolio worth S$1 billion (one billion Singapore dollars) and focus on shopping malls (*Business Times Singapore,* May 28, 2001, p. 2). According to Andrew Pridham, UBS Warburg's global real estate head, Singapore has the potential to develop into a regional hub for REITs and that as much as S$13 billion in Singapore commercial properties could be injected into REITs (*Business Times Singapore,* May 24, 2001, p. 30).

Although CapitalLand eventually cancelled what would have been Singapore's first REIT IPO because only 80% of its shares offered were subscribed (*Straits Times Singapore,* November 13, 2001, p. S13), many firms in the region are still actively considering REIT IPOs in the near future. For example, Keppel Land and Centrepoint Properties proposed to issue their own REITs even after the unsuccessful CapitaLand IPO (*AFX-Asia,* November 26, 2001). Meanwhile Ascendas, a JTC Corp unit, announced that it is entering into a joint venture with Australia's Macquarie Goodman Company to explore the potential of establishing a REIT (*Straits Times Singapore,* December 1, 2001, p. S19). More recently, a Dutch property fund Rodamco Asia is considering joining Singapore's list of potential REITs (*Business Times Singapore,* April 16, 2002, Money section). CapitaLand also said that it will relaunch its failed REIT IPO when market conditions improve and will prepare to launch additional REITs for its residential properties (*Business Times Singapore,* April 8, 2002, Money section).

Recent developments have regenerated interest in property trusts in Malaysia. Industry experts believe that, by learning from the U.S. experience with REITs and by borrowing the concept of U.S. REIT structure, Malaysia's property trust industry can be revolutionized. In March, 2002, the Association of Valuers & Property Consultants arranged a two-day seminar discussing the opportunity of creating REITs in Malaysia (*Global News Wire,* April 1, 2002). This is evidence of a revitalization in interest in REITs in Malaysia.

Taiwan has also been exploring the REIT concept for many years now, although the initial idea was to gather funds for the development of public infrastructures. The concept was not successful at first, probably because of the dearth of laws regulating trusts. However, with the recent passage of such laws, the growth of the REIT concept in Taiwan will probably gain some momentum in the future. This is especially true given that many of the large and distressed property companies in Taiwan may find it necessary to seek capital from the public equity market rather than from the private market.

Japan is also moving in the direction of launching a REIT stock market to revive its stagnant real estate markets. In November 1999, the Japan Nikkei jumped 2% when the Tokyo Stock Exchange (TSE) announced that Japan was considering such a move. In late November 2000, Japan released details of a new law that abolished its current legal ban on REITs and paved the way for the listing of REITs on the TSE (*Reuters,* November 22, 2000). In May 2001, a government study group proposed measures to promote REITs in Japan to kick-start the stagnant property market (*Jiji Press Ticker Service,* May 9, 2001). The report also points out that REIT capitalization in Japan could reach 4 trillion yen by March 2002. Japan's Ministry of Land, Infrastructure, and Transport also said that it will scrap its regulation on REIT minimum size in a bid to foster the new investment vehicle (*Jiji Press Ticker Service,* July 3, 2001).

The planned development of the Japanese REIT market has attracted significant attention from big U.S. rating agencies and investment banks. In May 2001, Standard and Poor's published a report outlining its fundamental policy toward rating Japanese REITs (*PR Newswire,* May 9, 2001). UBS, Nomura, and Morgan Stanley are among the investment banks looking to capitalize on Japan's REIT market. Morgan Stanley, for example, indicated that it plans to invest more than US$4.5 billion in the Japanese property market over the next three years in anticipation of a REIT-related upswing in property prices (*Financial Times London,* May 8, 2001).

The interest in establishing REITs has been strong among firms. For example, real estate giant Mitsui Fudosan Co. (and other Japanese real estate companies and financial institutions) as well as foreign financial institutions have already disclosed plans to embark on a REIT business (*AFX-Asia,* April 17, 2001). Mitsubishi Estate, a large Japanese real estate company, is expected to be among the first to launch a REIT in Japan, with a 100 billion yen portfolio made up of its own properties as well as offices owned by some insurance companies (*Financial Times London,* May 8, 2001). Japanese railway operator Tokyu Corp. and Tokyu Land Corp. indicated that they have agreed to join forces with Australia's Lend Lease Corp. to set up a REIT in 2002 with an initial portfolio of 100 to 200 billion yen (*Jiji Press Ticker Service,* June 28, 2001). Recently, the Nihon Keizai newspaper reports that Orix Corp planned to set up a REIT before the end of *2001 (AFX News Limited,* July 2, 2001).

Among all potential candidates, Japan Real Estate Investment Corp and Office Building Fund of Japan Inc. finally became the first batch of REITs to trade on the Tokyo Stock Exchange in 2001. Both REITs commanded a first trading day price higher or equal to their offering price (*Jiji Press*

Ticker Service, September 10, 2001). The next REIT that came on the market, Japan Retail Fund Investment Corp, was jointly established by Mitsubishi Corp. and UBS Realty of Switzerland (*Global New Wire,* February 26, 2002). Although the trading volumes of the three listed stocks have been thin since their listing, interest in REITs has not subsided. Brian Bremmer reports that an additional six or seven REITs, including a $757 million effort by Goldman, Sachs, & Co., are planned for IPOs during 2002 (*Business Week International Editions,* April 22, 2002, p. 53).

Given the size of the properties currently held by financial institutions, the size of the REIT market in Japan could be very large if it is established as planned. Some industry officials believe there is greater potential for REITs in Japan than in the United States or Europe because of the larger spread between real estate yields and deposit rates in Japan, which would give investors more incentive to invest in this vehicle. Some analysts predict that the market capitalization of Japanese REITs may grow to more than 3 trillion yen in the next five years (*Reuters,* November 22, 2000).

Another Asian country to observe a new REIT market is South Korea. After the successful establishment of a mortgage-backed securities market in South Korea in early 2000, the momentum for establishing a REIT market there is strong. Korea enacted the Real Estate Investment Trusts Act on April 7, 2001 and subsequently amended it on May 24, 2001 (*Global News Wire,* July 25, 2001). The act allows the establishment of REITs and Corporate Restructuring REITS (CR REITs), the latter having better tax benefits than REITs.

Kyobo Life Insurance and Meritz Securities Co. have jointly established the first CR REIT, Kyobo-Meritz First (*Business Korea,* October 23, 2001). The CR REIT subsequently traded on the Korea Stock Exchange on January 30, 2002. In the meantime, APAC REIT and Korea REITs also received approvals from the Ministry of Construction and Transportation to become a REIT company (*Global News Wire,* March 5, 2002). However, with an initial capitalization of 133 billion won (or US$ 101.44 million), Kocref CR REIT expects to become the largest CR REIT in the Korean REIT market to date (*Global News Wire,* March 11, 2002). The potential of the Korean REIT market is not small. Samsung Economic Research Institue predicts that if REITs are successful they will likely form a 30 trillion won market within five to six years (*Korea Economic Weekly,* May 8, 2000).

We should not leave out Hong Kong, Mainland China, and India. Hong Kong has recently established a mortgage corporation to develop its mortgage-backed securities market. Although Hong Kong has yet to develop a REIT market, approximately 30–35% of the constituent companies of Hong Kong's Hang Seng Index are property development companies. Lai and Wang (1999) report that the large development companies in Hong Kong also have significant holdings in land and properties. Given this, although Hong Kong currently does not have a REIT market, these property companies could establish such a market rather quickly by spinning off their property holdings. They have not done so yet because they have been very strong financially in the past and using the REIT format as a fund-raising tool seems unnecessary for them at this moment. However, economic conditions could change in the future. When the time is right, Hong Kong may be able to establish a REIT market very quickly because it already has the required infrastructure and legal environment in place.

It is probably too early to speculate about Mainland China because the history of the property market there is less than 20 years old. However, the Chinese historically have believed that all wealth comes from the ownership of land. Given the size of the property market in China, the enormous growth rate of the GNP, and the manner in which the country is embracing the concept of capitalism, we believe that China will have the largest REIT market in Asia in 20 years. According to a news report by *Asia Pulse* on June 12, 2000, India has also begun to explore the possibility of allowing REITs to start operations in the country in a move to stimulate its fledgling real estate market. The Association of Mutual Funds of India is currently reviewing the proposal.

REIT managers and investors in the United States should be aware of these changes and be prepared to meet the challenges ahead. At this moment, non-U.S. REITs are still offering dramatically different products when compared to U.S. REITs and may not be able to compete with them for U.S. funds. Even so, we should not underestimate the potential impact of such foreign competition. No one can know what is likely to happen in five to ten years. Judging from the U.S. experience with foreign competition with its textile, electronics, and automobile industries, U.S. REITs would be foolish to underestimate the potential impact of foreign REITs and should be prepared to face competition in the international arena.

The Fittest Survive

We are certain that the REIT concept will continue to thrive. However, it is also clear that the operating environment REITs face will force them to adapt their future strategies. Those REITs that still operate in a traditional mode will face tough competition from both domestic and foreign firms and will begin to lose their market share if they do not learn from past experience.

Indeed, there are no entry barriers to forming a REIT. When the market conditions are right, new REITs will flood the marketplace, as was made evident by their explosive growth in the 1990s. Given that there are still many unsecuritized properties available in real estate markets, those with the right management strategies that can attract the attention of REIT investors are more likely to form REITs to compete with the existing trusts.

Those REITs that have learned lessons from their past experiences will modify their management strategies to meet the challenges posed by the capital market and REIT investors. Only those that operate efficiently will perform well in the stock market. In our crystal ball, we see two types of REITs that might fit into this category.

The first has specialized knowledge in certain property types in certain geographical regions. Since real estate developments, by and large, are still local businesses, those REITs familiar with the development environment in certain cities or with specialized knowledge about the demand and supply conditions of certain property types can take advantage of the development opportunities that other REITs cannot identify. In addition, REITs that have good business relationships with their tenants and an awareness of the special needs of their customers will be able to identify development opportunities and provide profitable non–real estate related services to their tenants. However, we do not anticipate that this will be the mega-REIT, but more likely a relatively small type of REIT with focused operations and a specialized knowledge of its business.

The second type of REIT is larger sized, focuses on one property type, and holds a national or international portfolio. The economies of scale resulting from a large operation and a concentrated property type will allow these REITs to reduce their operating expenses. Their large holdings of properties will give them a special edge in serving the needs of national or international clients. The resulting information efficiency from concentrated property ownership will offer these REITs better opportunities to take advantage of property cycles and to identify undervalued properties.

Which types of REIT will dominate? We do not know. However, it is clear to us that the non-focused REITs with diversified portfolios will find it difficult to compete with other REITs. Smaller REITs that hire external advisors and do not establish their own niches will soon be out of favor. REITs that are willing to learn from past experience and that are willing to identify development strategies based on their strengths will be the REITs that will survive. Others will just fade away.

Concluding Remarks

If the past success of REITs is a harbinger of the future, we believe that the REIT concept will grow and prosper in a world filled with new opportunities for real estate companies and their investors. However, although the main REIT concept will remain, the future success of REITs will depend primarily on how effective REIT managers are in adapting to changes in the capital markets and finding new ways to improve profitability from their direct and non-direct real estate investments.

We expect to see REITs increasingly pursue alternative sources of revenue as a result of the recent tax-law changes embodied in REITSA and the RMA. These changes are likely to lead to both improved profitability for REITs as well as a decrease in the impact of real estate market cycles on

REIT stock prices. An increase in the use of technology as a means of reducing costs and improving REIT customer relations can be expected from the future, as well. REITs will also need to be prepared to compete in the international arena because they might have to invest abroad or face competition from foreign REITs.

Traditional REITs might find that it is not in their best interests to stay in the public capital market. Those that fail to learn from past experience might find it worthwhile to go private, and may be able to find some private capital providers who will still embrace the fund-like REIT investment strategy. In the public capital market, only the fittest REITs with dynamic management styles will receive attention and favorable consideration from financial analysts and REIT investors.

NOTES

1. See also Cymrot (1997), Prins and Denien (1999), and Carr (2000) for a discussion of the opportunities REITs have to explore providing products and services to their tenants.
2. See, for example, Saint-Pierre (1998) for a discussion on the foreign investment activities of REITs.
3. REITs that have undertaken investments in overseas real estate markets include ProLogis, CarrAmerica, Shurgard Storage Centers, Patriot American Hospitality, and Liberty Property Trust.
4. Some of the countries in which property trusts have tax benefits similar to those of U.S. REITs are Australia, Belgium, South Africa, Turkey, and the Netherlands.
5. See Harris, Foster, and U'ren (1998) for a discussion of investments in overseas markets.

REFERENCES

Baird, W. Blake, and Paul J. Donahue Jr. 1996. The future of REIT consolidation. *REIT Report* 17 (Autumn): 28.

Berkelder, M. 1997. Property trusts: Dutch property fund market. *Property Australia* 12 (1): 64.

Chan, Su Han, John Kensinger, Art Keown, and John Martin. 1997. Do strategic alliances create value? *Journal of Financial Economics* 96:199–221.

Cymrot, Allen. 1997. Real estate companies: At a crossroads for creating significant wealth. *REIT Report* 17 (Winter): 28.

Edwards, Tony. 1997. REITs simplified. *REIT Report 17* (Autumn): 35.

Edwards, Tony. 2000. At your service: REITs modernized. *Real Estate Portfolio* (March/April): 43.

Harris, David, John W. Foster, and Glen U'ren. 1998. The emergence of U.S. REITs viewed from a global perspective. In *Real estate investment trusts,* ed, Richard T. Garrigan and John F.C. Parsons, 447–66. New York: McGraw-Hill.

Lai, Neng, and Ko Wang. 1999. Land-supply restrictions, developer strategies, and housing policies: The case in Hong Kong. *International Real Estate Review* 2:143–59.

Maurer, Raymond, and Steffen Sebastian. 2002. Analysis of the inflation risk of European real estate securities. *Journal of Real Estate Research,* forthcoming.

Mueller, Glenn, and Michael Anikeeff. 2001. Real estate ownership and operating business: Does combining them make sense for REITs? *Journal of Real Estate Portfolio Management* 7:55–65.

Newell, Graeme, Mary Wong Yoke Ling, and Ting Kien Hwa. 2001. Development and performance of Malaysian property trusts. University of Western Sydney. Working paper.

Ong, Seow-Eng, Joseph Ooi, and Tien Foo Sing. 2000. Asset securitization in Singapore: A tale of three vehicles. National University of Singapore. Working paper.

Prins, Ronald W., and Mark A. Denien. 1999. Growing revenue from services: Opportunities and pitfalls. *KMPG LLP Real Estate Report* (Autumn): 6–8.

Raiman, L. 1999. The new world order of the REIT business. The REIT Center, New York University. Working paper.

Rayner, J. 1998. Property trusts: The South African experience. *Property Australia* 12 (4): 43.

Sahi, Winston, and Stephen Lee. 2000. The initial return performance of U.K. property company IPOs. University of Reading, England. Working paper.

Saint-Pierre, Paul. 1998. Crossing the borders: REITs in the international market place. *The REIT Report* 18 (Autumn): 46.

Appendix

Monthly Stock Returns and Performance Index of All Publicly Traded REITs (1962–2000 and 2001–2002)

This appendix reports the monthly return performance for all publicly traded REITs, and for different REIT types (equity REITs, mortgage REITs, and hybrid REITs). Equity REITs have more than 75% of their holdings in properties. Mortgage REITs have more than 75% of their holdings in mortgage- and debt-related instruments. Hybrid REITs invest in both properties and mortgage, but cannot be classified as either equity REITs or mortgage REITs.

The first and most important step in constructing the monthly stock return and performance index is to identify the list of all publicly traded REITs over time—not an easy task, because no existing publication provides a complete list. To overcome this problem, we use various publications by the National Association of Real Estate Investment Trusts, Inc. (NAREIT) together with other sources (primarily the Center for Research in Security Prices [CRSP] tapes).

The NAREIT publications include the following: 13 issues of the *REIT Fact Book* (1974 to 1986), the *State and Course of the 1987 Real Estate Investment Trust Industry; REIT Facts: A Statistical Profile of the REIT Industry in 1988;* the *REIT Sourcebook* (reports REIT statistics in the 1989–90 period); *REIT Formation: Getting the Deal Done* (reports REIT statistics in the 1991–92 period), and seven issues of the *REIT Handbook: The Complete Guide to the Real Estate Investment Trust Industry* (1993–2000). REIT information prior to 1974 was obtained primarily from the security-issuance (IPOs and secondary issues) information listed in the appendices of the 1974 *REIT Fact Book*. These publications serve as a very good starting point for identifying the list of REITs, but because the formats of these publications change over time, the list of REITs may not be complete (especially in the earlier years). Furthermore, there are several years for which the NAREIT publications do not report information on non-member REITs or on the tax-qualification status of individual REITs and their asset composition.

We use the CRSP tapes as another means to identify REITs for the list. CRSP uses standard industrial classification (SIC) codes to classify the industry to which a stock belongs. In the CRSP tapes REITs are normally classified under SIC codes 6798 and 6799. A search of the CRSP tapes using these codes yields a list of publicly traded firms that are candidates for possible inclusion on our REIT list. However, a careful examination of the firms classified as REITs by the CRSP tapes reveals that some of those firms are not, in fact, REITs. At the same time, a significant number of firms that are classified as REITs by the CRSP tapes are not listed in the NAREIT publications, and vice versa. In addition, some of the REITs listed in the NAREIT publications are not classified under the SIC codes for REITs by the CRSP tapes.

To overcome these problems we use additional sources, such as the firms' annual reports, *Standard and Poor's Stock Reports,* and the LEXIS-NEXIS database for further information. This process helps verify the tax-qualified status and the asset composition (equity, hybrid, and mortgage) of each listed REIT for every year during the 1962–2000 period.

Each firm included in the final REIT sample for constructing the monthly return index meets the following two criteria: It is confirmed to be a REIT, and it has stock-trading information in the CRSP tapes. A total of 486 REITs meet the criteria and have stock return data reported on the CRSP NYSE-Amex tapes and/or the CRSP Nasdaq tapes during the years 1962–2000. To the best of our knowledge, our REIT sample is larger than the REIT samples used by other studies. Our sample is free of survivorship bias and we have checked all possible information sources to identify the REITs contained in it.

Once we have identified the REITs for inclusion in our final sample, we use the permanent number given to each one by CRSP to generate their monthly returns (total return, income return, and capital appreciation return) and equity-market capitalization over the 1962–2000 period. The income component of the return (or *dividend yield*) is the dividend per share divided by the closing price of the security. The capital appreciation component of the return (or *capital gain*) is the percentage appreciation rate of the stock price. The total return is the sum of the income return and the capital appreciation return.

An equally weighted return for every month during the period is then computed using the returns of all REITs trading in those months. Table A.1 reports the equally weighted returns (total, income, and capital appreciation) and the average and total market capitalization in each month during the period. In the table we also calculate a total-return index for each month during the period. This index represents the holding-period return that an investor would have realized at the end of each period if he or she had invested $100 at the beginning of July 1962. Based on the index reported in table A.1, the investor's $100 investment at the beginning of July 1962 would have grown to $5,297 at the end of 2000.

One could also use the return index in the table to determine the holding-period return over any chosen period. For example, assume that an investor wants to know his or her total investment return from holding the REIT portfolio from the beginning of January 1990 to the end of December 1998. The investor can divide the return index at the end of December 1998 by the return index at the end of December 1989, subtract 1 from the result, and then multiply by 100 to convert the number to a percentage. Using this calculation, [($4,680.47 / $1,698.81) − 1] × 100, the holding-period return on the investment works out to be 175.5%. Figures A.1–A.3 plot the mean monthly returns (total, income, and capital appreciation) and show how the returns vary in each month over the 1962–2000 period.

Table A.2 reports the equally weighted monthly returns for different REIT types (equity, hybrid, and mortgage), which are as defined earlier. Figures A.4–A.6 plot the mean monthly total returns of these REITs over the 1962–2000 period and show how their returns vary in each month.

Readers may wish to note that NAREIT also publishes monthly (as well as daily) historical performance indexes for publicly traded REITs for the period from January 1972 to the most recent month in 2001 on their website: http://www.nareit.com. Our return series differs from NAREIT's series in that we include REIT data from 1962 onward, and we compute the returns using all the publicly traded REITs that we could identify from various sources for the 1962–2000 period. Since we do not have information on the number of REITs that NAREIT uses in its computation of returns, we can only speculate that the observed difference in the returns and in the return index between our series and NAREIT's may be due to sample-size differences. However, even if this is the case, the values of the return indexes generated by both series over the same time period (1972–2000) do not differ much. The tables we present in this appendix will be useful to investors who want to track the performance of REITs since the first one came on the market in 1962.

Constrained by the availability of data from the CRSP tapes, our return series cover data only up to 2000. However, we feel obligated to provide our readers with the most up-to-date information on REIT return performance. Thus, we examined NAREIT's website for the monthly return information for REITs from January 2001 to May 2002. The information from this source is summarized in table A.3. The reader is encouraged to visit the NAREIT website for details on how NAREIT constructs the return series and the sample of REITs used in its computation.

Table A.1 Mean Monthly Returns and Total Return Indices of Publicly Traded REITs (1962–2000)

		Equity Market Capitalization ($'000)		Return (%)				
	End of Month	Average	Total	Total	Income	Capital Appreciation	Return Index	Number of REITs
						—	100.00	—
1962	Jul	20,158	40,317	15.17	0.80	14.37	115.17	2
	Aug	20,278	40,556	−0.14	0.00	−0.14	115.01	2
	Sep	19,777	39,554	−3.81	0.00	−3.81	110.63	2
	Oct	19,491	38,982	−2.40	0.78	−3.18	107.98	2
	Nov	20,691	41,383	8.35	0.00	8.35	116.99	2
	Dec	21,010	42,020	4.83	0.00	4.83	122.64	2
1963	Jan	20,703	41,405	−1.57	0.74	−2.31	120.71	2
	Feb	20,850	41,700	2.78	0.00	2.78	124.07	2
	Mar	20,896	41,792	−1.36	0.00	−1.36	122.39	2
	Apr	23,415	46,830	10.52	0.77	9.75	135.26	2
	May	23,396	46,792	−0.18	0.00	−0.18	135.02	2
	Jun	23,124	46,248	−1.25	0.00	−1.25	133.33	2
	Jul	21,431	42,863	−6.91	0.62	−7.53	124.12	2
	Aug	22,828	45,655	7.94	0.00	7.94	133.98	2
	Sep	21,682	43,364	−5.60	0.00	−5.60	126.47	2
	Oct	21,692	43,385	−1.89	0.72	−2.61	124.08	2
	Nov	20,931	41,861	−2.83	0.00	−2.83	120.57	2
	Dec	20,637	41,274	−0.90	0.00	−0.90	119.48	2
1964	Jan	21,262	42,523	6.02	0.71	5.31	126.68	2
	Feb	20,593	41,187	−3.97	0.00	−3.97	121.65	2
	Mar	20,811	41,622	0.12	0.00	0.12	121.80	2
	Apr	20,698	41,396	1.76	0.71	1.05	123.94	2
	May	19,608	58,824	7.98	0.00	7.98	133.83	3
	Jun	19,257	57,772	−2.44	0.00	−2.44	130.57	3
	Jul	19,827	59,481	5.93	0.97	4.95	138.31	3
	Aug	19,909	59,727	0.04	0.00	0.04	138.36	3
	Sep	20,768	62,303	6.53	0.00	6.53	147.40	3
	Oct	20,515	61,545	−0.61	1.01	−1.62	146.51	3
	Nov	20,975	62,925	3.17	0.00	3.17	151.15	3
	Dec	21,073	63,219	−0.19	0.12	−0.30	150.87	3
1965	Jan	21,682	65,045	4.43	1.19	3.25	157.56	3
	Feb	22,020	66,059	2.27	0.12	2.14	161.13	3
	Mar	21,322	63,966	−3.47	0.14	−3.60	155.55	3
	Apr	21,220	63,661	1.03	1.33	−0.30	157.15	3
	May	20,995	62,985	−1.47	0.00	−1.47	154.84	3
	Jun	28,338	113,353	−0.39	0.11	−0.50	154.23	4
	Jul	28,632	114,528	1.10	1.37	−0.26	155.93	4
	Aug	31,795	127,179	8.73	0.12	8.62	169.55	4
	Sep	33,215	132,858	3.35	0.11	3.24	175.22	4
	Oct	32,119	128,477	−1.28	1.30	−2.59	172.97	4
	Nov	33,266	133,064	1.41	0.11	1.30	175.41	4
	Dec	33,138	132,554	−1.50	0.12	−1.62	172.78	4
1966	Jan	30,914	123,656	−1.55	1.29	−2.84	170.10	4

Table A.1 *Continued*

	Equity Market Capitalization ($'000)		Return (%)				
End of Month	Average	Total	Total	Income	Capital Appreciation	Return Index	Number of REITs
Feb	28,759	115,035	–4.08	0.12	–4.20	163.15	4
Mar	30,129	120,517	2.51	0.12	2.39	167.25	4
Apr	29,290	117,160	0.13	1.37	–1.24	167.47	4
May	27,429	109,718	–7.01	0.09	–7.10	155.72	4
Jun	26,848	107,391	–3.29	0.13	–3.42	150.60	4
Jul	25,543	102,173	–0.97	1.38	–2.35	149.14	4
Aug	24,247	96,986	–3.30	0.14	–3.44	144.22	4
Sep	25,496	101,985	3.33	0.11	3.22	149.03	4
Oct	25,489	101,957	–0.39	1.51	–1.90	148.44	4
Nov	27,274	109,095	3.14	0.11	3.02	153.10	4
Dec	26,993	107,974	–1.59	0.29	–1.88	150.67	4
1967 Jan	31,319	125,274	15.83	1.41	14.41	174.52	4
Feb	30,509	122,037	–0.03	0.14	–0.17	174.47	4
Mar	31,391	125,564	0.44	0.11	0.33	175.24	4
Apr	32,208	128,834	–0.33	1.44	–1.76	174.67	4
May	30,175	120,699	–2.78	0.15	–2.93	169.82	4
Jun	31,059	124,237	1.69	0.15	1.54	172.69	4
Jul	33,471	133,885	5.80	1.45	4.35	182.71	4
Aug	35,991	143,964	3.30	0.16	3.14	188.74	4
Sep	36,871	147,484	0.18	0.12	0.06	189.07	4
Oct	33,436	167,182	3.32	1.33	1.99	195.36	5
Nov	32,243	161,214	–3.67	0.00	–3.67	188.19	5
Dec	32,926	164,631	0.54	0.53	0.00	189.20	5
1968 Jan	34,727	173,636	11.68	1.16	10.52	211.30	5
Feb	35,087	210,521	1.79	0.09	1.70	215.09	6
Mar	34,167	205,004	–2.92	0.09	–3.01	208.81	6
Apr	36,034	216,205	3.24	1.35	1.89	215.57	6
May	39,154	234,926	9.32	0.40	8.92	235.65	6
Jun	38,933	233,597	3.13	0.09	3.04	243.02	6
Jul	44,522	267,133	9.44	1.01	8.43	265.96	6
Aug	45,810	274,863	3.87	0.32	3.54	276.24	6
Sep	55,826	334,958	9.78	0.34	9.43	303.24	6
Oct	56,549	339,293	3.80	0.69	3.11	314.76	6
Nov	61,727	308,633	–0.62	0.36	–0.98	312.81	5
Dec	68,379	341,895	0.38	0.10	0.28	314.01	5
1969 Jan	74,628	373,142	11.64	0.79	10.85	350.54	5
Feb	77,215	386,077	–2.14	0.31	–2.45	343.05	5
Mar	79,785	398,927	2.52	0.10	2.41	351.68	5
Apr	85,371	426,856	5.59	0.79	4.81	371.35	5
May	84,349	421,746	7.20	0.31	6.89	398.09	5
Jun	68,677	343,384	–7.09	0.09	–7.19	369.86	5
Jul	56,790	340,737	–5.21	0.55	–5.76	350.59	6
Aug	64,334	386,003	7.27	0.28	6.99	376.08	6
Sep	62,926	503,406	–3.77	0.23	–3.99	361.91	8
Oct	60,167	601,666	5.02	0.69	4.33	380.07	10

(*continued*)

Table A.1 *Continued*

	End of Month	Equity Market Capitalization ($'000) Average	Total	Return (%) Total	Income	Capital Appreciation	Return Index	Number of REITs
	Nov	58,616	586,159	−5.57	0.37	−5.94	358.90	10
	Dec	64,702	711,717	−4.52	0.38	−4.91	342.66	11
1970	Jan	60,335	724,018	5.16	0.76	4.39	360.32	12
	Feb	63,428	887,989	3.47	0.68	2.79	372.84	14
	Mar	58,452	935,230	−0.18	0.29	−0.48	372.16	16
	Apr	48,091	865,637	−13.11	0.71	−13.82	323.38	18
	May	46,897	937,948	−3.72	0.60	−4.32	311.36	20
	Jun	41,281	949,462	−4.26	0.34	−4.61	298.09	23
	Jul	43,269	1,038,451	4.55	1.03	3.52	311.66	24
	Aug	46,475	1,161,880	2.80	0.80	2.00	320.39	25
	Sep	49,680	1,241,999	6.96	0.73	6.23	342.68	25
	Oct	46,578	1,304,170	−0.57	0.76	−1.34	340.72	28
	Nov	47,181	1,415,433	2.84	0.64	2.20	350.40	30
	Dec	51,216	1,587,699	5.68	0.63	5.05	370.29	31
1971	Jan	57,517	2,013,106	8.89	0.91	7.98	403.20	35
	Feb	60,307	2,110,733	4.34	0.50	3.85	420.71	35
	Mar	69,431	2,568,946	10.65	0.71	9.94	465.52	37
	Apr	63,924	2,556,968	−2.50	0.41	−2.91	453.88	40
	May	58,792	2,645,637	−2.68	0.60	−3.29	441.70	45
	Jun	59,838	2,692,688	1.43	0.53	0.90	448.03	45
	Jul	60,341	2,836,024	−0.93	0.64	−1.57	443.84	47
	Aug	62,916	3,082,906	5.44	0.77	4.67	467.99	49
	Sep	65,583	3,344,746	6.49	0.47	6.02	498.36	51
	Oct	64,310	3,344,121	−0.01	0.70	−0.70	498.32	52
	Nov	58,213	3,027,051	−6.12	0.59	−6.71	467.82	52
	Dec	62,575	3,253,912	2.47	0.62	1.85	479.36	52
1972	Jan	71,908	3,811,122	2.90	0.86	2.04	493.25	53
	Feb	73,125	3,875,623	1.72	0.67	1.05	501.72	53
	Mar	75,061	4,128,379	0.39	0.50	−0.11	503.66	55
	Apr	75,360	4,295,495	−1.25	0.70	−1.95	497.35	57
	May	72,976	4,451,509	−0.04	0.62	−0.66	497.16	61
	Jun	70,167	4,350,369	−3.05	0.64	−3.70	481.99	62
	Jul	70,083	4,345,174	1.14	0.75	0.38	487.47	62
	Aug	71,954	4,461,133	1.80	0.67	1.13	496.26	62
	Sep	71,681	4,587,569	1.86	0.61	1.24	505.48	64
	Oct	74,715	4,781,743	4.62	0.90	3.71	528.82	64
	Nov	75,265	4,892,204	3.72	0.63	3.09	548.50	65
	Dec	59,823	6,939,422	0.20	0.40	−0.20	549.60	116
1973	Jan	60,009	7,141,019	1.88	0.78	1.10	559.95	119
	Feb	55,679	6,792,866	−4.84	0.45	−5.28	532.87	122
	Mar	55,482	6,879,821	0.13	0.73	−0.59	533.57	124
	Apr	51,503	6,592,369	−3.13	0.77	−3.90	516.88	128
	May	48,048	6,294,316	−5.87	0.58	−6.46	486.52	131
	Jun	48,064	6,344,444	1.26	0.78	0.48	492.66	132
	Jul	47,951	6,425,396	1.87	0.91	0.96	501.89	134
	Aug	45,379	5,944,689	−3.88	0.65	−4.53	482.40	131

Table A.1 *Continued*

	Equity Market Capitalization ($'000)			Return (%)			
End of Month	Average	Total	Total	Income	Capital Appreciation	Return Index	Number of REITs
Sep	49,090	6,479,880	6.31	0.75	5.56	512.86	132
Oct	48,917	6,457,061	0.41	1.05	−0.64	514.98	132
Nov	40,627	5,322,138	−16.94	0.53	−17.47	427.73	131
Dec	37,290	5,034,176	−9.57	0.82	−10.39	386.79	135
1974 Jan	37,832	5,145,125	5.63	1.06	4.58	408.58	136
Feb	38,235	5,161,663	1.26	0.78	0.47	413.71	135
Mar	34,692	4,718,048	−5.50	0.75	−6.25	390.96	136
Apr	29,018	3,946,425	−13.46	0.99	−14.45	338.34	136
May	25,453	3,410,652	−10.31	1.09	−11.40	303.46	134
Jun	21,356	2,819,018	−9.97	0.82	−10.79	273.21	132
Jul	19,785	2,572,103	−7.41	1.02	−8.42	252.98	130
Aug	15,261	1,968,701	−22.25	0.69	−22.94	196.68	129
Sep	14,227	1,835,286	−4.66	0.74	−5.40	187.51	129
Oct	14,761	1,889,452	−1.54	0.90	−2.44	184.63	128
Nov	13,548	1,720,581	−14.70	0.51	−15.21	157.48	127
Dec	11,912	1,548,590	−18.68	0.72	−19.40	128.05	130
1975 Jan	16,248	2,079,760	55.31	0.46	54.85	198.88	128
Feb	14,723	1,855,047	−12.43	0.48	−12.91	174.17	126
Mar	16,038	2,036,797	14.13	0.46	13.67	198.78	127
Apr	14,394	1,799,304	−9.72	0.28	−10.00	179.46	125
May	14,370	1,781,843	−0.54	0.47	−1.01	178.49	124
Jun	15,423	1,927,851	7.52	0.47	7.05	191.91	125
Jul	15,056	1,881,980	−0.66	0.45	−1.11	190.64	125
Aug	13,911	1,738,813	−7.84	0.33	−8.17	175.70	125
Sep	12,559	1,557,294	−8.90	0.39	−9.29	160.06	124
Oct	12,262	1,508,222	−7.82	0.36	−8.19	147.54	123
Nov	12,456	1,532,057	−4.46	0.22	−4.68	140.96	123
Dec	13,239	1,628,377	10.56	0.44	10.12	155.84	123
1976 Jan	15,218	1,871,770	24.42	0.37	24.06	193.90	123
Feb	16,281	1,953,692	17.66	0.19	17.47	228.15	120
Mar	15,705	1,853,179	−8.02	0.34	−8.36	209.84	118
Apr	15,255	1,815,379	−1.24	0.32	−1.56	207.25	119
May	14,990	1,813,832	−2.47	0.23	−2.70	202.12	121
Jun	15,299	1,897,090	−0.68	0.36	−1.04	200.75	124
Jul	15,360	1,889,325	2.11	0.32	1.80	204.99	123
Aug	15,369	1,890,377	−1.54	0.25	−1.79	201.83	123
Sep	15,614	1,904,892	−1.69	0.36	−2.04	198.43	122
Oct	15,522	1,893,698	−3.62	0.28	−3.90	191.25	122
Nov	16,210	1,993,776	5.98	0.28	5.69	202.68	123
Dec	18,048	2,219,856	20.04	0.36	19.68	243.31	123
1977 Jan	17,960	2,173,202	3.71	0.32	3.39	252.34	121
Feb	17,843	2,159,061	0.56	0.23	0.33	253.75	121
Mar	17,717	2,143,774	2.13	0.38	1.75	259.15	121
Apr	18,079	2,187,603	2.16	0.21	1.95	264.75	121
May	17,887	2,164,329	−1.04	0.30	−1.34	262.00	121
Jun	18,778	2,253,370	1.61	0.34	1.28	266.23	120

(continued)

Table A.1 *Continued*

	Equity Market Capitalization ($'000)		Return (%)				
End of Month	Average	Total	Total	Income	Capital Appreciation	Return Index	Number of REITs
Jul	19,521	2,322,970	6.31	0.28	6.03	283.02	119
Aug	19,320	2,299,021	2.73	0.29	2.44	290.74	119
Sep	19,327	2,261,223	0.67	0.22	0.45	292.69	117
Oct	18,977	2,201,357	−2.16	0.36	−2.52	286.37	116
Nov	20,687	2,420,426	14.68	0.25	14.43	328.41	117
Dec	20,399	2,407,057	0.84	0.33	0.52	331.19	118
1978 Jan	19,694	2,304,209	−1.34	0.36	−1.70	326.75	117
Feb	20,095	2,351,104	1.69	0.18	1.51	332.27	117
Mar	20,893	2,423,548	7.60	0.39	7.21	357.52	116
Apr	21,197	2,480,014	6.76	0.23	6.53	381.68	117
May	21,094	2,446,874	−3.25	0.27	−3.53	369.27	116
Jun	20,812	2,414,208	1.77	0.35	1.42	375.80	116
Jul	21,864	2,536,256	4.14	0.35	3.79	391.35	116
Aug	23,423	2,740,516	12.82	0.25	12.56	441.51	117
Sep	23,188	2,712,988	0.89	0.32	0.57	445.42	117
Oct	19,758	2,311,640	−15.64	0.31	−15.95	375.77	117
Nov	19,688	2,303,536	−3.16	0.25	−3.41	363.90	117
Dec	19,939	2,292,997	3.13	0.48	2.65	375.28	115
1979 Jan	21,415	2,484,094	11.91	0.47	11.44	419.96	116
Feb	21,275	2,467,906	0.41	0.27	0.14	421.68	116
Mar	23,862	2,791,832	12.71	0.41	12.29	475.25	117
Apr	23,966	2,780,077	4.57	0.39	4.19	496.99	116
May	24,263	2,790,282	2.91	0.32	2.60	511.48	115
Jun	26,705	3,017,672	7.46	0.36	7.10	549.63	113
Jul	27,492	3,079,156	0.85	0.37	0.48	554.33	112
Aug	29,201	3,241,336	10.66	0.36	10.30	613.43	111
Sep	28,158	3,125,500	−3.30	0.30	−3.60	593.21	111
Oct	24,530	2,722,867	−14.32	0.37	−14.69	508.28	111
Nov	25,480	2,777,280	5.13	0.41	4.72	534.37	109
Dec	25,499	2,804,876	0.91	0.42	0.49	539.25	110
1980 Jan	27,624	3,093,866	10.10	0.45	9.65	593.71	112
Feb	26,472	2,964,818	−1.70	0.38	−2.08	583.62	112
Mar	22,558	2,549,038	−15.63	0.41	−16.04	492.38	113
Apr	24,326	2,748,891	7.42	0.51	6.91	528.91	113
May	25,629	2,896,091	9.90	0.44	9.47	581.30	113
Jun	27,604	3,091,629	6.12	0.46	5.66	616.85	112
Jul	29,704	3,297,160	10.33	0.38	9.95	680.58	111
Aug	30,948	3,435,207	4.19	0.37	3.82	709.06	111
Sep	30,935	3,433,731	1.11	0.38	0.74	716.95	111
Oct	32,601	3,651,360	4.46	0.48	3.98	748.95	112
Nov	32,220	3,576,384	−0.75	0.29	−1.04	743.33	111
Dec	31,449	3,490,866	−3.02	0.52	−3.55	720.86	111
1981 Jan	29,143	3,118,286	3.25	0.44	2.82	744.32	107
Feb	29,475	3,153,831	0.44	0.28	0.16	747.58	107
Mar	31,292	3,254,361	6.96	0.56	6.40	799.59	104
Apr	31,927	3,288,499	−0.01	0.46	−0.46	799.54	103

Table A.1 *Continued*

		Equity Market Capitalization ($'000)		Return (%)				
	End of Month	Average	Total	Total	Income	Capital Appreciation	Return Index	Number of REITs
	May	30,905	3,183,168	−2.18	0.26	−2.44	782.11	103
	Jun	32,421	3,306,986	2.56	1.03	1.54	802.15	102
	Jul	32,016	3,297,617	−1.01	0.43	−1.44	794.07	103
	Aug	30,701	3,100,757	−4.62	0.35	−4.97	757.36	101
	Sep	27,033	2,676,296	−6.12	0.49	−6.61	711.01	99
	Oct	29,104	2,793,974	3.36	0.73	2.63	734.87	96
	Nov	31,614	2,971,698	5.00	0.34	4.67	771.62	94
	Dec	32,113	3,050,707	0.53	1.13	−0.59	775.73	95
1982	Jan	31,606	2,939,340	−0.35	0.51	−0.87	772.99	93
	Feb	30,652	2,850,650	−2.61	0.36	−2.97	752.81	93
	Mar	33,382	3,071,158	0.98	0.75	0.23	760.17	92
	Apr	35,870	3,335,887	3.33	0.54	2.79	785.48	93
	May	35,677	3,282,270	−0.73	0.34	−1.07	779.75	92
	Jun	32,587	2,965,423	−1.31	0.62	−1.93	769.53	91
	Jul	32,603	2,901,651	−0.55	0.52	−1.07	765.27	89
	Aug	35,677	3,139,537	4.46	0.59	3.86	799.37	88
	Sep	37,043	3,222,779	7.27	0.64	6.62	857.45	87
	Oct	42,241	3,717,226	8.47	0.73	7.74	930.05	88
	Nov	45,507	4,232,137	4.44	0.25	4.19	971.33	93
	Dec	46,337	4,170,314	2.51	0.53	1.98	995.67	90
1983	Jan	44,490	3,915,126	3.95	0.56	3.39	1035.02	88
	Feb	45,440	3,953,256	4.60	0.84	3.75	1082.61	87
	Mar	49,299	4,239,746	6.43	0.74	5.69	1152.21	86
	Apr	52,516	4,568,855	6.97	0.39	6.58	1232.53	87
	May	53,576	4,607,537	4.10	0.37	3.72	1283.02	86
	Jun	54,498	4,686,824	0.93	0.48	0.45	1294.92	86
	Jul	53,585	4,715,463	−0.77	0.42	−1.19	1284.97	88
	Aug	53,467	4,758,569	−1.30	0.51	−1.81	1268.25	89
	Sep	55,062	4,845,431	2.17	0.51	1.66	1295.72	88
	Oct	56,096	4,880,347	0.17	0.49	−0.32	1297.94	87
	Nov	56,705	4,819,887	1.37	0.41	0.96	1315.70	85
	Dec	58,615	4,982,276	0.50	0.60	−0.11	1322.21	85
1984	Jan	59,739	4,958,350	2.96	2.16	0.79	1361.31	83
	Feb	57,699	4,731,311	−2.25	0.39	−2.64	1330.73	82
	Mar	58,721	4,756,411	0.95	0.61	0.33	1343.31	81
	Apr	58,611	4,806,133	0.58	0.58	0.01	1351.16	82
	May	57,651	4,669,713	−2.99	0.39	−3.38	1310.75	81
	Jun	57,108	4,682,820	0.85	0.55	0.31	1321.91	82
	Jul	58,423	4,673,816	−0.22	0.66	−0.88	1318.97	80
	Aug	60,874	4,930,759	3.99	0.54	3.45	1371.65	81
	Sep	63,589	5,150,689	2.59	0.55	2.04	1407.19	81
	Oct	64,533	5,227,135	3.00	0.56	2.44	1449.43	81
	Nov	65,547	5,243,768	1.77	1.84	−0.07	1475.05	80
	Dec	70,218	5,757,841	1.01	0.99	0.02	1489.92	82
1985	Jan	74,027	6,070,217	6.49	0.73	5.76	1586.56	82
	Feb	73,788	6,050,645	1.73	0.41	1.33	1614.06	82

(continued)

Table A.1 *Continued*

	Equity Market Capitalization ($'000)		Return (%)				
End of Month	Average	Total	Total	Income	Capital Appreciation	Return Index	Number of REITs
Mar	76,903	6,536,730	0.12	0.71	−0.59	1616.07	85
Apr	75,998	6,687,832	−0.07	0.50	−0.57	1614.93	88
May	77,986	7,252,710	2.65	0.39	2.26	1657.68	93
Jun	76,960	7,234,286	2.03	0.56	1.47	1691.40	94
Jul	76,880	7,303,622	1.42	0.66	0.77	1715.47	95
Aug	74,995	7,274,469	−1.96	0.43	−2.39	1681.85	97
Sep	78,760	7,876,006	−2.71	0.45	−3.16	1636.27	100
Oct	78,124	8,124,853	2.28	0.73	1.54	1673.54	104
Nov	78,573	8,250,137	0.09	0.55	−0.46	1675.06	105
Dec	74,824	8,006,183	0.80	0.71	0.10	1688.54	107
1986 Jan	78,692	8,420,018	3.38	0.86	2.53	1745.69	107
Feb	81,531	8,642,280	2.40	0.43	1.96	1787.53	106
Mar	84,822	8,991,149	3.46	0.65	2.81	1849.46	106
Apr	84,689	8,977,044	0.82	0.76	0.06	1864.67	106
May	84,583	8,965,774	−0.98	0.38	−1.36	1846.35	106
Jun	88,217	9,439,271	1.90	0.65	1.25	1881.34	107
Jul	87,494	9,449,329	−0.42	0.77	−1.19	1873.44	108
Aug	90,935	9,821,030	2.71	0.50	2.22	1924.25	108
Sep	91,844	10,011,040	−1.69	0.49	−2.18	1891.72	109
Oct	94,281	10,088,029	2.09	0.82	1.27	1931.23	107
Nov	93,420	10,089,368	−0.08	0.41	−0.49	1929.73	108
Dec	91,518	10,158,482	−1.60	0.85	−2.46	1898.78	111
1987 Jan	91,553	10,436,997	3.30	0.84	2.46	1961.51	114
Feb	94,859	11,003,605	1.38	0.41	0.97	1988.66	116
Mar	95,818	11,306,565	0.70	0.73	−0.03	2002.55	118
Apr	93,212	11,092,284	−1.67	0.82	−2.50	1969.01	119
May	89,634	11,024,927	−0.68	0.43	−1.11	1955.58	123
Jun	94,197	11,586,266	1.42	0.76	0.66	1983.34	123
Jul	93,593	11,511,928	0.93	0.82	0.11	2001.77	123
Aug	91,624	11,269,723	−1.45	0.46	−1.91	1972.78	123
Sep	90,817	11,261,288	−2.35	0.85	−3.21	1926.33	124
Oct	77,183	9,570,687	−13.45	0.79	−14.24	1667.25	124
Nov	77,636	9,626,894	0.32	0.71	−0.39	1672.50	124
Dec	79,941	9,832,693	−0.58	1.32	−1.91	1662.73	123
1988 Jan	85,600	10,614,435	8.69	0.61	8.08	1807.30	124
Feb	87,232	10,903,993	3.03	0.75	2.28	1862.12	125
Mar	89,384	10,994,181	0.74	0.78	−0.05	1875.81	123
Apr	89,562	10,926,586	0.80	0.88	−0.08	1890.74	122
May	89,146	10,786,722	−1.41	0.71	−2.12	1864.15	121
Jun	91,910	11,213,051	2.42	0.87	1.54	1909.18	122
Jul	94,101	11,198,057	1.88	0.90	0.98	1945.09	119
Aug	93,105	11,265,671	−1.75	0.51	−2.26	1910.97	121
Sep	94,084	11,196,016	−0.19	0.82	−1.00	1907.43	119
Oct	91,365	11,146,585	−0.80	0.92	−1.72	1892.14	122
Nov	88,922	11,026,353	−1.60	0.49	−2.09	1861.94	124
Dec	89,918	11,149,880	−1.41	1.08	−2.48	1835.78	124

Table A.1 *Continued*

	End of Month	Equity Market Capitalization ($'000) Average	Total	Return (%) Total	Income	Capital Appreciation	Return Index	Number of REITs
1989	Jan	90,947	10,913,649	0.58	0.66	−0.08	1846.48	120
	Feb	88,720	10,646,393	−2.75	0.50	−3.25	1795.75	120
	Mar	89,367	10,724,033	−0.26	0.82	−1.08	1791.07	120
	Apr	93,991	11,090,922	0.90	0.75	0.15	1807.10	118
	May	95,570	11,277,313	2.98	0.62	2.36	1861.02	118
	Jun	96,382	11,469,478	0.21	0.78	−0.57	1864.95	119
	Jul	98,012	11,761,434	1.36	0.81	0.55	1890.36	120
	Aug	97,239	11,571,496	−1.27	0.43	−1.70	1866.41	119
	Sep	98,099	11,673,798	0.44	0.72	−0.28	1874.55	119
	Oct	94,948	11,203,914	−5.24	0.80	−6.04	1776.25	118
	Nov	93,246	11,096,248	−3.17	0.46	−3.63	1719.96	119
	Dec	94,854	11,287,613	−1.23	1.51	−2.74	1698.81	119
1990	Jan	92,412	10,904,575	−1.05	0.58	−1.62	1681.05	118
	Feb	88,685	10,464,824	−4.10	0.50	−4.60	1612.19	118
	Mar	90,827	10,717,636	1.30	1.01	0.29	1633.08	118
	Apr	89,187	10,434,879	−0.90	0.88	−1.78	1618.41	117
	May	88,752	10,383,967	−0.54	0.52	−1.06	1609.61	117
	Jun	88,594	10,365,509	−0.55	1.04	−1.59	1600.76	117
	Jul	83,965	9,823,854	−2.84	0.63	−3.48	1555.24	117
	Aug	78,080	9,213,385	−5.35	0.49	−5.85	1471.96	118
	Sep	71,937	8,488,619	−7.83	0.93	−8.76	1356.72	118
	Oct	68,854	8,124,774	−7.05	0.69	−7.74	1261.01	118
	Nov	72,907	8,603,010	4.18	0.58	3.60	1313.74	118
	Dec	72,426	8,473,844	−2.24	1.69	−3.94	1284.26	117
1991	Jan	78,253	9,155,586	8.75	0.35	8.40	1396.61	117
	Feb	82,170	9,531,680	8.55	0.49	8.06	1516.01	116
	Mar	86,329	10,445,775	9.87	0.99	8.89	1665.71	121
	Apr	87,594	10,598,889	2.58	0.55	2.03	1708.68	121
	May	89,312	10,806,709	1.10	0.79	0.31	1727.46	121
	Jun	89,484	10,827,566	−2.23	1.01	−3.24	1688.94	121
	Jul	89,954	11,064,356	0.49	0.53	−0.05	1697.14	123
	Aug	89,315	10,985,690	−1.12	0.43	−1.55	1678.13	123
	Sep	89,212	11,419,101	1.85	0.89	0.95	1709.11	128
	Oct	88,658	11,614,250	−1.92	0.43	−2.35	1676.27	131
	Nov	87,890	11,953,099	−2.64	0.30	−2.94	1632.01	136
	Dec	92,910	12,635,755	−0.17	1.15	−1.32	1629.27	136
1992	Jan	96,645	13,240,313	10.59	0.30	10.29	1801.79	137
	Feb	93,723	12,840,039	2.21	0.36	1.85	1841.69	137
	Mar	95,437	12,884,054	1.55	1.01	0.54	1870.22	135
	Apr	94,851	12,804,844	−2.61	0.45	−3.05	1821.46	135
	May	97,322	13,138,449	−0.10	0.75	−0.85	1819.62	135
	Jun	97,044	13,003,922	−1.60	0.96	−2.56	1790.56	134
	Jul	101,001	13,534,089	1.99	0.45	1.54	1826.23	134
	Aug	99,947	13,492,819	−0.78	0.30	−1.08	1811.93	135
	Sep	105,669	14,265,358	1.44	0.93	0.50	1837.98	135
	Oct	103,793	14,115,864	−2.79	0.63	−3.42	1786.72	136

(*continued*)

Table A.1 *Continued*

	Equity Market Capitalization ($'000)			Return (%)				
	End of Month	Average	Total	Total	Income	Capital Appreciation	Return Index	Number of REITs
	Nov	108,298	15,053,363	1.85	0.29	1.56	1819.82	139
	Dec	111,969	15,563,732	0.86	1.15	−0.29	1835.50	139
1993	Jan	117,722	16,481,098	7.59	0.29	7.30	1974.90	140
	Feb	125,337	17,923,199	7.53	0.32	7.22	2123.67	143
	Mar	139,033	19,881,688	6.88	0.97	5.91	2269.81	143
	Apr	135,508	19,377,701	−0.58	0.32	−0.90	2256.59	143
	May	136,797	20,109,129	−0.11	0.32	−0.43	2254.05	147
	Jun	146,155	22,069,438	2.51	0.89	1.63	2310.74	151
	Jul	150,537	23,032,187	3.26	0.32	2.94	2386.15	153
	Aug	162,628	26,020,472	2.00	0.27	1.72	2433.78	160
	Sep	174,793	28,316,486	4.65	0.71	3.94	2546.86	162
	Oct	175,773	29,881,340	1.87	0.35	1.52	2594.45	170
	Nov	172,569	30,544,759	−2.65	0.21	−2.86	2525.76	177
	Dec	177,075	32,758,840	1.15	1.15	0.00	2554.81	185
1994	Jan	180,693	34,873,699	2.46	0.27	2.19	2617.55	193
	Feb	188,457	37,125,940	3.22	0.27	2.95	2701.85	197
	Mar	182,465	37,222,930	−2.90	0.77	−3.67	2623.54	204
	Apr	190,677	39,660,824	0.55	0.42	0.14	2638.10	208
	May	193,038	40,730,990	1.96	0.51	1.44	2689.69	211
	Jun	196,732	43,084,297	−0.47	0.80	−1.27	2676.93	219
	Jul	196,922	43,913,514	0.54	0.38	0.16	2691.33	223
	Aug	200,023	45,405,201	0.56	0.49	0.06	2706.31	227
	Sep	196,935	44,704,249	0.92	0.93	−0.01	2731.30	227
	Oct	190,912	43,146,062	−3.24	0.48	−3.72	2642.85	226
	Nov	182,377	41,399,633	−3.47	0.38	−3.85	2551.10	227
	Dec	194,138	44,457,700	2.81	1.37	1.43	2622.68	229
1995	Jan	191,884	43,173,980	0.77	0.48	0.29	2642.87	225
	Feb	198,445	44,451,695	4.21	0.36	3.86	2754.18	224
	Mar	197,119	43,957,624	0.09	1.10	−1.01	2756.68	223
	Apr	201,050	44,633,092	1.39	0.60	0.79	2794.89	222
	May	212,343	47,352,399	3.34	0.48	2.86	2888.31	223
	Jun	217,173	48,863,854	1.82	0.89	0.93	2940.89	225
	Jul	225,767	50,346,132	0.50	0.40	0.10	2955.64	223
	Aug	227,586	51,206,919	1.60	0.41	1.19	3002.83	225
	Sep	232,504	52,545,862	2.43	0.91	1.52	3075.79	226
	Oct	229,887	51,954,416	−1.30	0.51	−1.81	3035.69	226
	Nov	235,521	52,756,724	0.26	0.42	−0.16	3043.71	224
	Dec	252,195	56,239,464	4.86	1.23	3.63	3191.62	223
1996	Jan	258,027	55,733,908	4.32	0.34	3.98	3329.62	216
	Feb	259,813	56,379,522	0.39	0.36	0.03	3342.49	217
	Mar	262,207	55,850,007	1.72	1.26	0.46	3400.07	213
	Apr	267,968	56,809,267	0.18	0.54	−0.36	3406.11	212
	May	277,512	58,555,049	3.25	0.42	2.83	3516.79	211
	Jun	287,947	59,893,007	2.33	1.07	1.26	3598.65	208
	Jul	297,529	61,291,066	0.25	0.46	−0.22	3607.47	206
	Aug	312,271	64,015,530	4.23	0.47	3.76	3760.08	205

Table A.1 *Continued*

		Equity Market Capitalization ($'000)		Return (%)				
	End of Month	Average	Total	Total	Income	Capital Appreciation	Return Index	Number of REITs
	Sep	325,206	66,016,788	2.50	0.87	1.63	3854.21	203
	Oct	346,504	70,340,308	1.88	0.50	1.38	3926.67	203
	Nov	363,752	73,841,671	3.52	0.48	3.05	4065.02	203
	Dec	409,898	83,209,306	7.80	1.12	6.68	4382.24	203
1997	Jan	423,502	84,700,471	3.69	0.34	3.35	4543.82	200
	Feb	426,785	86,210,494	0.06	0.86	−0.80	4546.69	202
	Mar	433,557	86,711,362	−0.53	0.83	−1.36	4522.54	200
	Apr	430,602	86,551,102	−1.69	0.35	−2.04	4446.14	201
	May	456,588	91,774,213	3.79	0.41	3.37	4614.59	201
	Jun	490,723	98,635,365	4.42	0.81	3.61	4818.67	201
	Jul	538,434	106,609,90	3.07	0.45	2.61	4966.43	198
	Aug	546,641	109,328,139	1.46	0.42	1.04	5038.74	200
	Sep	595,303	119,060,544	6.58	1.20	5.38	5370.20	200
	Oct	575,220	118,495,350	−1.24	0.37	−1.61	5303.61	206
	Nov	621,376	131,110,344	0.49	0.55	−0.06	5329.81	211
	Dec	630,108	132,322,628	2.40	1.34	1.06	5457.67	210
1998	Jan	632,648	133,488,730	0.67	0.27	0.40	5494.19	211
	Feb	622,720	133,262,029	−0.74	0.33	−1.07	5453.36	214
	Mar	683,521	148,324,073	2.34	0.97	1.38	5581.21	217
	Apr	662,313	146,371,238	−2.22	0.38	−2.60	5457.28	221
	May	678,844	152,060,994	−1.06	0.34	−1.40	5399.64	224
	Jun	699,546	154,599,738	−1.31	0.92	−2.23	5328.99	221
	Jul	660,856	144,066,661	−4.56	0.39	−4.95	5085.94	218
	Aug	603,014	132,059,989	−10.08	0.37	−10.45	4573.26	219
	Sep	647,269	140,457,308	6.08	1.07	5.01	4851.40	217
	Oct	629,418	136,583,778	−5.76	0.62	−6.38	4571.79	217
	Nov	639,300	138,088,832	2.72	0.35	2.37	4696.37	216
	Dec	635,573	138,554,856	−0.34	1.26	−1.60	4680.47	218
1999	Jan	624,508	136,767,254	−0.63	0.36	−0.99	4650.83	219
	Feb	611,587	134,549,207	−2.80	0.40	−3.20	4520.47	220
	Mar	607,549	133,053,301	−0.12	1.04	−1.16	4515.14	219
	Apr	679,816	148,879,776	7.58	0.64	6.94	4857.58	219
	May	690,898	151,306,764	2.99	0.51	2.49	5002.99	219
	Jun	678,875	147,315,919	0.94	1.09	−0.14	5050.15	217
	Jul	656,400	143,095,250	−1.99	0.54	−2.53	4949.51	218
	Aug	648,268	140,025,979	−3.34	0.43	−3.77	4784.21	216
	Sep	618,643	134,245,466	−2.12	0.96	−3.08	4682.70	217
	Oct	599,761	130,747,878	−2.21	0.73	−2.94	4579.03	218
	Nov	595,554	127,448,594	−1.05	0.97	−2.02	4531.05	214
	Dec	611,895	128,498,029	0.83	1.47	−0.65	4568.44	210
2000	Jan	608,871	127,862,852	0.36	0.46	−0.11	4584.83	210
	Feb	596,374	125,238,568	−1.26	0.43	−1.69	4526.85	210
	Mar	614,344	127,783,634	2.17	1.32	0.85	4625.24	208
	Apr	653,537	134,628,614	3.77	0.93	2.84	4799.43	206
	May	656,432	135,224,926	0.70	0.57	0.13	4832.97	206
	Jun	680,807	140,926,951	3.33	1.18	2.15	4993.82	207

(*continued*)

Table A.1 *Continued*

End of Month	Equity Market Capitalization ($'000) Average	Total	Return (%) Total	Income	Capital Appreciation	Return Index	Number of REITs
Jul	727,814	147,018,476	4.63	0.57	4.07	5225.24	202
Aug	696,366	140,665,946	−1.99	0.47	−2.46	5121.41	202
Sep	711,219	142,955,053	2.27	1.11	1.15	5237.41	201
Oct	684,351	135,501,533	−2.63	0.98	−3.62	5099.60	198
Nov	682,778	133,824,422	−0.63	0.56	−1.19	5067.47	196
Dec	725,714	140,062,860	4.54	2.28	2.26	5297.44	193
A. 1962–2000 period							
Mean	126,222	21,577,049	1.02	0.58	0.44		
Std. Dev.	179,549	39,804,515	5.72	0.35	5.72		
Maximum	727,814	154,599,738	55.31	2.28	54.85		
Minimum	11,912	38,982	−22.25	0.00	−22.94		
Number of Months	462	462	462	462	462		
B. 1962–70 period							
Mean	35,955	267,365	1.41	0.46	0.96		
Std. Dev.	17,147	340,622	4.97	0.46	4.88		
Maximum	85,371	1,587,699	15.83	1.51	14.41		
Minimum	19,257	38,982	−13.11	0.00	−13.82		
Number of Months	102	102	102	102	102		
C. 1971–80 period							
Mean	32,930	3,114,898	0.95	0.50	0.45		
Std. Dev.	19,967	1,422,171	9.19	0.22	9.23		
Maximum	75,360	7,141,019	55.31	1.09	54.85		
Minimum	11,912	1,508,222	−22.25	0.18	−22.94		
Number of Months	120	120	120	120	120		
D. 1981–90 period							
Mean	70,127	7,533,064	0.53	0.67	−0.13		
Std. Dev.	22,744	3,181,917	3.22	0.29	3.23		
Maximum	98,099	11,761,434	8.69	2.16	8.08		
Minimum	27,033	2,676,296	−13.45	0.25	−14.24		
Number of Months	120	120	120	120	120		
E. 1991–2000 period							
Mean	352,337	72,196,414	1.24	0.66	0.58		
Std. Dev.	230,718	51,087,657	3.23	0.35	3.20		
Maximum	727,814	154,599,738	10.59	2.28	10.29		
Minimum	78,253	9,155,586	−10.08	0.21	−10.45		
Number of Months	120	120	120	120	120		

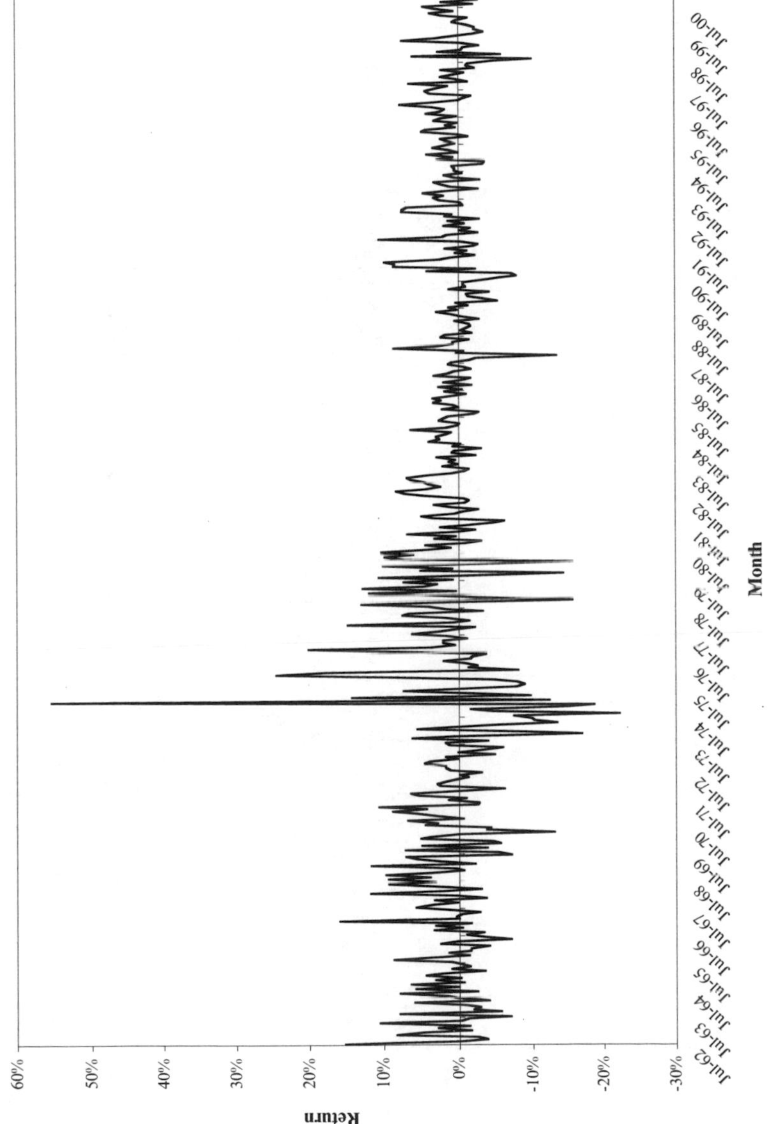

Figure A.1 Mean Monthly Total Returns for REITs

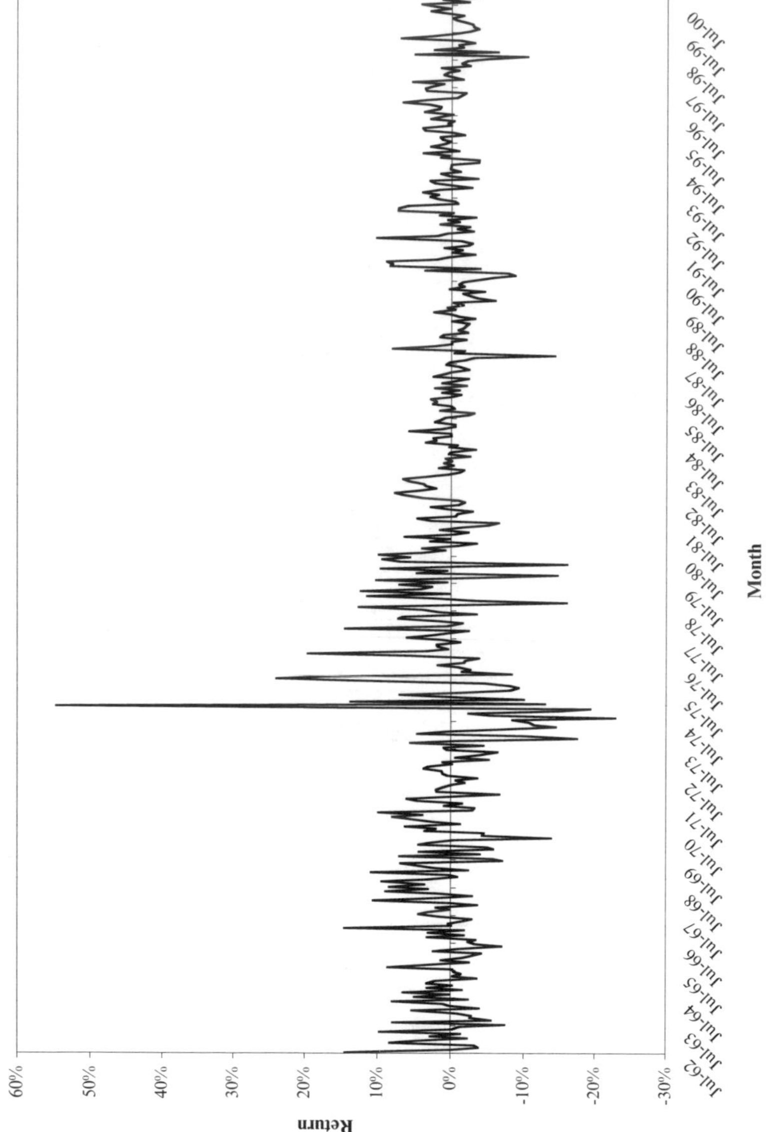

Figure A.2 Mean Monthly Capital Appreciation Return

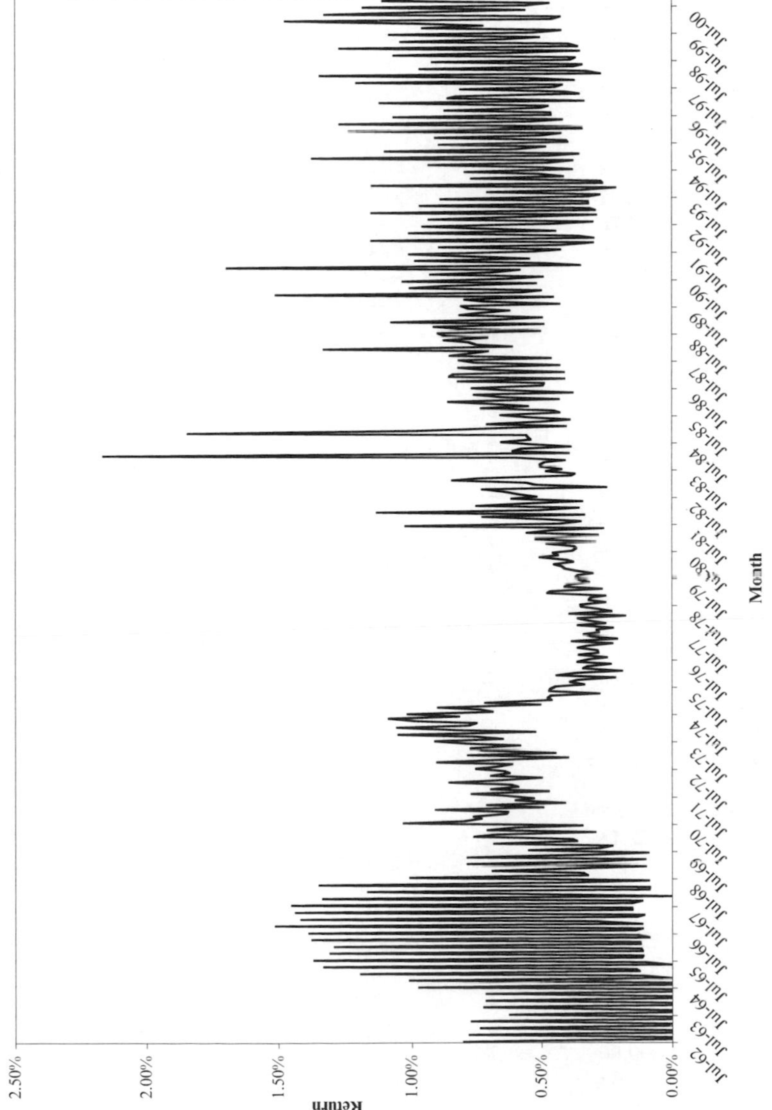

Figure A.3 Mean Monthly Income Return for REITs

Table A.2 Mean Monthly Total Returns by REIT Type (1962–2000)

		Equity REIT		Hybrid REIT		Mortgage REIT	
	Month	Mean Total Return (%)	Number of Obs.	Mean Total Return (%)	Number of Obs.	Mean Total Return (%)	Number of Obs.
1962	Jul	15.17	2	—	—	—	—
	Aug	−0.14	2	—	—	—	—
	Sep	−3.81	2	—	—	—	—
	Oct	−2.40	2	—	—	—	—
	Nov	8.35	2	—	—	—	—
	Dec	4.83	2	—	—	—	—
1963	Jan	−1.57	2	—	—	—	—
	Feb	2.78	2	—	—	—	—
	Mar	−1.36	2	—	—	—	—
	Apr	10.52	2	—	—	—	—
	May	−0.18	2	—	—	—	—
	Jun	−1.25	2	—	—	—	—
	Jul	−6.91	2	—	—	—	—
	Aug	7.94	2	—	—	—	—
	Sep	−5.60	2	—	—	—	—
	Oct	−1.89	2	—	—	—	—
	Nov	−2.83	2	—	—	—	—
	Dec	−0.90	2	—	—	—	—
1964	Jan	6.02	2	—	—	—	—
	Feb	−3.97	2	—	—	—	—
	Mar	0.12	2	—	—	—	—
	Apr	1.76	2	—	—	—	—
	May	10.90	2	2.13	1	—	—
	Jun	−0.01	2	−7.29	1	—	—
	Jul	8.72	2	0.35	1	—	—
	Aug	−0.51	2	1.14	1	—	—
	Sep	11.21	2	−2.81	1	—	—
	Oct	0.90	2	−3.62	1	—	—
	Nov	3.53	2	2.44	1	—	—
	Dec	0.91	2	−2.38	1	—	—
1965	Jan	2.11	2	9.07	1	—	—
	Feb	2.83	2	1.14	1	—	—
	Mar	−3.51	2	−3.37	1	—	—
	Apr	2.73	2	−2.39	1	—	—
	May	−0.09	2	−4.24	1	—	—
	Jun	−3.58	2	2.53	1	3.06	1
	Jul	1.93	2	−2.99	1	3.55	1
	Aug	2.57	2	10.39	1	19.42	1
	Sep	−0.90	2	7.06	1	8.13	1
	Oct	−0.82	2	−0.54	1	−2.96	1
	Nov	−0.62	2	−0.57	1	7.45	1
	Dec	−2.42	2	−2.27	1	1.09	1
1966	Jan	0.08	2	4.44	1	−10.79	1
	Feb	−0.68	2	−2.27	1	−12.70	1
	Mar	−0.37	2	0.00	1	10.80	1
	Apr	0.70	2	3.04	1	−3.93	1
	May	−6.64	2	−8.05	1	−6.73	1

Table A.2 *Continued*

	Month	Equity REIT		Hybrid REIT		Mortgage REIT	
		Mean Total Return (%)	Number of Obs.	Mean Total Return (%)	Number of Obs.	Mean Total Return (%)	Number of Obs.
	Jun	−5.81	2	−2.50	1	0.96	1
	Jul	1.52	2	0.72	1	−7.62	1
	Aug	−1.11	2	−2.60	1	−8.38	1
	Sep	−0.14	2	3.33	1	10.29	1
	Oct	−0.31	2	−6.43	1	5.48	1
	Nov	0.23	2	−1.41	1	13.50	1
	Dec	−1.25	2	−4.29	1	0.44	1
1967	Jan	15.35	2	12.87	1	19.75	1
	Feb	−1.70	2	8.11	1	−4.83	1
	Mar	−2.24	2	0.00	1	6.25	1
	Apr	−1.15	2	−8.08	1	9.06	1
	May	0.62	2	−1.39	1	−10.96	1
	Jun	−0.01	2	1.41	1	5.38	1
	Jul	3.54	2	2.16	1	13.96	1
	Aug	1.49	2	−2.78	1	12.99	1
	Sep	−1.94	2	0.00	1	4.60	1
	Oct	3.25	3	0.82	1	6.05	1
	Nov	−1.64	3	−8.70	1	−4.71	1
	Dec	0.58	3	−3.17	1	4.12	1
1968	Jan	10.89	3	22.19	1	3.55	1
	Feb	1.01	4	−4.11	1	10.82	1
	Mar	−6.23	4	8.57	1	−1.16	1
	Apr	4.28	4	−8.59	1	10.89	1
	May	9.09	4	10.29	1	9.25	1
	Jun	3.02	4	12.00	1	−5.32	1
	Jul	9.04	4	−2.90	1	23.38	1
	Aug	4.35	4	3.75	1	2.04	1
	Sep	1.20	4	16.87	1	37.00	1
	Oct	3.70	4	8.05	1	−0.06	1
	Nov	−1.42	3	4.85	1	−3.68	1
	Dec	−1.80	3	−1.85	1	9.16	1
1969	Jan	11.31	3	15.78	1	8.48	1
	Feb	−3.24	3	−9.09	1	8.12	1
	Mar	0.87	3	5.45	1	4.50	1
	Apr	1.82	3	13.58	1	8.93	1
	May	5.91	3	23.08	1	−4.79	1
	Jun	−7.40	3	11.88	1	−25.14	1
	Jul	−5.61	4	−7.39	1	−1.41	1
	Aug	4.59	4	7.32	1	17.94	1
	Sep	−8.17	4	3.11	3	−6.80	1
	Oct	2.03	5	1.48	3	17.78	2
	Nov	−6.07	5	−6.78	3	−2.51	2
	Dec	−8.11	5	−0.05	4	−4.51	2
1970	Jan	7.24	5	4.48	5	1.63	2
	Feb	3.25	5	2.82	7	6.30	2
	Mar	0.62	5	−2.22	9	6.99	2
	Apr	−6.92	6	−16.39	10	−15.22	2

(*continued*)

Table A.2 *Continued*

	Month	Equity REIT		Hybrid REIT		Mortgage REIT	
		Mean Total Return (%)	Number of Obs.	Mean Total Return (%)	Number of Obs.	Mean Total Return (%)	Number of Obs.
	May	−3.54	8	−2.76	10	−9.21	2
	Jun	−4.81	10	−3.29	11	−6.90	2
	Jul	4.36	10	5.34	12	0.83	2
	Aug	3.34	10	1.12	13	11.05	2
	Sep	1.97	10	9.56	13	15.02	2
	Oct	3.32	10	−1.99	15	−6.46	3
	Nov	3.58	10	1.91	17	5.65	3
	Dec	4.91	10	6.47	18	3.48	3
1971	Jan	8.41	10	10.70	20	2.62	5
	Feb	3.00	10	4.88	20	4.88	5
	Mar	5.60	10	12.30	22	13.51	5
	Apr	−1.28	12	−2.60	23	−4.98	5
	May	−3.55	13	−2.17	26	−3.01	6
	Jun	−1.03	13	3.00	26	−0.02	6
	Jul	−0.72	13	−1.01	27	−1.03	7
	Aug	3.48	13	5.17	29	10.22	7
	Sep	4.37	14	6.82	30	9.30	7
	Oct	−0.42	15	1.56	30	−5.85	7
	Nov	−2.97	15	−7.15	30	−8.48	7
	Dec	2.00	15	2.18	30	4.72	7
1972	Jan	4.27	15	2.94	31	−0.25	7
	Feb	1.51	15	1.75	31	2.03	7
	Mar	−0.56	17	1.42	31	−1.92	7
	Apr	−2.16	17	−0.89	32	−0.75	8
	May	0.23	19	−0.53	34	1.42	8
	Jun	−1.05	19	−3.77	35	−4.65	8
	Jul	0.66	19	1.36	35	1.29	8
	Aug	0.62	19	2.69	35	0.73	8
	Sep	1.66	20	1.58	36	3.58	8
	Oct	4.12	20	5.09	36	3.72	8
	Nov	2.24	21	4.51	36	4.05	8
	Dec	−0.41	44	0.51	58	0.84	14
1973	Jan	3.13	45	2.26	60	−3.70	14
	Feb	−3.80	46	−5.04	61	−7.18	15
	Mar	2.29	48	−1.76	61	0.91	15
	Apr	−2.94	50	−2.81	62	−4.94	16
	May	−6.13	52	−6.34	63	−3.20	16
	Jun	2.06	52	1.04	64	−0.45	16
	Jul	1.35	53	2.09	65	2.73	16
	Aug	−3.32	52	−4.02	63	−5.18	16
	Sep	4.20	52	7.68	63	7.71	17
	Oct	2.24	52	−1.12	63	0.50	17
	Nov	−14.17	53	−19.40	62	−16.60	16
	Dec	−6.91	54	−11.13	65	−12.22	16
1974	Jan	6.74	54	4.72	66	5.66	16
	Feb	1.77	53	0.45	66	2.90	16
	Mar	−1.96	54	−8.61	66	−4.63	16

Table A.2 *Continued*

	Month	Equity REIT Mean Total Return (%)	Equity REIT Number of Obs.	Hybrid REIT Mean Total Return (%)	Hybrid REIT Number of Obs.	Mortgage REIT Mean Total Return (%)	Mortgage REIT Number of Obs.
	Apr	−11.31	54	−15.48	66	−12.40	16
	May	−8.50	54	−12.53	64	−7.55	16
	Jun	−7.29	53	−12.82	63	−7.61	16
	Jul	−7.20	50	−9.60	64	0.74	16
	Aug	−15.87	50	−27.32	64	−21.94	15
	Sep	−5.18	50	−6.94	64	6.78	15
	Oct	0.32	49	−4.09	64	3.33	15
	Nov	−11.92	49	−17.37	63	−12.59	15
	Dec	−17.55	50	−20.54	65	−14.43	15
1975	Jan	43.35	49	67.58	64	42.03	15
	Feb	−7.82	49	−17.64	62	−5.91	15
	Mar	8.53	50	18.92	62	13.03	15
	Apr	−4.29	49	−14.25	62	−8.65	14
	May	−1.37	49	−0.64	61	2.84	14
	Jun	5.82	49	9.09	61	6.66	15
	Jul	1.93	51	−3.32	59	1.01	15
	Aug	−5.15	52	−10.56	59	−6.34	14
	Sep	−4.52	52	−13.12	59	−7.30	13
	Oct	−6.93	52	−10.00	58	−1.67	13
	Nov	−4.79	52	−4.51	58	−2.91	13
	Dec	5.68	52	16.72	57	3.63	14
1976	Jan	23.23	52	26.71	57	19.55	14
	Feb	8.96	51	25.75	55	17.55	14
	Mar	−3.89	51	−12.12	53	−7.54	14
	Apr	0.80	52	−3.68	53	0.46	14
	May	−1.35	53	−3.84	54	−1.47	14
	Jun	−1.21	54	−0.94	56	2.38	14
	Jul	1.69	52	1.60	57	5.77	14
	Aug	0.56	52	−3.89	57	0.22	14
	Sep	−1.91	51	−3.07	57	4.74	14
	Oct	−2.14	51	−5.81	57	−0.06	14
	Nov	8.51	52	4.17	57	3.92	14
	Dec	12.01	52	28.93	57	13.69	14
1977	Jan	9.88	52	−1.32	55	0.58	14
	Feb	1.01	52	−0.64	55	3.63	14
	Mar	3.15	52	1.85	55	−0.58	14
	Apr	2.86	53	1.74	54	1.11	14
	May	−0.98	52	−1.02	55	−1.30	14
	Jun	1.91	53	0.84	53	3.39	14
	Jul	4.24	53	8.59	52	5.68	14
	Aug	2.36	53	3.32	52	1.88	14
	Sep	1.65	53	0.91	50	−3.92	14
	Oct	−1.82	51	−2.97	51	−0.45	14
	Nov	11.68	52	18.47	51	12.06	14
	Dec	2.60	52	−0.11	52	−2.15	14
1978	Jan	0.13	51	−2.27	51	−3.15	15
	Feb	5.14	51	−0.90	52	−1.27	14

(*continued*)

Table A.2 *Continued*

	Month	Equity REIT Mean Total Return (%)	Equity REIT Number of Obs.	Hybrid REIT Mean Total Return (%)	Hybrid REIT Number of Obs.	Mortgage REIT Mean Total Return (%)	Mortgage REIT Number of Obs.
	Mar	6.03	50	9.10	52	7.66	14
	Apr	5.60	51	8.95	52	2.85	14
	May	−3.28	51	−3.23	51	−3.21	14
	Jun	1.60	50	0.88	52	5.68	14
	Jul	3.90	51	4.41	51	4.00	14
	Aug	8.85	52	18.39	51	7.25	14
	Sep	0.91	52	0.60	51	1.87	14
	Oct	−12.49	52	−18.84	51	−15.66	14
	Nov	−1.12	52	−6.03	51	−0.24	14
	Dec	2.08	51	5.43	50	−1.28	14
1979	Jan	11.62	51	11.66	51	13.81	14
	Feb	2.02	51	0.09	51	−4.30	14
	Mar	11.58	52	15.28	51	7.51	14
	Apr	4.65	52	5.80	50	−0.10	14
	May	1.04	52	5.48	49	0.92	14
	Jun	7.66	50	7.09	49	8.03	14
	Jul	1.43	50	0.56	48	−0.20	14
	Aug	10.73	50	11.12	47	8.85	14
	Sep	−0.25	50	−5.86	47	−5.57	14
	Oct	−10.43	50	−19.05	47	−12.31	14
	Nov	3.89	50	6.01	46	6.84	13
	Dec	0.87	51	1.47	46	−0.88	13
1980	Jan	10.67	53	9.29	46	10.66	13
	Feb	0.75	54	−2.41	45	−9.41	13
	Mar	−12.88	54	−19.79	45	−12.89	14
	Apr	6.10	54	6.79	45	14.51	14
	May	9.95	54	10.27	45	8.55	14
	Jun	7.22	54	4.26	44	7.70	14
	Jul	10.55	53	11.81	44	4.84	14
	Aug	4.17	54	5.63	43	−0.17	14
	Sep	−0.82	54	3.97	43	−0.22	14
	Oct	5.53	55	3.40	43	3.56	14
	Nov	0.46	56	−1.34	41	−3.87	14
	Dec	−1.06	55	−4.69	42	−5.76	14
1981	Jan	3.31	54	2.72	39	4.53	14
	Feb	1.58	54	−1.38	39	1.11	14
	Mar	5.50	53	10.07	37	4.24	14
	Apr	0.04	53	−1.08	36	2.57	14
	May	−1.19	53	−2.74	35	−4.40	15
	Jun	2.56	53	2.23	34	3.31	15
	Jul	−1.50	54	−2.06	34	3.14	15
	Aug	−4.33	53	−4.03	33	−6.97	15
	Sep	−5.24	53	−7.88	31	−5.59	15
	Oct	3.75	51	2.25	30	4.24	15
	Nov	4.88	50	4.64	29	6.11	15
	Dec	1.59	51	−1.39	29	0.65	15
1982	Jan	0.26	49	−0.67	29	−1.75	15

Table A.2 *Continued*

	Month	Equity REIT Mean Total Return (%)	Equity REIT Number of Obs.	Hybrid REIT Mean Total Return (%)	Hybrid REIT Number of Obs.	Mortgage REIT Mean Total Return (%)	Mortgage REIT Number of Obs.
	Feb	−2.17	49	−3.12	29	−3.07	15
	Mar	0.88	48	1.45	29	0.39	15
	Apr	3.35	51	2.79	27	4.23	15
	May	−0.27	50	−0.88	27	−2.00	15
	Jun	−1.79	49	−0.03	27	−2.05	15
	Jul	−1.34	49	−2.46	26	5.74	14
	Aug	4.89	49	0.50	26	10.73	13
	Sep	5.40	48	11.67	26	5.35	13
	Oct	7.06	48	10.50	27	9.45	13
	Nov	3.46	49	5.89	30	4.74	14
	Dec	3.48	48	1.16	29	1.92	13
1983	Jan	2.59	45	6.37	30	3.09	13
	Feb	3.93	45	5.84	30	4.02	12
	Mar	6.75	45	6.61	29	4.80	12
	Apr	7.23	46	7.78	29	4.03	12
	May	3.80	46	2.75	28	8.36	12
	Jun	1.21	46	1.40	28	−1.23	12
	Jul	−0.63	46	−0.50	30	−1.99	12
	Aug	−0.48	46	−0.97	31	−5.29	12
	Sep	1.81	46	2.48	31	2.77	11
	Oct	0.21	46	0.78	31	−1.90	10
	Nov	2.42	45	−0.03	30	0.84	10
	Dec	2.45	46	−0.74	28	−4.54	11
1984	Jan	2.99	45	2.81	27	3.20	11
	Feb	−0.43	45	−4.46	26	−4.43	11
	Mar	0.91	45	1.16	25	0.59	11
	Apr	0.09	45	1.40	25	0.72	12
	May	−1.25	45	−4.32	24	−6.83	12
	Jun	1.95	46	−0.40	24	−0.85	12
	Jul	−0.42	46	0.77	22	−1.28	12
	Aug	3.72	47	4.85	22	3.51	12
	Sep	2.40	47	2.69	22	3.18	12
	Oct	3.25	47	1.46	22	4.85	12
	Nov	2.20	47	2.51	21	−1.22	12
	Dec	1.00	47	0.77	21	1.38	14
1985	Jan	5.69	47	7.63	21	7.46	14
	Feb	1.40	47	1.73	21	2.85	14
	Mar	0.19	49	0.44	21	−0.52	15
	Apr	−0.29	50	1.34	21	−1.16	17
	May	2.47	55	3.31	21	2.42	17
	Jun	1.89	55	1.80	21	2.74	18
	Jul	1.90	57	0.77	21	0.63	17
	Aug	−1.38	58	−3.95	22	−1.38	17
	Sep	−2.14	58	−3.22	22	−3.80	20
	Oct	2.68	61	0.38	22	3.10	21
	Nov	−0.32	62	1.16	22	0.19	21
	Dec	0.69	63	3.72	22	−1.78	22

(*continued*)

Table A.2 *Continued*

	Month	Equity REIT		Hybrid REIT		Mortgage REIT	
		Mean Total Return (%)	Number of Obs.	Mean Total Return (%)	Number of Obs.	Mean Total Return (%)	Number of Obs.
1986	Jan	3.39	62	3.07	23	3.70	22
	Feb	0.96	61	4.58	22	4.11	23
	Mar	4.46	62	1.75	22	2.38	22
	Apr	−0.21	62	1.84	22	2.72	22
	May	−0.72	61	−0.74	23	−1.97	22
	Jun	2.94	60	2.19	23	−1.01	24
	Jul	−2.11	61	−1.24	22	4.44	25
	Aug	1.73	62	3.80	21	4.23	25
	Sep	−1.14	63	−2.34	21	−2.54	25
	Oct	1.42	62	3.03	20	2.98	25
	Nov	−0.48	63	0.85	20	0.19	25
	Dec	−2.33	65	−1.53	20	0.15	26
1987	Jan	4.63	68	1.06	20	1.56	26
	Feb	1.67	70	2.01	20	0.12	26
	Mar	0.99	72	−0.20	20	0.58	26
	Apr	−0.65	73	−3.10	20	−3.45	26
	May	−0.62	77	−0.34	20	−1.14	26
	Jun	1.73	77	−0.21	20	1.76	26
	Jul	0.59	77	1.32	20	1.62	26
	Aug	−1.47	77	−0.98	20	−1.73	26
	Sep	−2.04	77	−1.26	21	−4.17	26
	Oct	−14.10	77	−12.14	21	−12.59	26
	Nov	−0.40	77	2.67	21	0.55	26
	Dec	−0.44	76	−1.18	21	−0.53	26
1988	Jan	7.78	76	9.49	21	10.66	27
	Feb	4.14	76	2.53	21	0.41	28
	Mar	−0.26	75	4.22	20	0.92	28
	Apr	0.88	74	−0.61	20	1.59	28
	May	−1.42	73	−0.21	20	−2.23	28
	Jun	2.44	73	2.44	20	2.32	29
	Jul	3.30	70	1.17	20	−1.05	29
	Aug	−2.41	71	−0.90	20	−0.77	30
	Sep	−0.26	68	0.26	20	−0.32	31
	Oct	0.03	70	−0.69	20	−2.69	32
	Nov	−1.77	70	0.49	21	−2.55	33
	Dec	−0.83	69	−0.69	21	−3.00	34
1989	Jan	2.22	68	−0.19	21	−2.49	31
	Feb	−1.62	68	−1.37	21	−6.16	31
	Mar	1.61	68	1.09	21	−5.29	31
	Apr	1.24	69	1.24	21	−0.22	28
	May	2.66	69	0.60	21	5.56	28
	Jun	0.07	69	−0.47	21	1.04	29
	Jul	2.11	69	0.90	22	−0.07	29
	Aug	−1.41	68	−0.59	22	−1.45	29
	Sep	0.14	68	1.05	22	0.67	29
	Oct	−4.36	67	−6.46	22	−6.35	29
	Nov	−4.04	67	−3.79	22	−0.78	30

Table A.2 *Continued*

	Month	Equity REIT Mean Total Return (%)	Equity REIT Number of Obs.	Hybrid REIT Mean Total Return (%)	Hybrid REIT Number of Obs.	Mortgage REIT Mean Total Return (%)	Mortgage REIT Number of Obs.
	Dec	−1.67	67	−1.78	22	0.15	30
1990	Jan	−2.38	67	−0.72	21	1.70	30
	Feb	−2.77	67	−6.95	21	−5.05	30
	Mar	0.10	67	−1.84	21	6.15	30
	Apr	0.48	67	−0.54	21	−4.35	29
	May	−1.24	67	−1.49	21	1.75	29
	Jun	−0.87	67	−4.83	21	3.30	29
	Jul	−2.71	67	−4.80	21	−1.74	29
	Aug	−5.99	67	−6.85	22	−2.76	29
	Sep	−8.08	67	−6.41	22	−8.32	29
	Oct	−8.17	67	−3.03	21	−7.38	30
	Nov	5.39	67	2.81	21	2.44	30
	Dec	−2.46	67	−3.28	21	−1.00	29
1991	Jan	9.44	67	5.37	21	9.59	29
	Feb	5.51	66	13.51	21	11.87	29
	Mar	10.19	71	7.13	21	11.10	29
	Apr	1.82	71	4.55	21	3.01	29
	May	0.59	71	2.27	21	1.50	29
	Jun	−3.64	71	−3.02	21	1.79	29
	Jul	0.57	73	−0.45	21	0.96	29
	Aug	−0.79	73	−2.50	21	−0.94	29
	Sep	1.74	78	3.12	21	1.22	29
	Oct	−1.46	81	−2.66	21	−2.67	29
	Nov	−3.48	86	−5.47	21	1.90	29
	Dec	0.99	87	−1.22	21	−2.96	28
1992	Jan	9.58	88	8.56	21	15.29	28
	Feb	3.13	88	1.02	21	0.24	28
	Mar	2.70	86	1.44	21	−2.10	28
	Apr	−3.16	86	−4.51	21	0.50	28
	May	0.44	86	−3.51	21	0.81	28
	Jun	−1.03	86	−2.01	21	−3.09	27
	Jul	3.28	86	1.65	21	−1.85	27
	Aug	1.18	87	−1.35	22	−6.87	26
	Sep	1.85	87	0.38	22	0.97	26
	Oct	−2.70	88	−3.46	22	−2.52	26
	Nov	−0.67	91	7.94	22	5.53	26
	Dec	−0.21	91	3.44	22	2.42	26
1993	Jan	7.49	92	5.76	22	9.52	26
	Feb	10.76	95	6.77	22	−3.60	26
	Mar	8.81	95	7.17	22	−0.42	26
	Apr	0.35	96	−3.62	21	−1.58	26
	May	−0.41	100	2.09	21	−0.75	26
	Jun	3.43	103	1.50	21	−0.18	27
	Jul	2.27	105	7.96	21	3.48	27
	Aug	2.83	111	−0.57	21	0.61	28
	Sep	6.74	113	−0.20	21	−0.17	28
	Oct	1.64	120	4.93	21	0.60	29

(*continued*)

Table A.2 *Continued*

	Month	Equity REIT		Hybrid REIT		Mortgage REIT	
		Mean Total Return (%)	Number of Obs.	Mean Total Return (%)	Number of Obs.	Mean Total Return (%)	Number of Obs.
	Nov	−3.63	127	−2.41	21	1.49	29
	Dec	−0.31	134	7.37	21	3.32	30
1994	Jan	2.42	143	0.33	21	4.18	29
	Feb	3.62	148	1.71	21	2.25	28
	Mar	−2.61	155	0.29	21	−6.89	28
	Apr	0.38	159	1.03	21	1.19	28
	May	1.79	162	−0.92	21	5.07	28
	Jun	−0.18	170	−2.77	21	−0.57	28
	Jul	−0.04	174	1.64	21	3.34	28
	Aug	0.79	178	2.29	21	−2.25	28
	Sep	1.14	179	1.23	21	−0.76	27
	Oct	−3.31	178	−2.69	21	−3.22	27
	Nov	−3.57	179	−4.48	21	−2.01	27
	Dec	3.99	181	0.07	21	−2.98	27
1995	Jan	−0.34	178	2.78	21	6.72	26
	Feb	3.86	177	2.78	21	7.75	26
	Mar	−0.16	176	−1.60	21	3.15	26
	Apr	1.14	176	1.60	20	2.86	26
	May	3.13	177	1.81	20	5.94	26
	Jun	1.69	179	2.82	20	1.92	26
	Jul	0.90	177	−1.86	20	−0.40	26
	Aug	1.33	179	1.71	20	3.35	26
	Sep	2.52	180	3.64	20	0.90	26
	Oct	−1.62	180	0.33	20	−0.39	26
	Nov	0.38	180	−0.59	18	0.08	26
	Dec	5.13	179	2.26	18	4.81	26
1996	Jan	4.10	174	2.97	17	6.77	25
	Feb	1.01	175	−4.08	17	−0.92	25
	Mar	1.33	172	5.42	17	1.93	24
	Apr	0.09	171	1.30	17	0.02	24
	May	2.81	171	6.64	16	4.15	24
	Jun	1.96	169	0.86	16	6.07	23
	Jul	0.40	168	−0.13	16	−0.63	22
	Aug	4.27	168	2.46	16	5.30	21
	Sep	2.14	166	0.96	16	6.56	21
	Oct	1.89	167	2.25	15	1.56	21
	Nov	4.00	167	−0.47	15	2.58	21
	Dec	8.22	167	5.57	15	6.06	21
1997	Jan	1.87	164	11.00	15	12.65	21
	Feb	0.43	166	−3.07	15	−0.56	21
	Mar	−0.15	165	0.45	14	−4.17	21
	Apr	−1.69	167	−3.24	14	−0.61	20
	May	3.24	167	7.65	14	5.70	20
	Jun	4.61	167	1.05	14	5.22	20
	Jul	2.74	164	6.78	14	3.11	20
	Aug	1.02	166	2.19	13	4.43	21
	Sep	6.69	166	5.75	13	6.20	21

Table A.2 *Continued*

	Month	Equity REIT Mean Total Return (%)	Equity REIT Number of Obs.	Hybrid REIT Mean Total Return (%)	Hybrid REIT Number of Obs.	Mortgage REIT Mean Total Return (%)	Mortgage REIT Number of Obs.
	Oct	−1.34	169	1.77	13	−2.16	24
	Nov	0.57	172	0.79	14	−0.20	25
	Dec	2.62	171	1.52	13	1.35	26
1998	Jan	0.57	171	2.41	14	0.40	26
	Feb	−0.77	173	−0.37	14	−0.75	27
	Mar	2.27	174	1.26	13	3.27	30
	Apr	−2.84	176	2.38	15	−0.87	30
	May	−0.62	178	−1.40	14	−3.32	32
	Jun	−0.92	175	−3.69	14	−2.41	32
	Jul	−4.51	172	−1.88	14	−5.99	32
	Aug	−8.95	174	−8.06	13	−17.07	32
	Sep	6.99	173	6.59	13	0.79	31
	Oct	−2.24	173	−11.91	13	−22.83	31
	Nov	0.91	172	2.13	13	13.07	31
	Dec	−0.67	174	5.11	13	−0.76	31
1999	Jan	−1.91	175	0.53	13	6.08	31
	Feb	−2.95	176	−3.06	13	−1.84	31
	Mar	−0.20	175	2.24	13	−0.66	31
	Apr	8.06	175	2.42	13	7.05	31
	May	2.82	175	3.09	13	3.93	31
	Jun	1.20	173	1.03	13	−0.53	31
	Jul	−2.55	173	−0.75	14	0.56	31
	Aug	−2.65	172	−2.66	14	−7.61	30
	Sep	−2.52	172	1.08	15	−1.41	30
	Oct	−1.92	173	−3.36	15	−3.32	30
	Nov	−0.79	170	−1.06	15	−2.53	29
	Dec	1.02	167	0.92	14	−0.34	29
2000	Jan	0.52	167	1.17	14	−0.94	29
	Feb	−1.51	167	−2.58	14	0.80	29
	Mar	1.99	165	2.13	14	3.24	29
	Apr	4.85	165	1.45	13	−1.57	28
	May	0.98	165	−1.52	13	0.05	28
	Jun	3.16	166	5.27	13	3.40	28
	Jul	5.34	163	3.55	13	0.72	26
	Aug	−2.76	163	−2.13	13	2.92	26
	Sep	1.96	163	4.37	13	3.17	25
	Oct	−2.89	160	−1.03	13	−1.78	25
	Nov	−0.12	158	−2.61	13	−2.79	25
	Dec	5.00	156	4.57	13	1.51	24

(continued)

Table A.2 *Continued*

Month	Equity REIT		Hybrid REIT		Mortgage REIT	
	Mean Total Return (%)	Number of Obs.	Mean Total Return (%)	Number of Obs.	Mean Total Return (%)	Number of Obs.
A. 1962–2000 period						
Mean	1.03		0.93		1.15	
Std. Dev.	4.98		7.20		6.78	
Maximum	43.35		67.58		42.03	
Minimum	–17.55		–27.32		–25.14	
Number of Months	462		440		427	
B. 1962–70 period						
Mean	1.03		1.52		3.32	
Std. Dev.	4.88		7.09		10.09	
Maximum	15.35		23.08		37.00	
Minimum	–8.17		–16.39		–25.14	
Number of Months	102		80		67	
C. 1971–80 period						
Mean	1.21		0.72		0.74	
Std. Dev.	7.37		11.38		8.08	
Maximum	43.35		67.58		42.03	
Minimum	–17.55		–27.32		–21.94	
Number of Months	120		120		120	
D. 1981–90 period						
Mean	0.60		0.48		0.40	
Std. Dev.	3.18		3.65		3.91	
Maximum	7.78		11.67		10.73	
Minimum	–14.10		–12.14		–12.59	
Number of Months	120		120		120	
E. 1991–2000 period						
Mean	1.29		1.19		1.12	
Std. Dev.	3.33		3.78		4.92	
Maximum	10.76		13.51		15.29	
Minimum	–8.95		–11.91		–22.83	
Number of Months	120		120		120	

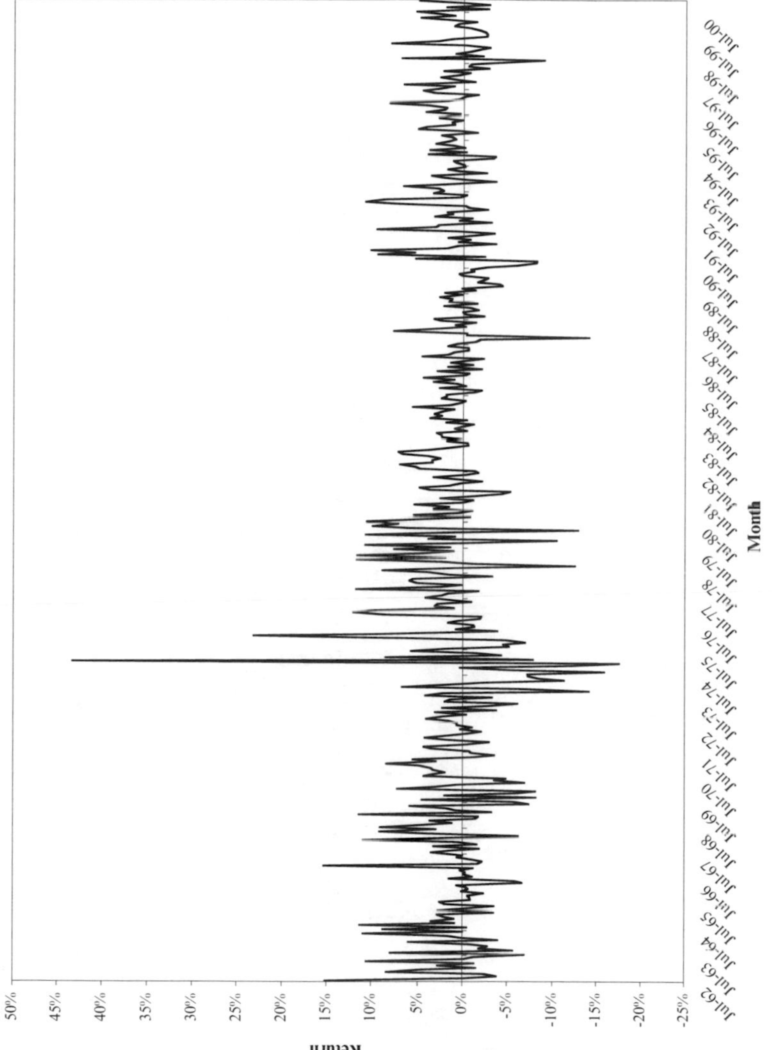

Figure A.4 Mean Monthly Total Return for Equity REITs

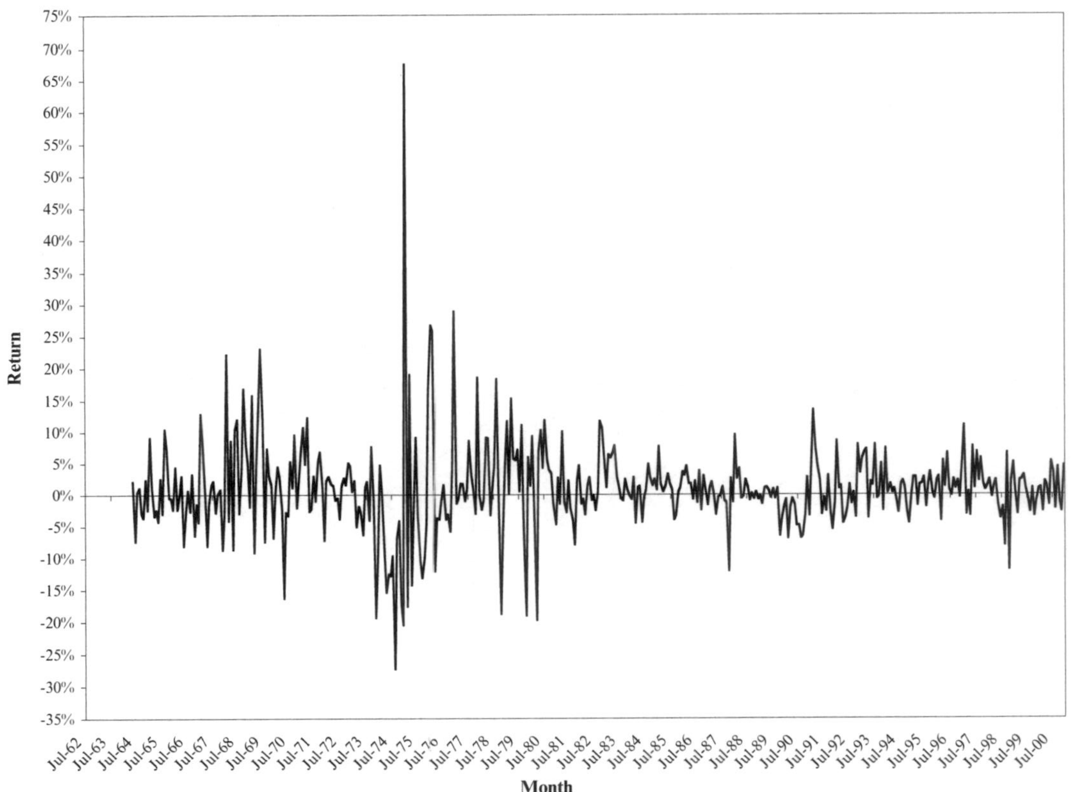

Figure A.5 Mean Monthly Total Return for Hybrid REITs

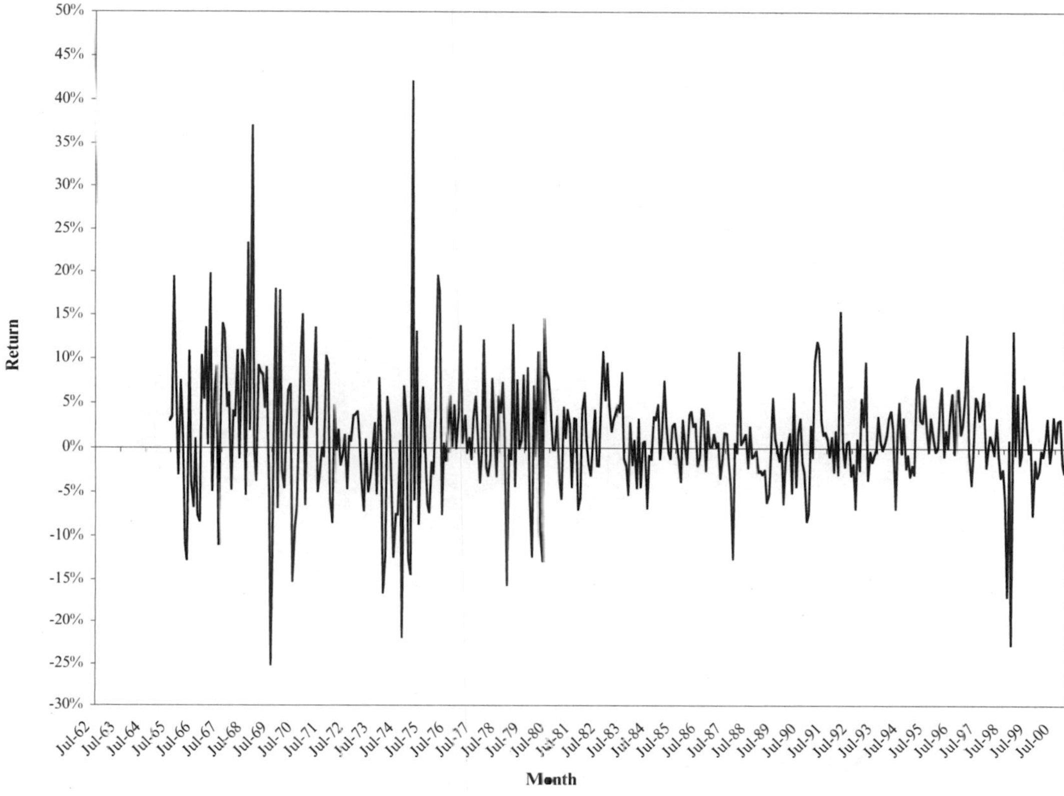

Figure A.6 Mean Monthly Total Return for Mortgage REITs

Table A.3 Mean Monthly Total Returns for All REITs (%) and by REIT Type (January 2001–May 2002)

	All REITs	Equity REITs	Hybrid REITs	Mortgage REITs
2001				
January	1.46	1.04	14.51	14.17
February	−1.30	−1.60	8.62	4.26
March	0.91	0.97	−3.04	3.35
April	2.63	2.39	9.01	8.04
May	2.53	2.42	2.89	8.41
June	5.85	5.86	7.06	3.45
July	−1.73	−1.99	2.53	6.25
August	3.39	3.66	0.15	−5.46
September	−4.01	−4.15	−4.53	4.16
October	−2.69	−2.86	−0.23	1.79
November	5.35	5.50	4.01	0.87
December	2.64	2.44	2.34	10.78
2002				
January	0.38	0.20	5.75	1.98
February	1.81	1.93	1.63	−2.06
March	5.99	6.00	6.71	5.04
April	1.31	0.85	7.17	10.32
May	1.45	1.35	−0.99	5.73

Source: NAREIT's website: http://www.nareit.com.

Index